Intrahousehold Resource Allocation in Developing Countries

Models, Methods, and Policy

EDITED BY LAWRENCE HADDAD, JOHN HODDINOTT,
AND HAROLD ALDERMAN

Published for the International Food Policy Research Institute

The Johns Hopkins University Press
Baltimore and London

© 1997 The International Food Policy Research Institute
All rights reserved. Published 1997
Printed in the United States of America on acid-free paper
06 05 04 03 02 01 00 99 98 97   5 4 3 2 1

The Johns Hopkins University Press
2715 North Charles Street
Baltimore, Maryland 21218-4319
The Johns Hopkins Press Ltd., London

Library of Congress Cataloging-in-Publication Data will be found at the end of this book.
A catalog record for this book is available from the British Library.

ISBN 0-8018-5572-1

Contents

Figures and Tables

Figures

Tables

Preface

The study of intrahousehold allocation—that is, understanding how rights, responsibilities, and resources are allocated among household and family members—is a relatively new field of study. The "new household economics" movement of the 1970s expanded the set of individual and household decisions that were examined by economists. The 1980s witnessed a growing chorus of dissenters when it came to treating all household members as if they behaved as one—as represented by a "unitary" model of household decisionmaking. Specifically, the dissenters argued that both altruism *and* conflict needed to be incorporated into household models for realistic predictions of individual behavior in response to prevailing incentives. The 1990s have, so far, seen four new developments. First, use of the unitary model to study intrahousehold issues increased. Second, there was a boomlet of alternative economic models of the household, or "collective" models of household decisionmaking. Third, a range of new methods—quantitative and qualitative—was developed to operationalize these new models. Finally, the relevance of intrahousehold issues for policymaking began to be articulated.

This book attempts to lead the reader through this sequence of events up to early 1997 in intrahousehold models, methods, and related policy applications, especially in the areas of poverty, agriculture, food security, and nutrition —areas that are critical to the mandate of the International Food Policy Research Institute (IFPRI). It also reviews those areas in which future research would be most valuable.

Although the writing of this book was not always conflict free, we did manage to draw upon enough altruism and cooperation to fill many household black boxes. Many individuals have contributed to the book's successful completion, and we are grateful to them all. A special note of thanks is due to those listed here.

First and foremost, we thank Roger Slade of the World Bank. This book is based on a three-day workshop organized by IFPRI and the World Bank and held in Washington, D.C., in February 1992. Roger deserves much of the credit for making that workshop happen through his intellectual, moral, and financial support.

The workshop was organized by Julia Addae-Mintah, Kimberly Chung, Laurie Goldberg, Rajul Pandya-Lorch, and Lisa Smith. Serving as discussants at the workshop were Jere Behrman, Lynn Bennett, Margaret Bentley, Sara Berry, Angus Deaton, Barbara Herz, Ravi Kanbur, Sandra Rosenhouse, Irene Tinker, and Patrick Webb. Other key participants included Mayra Buvinic, Anil Deolalikar, Raghav Gaiha, Marito Garcia, Margaret Grosh, Naila Kabeer, Eileen Kennedy, Shubh Kumar, Helzi Noponen, Michael Paolisso, Beatrice Rogers, and Ben Senauer.

We are grateful to the following individuals who served as reviewers for the individual book chapters: Ruth Alsop, Simon Appleton, Richard Blundell, Patrice Engle, Robert Evenson, Gillian Hart, Peter Hazell, Susan Horton, Christine Jones, Laurence Kotlikoff, Michael Lipton, Judith McGuire, Andrew McKay, Mark Montgomery, Jonathan Morduch, Martin Ravallion, Helena Ribe, Mark Rosenzweig, David Sahn, Amartya Sen, and Frances Woolley. Their input strengthened the volume considerably.

We are also grateful to two anonymous reviewers who plowed through the entire volume and generously shared their insights and thoughts with us.

Superlative word processing and editing were provided by Jay Willis at all stages of the volume. Uday Mohan copyedited an earlier version of the volume, Mary Snyder helped with the graphics, Peter Strupp of Princeton Editorial Associates performed the final edit, and Heidi Fritschel managed the book's production for IFPRI.

Financial and other support for the workshop and for the book has been generously provided by the Office of Women in Development at the United States Agency for International Development under Contract No. FAO-0100-G-00-5020-00 on Strengthening Development Policy through Gender Analysis: An Integrated Multicountry Research Program and under Contract No. BOA-4111-B-00-9112; the (then) Women in Development Division of the Department of Health and Human Resources at the World Bank; the Ford Foundation; and the Rockefeller Foundation.

Intrahousehold Resource Allocation in Developing Countries

1 Introduction: The Scope of Intrahousehold Resource Allocation Issues

LAWRENCE HADDAD, JOHN HODDINOTT, AND
HAROLD ALDERMAN

Most development objectives focus on the well-being of individuals. For example, policy targets are often related to the percentage of individuals that can read, are free from hunger, are in good health, can find gainful employment, and will avoid death from disease or violence. Although it is widely recognized that the welfare of an individual is, in large part, based on a complex set of economic and social interactions, development policies do not always acknowledge these. These interactions can affect, and be affected by, the creation, existence, and dissolution of institutions within which the individual is situated: family, household, business, club, or commune, to name a few. For the first two institutions in this list, both the processes by which resources are allocated among individuals and the outcomes of those processes are commonly referred to as "intrahousehold resource allocation."[1]

Taking this broad definition, this book surveys a diverse body of theory and evidence on intrahousehold allocation. In doing so, it seeks to achieve four objectives. First, it seeks to convince the reader that understanding the process by which household allocations occur is important for policy and project design. This point is discussed implicitly in many of the contributions to the first two parts of the book and is the dominant theme of Part III. Second, there is much confusion regarding the theoretical models that can be brought to bear on these issues, as exemplified by two common misunderstandings:

1. It is sometimes claimed that models in which the household is posited to act as a single decisionmaker (the "unitary" model) are silent on the issue of intrahousehold distribution. As discussed in this chapter and in the chapters by Pitt and Alderman and Gertler, this is simply wrong.

---

1. Models used for examining how resources are allocated among a group of individuals are most usefully employed if they can be applied to the group that exhibits the greatest social and economic interdependence. They can be characterized in a number of ways: coresident, eating from a common "pot," and blood relatives, to name three. Of equal importance to the usefulness of intrahousehold models is some knowledge of how the group of individuals came together in the first place. These issues are discussed in Chapter 8.

2. The suggestion that an alternative to the unitary model is a "bargaining" model neglects the important fact that there are at least four variants of these models (broadly termed "collective" models), as outlined here by Chiappori, McElroy, Lundberg and Pollak, and Carter and Katz.

Thus a second goal of the volume is to clarify the various theories that can be brought to bear on intrahousehold allocation. Part I of the book is devoted to outlining current thought on a variety of theoretical models.

A third objective is to indicate that, although substantial progress has been made on the theoretical front, a number of major measurement and econometric issues remain unaddressed. This point is emphasized in Part II of the book. The fourth objective is to suggest that further work on intrahousehold allocation will benefit substantially from interaction among researchers across a number of disciplines. For example, Guyer (Chapter 7) suggests that economics and anthropology appear to be heading toward a "new convergence of concern" around the nature and use of assets. Gittelsohn and Mookherji (Chapter 10) and Bouis and Peña (Chapter 11) illustrate how the measurement of intrahousehold allocations can be enhanced by drawing on techniques from anthropology and nutrition.

Certain topics relevant to this volume have been recently covered in detailed reviews (Hart 1995; Strauss and Beegle 1995; Strauss and Thomas 1995; Behrman 1996). As there should be, there has been much interplay between these reviews; we have benefited from having read them while preparing this overview. This volume is to be regarded as a complement to, not a substitute for, these works. In particular, more attention is devoted in this volume to a comparison of different collective models, to policy issues, and to the possibilities for collaboration across disciplines. In addition, by virtue of having worked with 19 contributors, we have been able to appreciate much of the breadth of the literature. In contrast, less attention is paid to detailed models of allocation within a unitary context, nor is there an attempt to provide a detailed review of the empirical literature in this area—fine reviews of these subjects can be found in Behrman and the two readings coauthored by Strauss. Such an emphasis should not be interpreted as a bias in favor of any one model of intrahousehold allocation, but rather as an illustration of how economists, sociologists, and anthropologists have begun to forge new tools to deal with the perceived inadequacies of existing methodologies.

A comment is also in order regarding the focus on developing countries. Many innovations in the theory of intrahousehold allocation have been formulated with developing countries in mind. Moreover, many of the empirical applications pertain to issues prevalent in low-income countries (for example, Pitt and Rosenzweig 1985, Jones 1986, and Thomas 1990). Since a function of this book is to provide a survey of this literature, it is natural that it draws heavily on this material. But as should be clear, there is much that economists and other social scientists whose geographic focus lies in the United States, Britain, and other developed countries can learn from these discussions.

The purpose of this chapter is twofold. The primary goal is to outline the models, methods, and policy tools associated with the analysis of intrahousehold resource allocation. In doing so, we explain how the individual chapters in this volume contribute to a better understanding of these issues. We have tried to convey the diversity of the theoretical approaches that can be taken, the degree of mathematical sophistication, the scope of intrahousehold issues, and the policy recommendations that can be made. In doing so, we seek to demonstrate that there is a range of models and tools that can address specific aspects of the broad question of how families and households allocate resources among members.

Models

Unitary Approaches to Intrahousehold Allocation

The idea that the household represents a locus of economic activity dates back at least to Chayanov's study of Russian peasants, first published in 1926 (Chayanov 1986). However, the economics of the family and the household was fully brought into the mainstream by Gary Becker, the 1992 Nobel Prize winner in economics, in the mid-1960s. The essence of Becker's approach was that, in accordance with a single set of preferences, the household combines time, goods purchased in the market, and goods produced at home to produce commodities that generate utility for the household (Becker 1965).

Until fairly recently, most economists have shared this view of the household. Though this approach originates in standard demand analysis, it has been extended to include the determinants of education, health, fertility, child fostering, migration, labor supply, home production, land tenure, and crop adoption. Particularly important in the context of developing countries has been the work by Singh, Squire, and Strauss (1986), who provide a joint model of production and consumption decisions. In Alderman et al. (1995), such models are called the "unitary" approach. They are sometimes referred to as the "common preferences" model, the "altruism" model, or the "benevolent dictator" model. The unitary model is so named because this label describes how the household acts (as one), whereas other such labels tend to reflect the means by which the household is hypothesized to act as one.

The unitary model offers a number of important theoretical perspectives on the question of intrahousehold distribution. Consider parental investment in children. Assume the existence of a welfare function that reflects parental preferences, defined over their own consumption, the adult income of each child, and the size of transfers made to each child (Behrman 1996). This is maximized, subject to two constraints: a parental budget constraint and the earnings production function for each child, itself a function of human capital investments made in that child by parents and that child's initial endowment. Behrman (1996) refers to this very general framework as the "parental altruism model." Placing restrictions on this general approach yields several models of intrahousehold resource allocation.

One restriction, originally due to Becker and Tomes (1976), assumes that parents are concerned solely with their children's total level of wealth and exhibit equal concern for each child. Human capital investments are made in children best placed to generate a higher rate of return on these. That is, parents invest in their children in such a way as to reinforce differences in child endowments. Transfers are made to more poorly endowed offspring in order to equalize children's wealth. Behrman (1996) refers to this approach as the "wealth model." A second approach is the "separable earnings-transfers model" (Behrman, Pollak, and Taubman 1982). By assuming that children's income as adults and parental transfers to children are separable within the parental welfare function, attention can be focused on the determinants of investment in children. These are guided by two concerns. First, parents may be interested in ensuring that all children are equally well off. Alternatively, they may have preferences for particular children; for example, boys over girls, firstborn over latter born, their own children over those whom they raise as foster children. These can be called "equity" concerns, though it is entirely possible that parents prefer unequal outcomes among their children. As in the wealth model, parents also desire to maximize the return on the investment in their children. These are "efficiency" concerns.

Suppose parents care only about equity and have no concerns regarding efficiency. Such preferences imply that they will seek to equalize their children's future earnings but do not imply that all children will be treated equally. Consider the case of parents who want their daughter and son to receive equal earnings but recognize that the daughter will face discrimination in the labor market; specifically, her wages will be less than those of her comparably qualified brother doing the same work. Here parents will devote more resources to their daughter (for example, by providing her with more education) in order to equalize future earnings. Conversely, where parents seek to maximize the total future earnings of their offspring, they invest relatively more in those children with the best future prospects. In the example considered here, parents would invest more in their son than in their daughter. That is, parents "reinforce" existing inequalities in child endowments. It is also possible to construct intermediate cases in which both equity and efficiency concerns play a role.

Mark Pitt's chapter is situated within this literature. Pitt asks how the allocations to one household member affect the allocations to others. Conceptually, demand for each good (including home-produced goods such as health) for each individual can be treated as demand equations conditional on the demand for goods allocated to other individuals. However, identification of such models is hampered by the fact that there are more person-specific goods than there are prices, and identification restrictions are required. Pitt illustrates two approaches. One involves cross-individual restrictions on parameters. The other estimates individual endowments that assist in identification of individual caloric demand if the errors in health production functions are uncorrelated with those in the reduced-form demand equations.

Collective Approaches to Intrahousehold Allocation

Fundamental to the unitary model is the assumption that there exists a parental, or household, welfare function and that all resources—capital, labor, land, and information—are pooled. Although most researchers acknowledge that the problem of how the common actions come about is not solved, many argue that the unitary model is a useful approximation and that an exploration of the underlying decisionmaking process yields no additional useful information. Others are more troubled by this assertion. These concerns have spawned a set of approaches—the "collective" approaches (Alderman et al. 1995)— which are examined in this section. However, it is important to be clear about the distinction between these approaches. As Alderman and Gertler (Chapter 14, this volume) note, even if a collective approach is used, it is still necessary to explain why a particular household member chooses to invest more in one child than another. The dispute thus centers on whether the unitary model is sufficient to account for all aspects of intrahousehold distribution.

If individual household members have different preferences, the assumption of a household welfare function requires that these differing preferences be aggregated. How can this be accomplished? One possibility, outlined by Samuelson (1956), is that the household welfare function reflects a consensus among members. In a similar vein, Evenson, Popkin, and King-Quizon (1979) have suggested that the household welfare function means that the household members agree to follow certain rules when distributing resources within the household. However, this definition does not indicate how such a consensus is to be reached.

A second approach applies Sen's (1966) model of cooperatives to the household. Here family welfare is the weighted sum of the net utility of all members. But in the absence of a dictator, or "symmetric sympathy," it is unclear how these weights are to be determined. In addition, the aggregate household weights will not be equivalent to a welfare function unless they are independent of prices and incomes, a very strong assumption. Other solutions include assortative mating and internal household market equilibria at implicit pricing (Becker 1973). But assortative mating is less appealing with respect to shared preferences across generations. Moreover, a model of implicit contracting within a household must still address the problems of monitoring and incentives related to such agreements.

One additional attempt to resolve the problems of aggregation and enforcement is Becker's (1974b, 1981) "rotten-kid theorem." Becker considers the case of a household with two members, a benefactor and a recipient. The recipient is selfish in that he or she derives utility solely from his or her own consumption. The benefactor, as an altruist, can increase his or her own utility by transferring some of his or her own consumption to that of the recipient. Now suppose the recipient undertakes some action that raises his or her own consumption but lowers that of the benefactor. The benefactor could respond by lowering transfers to the recipient, so much so that the recipient's new level of consumption is below his or her original level. Consequently, the recipient will not behave rottenly in the first place. Thus the preferences of the altruist and the preferences of the household converge. This is an attractive result; the preferences of the altruist become the preferences of the household; the household's maximand becomes the utility function of the altruist. However, the rotten-kid theorem only holds under restrictive circumstances.

First, the benefactor must be altruistic over all levels of the consumption of others. If consumption by others is either an inferior or a luxury good, the threat of reduced transfers may not be credible over all levels of consumption. Moreover, the theorem assumes that any attempt by the recipient to disrupt the given distribution of consumption is small relative to that available to the altruist. That is, a kid could not be so rotten that he reduces the altruist's consumption below his initial endowment while raising his own above its previous (endowment plus transfer) level. Furthermore, not only must the resources of the altruist be larger than those of any one individual, they must also be larger than those of any coalition of household members. If this were not the case, it might be possible for a group of individuals to behave rottenly, increasing their collective consumption at the expense of others. (Pollak [1985] discusses these issues more formally.)

Hirshleifer (1977) has suggested that Becker's result is dependent on who makes the last move. If the rotten kid can act after the benefactor has transferred consumption (as in *King Lear*), he can behave selfishly without fear of retribution. Bernheim and Stark (1988) and Bruce and Waldman (1990) develop a line of criticism known as the Samaritan's Dilemma. Assume there are two household members who live for two periods. One is altruistic whereas the other is selfish. Both consume a portion of their endowment in the first period. In the second period, the altruist divides her remaining resources between herself and the other person. The selfish member consumes the rest of his endowment and the transfer from the altruist. However, because the selfish agent knows that the altruist will make a transfer to him, he consumes more in the first period than he would have in the absence of a transfer. The altruist can prevent such behavior by consuming more in the first period than she would otherwise, but, in doing so, reduces her utility. Bergstrom (1989) generalizes these results and shows that the rotten-kid theorem collapses when a second commodity is introduced. Only under the strong condition of transferable utility does it continue to hold.

Concerns over the theoretical underpinnings of the unitary model have given impetus to a number of approaches that focus on the individuality of household members and explicitly address the question of how individual preferences lead to a collective choice. They do not require any unique household welfare index to be interpreted as a utility function, thereby allowing the index to be dependent on prices and incomes, as well as "tastes." Though many of these approaches are referred to as bargaining models, the more generic label of "collective" models is preferred, partly because some important collective models do not explicitly address bargaining and because the phrase can be neatly juxtaposed with the term "unitary" models. The collective approach to the household can be subdivided into two broad categories: those models that rely on cooperative solutions to bargaining among individuals and those that rely on noncooperative game theory. It is possible to show that the unitary model is a special case of the collective class of models.

The cooperative approach begins by noting that individuals form a household when the benefits associated with doing so exceed those obtainable from remaining alone. This situation could occur because of the existence of economies of scale associated with the production of certain household goods, or because there are some goods that can be produced and shared by married couples but not single individuals. In any case, household formation generates a surplus that will be distributed across the members. Much of this description is in common with that of unitary models; the point of departure comes from the rule governing this distribution.

Broadly speaking, there are two types of cooperative approaches. Models in the first category suppose only that household decisions are always efficient in the Pareto sense (Apps 1981, 1982; Apps and Rees 1988; Chiappori 1988b, 1992; Kooreman and Kapteyn 1990; Browning et al. 1994; Browning and Chiappori 1995). In particular, nothing is assumed a priori about the nature of the decision process, or equivalently, about the location of the final outcome on the household Pareto frontier. As Pierre-André Chiappori explains in his chapter, even if evidence were to suggest that the unitary approach (which he calls the "traditional" approach) were not correct, this mere fact does not support any particular alternative model. The only way to support a particular collective setting empirically is to derive from that framework conditions that potentially can be, but are not actually, falsified by empirical observation. Chiappori argues that the household's income-sharing rule will depend on the income of individual A, the income of individual B, and income received collectively by the household. Then the ratio of the impact of A's income upon the demand for commodity i and the impact of B's income upon the demand for commodity i

should be identical for all goods. These restrictions can be tested by incorporating them into a demand function that permits the coefficients on income from individual A and individual B to vary by commodity. Using a sample of French households in which both the husband and the wife work full time, and a sample of nine consumption goods, Chiappori finds that the restrictions implied by the collective model cannot be rejected.

A second category of cooperative models differs from this approach by imposing more structure by representing household allocations as the outcome of some specific bargaining process and applying to this framework the tools of game theory (Manser and Brown 1980; McElroy and Horney 1981; McElroy 1990). Marjorie McElroy begins her chapter by briefly outlining this approach. Suppose two individuals are considering forming a household. They both have a level of personal utility within marriage based on consumption of household public goods, individual consumption of goods, and leisure. Similarly they have levels of personal utility for their unmarried state that reflect both their endowments and "extrahousehold environmental parameters" (EEPs), factors that shift individuals' threat points. They include measures of the relevant marriage and remarriage markets, laws concerning alimony and child support, changes in tax status associated with moving between marital states, and the ability of each person to receive assistance from his or her own family (itself perhaps a function of parental wealth). Both individuals gain from household formation when their utility within marriage exceeds that outside it. The critical question becomes the mechanism by which these gains are apportioned.

In McElroy's model, these individuals maximize the product of the gains in utility from marriage (a "Nash" solution) for both individuals, subject to a joint full-income constraint. The resultant Marshallian demand functions include, as arguments, all prices, nonlabor income, and EEPs. As McElroy emphasizes, the unitary model is a special case of this Nash model, with the parameters on nonlabor income and EEPs set equal to zero. Note that McElroy's use of a Nash solution differentiates her approach from that taken by Chiappori (1988a), who advocates a more general approach. An attractive feature of McElroy's model is that policy interventions enter directly into demand functions by way of the EEPs. Furthermore, the use of a Nash cooperative solution is not especially restrictive. As she notes, it can emerge from a number of noncooperative frameworks. Yet at another level reliance on the Nash solution is troubling—the failure of an empirical model to differentiate between competing approaches could reflect the genuine absence of a difference or merely the inappropriateness of the bargaining model adopted.

An innovative aspect of McElroy's chapter is her demonstration of the complementarity of the partial-equilibrium Nash bargaining models with general-equilibrium marriage market models. McElroy shows that the predictions of the marriage market model complement the predictions of the Nash bargaining models. Specifically, if an increase in women's ability to maintain themselves outside marriage does not come at the expense of the ability of men to maintain themselves outside marriage, this generally increases and never decreases the income of married women. However, when the increased ability of women to maintain themselves comes at the expense of men, this generally increases (never decreases) women's income and generally decreases (never increases) men's income. For policies that, unintentionally, increase men's control over income while simultaneously undercutting women's control, the marriage model indicates that this leads directly to the long-term deterioration of the well-being of women. Even policies that promote market gains for women that are not at the expense of men may well be resisted by men, since under these policies their long-term share of marital income would decline.

In McElroy's model, the issue of enforcement is resolved in several ways. The threat of marital dissolution is a possibility in the context of long-term decisions but, as she notes, "In the context of small daily decisions, it is not credible for either spouse to threaten to leave the marriage." She suggests that decisions regarding short-run issues can be motivated by time preferences (the loss associated with delays in settling disagreements).

Shelly Lundberg and Robert Pollak take issue with the divorce-threat version of the Nash bargaining model in their chapter. They argue that the divorce threat is not always credible and that the outcome of marital non-cooperation can take some other form. They lay out what they call a "separate-spheres" model of the household. Like the divorce-threat version of the Nash bargaining model, the model is a bargaining model that views marriage as a cooperative game, but with a threat point that is a noncooperative equilibrium within marriage, based on traditional gender roles. They show how a child allowance scheme has no distributional implications in a two-parent family under the unitary or divorce-threat version of the Nash bargaining model, but does under their separate-spheres model. However, their work shares an important similarity with that of McElroy. In both chapters, attention is drawn to the importance of the effects of policy in a general equilibrium setting. In McElroy's model, policies (such as child-care subsidies in cases in which women always obtain custody of children on divorce) that improve an individual's allocation within the household also improve his or her opportunities outside it. In Lundberg and Pollak's model, the payment of child allowances to women initially improves the intrahousehold distribution of resources in favor of women. But they point out that, if household formation is preceded by some form of binding agreement (such as a prenuptial contract) that includes the promise of transfers from husband to wife (net transfers in the Carter-Katz model, discussed later, are an example of this), husbands may reduce their transfers by an amount equivalent to the shift in child allowances.

In contrast to cooperative models, the noncooperative approach does not assume that members necessarily enter into binding and enforceable contracts with each other. Examples of this approach include Leuthold (1968), Ashworth and Ulph (1981), Ulph (1988), Woolley (1988), Kanbur (1991), and the chapter by Michael Carter and Elizabeth Katz. They assume that individuals within the household not only have differing preferences but also act as autonomous subeconomies. The household is depicted as a site of largely separate gender-specific economies linked by reciprocal claims on members' income, land, goods, and labor. They consider a two-person household in which each individual controls his or her own income and purchases commodities, subject to an individual (nonpooled) income constraint. A net transfer of income between individuals establishes the only link between them. Each individual has a utility function of goods he or she exclusively consumes and a good consumed in common, conditional on the level of net transfers. When making decisions, each person takes net transfers as given and chooses the goods he or she will exclusively consume in order to maximize his or her own utility, subject to the constraint that purchases are less than own-income plus net transfers. This yields a demand function for the goods consumed, which is a function of prices and net transfers. The Nash equilibrium (no household member has an incentive to deviate from his or her set of actions given that no other member deviates) is the level of goods consumed by both individuals that satisfies both demand functions simultaneously. An attractive aspect of this approach is that it is not assumed that income is pooled—a feature in agreement with many of the empirical studies reviewed later in this chapter.

An anthropologist has the last word in Part I of this volume. If the first section of the volume has so far been devoted to a comparison of different economic models, Jane Guyer begins to expand on the potential for multidisciplinary research on intrahousehold issues, specifically from a measurement point of view. Guyer ends this section by exploring some of the intellectual bases for the different approaches economists and anthropologists use when studying and measuring the same household phenomena. In addition, Guyer suggests that economics and anthropology appear to be heading toward a "new convergence of concern" around the nature and use of assets or endowments. Guyer argues that economists should be more concerned with the process of endowment or asset formation instead of regarding it as exogenous and static. Even when economists do use dynamic models, the focus tends to be on asset management from year to year, rather than asset creation, destruction, or delegitimatization, sometimes beyond an individual's own life cycle. Having established the importance of assets to economists and anthropologists—although important in different ways—Guyer emphasizes that the study of assets will help economic models be more open to the incorporation of the anthropological view of "endowment." In this way, she adds, the anthropology of value could be similarly opened up to the economics of investment.

Methods

Part II begins with a critical evaluation of the empirical evidence—both informal and formal—that casts doubt on the unitary model. We examine the results of a series of tests of restrictions implied by the unitary model: Is unearned income pooled? Is income pooled across genders or generations? Are cross-wage labor supply effects identical across gender? Do parents manipulate their adult children? Are male heads of household altruistic? How convincing is the empirical evidence? We note that evaluation is hindered by the fact that much observed behavior lends itself to interpretations consistent with more than one household model. Indeed, a classic exchange in the literature on intrahousehold allocation between Folbre (1984) and Rosenzweig and Schultz (1984) centered on the interpretation of the relationship between gender differences in expected wages and gender bias in child mortality. Both sets of authors accepted the existence of a relationship; they differed on whether this reflected efficiency concerns by parents or relative bargaining power in household decisions—both of which are presumed to parallel wage rates. Indeed the difficulty in distinguishing between "endowment" effects and "bargaining" effects has yet to be satisfactorily resolved. It is also an area in which interaction between the unitary approach (in which the identification of endowments is central) and collective models may prove fruitful. Mindful of this and a number of other caveats, we argue that the existing evidence should be seen as shifting the burden of proof to an approach in which assumption of income pooling is defended rather than maintained.

In the next chapter, Duncan Thomas discusses this further, using data from Brazil; in so doing, he addresses some of the econometric issues raised in reply to his earlier papers on the topic. Using nonlabor income data, Thomas rejects the income-pooling hypothesis. For example, an additional crusado in the hands of a woman raises the share of the household budget spent on education, health, and household services (mostly domestic services) by a factor of between three and six compared with an additional crusado in the hands of a man. In addition, the income of women is associated with higher per capita calorie and protein intake. When Thomas restricts his analysis to those households composed of an intact couple, there is still some evidence suggesting that income effects differ between men and women. If, however, the sample is further restricted to those couples in which both members participate in the labor force, then there is no evidence that treating these households as a single agent is an invalid empirical strategy. This approach suggests that this understanding of household resource allocation may be improved if household composition and labor supply choices are simultaneously taken into account.

Joel Gittelsohn and Sangeeta Mookherji outline how anthropological techniques can be used to lay the foundation for quantitative work on intrahousehold allocation by anthropologists and economists. However, Gittelsohn and Mookherji note that although qualitative research can lay the foundation for quantitative research, economists should not regard this as its sole purpose. They provide specific examples in which anthropological methods can be applied: improvements in survey design, insight into community interventions, and measurement and monitoring of changes over time. They conclude by noting that anthropologists have been less successful in predicting patterns of intrahousehold allocation of such resources as food, and that this is a potentially fruitful area of collaboration with economists.

Even if appropriate methods for collecting food consumption data exist, Howarth Bouis and Christine Peña suggest that current measures of discrimination focus too much on calories. They propose a new indicator for examining discrimination in the intrahousehold distribution of food. They argue that inequality among household members in terms of intake relative to requirements is least likely to be manifested in calorie adequacy or hunger. Rather it is the allocation of micronutrients, associated with higher-status foods, that will be unequally distributed. Bouis and Peña propose an indicator of inequality that is the ratio of an individual's proportion of household micronutrient intake to his or her proportion of household calorie intake. A ratio exceeding one indicates either favoritism or strong bargaining power for a particular household member. For a Philippine sample, Bouis and Peña find no discernible differences in these ratios between girls and boys, but they do find that preschoolers of both sexes are favored in the intrahousehold distribution of food. This is a conclusion different from that reached by comparing only calorie adequacy levels—both unadjusted and adjusted for activity patterns.

Barbara Harriss-White provides a cautionary tale on the measurement of intrahousehold food allocation. Harriss-White assesses the policy recommendations that emerge from five studies of intrahousehold nutrient distribution, each of which uses data collected from the same set of study households in southern India. The studies differ in their conclusions for a number of reasons: the individual classifications of data (for example, different age group classifications), different treatments of seasonality, different nutrients studied (see the discussion of the previous chapter), different aggregations of households (for example, different hectare cutoffs on what constitutes a smallholder), and, finally, different groups of individuals studied. Harriss-White notes that the disagreements among the studies are not trivial in magnitude, and that a policymaker would be "right to be intervention-averse," but she concludes that even if a unified message were to have emerged from the five studies, how it would feed into the policy process is unclear. She concludes that "not only do households need unpacking, so does the policy process."

Judith Bruce and Cynthia Lloyd conclude the section on measurement issues by pointing out that when households are unpacked, a clearer picture of other family relationships might emerge. Their chapter underscores the need for policy to look beyond households to family relationships. They argue that the poverty of mothers and children may be determined less by their normatively ascribed household type than by the degree to which fathers—regardless of marital or residential arrangements—contribute economically to children. They stress that living arrangements or household structures alone may be insufficient to explain children's welfare status. In doing so, they emphasize that households and families contain overlapping, but not necessarily identical, memberships. As such, measurement exercises that focus on, say, households may miss important contributions made by family members not resident in the household.

Policy

Even if policymakers are agnostic about the usefulness of any specific household model, unitary or collective, they neglect patterns of intrahousehold inequalities at their peril. Consider a common policy situation: a government attempts to target a program to individuals by age or gender, rather than to households. Many examples exist in which governments assume either (1) that amelioration of household poverty is sufficient for the alleviation of individual poverty or (2) that individual poverty can be alleviated without regard to the actions of other household members. These assumptions will lead to policy failure, irrespective of the choice of resource allocation model.

Consider a nonwelfarist approach to raising the food consumption of undernourished individuals through an in-kind transfer to undernourished households.[2] Haddad and Kanbur (1990) demonstrate that the undernourishment rankings of various socioeconomic and geographic household groups can change when individual-level food consumption information is used instead of household-level information. For example, although individual-level data may indicate that individuals from certain households are an important food poverty group, a reliance on household-level data might imply that they are not an important group. This result occurs when patterns of intrahousehold inequality differ between different household groups. If inequality were similar in all groups, food poverty rankings would be identical, whether or not individual-level data were used to target the transfer.

Two other studies explicitly dispel the notion that the improvement of household nutrition is sufficient for the improvement of preschooler nutrition. Pelletier, Msukwa, and Ramakrishnan (1991) test the hypothesis that the nutrition status of older household members is strongly reflected in that of young children and that associated socioeconomic factors are the same for both age groups. The study shows that, in a Malawian sample, the first assumption is

---

2. A welfarist approach to poverty assumes that the level of income indicates the welfare of the individual or household in question, regardless of how that income is spent. A nonwelfarist approach focuses on the consumption of one or more goods or services without direct invocation of the household's own assessment of the utility of consuming that commodity.

more valid than the second, but then only during acute food shortages. Work by Senauer and Garcia (1992) in the Philippines arrives at similar conclusions: if intrahousehold food allocation patterns are inequitable relative to requirements, then targeting preschoolers based on household-level indicators may be a very costly way of raising preschooler food intake.

Programs that do rely on individual-level data for targeting purposes are prone to another type of error of neglect of household decisionmaking. These programs often confuse the need to isolate the individual outcome with the assumption that the food allocation mechanism within the household can be ignored. Suppose there is concern regarding the nutrition of children. A possible policy response is the implementation of a school meals program in which children who are recorded as being particularly undernourished receive extra food. The success of this intervention cannot be ascertained in the absence of information on the pattern of food allocation among household members. Households might respond to this program by reducing the amount of food the targeted child receives at home (and increasing the amount of food consumed by other household members). Indeed this was the conclusion of Beaton and Ghassemi's (1982) review of international experience with supplementary feeding programs (see also Kennedy and Alderman 1987). Ironically, the naive approach to targeting individuals in isolation from the household is an extreme version of a child as a "separate sphere" and thus is inconsistent with the unitary model, among others. Although these examples pertain to nutrition programs, the issue is more general. For example, Apps and Savage (1989) show that welfare orderings of Australian households are very sensitive to the neglect of intrahousehold inequality. Moreover, the rankings are also sensitive to the method of measuring intrahousehold resource allocation. This finding has implications for the design of a tax and welfare system.

The issue is not confined to either gender inequalities or the welfare of young children. Many countries have designed programs to meet the needs of the elderly. Few of these programs are fully financed from individual contributions (World Bank 1994). The appreciable wage taxes that are earmarked for such programs represent a transfer from one generation to another. However, too little is known about either the poverty of the elderly or how their needs are met by intrafamily transfer to be able to access fully the implications of various social security policies. The full impact of targeting programs to the elderly can only be effectively assessed if the responses of other family members are taken into consideration (Cox and Jimenez 1992).

Within this context, Part III of the book considers a number of policy issues in the context of intrahousehold allocation. Harold Alderman and Paul Gertler argue that price policy is not silent on intrahousehold health-seeking behaviors in Pakistan. They find that there is a tendency to use high-quality providers (private doctors) more often for males than for females. These differences, though, disappear as income rises. The authors argue that although the differences in health care are not dramatic, they pertain to an environment in which the price of health care is low. Moreover, most of the illness incidents from which their estimates are derived are the general day-to-day ailments to which children are susceptible. They suggest that the comparatively high price for life-threatening treatments that often require more expensive hospitalization may lead to more gender discrimination and possibly fatal delays in seeking care.

At the program level, Jennie Dey Abbas also emphasizes the importance of knowing intrahousehold resource allocation patterns prior to intervention design. Using a Gambian case study, she points out that any evaluation of a project or policy to raise male and female labor productivity in agriculture must take into account differences in rights to accompanying resources, as well as unobserved labor obligations to other household members. The obligations of women to men are usually asymmetric, and they afford ample scope for male opportunism.

Nancy Folbre picks up the theme of asymmetric rights and obligations in a more general way, arguing that most discussions of public policy and intrahousehold inequality tacitly assume that policymakers are able to abstract themselves from societal biases. Such a view is at odds with new political economy theories that emphasize how policies are shaped by activities undertaken by political coalitions (though she is cautious about carte blanche application of these models to family and social policy). Folbre provides evidence that public policy in many countries, but especially in the developing world, reinforces intrahousehold and intrafamily inequality. Folbre calls for additional research on extrahousehold factors that shape, and are shaped by, intrahousehold processes—family law and social entitlements, for instance.

The final chapter of Part III concludes the book. The chapter acknowledges that the unitary model is a powerful tool that can be readily adapted to explain complex patterns of intrahousehold inequality. Is the investigation of alternative models, then, merely a matter of academic intrigue? We argue that the intrahousehold issues are as relevant to policymakers as they are to researchers. Specifically, at least four types of policy failures that will be precipitated by neglect of intrahousehold decisionmaking processes are identified.

The first concerns the effect of public transfers made to the household. The unitary model predicts that the impact of such transfers is unaffected by the identity of the recipient, because all household resources are pooled. For a household that behaves in a manner consistent with a collective model of the household, the welfare effects of a transfer may be quite different if the recipient is, say, a man as opposed to a woman. Second, not only is the identity of the recipient important, the response of nonrecipients must be considered. The extent to which public transfers are mitigated or enhanced by changes in private behavior is determined by whether intrahousehold interactions are best described as intergenerational altruism (a form of the unitary model) or a collective model with exchange motives. Third, at the project level, the unitary model implies that it does not matter to whom policy initiatives are directed. This "information source independence" arises because the unitary model assumes that not only is nonlabor income pooled, so too is information. However, the assumption that the self-declared head of household has detailed knowledge of the activities of other relevant household members will invariably lead to such policy failures as (1) the nonadoption of particular policies and (2) unintended costs arising from policies that are adopted. Failure to facilitate the adoption of new technology or of practices that retard environmental degradation, or the adoption of projects that make the target group worse off, exemplifies faulty policy assumptions.

The final and perhaps most important drawback of relying on the unitary model for policy guidance is that a number of potentially powerful policy handles are disabled. Under the unitary model, policymakers affect intrahousehold resource allocation primarily through changes in prices. Some collective approaches suggest that additional policy handles, often with a very long reach, are available to the policymaker. Examples of these policy handles include changes in access to common property resources, credit, public works schemes, and a general strengthening of legal and institutional rights.

The importance of collective models in policy analysis does not imply that the indiscriminate adoption of a model simply because it is a member of the collective class is advocated. Despite numerous rejections of income pooling and of polar cases of altruism within a family, to date no one model of collective behavior has dominated the alternatives posed. In fact, most arguments for the policy relevance of model choice are based on the failings of the unitary model rather than the strengths of a particular collective model. Put another way, collective models may resolve a number of the anomalies that have accrued under the unitary model, but further work is necessary to improve their predictive power. The final chapter concludes by outlining where such work might be most fruitful.

PART I

Modeling Intrahousehold Resource Allocation

2 Specification and Estimation of the Demand for Goods within the Household

MARK M. PITT

There is a large empirical literature in which household or individual data are used to estimate the demands for both market goods and nonmarket goods, such as health and human capital. For example, Pitt and Rosenzweig (1985) have estimated the effect of food prices and access to health programs and clean water on the health of individuals (as measured by recent morbidity) and on the quantity of food nutrients consumed by households in Indonesia. Studies such as these inform policymakers how changes in food prices and program provision affect the health of individuals. If separate demand equations are estimated for different types of individuals, perhaps differentiated by age and gender, even more is learned about the distribution of the effects of policy changes. Pitt and Rosenzweig found that the effects of price changes on recent morbidity differed between male heads of household and their spouses in Indonesia. As useful as such studies may be, they tell almost nothing about how households allocate resources among their members. As demonstrated in this chapter, it is quite difficult to estimate the demand for goods within the household.

A useful way of approaching the problem is to formulate it in terms of intrahousehold conditional demand equations. Such equations ask how the allocations provided to one household member affect the allocations of others. For example, how does one person's health, time allocation, or food consumption affect that of another? And how does the allocation of each of these goods affect the allocation of the others?

I begin with a restatement of the simple model of demand in which a single consumer chooses among a set of market goods. The concept of a conditional demand equation, first considered by Pollak (1969), is introduced in this simple framework before multiperson households and nonmarket goods are considered. I stress the problem of finding believable and theoretically justified restrictions that enable the researcher to identify cross-person demand relationships within the household statistically, and I show why it is, in general, impossible to identify these demand relationships based upon the usual

19

exclusion restrictions. Some approaches to estimation are considered, and examples drawn from my work with Mark Rosenzweig are used to illustrate these methods.

Conditional Demand in a Simple One-Person Household

Consider the simplest possible case of a one-person household with fixed (exogenous) income, M, and a utility function having only market goods, x_i, as arguments. The household's problem is

$$\max U = U(x_1, x_2, \ldots, x_K), \quad \text{subject to} \sum_{i=1}^{K} p_i x_1 = M \tag{2.1}$$

where p_i is the market price of good i, taken parametrically by the household. The uncompensated (Marshallian) demand equations resulting from this problem are

$$x_i = d_i(p_1, p_2, \ldots, p_K, M), \quad i = 1, \ldots, K \tag{2.2}$$

Dual to this problem is the problem of minimizing the cost, c, of obtaining a given level of utility, U:

$$\min c = c(p_1, p_2, \ldots, p_K, U) \tag{2.3}$$

The partial derivatives of the cost function are the compensated (Hicksian) demand equations:

$$\frac{\partial c}{\partial p_i} = x_i = q_i(p_1, p_2, \ldots, p_K, U), \quad i = 1, \ldots, K \tag{2.4}$$

Consider the problem of this single-person household if the allocation of one or more goods is rationed and the ration is binding. That is, given the household's income and the prices it faces, it would wish to consume at least as much as the rationed quantity if it could freely choose consumption levels. In this case, consumption of the rationed good exactly equals the ration amount. For simplicity, good x_1 will be treated as the rationed good, and the rationed quantity is $\bar{x}_1$. The consumer's problem is now

$$\min c^1 = c^1(\bar{x}_1, p_1, p_2, \ldots, p_K, U) \tag{2.5}$$

where c^1 denotes the cost of utility, conditional on consumption of the rationed quantity $\bar{x}_1$. One can view the consumer's problem as choosing consumption levels of all goods except x_1 so as to maximize utility subject to consuming $x_1 = \bar{x}_1$ and to having income of $M - p_1\bar{x}_1$ to spend on the other $K - 1$ goods. Formally the rationed household's problem is

$$\max U = U(\bar{x}_1, x_2, \ldots, x_K), \quad \text{subject to} \sum_{i=2}^{K} p_i x_i = M - p_1 \bar{x}_1 \quad (2.6)$$

From the rationed problem equation (2.6), it can be seen that the only way in which the price of the rationed good p_1 affects demand is through the term $p_1 \bar{x}_1$ on the right-hand side of the budget constraint. A fall in the price of the rationed good just increases the income available for purchasing all other goods, that is, the price change only induces an income effect. There is no substitution effect resulting from changing the price p_1 as long as the ration remains binding. Thus the derivatives of the conditional cost function, equation (2.5), which are the conditional compensated (Hicksian) demand equations, do not depend on p_1:

$$\frac{\partial c^1}{\partial p_i} = x_i = q_i^1(\bar{x}_1, p_2, p_3, \ldots, p_K, U), \quad i = 2, \ldots, K \quad (2.7)$$

where q_i^1 is the demand for good i, conditional on the ration $\bar{x}_1$.

If the rationed good is food these conditional demand equations tell how a change in the consumption of food alters the consumption of the other goods, such as time allocation and nonfood goods consumption. In the absence of actual rationing, the conditional demand equation (2.7) would never have to be estimated. The integrability of demand systems means that everything about preferences that can be learned is learned by estimating the unconditional demand equation (2.4). The parameters of the conditional demand equations can be constructed from the parameters of the unconditional demand equations. Furthermore the reverse is also true: the unconditional cost function can be recovered from the conditional cost function (Browning 1983).

Nonetheless consider how to estimate empirically the effect of changing the level of consumption of one good in a single-person household on the demand for all other goods. This is exactly the problem of estimating the conditional demands, equation (2.7), in the absence of rationing. To make the problem realistic, assume that estimation will use data from single-person households having heterogeneous preferences. If the preference heterogeneity results in additive stochastic terms appended to the conditional demand equations, least squares estimation will result in heterogeneity bias. The level of observed consumption of the good conditioned upon x_1 is a regressor that will likely be correlated with this preference-based error. Consumers with above-average preferences for good x_1 will consume more of it and consequently have less income remaining to spend on all other goods. One obvious approach to estimating models with endogenous regressors is to use instrumental variable methods. From equations (2.4) and (2.7) there is a single, theoretically justified exclusion restriction, the price p_1, that is a determinant of x_1 in equation (2.4) but does not appear in the demand equation (2.7) conditional on x_1. It is straightforward to extend this example by conditioning on more than one good. Conditioning on the quantity of more than one good consumed results in conditional demand equations that exclude the prices of all conditioned goods as arguments (regressors), thus assuring exact identification of exclusion restrictions for instrumental variable estimation.

Conditional Demand in a Multiperson Household

The problem for a multimember household analogous to the one described in equation (2.1) is

$$\max U = U(x_{11}, x_{12}, \ldots, x_{1J}, x_{21}, x_{22}, \ldots, x_{2J}, \ldots, x_{KJ}),$$

$$\text{subject to } \sum_{i=1}^{K} \sum_{j=1}^{J} p_i x_{ij} = M \qquad (2.8)$$

where x_{ij} is the consumption of good i by household member j in a household composed of J members. The key difference between the single-person and multimember household models is not the larger number of person-specific goods but the fact that there are more goods than there are prices. There are K market goods and J household members yielding KJ person-specific goods, but still only prices for K goods.[1] The cost function, conditioning on the consumption of one good by one member of the household, is then

$$c^{11} = c^{11}(x_{11}, p_1, p_2, \ldots, p_K, U) \qquad (2.9)$$

where indexes are innocuously chosen such that the cost function c^{11} is conditional on the consumption of good 1 by household member 1 (x_{11}). In the multimember household, unlike the single-person household, a reduction in the price of the rationed good p_1 can have substitution effects on demands for all other goods. To see this, note that the household's problem is to allocate $KJ - 1$ person-specific goods so as to maximize utility subject to consuming $x_{11} = \bar{x}_{11}$ and remaining income $M - p_1\bar{x}_{11}$:

$$\max U = U(\bar{x}_{11}, x_{12}, x_{13}, \ldots, x_{1J}, x_{21}, x_{22}, \ldots, x_{2J}, \ldots, x_{KJ}),$$

$$\text{subject to } \sum_{j=1}^{J} \sum_{i=2}^{K} p_i x_{ij} + p_1 \sum_{j=2}^{J} x_{1j} = M - p_1\bar{x}_{11} \qquad (2.10)$$

---

1. Of course, restrictions placed on the utility function can lead to the aggregation of goods across persons, reducing the excess number of "goods" relative to prices, but cannot eliminate the excess number altogether, except in the limiting case.

Time is one good that likely has person-specific prices (wages). This fact has been exploited by Rosenzweig (1986a) and others to estimate intrahousehold cross-wage effects. It is difficult to think of important classes of other market goods for which person-specific prices exist, although the shadow prices of goods produced in the household, such as health, are likely to vary across or within a household. These issues are addressed later in the chapter.

In equation (2.10) the price p_1 still appears on the left-hand side of the budget constraint as it reflects the prices for the $J - 1$ "unconstrained" goods $x_{12}, x_{13}, \ldots, x_{1J}$. The derivative of the conditional (and unconditional) cost function with respect to a price p_1 is not the compensated demand for a person-specific good as it was in the single-person household, because p_1 is the common price of J (or $J - 1$ for p_1) person-specific goods in equation (2.10). The conditional demand for person-specific good x_{ij} is

$$x_{ij}^{11} = q_{ij}^{11}(\bar{x}_{11}, p_1, p_2, \ldots, p_K, U) \tag{2.11}$$

In this case identifying exclusion restrictions are not available to carry out instrumental variable estimation, since the price p_1 of the conditioned good x_{11} is not excluded from the conditional demand equation. All the goods x_{1i} have the same price. Furthermore one cannot infer the conditional demand equations by estimating the unconditional demand equations. The unconditional demand equations for person-specific goods are themselves not identifiable because person-specific prices do not exist for all goods.

The problem of the multimember household can now be generalized to include home-produced goods, such as health, and the time allocation of household members. The household's problem is now

$$\max U = U(x_{11}, x_{12}, \ldots, x_{1J}, x_{21}, x_{22}, \ldots, x_{2J}, \ldots, x_{KJ}),$$
$$\text{subject to } h_j = h_j(x_{1j}, x_{2j}, \ldots, x_{kj}, l_1, l_2, \ldots, l_j, z_j, \mu_j), j = 1,$$
$$\text{and } \sum_{i=1}^{K} \sum_{j=1}^{J} p_i x_{ij} + \sum_{j=1}^{J} w_j l_j + \sum_{j=1}^{J} p_z z_j = v + \sum_{j=1}^{J} w_j T \tag{2.12}$$

where

l_j = home time of household member j,

h_j = quantity of home-produced good h (health) allocated to person j,

w_j = market wage of member j,

z = an input into the production of the home-produced good,

p_z = its price, and

v = nonearnings (exogenous) income.

The term μ_j represents person-specific endowments, such as innate healthiness, which are fixed and not changeable by the household. The health production functions given in equation (2.12) are general in that they allow for the technology producing h to be different for every household member and for own-consumption of the market goods x and the home time l of every household member to be inputs into the production of h. But by treating home time as a household public good—that is, by not distinguishing among the allocations of person j's time to the production of each household member's home good—the treatment of home time in the technology is not perfectly general. If home time were a private good allocatable to each person, there would be J^2

home time allocations and home time demand equations. In that case even the wage would not be a good-specific price, since the price of the home time of the jth person devoted to the production of each of the household's J members would be identically w_j.[2]

Consider the nature of the conditional demand equations corresponding to equation (2.12) in the case of a single-person household. Even though the h good is not a market good, there is a market good z that does not provide utility directly but only enters into the unconditional demand equations through its effect on h. The price of this good acts as the "price of health." Conditioning on $h = \bar{h}$, the conditional demand equations for the single-person household do not depend on p_z, and thus p_z is available as an identifying exclusion restriction for the instrumental variable estimation of the conditional demands. If there is a vector of health inputs like z, then there are overidentifying restrictions.

Unfortunately, as in the case with only market goods available, in a multimember household when the price p_z is not person-specific, p_z does not disappear from demand equations that condition on the level of h provided by any one household member or subset of household members.[3] Thus, except in the case of time allocation, the problem of more person-specific goods than prices precludes the estimation of person-specific unconditional demand equations as well as the use of instrumental variable methods to estimate intrahousehold conditional demand equations.

Some Approaches to Estimation

In spite of this gloomy theoretical outlook, many studies have indeed estimated intrahousehold conditional demand equations. Four approaches have been followed.

Ignoring Unobserved Heterogeneity

One approach is essentially to ignore the problem, treating the conditioned-upon behaviors as exogenous. In some of the literature the labor supply of women has been regressed on the number of children or their health without regard to the possible effects of unobserved heterogeneity on the estimates.

---

2. In this discussion, I assume interior solutions for time allocation—that is, the opportunity cost of time is the market wage. If no time is spent in the market, the market wage is not the shadow price of time and there is one less exogenous variable in the demand equations. Estimation of demand systems with corner solutions is essentially the estimation of conditional demand equations with binding rations of zero (Lee and Pitt 1986).

3. It is likely that there are some "Z goods" that are only inputs into the production of the home-produced good h for certain types of household members. For example some inputs into the care of infants (diapers, infant formula, certain inoculations) are not also inputs into the care of older household members. There may be gender-specific health inputs reflecting the different biologies of men and women. In practice these prices are not often measured and more than one household member is of the same type.

Identification with Exclusion Restrictions

A second approach is to make exclusion restrictions necessary for the use of instrumental variable methods, even though, as demonstrated previously, it is difficult to find such restrictions that are not inconsistent with a general theory of household behavior. Pitt and Rosenzweig (1985) estimate the way in which the health of male heads of farm households in Indonesia affects their labor supply. They use the prevalence of health programs, such as public health clinics and sanitation facilities, as identifying instruments (corresponding to p_z). A Hausman-Wu test "confirms" the endogeneity of health in this conditional labor supply equation. But in these multimember households health programs and facilities must also affect the health of the head's wife and other household members. Interpreting these estimates as the supply of labor conditional on own-health, as Pitt and Rosenzweig do, requires either that health prices affect the health of the household head but not that of other household members, or that the health status and time allocation of other household members have no effect on the head's labor supply (as in the single-member household); neither of these situations is very believable.

Identification through Cross-Person Restrictions on Demands

A third approach is to put additional structure on the model that, although not necessarily consistent with a general model of household behavior, involves restrictions less onerous than the zero exclusion restrictions of the second approach. Pitt and Rosenzweig (1990) use this method to estimate the effects of infant mortality on the allocation of time in Indonesian households. The linearized demand equations for the home time of two household members, i and j, conditional on the health of family member k, are

$$l_i = \alpha_{0i} + \alpha_{1i}p_1 + \alpha_{2i}p_2 + \ldots + \alpha_{Ki}p_K + \beta_{1i}w_1 + \beta_{2i}w_2 + \ldots$$
$$+ \beta_{Ji}w_J + \gamma_i p_z + \lambda_i h_k + \varepsilon_i \tag{2.13}$$

and

$$l_j = \alpha_{0j} + \alpha_{1j}p_1 + \alpha_{2j}p_2 + \ldots + \alpha_{Kj}p_K + \beta_{1j}w_1 + \beta_{2j}w_2 + \ldots$$
$$+ \beta_{Jj}w_J + \gamma_j p_z + \lambda_j h_k + \varepsilon_j \tag{2.14}$$

where ε_i is an error term that includes the effects of the J health endowments $\mu_1, \ldots, \mu_J$, and the remaining Greek letters are unknown parameters. Pitt and Rosenzweig impose the restriction that $\gamma_i = \gamma_j$. The plausibility of this restriction depends on the characteristics of the individuals i and j. If behavior is age dependent then the restriction is plausible if the individuals i and j are of approximately the same age. If behavior is gender dependent then the restriction is more plausible if i and j are of the same gender. Unconditional demand equations that demonstrate differences in price response by gender do not necessarily invalidate this restriction, since gender differences in price response in unconditional demand do not necessarily imply a different price response when conditioned on infant health (or any other behavior). In Pitt and Rosenzweig's study this equality restriction is made for three member types: the mother of the infant whose health status is conditioned and the infant's male and female teenage siblings.

Time allocation is measured as principal activity in the week prior to the date of the survey, the 1980 National Socioeconomic Survey of Indonesia (SUSENAS). Four mutually exclusive principal activities are distinguished: work, school, home care, and leisure. The linearized conditional demand equation for family members in a household containing a mother and her teenage son and daughter is

$$l_{ij}^* = (\alpha_{iM} + \delta_{ij}^A D_j)'A_j + (\gamma_{iM} + \delta_{ij}^h D_j)h^* + (\beta_{1M} + \delta_{ij}^x D_j)'X + Z\lambda_{ij} + \varepsilon_{ij} \quad (2.15)$$

where

l_{ij}^* = level at which household member j undertakes activity i,

D_j = 1 in the equation for j and 0 otherwise in the son and daughter equations,

h^* = the endogenous health of the mother's infant child,

A = a vector of member-specific exogenous variables, and

X and Z are vectors of household-specific exogenous variables,
  to be distinguished later.

The Greek letters, except ε, represent parameters to be estimated, and ε_{ij} represents error terms having a multivariate distribution with zero means and covariance matrix Σ. The vector of exogenous variables Z is that for which equality restrictions are imposed:

$$\lambda_{ij} = \lambda_{ik} \qquad i \neq k; \ i, \ k = \text{member type} \tag{2.16}$$

The vector Z consists of two subsets of regressors: 26 prices or price indexes for goods and a set of 16 community characteristics, including health facilities and programs, public waste facilities, and drinking water sources.

Neither h^* nor the activity variable l_{ij}^* is observed in the data, only sets of dichotomous indicators indicating whether an infant had been sick or not and the primary time activity of the household member. The model was estimated using an instrumental variable household fixed-effects method (Chamberlain 1980). The fixed-effects procedure greatly reduces the computational burden, reduces the effects of heterogeneity across households, and eliminates the sample selection problem under suitable assumptions. It does not, however, permit identification of the parameters λ_{ij}, and only the differential effects δ are identified for the regressors X and h^*. But the parameters δ are required to test the hypothesis about intrahousehold distribution, and the parameters λ_{ij} are

TABLE 2.1 Differential effects of infant illness on household activities of daughters, sons, and mothers relative to home care

Household Pair/ Infant Illness	Alternative Activity to Home Care					
	Labor Force		School		Leisure	
	Exogenous	Endogenous	Exogenous	Endogenous	Exogenous	Endogenous
Daughter versus son	2.84	−1.25	3.21	−1.07	3.23	−1.11
	(1.40)[a]	(2.23)[b]	(1.58)[a]	(2.03)[b]	(1.58)[a]	(1.88)[b]
		[3.23][c]		[2.85]		[2.57]
Daughter versus mother	−.348	.072	...	...	...	...
	(1.87)	(0.49)				
		[0.60]				
Son versus mother	−3.19	1.32	.·.·	...	...	...
	(1.57)	(2.32)				
		[3.20]				

SOURCE: Pitt and Rosenzweig (1990), p. 981.
[a]Asymptotic *t*-ratios are in parentheses.
[b]Asymptotic *t*-ratios corrected for use of stochastic regressors, estimated from first stage, are in parentheses.
[c]Uncorrected *t*-ratios computed directly from information matrix are in brackets.

maintained not to affect time allocation differentially and thus are of little interest.

Table 2.1 presents estimates of the δ_{ij} parameters, which capture differential activity effects of child illness relative to the household care activity. These parameters were estimated from maximizing a single multinomial logit fixed-effects likelihood containing predicted values of infant health from a first-stage maximum-likelihood binary logit regression. In the first-stage equation, the sets of regressors upon which identification rests—area-level food prices ($\chi^2[26] = 80.6$), programs and health facilities ($\chi^2[7] = 17.6$), and water supplies ($\chi^2[5] = 18.4$)—are statistically significant.

Parameters from two specifications are presented in Table 2.1: those from a single-stage multinomial fixed-effects logit that treats infant health as exogenous in the differential allocation of time, and one in which instrumental variable methods are applied. The two sets of estimates are not directly comparable since actual health is a dichotomous indicator of morbidity, whereas predicted morbidity is a continuous estimate of a latent variable. Nonetheless the signs of the parameters differ in every case. Treating infant health as exogenous results in the (false) inference that there is no statistically different effect of infant health on the activity responses of teenage siblings. In the consistent instrumental variable estimates, infant health does significantly influence differential time allocation. The hypothesis that the responses of sons and daughters to own-age, infant illness, and the number and sex composition of household teenagers are identical is strongly rejected ($\chi^2[15] = 73.6$). However, the hypothesis that the responses of daughters and mothers are not different cannot be rejected ($\chi^2[6] = 14.5$), whereas it is rejected in a comparison of sons and mothers ($\chi^2[6] = 69.3$). The differential responses are thus based more on gender than on age.

Interpretation of the parameters is somewhat complicated since they represent the effect of a change in infant health on the allocation of time to one activity relative to another activity (home care) for one person-type relative to another. The consistently estimated parameter in the first row, second column of Table 2.1 (-1.25) indicates that increases in the latent illness of an infant reduce the daughter's time in the labor force, as compared with home care, more than the son's. Furthermore, increases in latent infant illness also reduce schooling and leisure time (relative to home care) for daughters more than for sons. These results suggest that reductions in infant morbidity would reduce gender-based inequality among teenagers in Indonesia. Assessing the quantitative importance of the level as opposed to the differential effect of latent infant illness requires at least one additional restriction. In Pitt and Rosenzweig (1990) quantitative estimates of level effects are obtained under the assumption that teenage boys do not alter their time devoted to household activities in response to the illness of an infant sibling.[4]

The "Endowment Method"

The fourth approach to identifying intrahousehold conditional demand equations relies on treating the endowment μ_j as an implicit person-specific "price" for the home-produced good h in equation (2.12). To see this, note that

---

4. Recently I have implemented a somewhat related approach that permits the identification of all the level regression parameters without placing cross-equation restrictions on regression parameters (Pitt 1996). The approach is a generalization of the methods developed by Chamberlain (1977a, 1977b) and Chamberlain and Griliches (1975) that identify models of the returns to schooling through the imposition of error covariance restrictions across a set of schooling, earning, and occupational choice behaviors for siblings. In Pitt (1996) the idea is to place a factor-analytic structure on the residuals of a set of sex-specific regressions for weight, height, and arm circumference for siblings of both sexes and the residuals of the choice equations of their father's and mother's decision whether to participate in a group-based credit program in Bangladesh. The model allows individual-specific error components to be correlated across children within the family without loss of identification. The imposition of the factor-analytic structure alone is sufficient to identify separately the effect of credit program participation by gender on the health outcomes of boys and girls. Estimation is essentially maximum likelihood generalized least squares with a restricted covariance matrix. This estimation is fairly complex since eight equations are estimated simultaneously—three nutritional outcomes separately for boys and girls plus credit program participation for men and women. This estimation involves not only a large number of regression parameters of the usual sort but also a rather large number of parameters describing the correlation structure of the residual variance-covariance matrix. In addition, the number of boy and girl children in each household varies across households, resulting in an "unbalanced" design. The likelihood is tailored to include all sampled children and not just a fixed number per household.

the shadow price associated with an allocation ("ration") of a home-produced good to household member 1 is

$$p_{h1}^* = \frac{\partial U / \partial h_1}{\partial U / \partial v} \tag{2.17}$$

where p_{h1}^* is the shadow price of the allocation $h_1 = \bar{h}_1$, and v is, as before, nonearnings income. The shadow price of h_1 is the reduction in the (minimum) cost of obtaining the prior level of utility as a result of the increase of health by one unit. The shadow price associated with an increase in the endowment μ_1 of household member 1 is similarly

$$p_{\mu 1}^* = \frac{\partial U / \partial \mu_1}{\partial U / \partial v} = \frac{(\partial U / \partial h_1)(\partial h_1 / \partial \mu_1)}{\partial U / \partial v} \tag{2.18}$$

If the endowments μ_j are additive in the household technologies (equation [2.12]), then $\partial h_1/\partial \mu_1 = 1$ and $p_{\mu 1}^* = p_{h1}^*$. Simply put, a unit increase in the endowment μ_j implies a unit increase in h_j when all input allocations are unchanged. The μ_j are exogenous person-specific determinants of the shadow price of h_j and thus are valid instruments for the estimation of demand equations conditional upon the household allocation of the h good among its members.

In practice none of the studies that have used the endowment method has estimated conditional demand equations with μ_j as an identifying instrument. Instead they have estimated reduced-form demand equations with the estimated μ_j added to the set of exogenous regressors. These are unconditional demand equations, but now with an individual-specific exogenous component to health, μ_j, as an implicit person-specific price. The conditional demand equations can thus be fully recovered from the full set of unconditional demand equations. Regularity conditions of demand theory imply that the sign on μ_j in a reduced-form (unconditional) demand equation for the ith input provided person j, x_{ij}, must be the same as the sign on h_j in a conditional (on h_j) demand equation for x_{ij}, with μ_j as an identifying instrument. In particular, regularity requires that

$$\frac{dh_j}{d\mu_j} = \sum \left(\frac{\partial h_j}{\partial x_{ij}} \frac{\partial x_{ii}}{\partial \mu_j} \right) + \frac{\partial h_j}{\partial \mu_j} \geq 0 \tag{2.19}$$

which implies that an individual's health is never made worse by the acquisition of exogenous health. The household may "tax" away some of the exogenous health by reducing health inputs x_{ij} but will not tax away more than all of it.

The problem with any empirical methodology that estimates cross-person effects using endowments is that the μ_j is not directly observed. However, if the technology is known, it can be calculated as $\mu_j = h_j - h_j(^*)$, where $h_j(^*)$ is shorthand for the technology found in equation (2.12) and additive endowments are assumed. In practice the technology is not known but must be specified and consistently estimated from nonexperimental data, subject to errors of measurement and other sources of stochastic variation.

Consider the (trivial) case of the single-person household and the problem of determining the effect of an exogenous increase in the health of an individual on that individual's demand for the single health input z. If the health technology and health input demand equation are linear in the parameters, the result is

$$h_j = \alpha + \beta z_j + \mu_j + \varepsilon_j$$
$$z_j = \pi p_{zj} + \gamma \pi_{xj} + \lambda \mu_j + e_j \tag{2.20}$$

where μ_j is the health endowment of person (household) j, p_x is the price of a market good that does not affect health, and ε_j and e_j are random errors for which $E(\varepsilon_j, e_j) = 0$, $E(\varepsilon_j, \mu_j) = 0$, and $E(e_j, \mu_j) = 0$. These restrictions on the error components imply that the only source of error correlation in the two equations (2.20) arises from the health endowments. The covariance between the residuals of these equations is thus $\mathrm{cov}(\mu + \varepsilon, \lambda \mu + e) = \lambda \sigma_\mu^2$ and is straightforward to estimate. Since σ_μ^2 is nonnegative, the sign of this term is the sign of λ. A negative λ implies compensatory behavior on the part of the household—an exogenous increase in health induces a reduction in health input demand, which would not be a very surprising result. Identification of the magnitude of λ requires knowledge of σ_μ^2.

Knowledge of the signs of person-specific λs is of more interest in the multiperson household framework, where reinforcing behavior is more likely (Pitt, Rosenzweig, and Hassan 1990), but identifying these signs becomes problematic even if strong restrictions are placed on the error covariances (as above) and on the health technologies. Consider the simple case of a two-person household in which both person-types (j and k) have identical health technologies,

$$h_j = \beta z_j + \mu_j + \varepsilon_j$$
$$h_k = \beta z_k + \mu_k + \varepsilon_k \tag{2.21}$$

and the demand equations for health input provided persons j and k would be estimated

$$z_j = \pi_j p_z + \gamma_j p_x + \lambda_j \mu_j + \lambda_{kj} \mu_k + e_j$$
$$z_k = \pi_k p_z + \lambda_k p_x + \lambda_{jk} \mu_j + \lambda_k \mu_k + e_k \tag{2.22}$$

from a sample of households (where the household subscript is dropped for simplicity). The parameter λ_{kj} represents the effect of person k's exogenous health on person j's allocation of good z. If, as before, the only source of residual covariation is through the μs, and if $E(\mu_j, \mu_k) \neq 0$, as seems likely, identification of the three λs requires knowledge of the variances and covariances of the μs.

Assuming that $\sigma_\varepsilon^2 = 0$ for both j and k—that is, that the residual variance of the health technologies is identical to the variance of the endowment (no measurement error exists)—is sufficient for identifying the λs. Rosenzweig and Schultz (1983), the first to apply the endowment method to the estimation of intrahousehold demand equations, treated the estimated residuals from the health technology as measured-with-error estimates of the endowments μ_j and included them as regressors in the demand equations (2.21).[5] Under the assumption that the "measurement error" ε_j was uncorrelated with the error e_j, classical errors-in-variable bias results: parameters are biased toward zero. Thus Rosenzweig and Schultz interpret their estimates as lower bounds on the true absolute values of the regression coefficients.

The problem is that there is often reason to believe that this measurement error is not orthogonal to the errors ε_j of the demand equations. If the source of the error ε_j is only measurement error on health or human capital outcome h_j, then the orthogonality condition is not unbelievable. But if the source of the measurement error arises from the input z_j, then a very difficult form of bias arises in the estimation of the conditional demand equation (2.21). To see this problem consider the linear health-production function for person j in equation (2.21) as consisting of measured-with-error output h_j and input z_j. The true (measured-without-error) endowment is

$$\mu_j^* = h_j^* - z_j^* \beta \tag{2.23}$$

where h_i^* and z_i^* are the (unobserved) true values of health and the health input, respectively. If both health and the input z have measurement errors η_i and v_i with classical errors-in-variables properties, that is,

$$h_j = h_j^* + \eta_j \tag{2.24}$$

$$z_j = z_j^* + v_j \tag{2.25}$$

where $E(h_i^*, \eta_j) = 0$, $E(z_i^*, v_j) = 0$, and $E(\eta_j, v_j) = 0$, then the estimated endowment, $\hat{\mu}_j$, is

$$\hat{\mu}_j = (h_j^* + \eta_j) - (z_j^* + v_j)\hat{\beta}$$
$$= \mu_j^* + \eta_j - v_j\hat{\beta} \tag{2.26}$$

where $\hat{\beta}$ is a consistent estimator of β. Thus the health endowment measurement error is $\eta_j - v_j\hat{\beta}$ and the demand for the good z by person j is

$$z_j = \pi_j p_z + \lambda_j \hat{\mu}_j + \lambda_{kj} \hat{\mu}_k + (v_j + e_j) \tag{2.27}$$

---

5. Pagan (1984) has shown that ordinary least squares estimates of regression equations having an estimated residual as a regressor provide consistent estimates of the parameter covariance matrix as long as the estimated residuals are orthogonal to the regression residuals.

If the marginal product of the health input is positive($\beta > 0$), then the measurement errors of v_j and v_k are systematically negatively correlated with the error of the person-specific input demand equation (2.27). Simply put, any error in the measurement of a production function input will impart a proportional measurement error to the estimated endowment. A subsequent regression of this input on estimated endowments will have spurious correlation arising from their common measurement error.

Consistent parameter estimates in the presence of measurement error in the regressors can be obtained by instrumental variable methods. Notice that estimation of the health technology typically requires instrumental variable estimation anyway, as long as there is any endowment heterogeneity ($\sigma_\mu > 0$) and household allocations are influenced by differential endowments ($\lambda_j \neq 0$, $\lambda_{kj} \neq 0$). Prices for health inputs (p_z), including foods and medical care, are appropriate identifying instruments. However, prices are not valid instruments for $\hat{\mu}_j$ in the estimation of the demand equation (2.27), since they are by construction uncorrelated with the endowments. The only instruments possible are repeated (noncontemporaneous) measures of health and health inputs, inclusive of noncontemporaneous alternative measures of health. The validity of these instruments requires that the period-specific measurement errors be uncorrelated across periods. This was the approach followed by Pitt, Rosenzweig, and Hassan (1990) in their study of the intrahousehold allocation of food in rural Bangladesh.

In that study weight-for-height endowment measures were estimated for all members of a sample of Bangladeshi households and used to study the intrahousehold allocation of calories. The study explicitly modeled and estimated the link among food consumption, health, labor-market productivity, occupational choice, and individual heterogeneity. Table 2.2 presents estimates of weight-for-height production functions, estimated with a sample of 1,737 individuals. Inputs include measured (not reported) calorie consumption over a 24-hour period, measures of the energy intensity of effort, age, age squared, age-sex interaction, dummy variables for pregnancy and lactation, and the quality of drinking water. Calorie consumption, energy intensity of effort, and pregnant/lactating status are considered endogenous in the two-stage least squares estimates. Instruments include household head's age and schooling level, landholdings, and the prices of all foods consumed, interacted with individual age and sex variables, land, and head's schooling and age. The first column of Table 2.2 presents (inconsistent) ordinary least squares (OLS) estimates of the production function. A comparison with the consistent two-stage least squares (2SLS) estimates of the second column reveals the importance of heterogeneity bias. Using OLS, the calorie elasticity is seriously underestimated and the effects of the energy intensity of effort are opposite in sign to the 2SLS estimates. The 2SLS estimates reveal the important effect of calorie consumption on weight-for-height and the depleting effect of active occupations.

TABLE 2.2 Effects of calorie consumption, activity level, and pregnancy status on weight-for-height

Variable[a]	Ordinary Least Squares Estimates[b]	Two-Stage Least Squares Estimates[b]
Calorie consumption[c]	0.0295	0.136
	(4.09)	(3.37)
Very active occupation[c]	0.0859	−0.0119
	(5.34)	(0.23)
Exceptionally active occupation[c]	0.0668	−0.0817
	(3.43)	(1.26)
Pregnant[c]	0.262	0.326
	(7.69)	(1.34)
Lactating[c]	0.144	0.513
	(9.28)	(4.65)
Age	0.284	0.0987
	(16.6)	(1.90)
Age squared	−0.00456	0.0174
	(1.44)	(2.37)
Sex (male = 1)	0.00196	−0.0578
	(0.08)	(1.81)
Age × sex	0.0152	0.0687
	(1.74)	(4.04)
Water drawn from tube well	−0.0478	−0.0406
	(3.13)	(2.10)
Water drawn from well	−0.0720	−0.0693
	(4.11)	(3.15)
Water drawn from pond	−0.0460	−0.0649
	(2.30)	(2.55)
Constant	−2.56	−3.12
	(52.4)	(13.9)
N	1,737	1,737
R^2	0.775	. . .
F	395.1	. . .
H_0: No influence of calcium, carotene, thiamine, and riboflavin consumption (F)	. . .	1.23
H_0: No difference in effect of calorie consumption by sex (F)	. . .	2.16

SOURCE: Pitt, Rosenzweig, and Hassan (1990), p. 1150.

[a]All variables in logs, except sex, water sources, and activity level.

[b]Asymptotic t-ratios in parentheses.

[c]Endogenous variable; instruments include household head's age and schooling level, landholdings, and prices of all foods consumed, used in interaction with individual age and sex variables, land, and head's schooling and age.

The individual endowments were estimated based on the technology parameter estimates and the actual resources consumed or expended by each individual. In order to deal with the possibility of systematic measurement error in the measured endowments, a longitudinal subsample of households that were surveyed in four rounds over a 12-month period was used for the estimation of the intrahousehold calorie allocation equations. In addition to repeated measures of weight and height, individuals also had measurements of midarm circumference and skinfolds taken in every round. Production functions for these health outcomes were estimated by two-stage least squares containing the same regressors and instruments as the weight-for-height production function. The instruments for an individual's weight-for-height endowment in any period are the estimated endowments of the three health attributes averaged over all other periods. The estimated effect of an individual's own endowment on his or her calorie allocation was found to be negative without using instruments for measurement error. The effect became positive when instrumental variable methods were applied. These results clearly support the existence of systematic measurement error in the estimated endowments.

A problem that arises in the specification of demand models that include cross-person effects is that households are of different size and demographic composition. If households had only two individuals, each of a different type (for example, male and female), then it would be easy to specify the demand for goods by person j as a function of the person-specific prices, endowments, and observed exogenous characteristics of family member k as well as own characteristics and prices. But samples of households with differing numbers of individuals by type are unbalanced in that the attributes of a second son, for example, can only influence allocations in households that have a second son. Pitt, Rosenzweig, and Hassan (1990) handled this problem in two ways. First the intrahousehold distribution of exogenous characteristics was summarized as moments of distributions. Regressors included the mean weight-for-height endowments, mean age, proportion of male family members, and variance of ages of family members. Higher moments did not significantly improve the fit. Cross-gender effects were estimated by introducing the mean weight-for-height endowment separately for males and females. Only in same-sex households are cross-effects not estimable.[6]

---

6. Estimation of a "true" cross-effect would require that the calculated moments of the intrahousehold distributions not include own characteristics. If they do, the estimates conform to the experiment in which a transfer of characteristics (endowment, age, gender) occurs within the household that leaves mean endowment unchanged.

A fully parameterized model would require estimation of demand equations for each demographic mix characterizing households in the sample. If the slopes of demand equations were thought to vary only with gender, then, even in households of four persons, there would be five possible demand regimes corresponding to the number of females or males that can be found in households of four persons. In households with differing numbers of members, there would be

Second, a household fixed-effects two-stage generalized least squares estimation was applied to the sample of individuals, divided by gender. The advantage to the household fixed-effects procedure is that it deals perfectly with cross-person effects, since the demographic composition of a household is a fixed effect to each household member.[7] Table 2.3 presents parameter estimates of individual calorie consumption equations estimated with this method. Interestingly the parameter estimates diverge little from those obtained by specifying cross-effects separately for males and females, using moments of the distribution of ages and endowments. Columns 2 and 4 of Table 2.3 allow the parameters to vary by both age and gender. The pattern of estimated own endowments matches up well with the pattern of activities that individuals of these age and gender groups predominantly perform. Young children (less than 6 years of age) are not economically productive and thus there is no (current) labor market (productivity) return on additional calorie consumption for them. As a consequence calorie compensation dominates—part of the better health derived from a higher endowment is taxed away via a reduction in calorie allocations.

Male and female children 6–12 years of age exhibit calorie reinforcement. During these ages both genders have the ability to choose among activities of varying levels of energy intensity (and economic return) for which there are apparent returns to health. A 10 percent increase in the health (weight-for-height) endowment increases calorie consumption by 9.2 percent for males and 18.6 percent for females. This is consistent with activities data that show that girls have a greater diversity of activities as characterized by energy intensity of effort than boys. Adult males have the greatest calorie reinforcement of all household member-types, whereas adult females, with limited choices of activity, have an endowment response that is essentially zero.

Not many data sets contain information on person-specific health inputs, in particular food intake. Individual-level food intake data are seldom collected because of the great difficulty and cost of doing so. When they are collected, enumerators most often ask respondents to recall their consumption of a list of common foods during the prior 24 hours (as in the village surveys of the International Crops Research Institute for the Semi-Arid Tropics). Estimation of health production functions (typically using anthropometric measures of health as dependent variables) using data collected in this way, have not always

---

additional regimes to be estimated, because the effect of a change in an individual's endowment on the resources allocated to that individual depends on how many other members are available for reallocation. If household size and composition are endogenous, if for no other reason than the response of fertility to endowments, it is a switching-regimes model with endogenous regimes.

7. Although treating household composition as a fixed effect seems less arbitrary than trying to specify parsimonious functional forms, such as moments of distributions, it is valid only if the underlying parameters of the individual-specific demand equations are themselves not functions of the demographic composition of the household.

TABLE 2.3 Effects of personal characteristics on individual calorie consumption

Variable[a]	Fixed-Effects Two-Stage Generalized Least Squares Estimates[b]			
	Males		Females	
	Endowment Effects Constant	Endowment Effects Vary with Age	Endowment Effects Constant	Endowment Effects Vary with Age
Own endowment[c]	0.447	. . .	–0.0278	. . .
	(3.58)		(0.15)	
Age < 6[c]	. . .	–0.435	. . .	–0.314
		(1.35)		(0.46)
6 ≤ age < 12[c]	. . .	0.923	. . .	1.86
		(2.29)		(2.13)
Age ≥ 12[c]	. . .	1.21	. . .	0.0894
		(2.69)		(0.13)
Age	1.44	1.31	1.34	1.35
	(22.9)	(14.9)	(18.1)	(17.9)
Age squared	–0.201	–0.170	–0.199	–0.206
	(16.7)	(9.16)	(13.4)	(13.7)
N	429	429	371	371
χ^2 (no individual error components)	46.5	48.35	32.36	26.17
Individual error variance/ total error variance	0.287	0.300	0.258	0.282

SOURCE: Pitt, Rosenzweig, and Hassan (1990), p. 1152.

[a]All variables in logs.

[b]Asymptotic *t*-ratios in parentheses.

[c]Instrumental variables used are means of individual and family endowments for weight-for-height, skinfold thickness, and arm circumference calculated over all survey rounds, excluding the round from which observation was drawn.

been successful. In the Nutrition Survey of Rural Bangladesh, used by Pitt, Rosenzweig, and Hassan (1990), trained female enumerators resided with each household and physically weighed and measured the food consumption of each household member over a 24-hour period. These data seem "better" than recall data in that they are statistically significant determinants of weight-for-height, but they still suffer from at least two drawbacks (besides the cost of data collection). First, the typical reference period of 24 hours is rather short, so that even if enumerators measured the day's consumption without error, food consumption on other days would be unlikely to be the same. A single day's observation may be a noisy measure of even a short-term level of food intake. This is perhaps less of a problem for investigating the determinants of weight-for-height, an indicator of short-run health, than for other measures of health, such as morbidity. The second problem is that inserting an enumerator into a household to weigh and measure each individual's food intake, certainly an intrusive procedure, may cause the household to alter the level and allocation of food intake in order to please the enumerator. Recent evidence from the Philippines, where enumerators physically measured the food consumption of each individual in sampled households for a 7-day period, suggests that households consumed much higher levels of high-cost status foods, such as eggs and milk, during the first days of an enumerator's observations, but substantially less as the week wore on.

In Pitt and Lavy's (1995) study of the allocation of preventive medical care in Ghana, endowment measures derived from a morbidity technology, rather than from a nutritional status (weight-for-height) technology, are more likely to capture those components of innate healthiness associated with medical care decisions. Anthropometric measures, such as weight-for-height, are specified as inputs capturing the effects of individual-specific food consumption on morbidity. Weight-for-height is thus treated as an aggregator of the food intakes in the health technology, with the assumption that food consumption affects morbidity h only through weight-for-height. Weight-for-height is expected to suffer much less from the measurement error problems associated with individual-level food consumption information.[8]

One might ask how it can be claimed that it is in general "impossible" to find theoretically justified restrictions that can identify intrahousehold conditional demand relations, yet the endowment method seems to do just that. Although it is true that the endowment method is consistent with the theory of the household presented previously, a strong restriction (in the sense of not being very believable) is nonetheless required for the statistical consistency of estimates based on the use of estimated endowments. Essentially the restriction is that the researcher know the correct specification of the technology from which inputs are to be estimated. If the wrong functional form is chosen or if relevant inputs are omitted, the use of estimated endowments will not estimate the intrahousehold demands without bias. Since one can seldom claim to know the "true" functional form for any structural relationship, functional form misspecification is not an issue peculiar to this problem. The problem of omitted inputs is a much more difficult one to brush aside. Go back to the simple example of the single-person household having a linear health technology with a single input as in equation (2.20), but now allow for a second input, q_j, unmeasured or unknown to the researcher:

$$h_j = \alpha + \beta z_j + \gamma q_j + \mu_j + \varepsilon_j$$
$$z_j = \pi p_{z_j} + \delta p_{q_j} + \gamma_j p_x + \lambda \mu_j + e_j \qquad (2.28)$$

---

8. The endowment method has been applied in new and interesting ways in Rosenzweig and Wolpin (1991), Behrman, Rosenzweig, and Taubman (1994), and Filmer (1995).

where p_q is the price of input q. It is clear that the production function (2.28) estimated without q_j as a regressor will have residuals that include the effects of q_j as well as the bias to the other parameters caused by its omission, since it is likely that z_j and q_j are correlated. Bias will result, for the estimated endowments obtained from those residuals will now be correlated with the prices in the demand equation for z_j, since the demand for q_j, like the demand for z_j, depends on the price of inputs. The endowment method thus relies on a covariance restriction for identification: the errors of the production function are uncorrelated with those of the reduced-form demand equation. An omitted variable makes that correlation nonzero and the restriction invalid.[9] Any reasonable application of the endowment method must make a convincing case that it has reasonably complete data on production inputs.

Summary

This chapter has set out the problem of specifying and statistically identifying the demand for goods within the household, making use of the concept of conditional demand introduced by Pollak (1969). Essentially the identification problem arises from the absence of prices for most person-specific goods. These prices are required to estimate demand equations having cross-person effects. Two methods for estimating intrahousehold demands were discussed. One method called for restrictions on parameters that may be inconsistent with a general model of household behavior. It was suggested that cross-person restrictions on parameters might be less onerous than the usual exclusion restrictions. The second method, known as the endowment method, involved making covariance restrictions, which, although not at odds with a theory of behavior, required rich data on individual-specific inputs. Both methods were illustrated with empirical examples, using data from developing countries.

---

9. The instrumental variable method for dealing with measurement error in the endowments is not applicable here, since the omitted variable is omitted in every period.

3 "Collective" Models of Household Behavior: The Sharing Rule Approach

PIERRE-ANDRÉ CHIAPPORI

In the traditional approach of microeconomic theory, households are considered elementary decision units. They are modeled as "consumers" in the usual sense, characterized by a single utility function that is maximized under a budget constraint. This amounts to assuming either that the topic of intrahousehold resource allocation is irrelevant or that it can be conveniently addressed within the fiction of a dictatorial decisionmaking process.

This view has been recently challenged by a number of authors who claim that households should be understood as collective decision units, that intrahousehold decisionmaking processes are complex phenomena deserving particular attention, and that the single-utility hypothesis is essentially an ad hoc justification for disregarding these issues. As a consequence, collective models of household behavior have been developed.[1] My first goal in this chapter is to discuss the kinds of models that have been offered and emphasize the (sometimes technical) differences between them. My second goal is to present a particular approach to understanding intrahousehold decisionmaking, based upon the general concept of "sharing rule." The basic principle behind this concept will be reviewed and then the empirical consequences discussed. The dispute between the traditional and the collective approaches must not remain within the field of theory; empirical issues are also involved. But what can data tell us about the empirical relevance of the two classes of models? This question will be answered in the last part of the chapter.

---

1. Among early contributors, one can mention Apps (1981, 1982), Apps and Jones (1986), and Chiappori (1988b, 1990a), who introduced cooperative models, whereas Ashworth and Ulph (1981), Bourguignon (1984), Ulph (1988), Kooreman and Kapteyn (1990) referred to noncooperative game theory and Kapteyn and Kooreman (1992) simultaneously considered both settings. Manser and Brown (1980), McElroy and Horney (1981, 1990), and more recently Haddad and Kanbur (1990, 1992, 1993) have discussed models based upon bargaining theory.

Collective Models: Some Basic Distinctions

Collective versus Traditional Approaches

The first and most basic distinction among models is the one between collective and traditional approaches. Either one assumes that households behave as if they were single consumers and then works within the traditional, single-utility framework, or one explicitly recognizes the existence of several decisionmaking units, with potentially different preferences that do not systematically aggregate into a unique household utility function, and works in the collective line.

Clear as this separation may seem, two remarks must be made at this point. First, the fundamental discrepancy does not involve the number of decisionmakers within the household. Some models belonging to the traditional line—for example, Becker's "altruistic" models or Samuelson's collective welfare index—are compatible with the existence of several decisionmakers. However, aggregation theory says that a group does not behave as a single person, apart from highly peculiar cases. As McElroy (Chapter 4, this volume) notes, the reconciliation of the existence of several individuals with a unique utility function requires strong assumptions. Second, the specific assumption of the traditional approach is not the maximization (under budget constraint) of a unique welfare index. Indeed many collective frameworks, including bargaining models, imply such a maximization (and, in a sense, many reasonable decisionmaking processes share this property). The specificity of traditional settings lies in the fact that this maximand can be interpreted as a utility function; it is independent of prices and incomes—the latter appearing only in the budget constraint. In all collective models, conversely, the maximand is price dependent.[2] In particular, in single-utility models, wages or nonlabor incomes can affect behavior only through usual income and substitution effects, whereas much more complex influences can be taken into account within a collective framework.

Cooperation versus Conflict

First consider the class of cooperative collective models. Here "cooperation" should be understood in the sense of game theory. Cooperative decisionmaking processes have outcomes that are Pareto efficient; thus the central assumption is that households will never adopt a decision that is Pareto dominated. This class of models includes, in particular, bargaining models, at least when information asymmetries are assumed away. Conversely one may think of several kinds of collective processes that are formally different from bar-

---

2. In particular, all such models are particular cases of "price-dependent preferences." The difficulty, however, is to generate testable restrictions, a goal that obviously implies some restrictions on the form of the maximand.

gaining, yet still always generate Pareto-efficient outcomes (this is the case, for instance, for "matching" models of the marriage market; see McElroy [Chapter 4, this volume]). Thus though Nash bargaining models are nested within the set of cooperative models, the converse is in general not true.

Two avenues can be explored. One is to stick to the sole-efficiency assumption and try to derive testable restrictions upon behavior; this line has been followed by, among others, Chiappori (1988b, 1992), Bourguignon et al. (1993), Browning et al. (1994), and Browning and Chiappori (1995). Or, following Manser and Brown (1980) and McElroy and Horney (1981), a priori further restrictions can be imposed upon the decisionmaking process—typically a particular bargaining concept, for instance Nash—and the additional implications this specification introduces can be investigated.

These lines of study have given rise to two related but different research programs. Although these programs may converge in the future this has not yet happened. The advantages of the first approach, in terms of generality and comprehensiveness, must be traded off against the increased predictive power that should typically result from more restrictive assumptions. Again the comparison of empirical consequences turns out to be a central issue.

Assumptions on Commodities and Preferences

Quite apart from the formalization of decisionmaking processes, models may differ in the particular assumptions they make regarding the form of preferences and/or the nature of the commodities. For instance it may be assumed that some goods are privately consumed whereas others are "public" within the household. But it may be argued that even private consumption by one of the members will generally enter the utility function of the other—say, because the latter is altruistic or because externalities are generated. Though these assumptions are in a sense rather technical, they still should be considered with care, because the properties of the model—that is, its ability to generate testable restrictions or the identifiability of the structural framework—will crucially depend on the particular formulation adopted.

To be a little more specific consider a household of two members, A and B, with respective preferences, U^A and U^B. The household can consume $n + N$ goods, among which n are consumed privately by each member, whereas N are public goods for the household. Let $x^A = (x_1^A, \ldots, x_n^A)$ and $x^B = (x_1^B, \ldots, x_n^B)$ denote the respective private consumption bundles of A and B, and $X = (X_1, \ldots, X_n)$ denote the household consumption of public goods. Hence, U^A and U^B map R^{n+N} to R and can be written, respectively, as $U^A(x^A, X)$, $U^B(x^B, X)$. A polar case, considered for instance, by Chiappori (1988b), is $N = 0$; all goods are privately consumed, and preferences are said to be egoistic. At the other extreme one might assume, as in McElroy and Horney (1981), that the total consumption of any member enters both members' utility function; that is, all consumptions are public goods within the household. Then the preferences will be said to be altruistic and take the form $U^A(x^A,x^B,X)$, $U^B(x^A,x^B,X)$. Of course the altruistic setting is more general. Not surprisingly the price paid for this generality is that it is less testable, and the uniqueness of the structural model underlying a given demand function is more difficult to guarantee.[3] In particular it can readily be seen that altruistic models encompass, as particular cases, single-utility frameworks (just take $U^A = U^B$). This is not true, however, for egoistic models, since these exhibit a separability property between each member's private consumption bundle.

An intermediate case of interest is Becker's notion of caring. Here each member is assumed to maximize a welfare index that depends on both his or her own "egoistic" utility and his or her companion's; technically the preferences are of the form $W^A[U^A(x^A,X),U^B(x^B,X)]$, $W^B[U^A(x^A,X),U^B(x^B,X)]$. Interestingly enough the properties of the "caring" framework are, at least under the assumption of Pareto-efficient decisions, much closer to the egoistic than to the altruistic case. The basic reason is that the set of Pareto-efficient allocations of the "caring" model is a subset of that of the "egoistic" model.

A last distinction relevant for private consumption is that among exclusive, assignable, and nonassignable goods. A good is exclusive when it is consumed by only one member; a typical example is labor supply (or leisure), at least insofar as it is not a public good for the household. A nonexclusive good is assignable when each member's consumption can be observed independently; otherwise it is nonassignable. The existence of either an assignable good or a pair of exclusive goods typically increases the predictive power of models. Note as well that the observation of two exclusive consumptions will in general yield more information than that of an assignable good; this is because the prices of the exclusive goods will be different, whereas the assignable good has a single price, whatever the number of consumers.

In the notation that follows, $p \varepsilon R^n$ denotes the price vector of the private (and public, $P \varepsilon R^N$) goods, and y denotes the household's total income, so that the overall budget constraint is

$$p(x^A + x^B) + PX = y \tag{3.1}$$

In some cases, each member's income can be independently observed; that is

$$y = y^A + y^B \tag{3.2}$$

The Sharing Rule Interpretation

When preferences are of the egoistic or caring type the efficiency hypothesis can be given a nice, intuitive interpretation. Specifically if $\bar{x}^A(p,P,y)$,

---

3. For a detailed discussion see Chiappori (1988b, 1990a). The intuition is that although the set of altruistic utility functions contains that of egoistic ones, it is by far much larger. Hence testable properties that are fulfilled by all functions of the smaller set may not exist for some function of the larger. In addition uniqueness may be true within the subclass of egoistic preferences but not within the general class of altruistic utilities.

$\overline{x}^B(p,P,y)$, $\overline{X}(p,P,y)$ is the chosen consumption bundle, then there exists a sharing rule $\theta(p,P,y)$ such that

$$\overline{x}^A(p,P,Y) \text{ is the solution of max } U^A(x^A,\overline{X}), \quad p^A x^A = \theta(p,P,y)$$
$$\overline{x}^B(p,P,y) \text{ is the solution of max } U^B(x^B,\overline{X}), \quad p^B x^B = y - P\overline{X} - \theta(p,P,y)$$

For the proof, see Bourguignon et al. (1993).

The interpretation is as follows. Once the household has decided upon the expenditures, PX, for public goods, the remaining income, $y - PX$, must be allocated among the members' private consumptions. Then the efficiency assumption implies that members agree upon the respective amount each of them is allowed to spend. This is exactly what is meant by a sharing rule. Note that the rule will in general depend on all prices and incomes, and that, at least in the general framework, no assumption is made about the form of the rule—it is simply assumed that such a rule does exist. Each member will allocate the amount thus defined so as to maximize his or her utility.[4]

The sharing rule property is quite general: it can be used, with egoistic or caring preferences, to interpret any efficient decisionmaking process.[5] Conversely any arbitrarily chosen rule will generate efficient decisions when preferences are egoistic. This, however, does not hold in the "caring" case for "too unfair" sharing rules.[6] Remember as well that the Nash bargaining approach is embedded within this framework. With caring preferences, Nash bargaining models essentially generate additional restrictions upon the sharing rule.

Finally an attractive property of the sharing rule interpretation is that it provides a description of the decisionmaking process that is independent of the particular, cardinal representation of preferences; that is, the demand functions it generates are not modified when U^X is replaced by $F[U^X]$, where F is some nondecreasing mapping (and X = A or B). This is especially convenient

---

4. Note that the choice of the private consumption bundle will in general be made conditionally on the choice of public goods, because the latter does enter the utility function. This effect can be avoided by assuming that private consumptions are separable from public consumptions within each member's utility; that is, $U^i(x^i,X) = \overline{U}^i[u^i(x^i),X]$, $i = A,B$. Then,

$$\overline{x}^A(p,P,y) \text{ is the solution of max } U^A(x^A), \quad p^A x^A = \theta(p,P,y)$$
$$\overline{x}^B(p,P,y) \text{ is the solution of max } U^B(x^B), \quad p^B x^B = y - P\overline{X} - \theta(p,P,y)$$

5. With altruistic preferences, however, the sharing rule interpretation is no longer equivalent to efficiency in general. In that case all individual consumptions are public goods—they all enter both utility functions. However, decentralized decisions will not generally be efficient because the effect upon the other member's welfare will not be adequately taken into account. Of course the fact that the sharing rule idea is not compatible with efficiency does not necessary imply that it is irrelevant; see for instance Lundberg and Pollak (Chapter 5, this volume).

6. The idea is that, when the allocation prescribed by the rule is highly unequal, reducing inequality by departing from the rule may increase both welfare levels; indeed, the favored member, being caring, will be made better off as well.

because it is very difficult to distinguish empirically between ordinally equivalent but cardinally different utility functions.

Nash Bargaining

Here the first step is to define for each member a "reservation utility" or "threat point," $V^X(p,P,y)$ (X = A,B), representing the minimum welfare level X could obtain in any case (and especially if no collective agreement could be reached). Of course, this will depend on the economic environment, that is, prices (including wages) and incomes. Then the surplus arising from cooperation is shared geometrically between the members; that is, the household maximizes $[U^A - V^A][U^B - V^B]$ under budget constraint.

Several problems must be solved at this point. One is the choice of threat points. Should one take utilities when divorced, as in McElroy (1990), or rather noncooperative equilibrium within the household, as argued by Ulph (1988) and Lundberg and Pollak (Chapter 5, this volume)? In both cases estimating the model is by no means an easy task. Simultaneous estimation of preferences and threat points from data on married couples may be quite difficult.

One solution, advocated by McElroy (1990), might be to estimate threat points from data on the behavior of divorced individuals. But the problem here is that, in contrast with the sharing rule approach discussed earlier, the concept of Nash bargaining equilibrium requires a cardinal representation of preferences. The latter concept is not invariant through an increasing transformation of utilities, threat points, or both. Indeed the Nash bargaining equilibrium concept amounts to assuming that the gains obtained through the agreement, with respect to some given reference point (the threat point), are shared "equally" in some sense. But the gains are expressed in utilities; if the evaluation of one member's welfare is changed—and this is exactly what the transformation would do—the allocation of the surplus will be modified as well. Empirically this is bad news, because such a transformation does not affect preferences, hence observed behavior (at least in the absence of uncertainty). In other words, for any given consumption or labor supply function, the choice of a particular cardinal representation (among the infinity compatible with observed behavior) is essentially arbitrary; the conclusion will then crucially depend on this choice.[7]

Despite these technical difficulties, however, the Nash bargaining approach may (once adequately designed) provide useful insights into the conse-

---

7. Assume that member A's utility when divorced is of the form $U^A - s^A(p,P,Y)$ (that is, that divorce has a cost per se—not an unrealistic assumption). Then s^A cannot be identified from data on divorced individuals but will clearly play a key role in the Nash bargaining procedure. The same is true, more generally, for preferences of the form $F(U^A,p,P,y)$; the argument is very similar to the analysis of equivalence scales in Blundell and Lewbel (1991). Another solution would be to use direct information on preferences collected from interviews or experiments (Kapteyn and Kooreman 1992).

quences of taking into account intrahousehold decisionmaking processes. For instance Haddad and Kanbur (1992, 1993) emphasize the impact of intra-household allocation issues for the targeting of welfare policies. The design of an optimal, in-kind benefit will crucially depend on who exactly in the house-hold receives the benefits. Targeting a food supplement to, say, children be-tween the ages of 3 and 10 is meaningless if the corresponding increase is offset by a reduction in the child's share of food at home. Another consequence is that the scope of a given policy may be much broader than that suggested by the number of people who actually receive it. A minimum wage, for instance, will typically modify the threat point for nonworking spouses and thus, accord-ing to the bargaining ideas, influence the sharing rule, even in households that do not seem directly concerned by the regulation.

Last it must be emphasized that the spirit of bargaining processes can be captured, even in the absence of a specialized model, by introducing within the general Pareto framework some specific and testable assumptions. The sharing rule approach is especially convenient for this purpose. For instance any variable that is likely to be positively correlated with the bargaining power of one spouse (say, his or her wage or nonlabor income) should have a positive effect on the latter's share; conversely any factor that favors the partner's threat point should have a negative effect. Such conclusions can readily be empiri-cally tested in the collective framework, as argued in the next section.

Testable Implications of the Sharing Rule Approach

As McElroy and Horney (1981), Horney and McElroy (1988), Schultz (1990), and Thomas (1990, 1992) have emphasized, the single-utility approach has consequences that can readily be tested. In addition to well-known proper-ties that have been repeatedly analyzed in the literature, such as homogeneity or Slutsky relations, these authors have concentrated upon an important conse-quence of the traditional approach, namely income pooling. Whenever in-comes do not affect preferences but only the budget constraint, then only total income, and not income composition, should matter. Empirical evidence sug-gests that this property does not hold (see Hoddinott, Alderman, and Haddad, Chapter 8, this volume).

However, these results must be interpreted carefully. They must definitely not be seen as supporting the collective approach in general or, even worse, some of its particular versions. Although any evidence against income pooling does suggest that the traditional approach is not correct, this finding does not support any particular alternative model. There are certainly hundreds of ad hoc assumptions that could explain the observed results within the traditional approach[8] and thousands of more or less funny alternative models that could

---

8. For instance endogeneity bias or differences in volatility of various income sources.

justify them outside it. The only way to support empirically the collective setting is to derive, from the collective framework itself, conditions that can potentially be, but are actually not, falsified by empirical observation.[9] This requirement should be kept in mind when constructing the model.

Hence the next question: is it possible to derive testable restrictions from the sharing rule framework? The answer is essentially positive. To elaborate on this point two particular settings will be considered: general demand systems on cross-section data (in which the emphasis is put on income effect, thus generalizing the income pooling literature) and general demand systems on panel or pseudo-panel data (in which attention is concentrated upon *price* effects).

Cross-Section Data and Income Effects

The simplest presentation of the argument is given in Browning et al. (1994). Assume that income can be decomposed into three exogenous sources, $y = y^A + y^B + y^o$, according to whether it is received by member A, by member B, or collectively by the household. The decision process will in general be a function of y^A, y^B, and y^o; by a simple change in variables, it can be expressed as a function of y^A, y^B, and y.

If Pareto efficiency is assumed, demands are a solution of a problem of the form

$$\max = \theta U^A(x^A,x^B,X) + (1 - \theta)U^B(x^A,x^B,X) \qquad \text{subject to } px = y \qquad (3.3)$$

where $\theta(y^A,y^B,y)$ represents member A's "weight" in the process.

Now the key idea is that the specific effects of individual incomes y^A and y^B operate exclusively through the "weighting factor," θ. In particular, they should have similar properties across goods. Assume, for instance, that it is observed that an additional dollar given to the husband decreases some given consumption—say, health care—by the same amount as 50 cents withdrawn from the wife (remember that total income y is held constant, so that y^o must decrease or increase accordingly). This means that within the decision process the husband's implicit weight is modified (say, decreased) in exactly the same way by both transfers and, in addition, that the wife's propensity to consume health care is larger than the husband's. Whereas the latter conclusion is specific to the good, the former is not; that is, it should be observed that an additional dollar given to the husband has the same effect, upon any (nonassignable) consumption, as 50 cents withdrawn from the wife. Technically this property can be translated for all goods as follows:

$$\frac{\partial x_i / \partial y^A}{\partial x_i / \partial y^B} = \frac{\partial \theta / \partial y^A}{\partial \theta / \partial y^B} \qquad (3.4)$$

---

9. Specifically the new approach should have unexpected empirical implications—consequences that must be true under the new theory but false under the old one.

where the right-hand side is independent of i. Note that this conclusion does *not* require any assumption whatsoever regarding preferences; it stems from the sole efficiency assumption. Hence this is a simple and powerful test of the collective approach. It should also be emphasized that y^A and y^B could be replaced by any exogenous variable that may affect the decision process, such as laws on divorce, market for marriage, or minimum wages.

Empirical Test

This property can clearly be tested empirically. As an illustration Bourguignon et al. (1993) consider the following polynomial functional form for household demand:

$$x_i = a_i y + \gamma_i [by^2 + cy^A + dy^B + e(y^A)^2/2 + f(y^B)^2/2 + gy^A y^B] \qquad (R2) \quad (3.5)$$

where z includes sociodemographic variables like age, education, the presence of one child, the living area, or home ownership status. In that framework, testing the pooling hypothesis is equivalent to testing that all the coefficients of terms, including the variables y^A and y^B, are zero. Indeed for any given value of total income y, individual incomes should not matter. Note, incidentally, that one could have taken y^A, y^B, and y^o (instead of y^A, y^B, and y) as variables; the pooling hypothesis would then have implied that only the sum mattered.

When estimating this model, a technical difficulty arises because substitution effects between leisure and consumption must be avoided. Indeed if individual incomes result from an endogenous labor supply decision, higher income may reveal more working hours, which, in turn, will affect consumption through substitution effects, so that the income pooling conclusion is not guaranteed. So incomes must be exogenous. Several solutions can be considered. Thomas (1990, 1992), for instance, considers various sources of nonlabor incomes. In the Bourguignon et al. (1993) model considered here, y^i is taken as member i's labor income, but a sample of French households in which both members work full time is used. Then labor supply is constrained at the legal maximum, so that the number of hours is taken to be exogenous. Table 3.1 gives the unrestricted ordinary least squares estimates obtained for the nine goods included in the analysis, as well as the results of the log-likelihood ratio test of the hypothesis that all coefficients c_i, d_i, e_i, f_i, and g_i are equal to zero. This amounts to 45 restrictions and the corresponding χ^2 value leads to the clear rejection of the pooling hypothesis.

In order to test the cooperative hypothesis, it is first necessary to derive the restriction on the coefficients implied by the general restrictions stated previously. The latter can actually be shown to imply that demand must take one of the two following forms:

$$x_i = a_i y + \lambda_i [y^A + ky^B + Ky^2] + \mu_i [(y^A + ky^B)^2 + Ly^2] \qquad (R1) \quad (3.6)$$

or

TABLE 3.1 Tests of the consumption models

			Restriction	
	Unrestricted	Pooled	R1	R2
2 log likelihood	471.82	544.70	515.00	525.18
χ^2	...	72.88	43.18	53.36
Number of restrictions	...	45	33	40
Probability (percent)	...	0.5	11.1	7.7

SOURCE: Bourguignon et al. (1993).

$$x_i = a_i y + \gamma_i [by^2 + cy^A + dy^B + e(y^A)^2/2 + f(y^B)^2/2 + gy^A y^B] \qquad \text{(R2)} \quad (3.7)$$

where k, K, and L, on the one hand, and b, c, d, e, f, and g, on the other, do not depend on the good, i, that is considered.

Table 3.1 gives the log-likelihood ratios corresponding to the restriction equations (3.6) and (3.7) imposed on the ordinary least squares estimates of the nine consumption equations. The corresponding χ^2 tests involve 33 and 40 degrees of freedom, respectively, and they are both above the critical 5 percent probability level. So it cannot be rejected that the data satisfy the cooperative hypothesis.

Another interesting consequence is that most conclusions stemming from bargaining ideas can be empirically tested along this line from readily available data. For instance a threat point interpretation implies that, when total income is kept fixed, Θ should increase with y^A and decrease with y^B; hence the ratios of partials of Θ with respect to y^A and y^B should be negative. But from the developments mentioned previously, the same should then be true for the partial ratios of x_i as well. This latter conclusion can be tested from any data set with different income sources. (Incidentally, the ratios appeared to be always nonnegative and, in several cases, significantly positive in the Bourguignon et al. [1993] estimation.)

Price Effects

As is well known, the "unitary" models have precise implications for the effects upon demands of price changes; specifically the Slutsky matrix of compensated price effects must be symmetric. This conclusion, however, is regularly rejected on household data (see for example Browning and Meghir [1991]). Usually this rejection has either been seen as a rejection of utility theory or been attributed to technical problems (inadequate functional forms, inappropriate separability assumptions, misspecification of the stochastic structure, and so on). Thus it has been concluded either that utility theory is false or that it is untestable. The collective approach, however, suggests a different interpretation: the repeated rejections of substitution symmetry in empirical work may occur because household decisions cannot be stuffed into an overly restrictive unitary framework. This remark immediately leads to a basic question: can one derive restrictive, testable implications of the collective framework for demand functions that could be seen as the counterpart, or more precisely the generalization, of Slutsky symmetry and negativeness in the unitary case?

This problem is solved by Browning and Chiappori (1995).[10] They consider a very general framework. For example, any commodity may be either public, or private, or both, and individual private consumptions are assumed to be unobservable. Similarly no particular assumption on individual preferences is introduced—except that they can be represented by conventional utility functions. This approach allows for intrahousehold consumption externalities, for any form of altruism, and so on. Despite this explicitly minimalist set of assumptions, the authors show that one can make very specific predictions about household behavior.

The principal theoretical result of the Browning and Chiappori (1995) paper is the following. Let $x_i(p,y)$ be the observed demand function (where y denotes household income and p the price vector; note that different income sources are no longer needed). Define, as usual, the Slutsky matrix $S = s_{ij}$ by

$$s_{ij} = \frac{\partial x_j}{\partial p_j} + x_j \frac{\partial x_i}{\partial y}$$

Then the collective framework has the following implication: S *is the sum of a symmetric, negative matrix* Σ *and a matrix* R *that has at most rank 1.* That is, it can be written in the form

$$S = \Sigma + uv'$$

where u and v are n vectors and $R = uv'$.

In the unitary framework, S was symmetric, which corresponds to the particular case $R = 0$. Hence this "symmetric plus rank one" (SR1) condition is a straightforward generalization of Slutsky. A geometric interpretation of SR1 is the following. Note first that for any given pair of utilities the budget constraint defines the Pareto frontier as a function of the price-income bundle; then θ determines the location of the final outcome on the frontier, as in (3.3). Assume now that prices and income are changed. This action has two consequences. For one thing, the Pareto frontier will move. Keeping θ constant, this would change demand in a way described by the Σ matrix. Note, however, that

---

10. It should be remembered that axiomatic models of bargaining with symmetric information generally generate efficient outcomes (this is the case, for instance, with all models developed so far in the Nash bargaining literature); hence the collective framework encompasses all cooperative models existing in the literature. As a consequence the conditions derived from the efficiency assumption alone do apply, a fortiori, to all these models as well.

this change will *not* violate Slutsky symmetry, that is, its nature is not different from the traditional, unitary effect. The second effect is that θ will also change; this effect will introduce an additional move of demand *along* the (new) frontier. This change (as summarized by the *R* matrix) *does* violate Slutsky symmetry. But moves along a one-dimensional manifold are quite restricted. For instance, the set of price-income bundles that lead to the *same* θ is likely to be quite large in general; indeed, under the smoothness assumption, it is an $(n - 1)$-dimensional manifold. Considering the linear tangent spaces, this means that there is a whole hyperplane such that, if the (infinitesimal) change in prices and income belongs to that hyperplane, then no deviation from Slutsky symmetry can be observed. In other words, *the SR1 condition is a direct consequence of the fact that, in a two-person household, the Pareto frontier is of dimension 1, whatever the number of commodities.*

Testing for SR1 is an interesting problem. The basic idea is that a matrix *S* is SR1 if and only if the matrix $M = S - S'$ is of rank at most 2. The empirical strategy is thus the following:

- Estimate demands functions.
- Derive an estimation of *M*.
- Test for the rank of *M*.

Browning and Chiappori (1995) provide a first test on Canadian data. They divide the sample of households without children into three subsamples: single males, single females, and couples. They find that Slutsky symmetry is strongly rejected for couples, *but not for singles*—quite an interesting result, since it is probably the first time the property is tested on a sample of consumers (as opposed to households). In addition the SR1 conditions are not rejected for couples, a finding that indicates that the collective model may indeed help understand the rejection of Slutsky symmetry.

Estimating the Model: The Case of One Assignable Good

Finally estimation issues should be considered. Stronger assumptions are needed for this purpose; essentially preferences must be either "egoistic" or "caring," and private consumption must be separable, so that the sharing rule interpretation does apply. It is assumed here that one good (say, good Λ) is assignable. In that case, the effect of member *i*'s income upon member *j*'s consumption can be directly recorded. In fact not only do new conditions appear, but the sharing rule itself can be recovered up to an additive constant. To see why, note that if good 1 is assignable, then:

$$\frac{\partial x_1^A / \partial y^A}{\partial x_1^A / \partial y} = \frac{\partial \theta / \partial y^A}{\partial \theta / \partial y} \tag{3.8}$$

$$\frac{\partial x_1^A / \partial y^B}{\partial x_1^A / \partial y} = \frac{\partial \theta / \partial y^B}{\partial \theta / \partial y} \tag{3.9}$$

and

$$\frac{\partial x_1^B / \partial y^A}{\partial x_1^B / \partial y} = \frac{-\partial \theta / \partial y^A}{1 - \partial \theta / \partial y} \qquad (3.10)$$

$$\frac{\partial x_1^B / \partial y^B}{\partial x_1^B / \partial y} = \frac{-\partial \theta / \partial y^B}{1 - \partial \theta / \partial y} \qquad (3.11)$$

Then $\partial\theta/\partial y^A$, $\partial\theta/\partial y^B$, and $\partial\theta/\partial y$ can be recovered, and Θ is known up to an additive constant. The intuition is that by looking at the assignable good it can be directly observed how changes in the various components of income affect each member's consumption (rather than the sum of the two). Given that any variation of member A's consumption that results from, say, an increase in his or her share must correspond to a decrease in member B's share, and hence to a specific response in terms of member B's consumption, a number of insights about the sharing rule become available. In fact the way in which the sharing rule varies in response to changes in incomes can be exactly identified. The only remaining ambiguity concerns the initial level (the constant) from which these variations take place.

The strong conclusion is that identification of one assignable good is sufficient for recovering the entire decision process. Under the specific assumptions that have been made—that is, egoistic or caring preferences, Pareto efficiency, and different exogenous income sources—each member's total consumption in private goods can be deduced. As a matter of fact each member's consumption of each private good can be ascertained—by simply observing how the consumption of one single private good is distributed within the household. Even stronger results can be established. For instance it can be shown that the observation of one member's private consumption of some exclusive good is sufficient for recovering the sharing rule up to a constant (see Browning et al. 1994). For an empirical application, see Browning et al. (1994).

Conclusion

The set of "collective" approaches to household behavior developed so far is the starting point of a general and coherent research program. In traditional, single-utility models, households are black boxes, formally identical to individuals. Behavior depends, in particular, only on total income. The first step has been to establish empirically that the black box was functioning in a more complex way than suggested by traditional models—and that the distribution of income also mattered. Much progress has recently been made in this direction. There are now serious reasons to believe that the standard approach may miss some essential aspects of household behavior. The second step is to open the black box. Here the question is: can one define theoretically, and recover empirically, some kind of stable structural pattern that underlies (collective) household behavior? The concept of the sharing rule is proposed as a candidate for this purpose.

In any case the most urgent task now is to test empirically the various collective models at stake. It should then be possible to draw policy conclusions. However, this step cannot be taken before completion of the second step—a goal that is far from being achieved. Although a few estimations have been performed, most of the work is still ahead.

4 The Policy Implications of Family Bargaining and Marriage Markets

MARJORIE B. McELROY

Recent studies have raised doubts that the economic progress of women in the labor market translates into progress in their well-being at home (see Goldin [1990:211–13] for a succinct review of U.S. evidence and Schultz [1990] for a review of development policies and the status of women in developing countries). More generally how does economic progress in conjunction with a variety of policies translate into changes in the well-being of individual family members? When do the gains accrue primarily to wives, to husbands, or to children?

To date most of the analysis of intrahousehold distributions has rested on partial-equilibrium models of optimizing individuals or households. The partial-equilibrium analysis includes the work of Becker (1981 and elsewhere) based on altruism; the use of cooperative-bargaining models by Manser and Brown (1980), McElroy and Horney (1981), and others; work on collective decisions by Chiappori (1988a) and coauthors; and the use of noncooperative models by Lundberg and Pollak (Chapter 5, this volume), Ulph (1988), and others.

In contrast little analysis has been based on the appropriate general-equilibrium framework, the marriage market. In Becker's (1973, 1974a) seminal work on marriage markets, the emphasis was on assortative mating (who marries whom), rather than on the allocation of the gains from marriage (who gains what). Although Becker analyzed the core of the marriage market (the set of all equilibrium-allocation markets), there has been, to this author's knowledge, no work on the comparative statics of the allocation of the gains from marriage. Moreover, apart from a sentence or two in Becker (1981), there exists virtually no discussion of the formal links between partial- and general-equilibrium approaches to intrahousehold distributions.

This research was supported by National Science Foundation grant SES-91–02331. I thank Pierre-André Chiappori and John Hoddinott—as well as other participants in the World Bank–IFPRI conference "Intrahousehold Resource Allocation," held in Washington, D.C., February 12–14, 1992—for their comments.

One reason for this inattention is undoubtedly the nonuniqueness of core solution allocations. In this chapter I take a first step toward the comparative static analysis of intrahousehold distributions in a general-equilibrium setting. The key is to define "sympathetic" solutions, a class of unique marriage market solutions that respond in predictable ways to changes in the economic opportunities outside marriage. Under sympathetic solutions, an individual's allocation within marriage directly reflects that individual's opportunities outside marriage. Many of the unique marriage market solutions found in the game theory literature are sympathetic precisely because sympathetic solutions embody certain notions of "fairness."

An interesting result emerges from this analysis. Under sympathetic solutions, anything that makes an individual better off outside marriage tends to increase (and never decreases) that person's equilibrium "price" or share of marital income. There is a well-known parallel result from partial-equilibrium cooperative-bargaining models: anything that makes the individual better off outside marriage increases that person's bargaining power within the marriage and thereby increases that person's utility within the marriage. Therefore there exists a deep complementarity between general-equilibrium sympathetic–marriage market models and partial-equilibrium cooperative models of family decisions. Each reinforces the conclusions of the other: the distribution of well-being among family members reflects their individual economic opportunities outside that family.

The first section of this chapter reviews several competing partial-equilibrium models of family decisions. A new analysis is presented of intrafamily distributions based on a general-equilibrium marriage market model. The deep complementarity between models of Nash-bargained family decisions and marriage market models is demonstrated. For simplicity this chapter discusses only two-person husband-wife families, although in many cases more general results are available.

Partial-Equilibrium Models of Family Decisions

Family Utility Models

Family utility models are defined here as models in which family decisions are observationally equivalent to decisions made by a single utility-maximizing agent subject to a family budget constraint. Although there exist several formal justifications for this model, the only satisfactory economic rationale is put forward by Becker (1973, 1974a, 1981). Other rationales for assuming that a family behaves as if guided by a single utility function are that (1) family members have identical preferences, (2) a family welfare function and a particular rule for the intrafamily distribution of income exist, and

(3) one family member is a dictator. Although technically correct, none of these rationales for a single utility function is economically justified.[1]

Becker's approach is based on a particular form of altruism. In his setup a single commodity is to be distributed between husband and wife. Each cares about his or her own consumption of this commodity and also about the utility derived from the consumption of his or her spouse. The family commodity endowment of each spouse is determined in the marriage market.[2] These endowments play a crucial role. If one spouse has a sufficiently high endowment relative to the other, then, owing to altruistic preferences, there may be scope for a Pareto move in which the relatively well-endowed spouse transfers commodity income to his or her partner. Becker described this process as an "effective altruist" transferring income to his or her "beneficiary." The transfer is complete when no further Pareto moves are possible, that is, when, subject to the family budget constraint, the altruist's utility is maximized.

Under certain assumptions, effective altruism solves the coordination problem and thereby allows separate analysis of family production and consumption.[3] Hence it is in the interest of all family members to produce and, in general, act so as to maximize family income regardless of the consequences for their own individual incomes. What influences each individual's welfare is (1) how far out the family budget constraint can be pushed and (2) how much the effective altruist values each beneficiary's welfare. There is nothing in the

---

1. At least four other names for family utility models appear in the literature. The first is "reduced form neoclassical models" or simply "neoclassical models" (for example, McElroy and Horney 1981). Adoption of this terminology was motivated by the nesting of "neoclassical models" within Nash-bargained models. As pointed out by an irritated referee who persuaded this author to switch from "neoclassical" to "altruistic," bargaining models should not be contrasted with "neoclassical models" because bargaining models are in the neoclassical tradition. The other names include "altruistic models" in McElroy (1990) and "family utility models" (Lundberg 1988), which hark back to the labor supply literature; the value-laden term "dictatorial model" (Lundberg and Pollak, Chapter 5, this volume), which emphasizes the observational equivalence of the altruistic and dictatorial rationales; and "unitary preference model" or "unitary model," as used by Schultz (1990), Thomas (1990), and Alderman et al. (1995). The latter avoids the criticisms of the preceding terminologies and seemed to be the consensus of participants at the World Bank–IFPRI conference, including the author. In retrospect, however, the phrase conjures up images of a family whose members have identical and thereby nonconflicting preferences. Therefore, I have defected from the consensus.

I prefer the term "family utility model" because it subtly reminds one that the concept, sans Becker's rationale, makes no economic sense, and also because it links it to the labor supply literature, the place where such models have received the most use.

2. The wife's endowment is "the [commodity] income that would be imputed to w [the wife] by the marriage market if she had married a selfish person otherwise identical to h [her husband]." The husband's endowment is determined analogously (see, for example, Becker 1981:172–173).

3. Bergstrom (1989) showed that Becker's "rotten-kid theorem" requires transferable utility. He also exhibited a class of utility functions that are necessary and sufficient for transferability to obtain. In the one-commodity world assumed here, transferable utility automatically obtains.

model that forces the effective altruist to be "generous" or "egalitarian" or "kind" to beneficiaries. Nor does the model preclude such characterizations. It accommodates "stingy" effective altruists who provide just enough to each family member to coordinate efficient production and consumption as well as "generous" effective altruists who value the consumption by beneficiaries almost as much as or as much as (but no more than) their own consumption.

In this setup, how does the economic progress of women in the labor market translate into improvements in their well-being at home? Consider a "small" increase in women's wages—small enough so that the optimal sorting in the marriage market remains unchanged, and small enough so that comparative advantages in market and home production do not switch. Such a wage increase would increase the full family income of each family by swinging out the budget constraint. It would cause some wives to enter the labor force and (assuming positive supply elasticities) other wives to work a little more in the market. In these women's families, goods would be substituted for time in home production, and commodity output would rise. This increase in commodity output would be distributed among family members according to the preferences of the altruistic head. It would not be distributed any differently than would an equivalent increase in commodity output due to an increase in the wage rate or the nonwage income of any other family member. Each member of a working woman's family would be at least a little bit better off. However, wives themselves are not predicted to benefit relatively more or less than would other family members.

It is precisely this wide latitude of the effective altruist that makes this model an impenetrable black box with respect to the intrafamily distribution of income. Suppose that family income increases because of the purposeful activities of, good luck of, inheritance of, rise in wages for, or government transfer to the wife. This increase is divided among family members solely according to the dictates of the effective altruist. Unless the wife is the effective altruist, no nontrivial increase in her well-being is guaranteed. The same holds for every member. More generally, for a small rise (fall) in wages, the altruist would allocate any resultant increase (decrease) in commodity output in a manner that is independent of who earned it. Similarly, for a small increase (decrease) in unearned income, the altruist would allocate any resultant increase (decrease) in commodity output in a manner that is independent of who received it.

The preceding analysis applies to small exogenous changes that result in small changes in interior solutions. Such changes are either consistent or inconsistent with one-person constrained utility maximization. If consistent, then behavior may be rationalized via an effective altruist, but the identity of the effective altruist and the effects on intrafamily distributions go unanalyzed. If inconsistent, then changes in the identity of the altruist and/or alternative models of family behavior must be considered. In contrast, sufficiently large changes can lead to changes in the identity of the family altruist (for example, a switch from husband to wife) and even a new and different matching in the marriage market. Although such switches are a logical possibility, when an investigator invokes altruism and specifies a single utility function for a family, that investigator is examining small changes, thereby precluding identification of the altruist and of the intrafamily distribution of income and well-being.

Cooperative Bargaining Models

Very recently, especially in development economics, attention has shifted from altruistic models to bargaining models. Here the most highly developed model is the Nash cooperative-bargaining model of family behavior, introduced independently by Manser and Brown (1980) and McElroy and Horney (1981).[4] The comparative statics of this model generalize those of a one-person neoclassical constrained utility maximization. Changes in demand result not only from shifts and twists in the budget constraint but also from changes in the objective function due to relative changes in power. These changes are determined by opportunities of each family member outside the family.

In the Nash bargaining model, two individuals, m and f, solve a joint allocation problem. The Nash model maintains that m and f jointly allocate the commodity x so as to maximize the product of their individual gains from marriage:

$$N \equiv \left[U^m(x) - V_0^m(p_0, p_m, w_m, I_m; E_m) \right]\left[U^f(x) - V_0^f(p_0, p_f, w_f, I_f, E_f) \right] \quad (4.1)$$

subject to full household expenditures equaling full household income,

$$p_0 x_0 + p_m x_m + p_f x_f + w_f l_f + w_m l_m = (w_m + w_f)T + I_m + I_f \quad (4.2)$$

Here x_m is a good consumed by m, x_f is a good consumed by f, l_m is the leisure time of m, l_f is the leisure time of f, and x_0 is a household good (a Samuelsonian pure public good within the household); p_0, p_m, p_f, w_m, and w_f are the corresponding prices. I_m and I_f are m and f's respective and separate nonwage incomes. Nonwage income, in turn, is all income that is independent of the allocation of time between market work and other activities. The vectors E_m and E_f are "extrahousehold environmental parameters" (EEPs) and are discussed shortly. Finally, $V_0^m(p_0, p_m, w_m, I_m; E_m)$ is m's threat point as determined by his maximized indirect utility (in the unmarried state); $V_0^f(\cdot)$ is analogously defined. The reader is referred to McElroy (1990:5–10) for details.

The solution to maximization of equation (4.1) subject to equation (4.2) is a system of demand equations (for goods and leisure):

$$x_i = h_i(p, I_m, I_f; E_m, E_f), \qquad i = 0, m, f$$
$$l_i = g_i(p, I_m, I_f; E_m, E_f), \qquad i = m, f \quad (4.3)$$

---

4. Other cooperative-bargaining models were proposed by Clemhout and Wan (1977), who used a Lindahl solution, and Manser and Brown (1980), who explored a Kalai-Smorodinsky solution.

The arguments of these demand functions include all prices, separate measures of nonwage income for m and f, and the EEPs, E_m and E_f.

McElroy (1990) gave a comprehensive statement of the empirical content of Nash-bargained household behavior, including the comparative static results for EEPs. EEPs are pure threat-point shifters. They include, for example, measures of the size of the relevant marriage or remarriage market for an individual, which, in turn, could include rural-urban dummies; the sex ratio for the relevant age group; dummies for religion, caste, and unusual traits (deviant height, IQ greater than 160, and so forth); and measures of mobility. EEPs would also include wealth or permanent income and productivity outside marriage. In addition to own wages and nonwage income, these measures would include measures of employability (for example, dummies for various degrees of prohibition on market work by gender) and measures of wealth of one's family of origin. They would also include parameterizations of variations in the rules for property settlements and of the rules governing marriage and divorce that help to determine child support, custody, and alimony. For example, individual states in the United States may be characterized as permitting no-fault divorce or requiring mutual consent for divorce (H. E. Peters 1986). Finally, all taxes and transfers that are conditioned on marital status can be used as EEPs, as well as variations in child allowances and in the subsidization of child care. In cross-state or cross-country comparisons, even the unit of taxation (family versus individual) may play the role of an EEP.

This menu of potential EEPs is long, and a few comments are in order. First, it may be augmented with the more detailed examples of comparative static marriage markets mentioned later in this chapter. As noted in the introduction, changes in EEPs are precisely those changes whose effects one analyzes in studying the comparative statics of marriage markets. Second, this listing of EEPs is certainly not exhaustive of all parameters that affect the welfare of individuals outside marriage. Rather it indicates the types of variables that may serve as EEPs in empirical work. Third, empirical work requires variation in these variables. But, in any given cross-section or time-series data for a given locale, most of these variables remain fixed. Finally, interpreting the coefficients associated with EEPs is often a delicate business. There are issues of endogeneity (for example, nonwage income is the result of past decisions) and identification (for example, parental wealth plays a role in marital selection as well as in intrafamily income distributions). For a more comprehensive discussion of EEPs, see McElroy (1990:566–568).

In the Nash model, the threat points of m and f play a key role. As noted above, f's threat point (V_0^f) is the maximal level of utility that f can obtain outside the marriage. This level, in turn, depends on the prices of f's goods, the wage rate for her labor, her nonwage income, and her EEPs; m's threat point is analogously determined. An increase in the threat point of either spouse results in family demands that more strongly reflect the preferences of that spouse.

Hence the demand functions in equation (4.3), inheriting their arguments from the threat points, include as arguments not just all prices and wages but the nonwage income of each spouse (as opposed to the spouses' pooled nonwage income), as well as the EEPs.

Some Relationships between Noncooperative and Cooperative Models

Cooperative-bargaining models require that the threat points represent credible threats. In the context of small daily decisions, it is not credible for either spouse to threaten to leave the marriage. Ultimately only credible threats ensure that the cooperative solution agreement is enforceable. Ulph (1988), explicitly, and Lundberg and Pollak (Chapter 5, this volume), implicitly, recognize this point by producing noncooperative models of family decisions. In particular, both made the interesting point that the noncooperative solution could be used as the threat points for a cooperative Nash game.

Ulph's proposal dovetails with the game-theoretic results of Binmore, Rubinstein, and Wolinsky (1986). They showed that the cooperative Nash solution is the limiting (as time between offers goes to zero) subgame perfect equilibrium for a noncooperative game of alternating offers.[5] Hence the enforceability of the cooperative Nash agreement follows from the self-enforcing property of an appropriately specified noncooperative game.

Binmore, Rubinstein, and Wolinsky (1986) showed that the appropriate specification of the threat points in the underlying noncooperative game depends on the players' motives (risk aversion or time preference) to settle. For Nash-bargained household decisions, this insight distinguishes models of short-run decisions from models of long-run decisions.

Short-run family decisions can be thought of as responses to small serial shocks. For these decisions, time preference motivates the spouses to settle. Here the solution to a noncooperative game such as that of Ulph (1988) emerges as the natural specification of the status quo as threat point. In contrast, for long-run decisions, the loss of the opportunity to marry in the first place and the risk of one partner's leaving the marriage motivate the specification of threat points that reflect each spouse's best opportunities outside the marriage.

Threat points reflecting opportunities outside marriage are in line with those currently specified in Nash bargaining applications. These specifications measure men's and women's independent economic viability and marriage or remarriage prospects. Hence one would expect these outside opportunities embedded in the threat point to explain long-term, "marriage-cycle" decisions such as fertility, investments in the health and human capital of children, and

---

5. Harsanyi and Selten (1988) provide support for the Nash cooperative-bargaining approach by arguing that the Nash cooperative criterion function emerges naturally under a wide range of interesting noncooperative setups.

the joint allocation of time between the market and household production. These threat-point specifications should not be expected to work well in explaining evolving responses to small serial shocks.[6]

In sum, unlike family utility models, Nash-bargained household decisions translate women's increased economic independence directly into increased welfare within their families. This increase in welfare should be observable in terms of long-term, "marriage-cycle" decisions, but not in responses to small serial shocks.

Other Approaches

In addition to the family utility and bargaining models, at least two other types of models deserve mention. The first is Pollak's (1985) "transactions cost approach" to family decisions. The other is a Pareto-only approach by Chiappori (1988b; Chapter 3, this volume). Neither the transactions cost approach nor the Pareto-only approach was designed to focus on the link between women's economic independence and their well-being within families. However, such linkage would be consistent with both models.

The Relationships among Models

Figure 4.1 depicts the relationships among static, partial-equilibrium models of family decisions and intrafamily distributions. (The shapes and sizes of the sets are not to scale!) The largest rectangle represents the set of all possible models of household decisions. It contains the largest circle, representing the set of all bargaining models of household behavior, including cooperative and noncooperative models. The largest square also contains the rectangle that is meant to suggest an open book, with a left-hand page and a right-hand page. This rectangle intersects the circle. The entire rectangle (including both "pages") represents the set of all possible models resulting in Pareto-optimal allocations within families. The right-hand page represents all Pareto-optimal models that exclude the effects of EEPs; this would include Chiappori's (1988b) model. The left-hand page represents all Pareto-optimal models that include the effects of EEPs. Continuing to work inward, the book contains the ellipse that represents the set of all Nash cooperative models.

The relationship between Chiappori's model and the Nash bargaining model is interesting. Formally, Chiappori's model contains the Nash bargaining model so long as EEPs are identified as determinants of the bargaining rule. However, his model lacks a compelling economic rationale for EEPs as he does not analyze the sources of bargaining power. Hence the Nash bargaining

---

6. The author owes both the Binmore, Rubinstein, and Wolinsky (1986) reference and this distinction between the threat points for short-term and long-term decisions to Peter Cramton and Kenneth Kletzer and, in turn, to T. Paul Schultz, who arranged for them to discuss an earlier paper of mine at a Yale University conference.

FIGURE 4.1 Relationships among partial-equilibrium models of family decisions

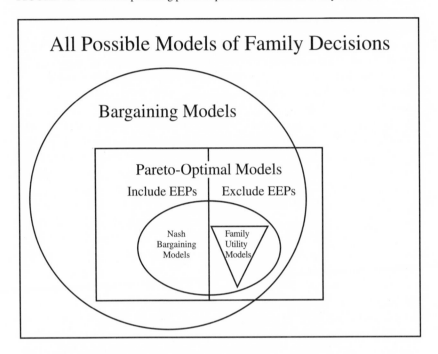

model complements his approach by giving an economic rationale for EEPs and thus insight into their empirical specification.

Returning to the ellipse, which represents the set of all Nash cooperative models, some of these include EEPs and lie on the left-hand page and some of them may exclude EEPs. In the world of testing, excluding EEPs means that the highest available utility levels outside a particular marriage are unresponsive to EEPs ($\partial V_0^k / \partial E_k = 0$ for $k = m, f$, and likewise for all higher derivatives) and, therefore, EEPs do not appear as arguments in family demands for goods and leisure (E_f and E_m may be excluded from the arguments of equation [4.3]). It is still possible, however, that income pooling may not hold. If, in addition, income pooling is imposed, then the Nash cooperative model collapses to the family utility model. This is shown as the triangle on the right-hand side of the ellipse. The family utility model is clearly the least general of all of the classes of models under discussion.

Marriage Markets

The altruism and bargaining models share a common feature. Both models are conditioned on the existence of a given family unit. Becker (1981) tied his altruism model directly to the marriage market by conditioning the initial (pre-redistribution via altruism) "endowment" of each spouse; these initial endowments are the allocations imputed to each one in the marriage market (see note 3). But the connection of both altruism and bargaining models to the marriage market is weak because neither deals, either implicitly or explicitly, with the fact that marriage markets do not in general yield unique solutions, but rather a set of solutions, the core. In linking the economic independence of women to their well-being in families, this connection is a key issue.

The analysis presented in this section by no means solves this problem of nonuniqueness. Nor does it provide an entirely satisfactory link between bargaining models and the core. It does, however, provide some insight into this link. For whatever justification there may be for the Nash bargaining model using opportunities outside the marriage as credible threats vis-à-vis long-run decisions, this justification must be ultimately grounded in marriage market analysis. What emerges from this section is a picture wherein the conclusions of Nash and marriage market models reinforce each other: for both, the economic independence of husband and wife has a direct effect on their respective incomes within the marriage.

The remainder of this section derives novel and important comparative static results that link the economic independence of women (and their marriageability) directly to their share of the intrafamily distribution of income and, therefore, to their welfare as wives. The setting is the monogamous marriage market of Becker. The theoretical underpinnings come from the pure game-theoretic theorems of Demange and Gale (1985). Although this section employs an extremely simple example, the results hold quite generally.

Setup

Marriage markets are so-called "two-sided" markets (for example, of firms and workers, of buyers and sellers, or, in our case, of women and men). Participants on both sides of the market are motivated by potential gains that can be realized only by being matched with (for example, marrying) someone from the other side. Marriage markets answer two questions: (1) who is matched with whom (and who remains unmatched) and (2) how is the total surplus from each marriage allocated between the spouses.

In a marriage market of men and women, the gains to each participant take the form of commodity income. Commodity income is measured in terms of a single Beckerian commodity, z, which is produced from purchased goods and household time. As in national income accounting, all output is consumed by individuals, and in this context it is called income. A participant's gain from the marriage market is the income that person receives over and above what he or she would receive if he or she did not participate. It is assumed that participants act to maximize their own individual incomes.

For purposes of exposition, assume that there are only two men, M_1 and M_2, and two women, F_1 and F_2. Without loss of generality, assume that if M_i (or F_j) remains single, his (her) commodity income is zero (this normalization is inessential to the results of the analysis).[7] Furthermore, assume that if M_i and F_j marry, their total gain (or surplus) in marriage is given by z_{ij}, and that these gains are arrayed as follows:

Baseline case	F_0	F_1	F_2
M_0	0	0	0
M_1	0	z_{11}	z_{12}
M_2	0	z_{21}	z_{22}

This array indicates, for example, that if M_1 marries F_2, their total commodity output would be z_{12}. If M_1 remains unmarried (that is, marries F_0), his commodity income is normalized to be 0.

In this simple setup, there are only two possible matchings. One is the diagonal matching, in which M_1 marries F_1 and also M_2 marries F_2. It is denoted by ([1,1],[2,2]). The other is the off-diagonal matching; it is denoted by ([1,2],[2,1]). Without loss of generality, assume that the indexes were chosen so that the diagonal matching is the equilibrium matching. In the present example, this amounts to assuming that[8]

$$z_{11} + z_{22} \geq z_{12} + z_{21}$$

If M_i and F_j marry, let m_{ij} and f_{ij} indicate their respective incomes. Then if the diagonal matching is the equilibrium matching, it must be feasible, that is,

$$m_{11} + f_{11} = z_{11}$$
$$m_{22} + f_{22} = z_{22} \tag{4.4}$$

Furthermore, the marriage is rational for each individual only if

$$m_{11} \geq 0, \quad f_{11} \geq 0$$
$$m_{22} \geq 0, \quad f_{22} \geq 0 \tag{4.5}$$

Finally, this matching is stable only if

$$m_{11} + f_{22} \geq z_{12}$$
$$m_{22} + f_{11} \geq z_{21} \tag{4.6}$$

---

7. Formally, for convenience, the "dummy" participants, F_0 and M_0, were created. Then if M_i is "matched" with F_0, this is interpreted as M_i being single, with normalized income of zero, and so forth.

8. A theorem from linear programming applies to this problem whereby (1) the primal solution is the matching that maximizes the grand total income as found by summing over all couples and (2) the dual solution is the set of core allocations (see, for example, Roth and Sotomayor 1990).

FIGURE 4.2 Baseline case

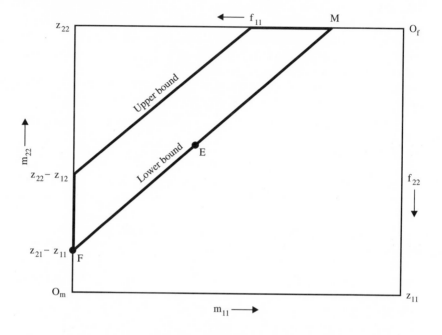

The first inequality in equation (4.6) is interpreted thus: suppose M_1 is married to F_1 and receiving m_{11}, and F_2 is married to M_2 and receiving f_{22}. Stability requires that the total of their incomes ($m_{11} + f_{22}$) must be at least as great as what they could get if they married each other (z_{12}). Otherwise it would pay them to leave their respective marriages and marry each other. Using equation (4.4), these stability conditions may be reexpressed as

$$m_{22} \leq (z_{22} - z_{12}) + m_{11}$$
$$m_{22} \geq (z_{21} - z_{11}) + m_{11} \tag{4.7}$$

A solution is a matching along with an allocation of the marital outputs that is feasible, individually rational, and stable. Hence if the diagonal matching is the solution matching, the solution allocation (m_{11}, f_{11}, m_{22}, f_{22}) must satisfy equations (4.4), (4.5), and (4.7).

Figure 4.2 graphs the set of core allocations for a particular array of z_{ij}s given by[9]

$$Z = \begin{bmatrix} 8 & 4 \\ 9 & 7 \end{bmatrix}$$

---

9. This numerical example coincides with that used by Becker.

Here, O_m is the origin for the men and O_f is the origin for the women. An allocation of z is given by $(m_{11}, f_{11}, m_{22}, f_{22}) = (m_{11}, z_{11} - m_{11}, m_{22}, z_{22} - m_{22})$. Hence any point in the rectangle between O_m and O_f represents a unique, feasible, and individually rational allocation (that is, it satisfies equations [4.4] and [4.5]). Stability (equation [4.7]) adds an upper and a lower bound for m_{22}, represented by the two bold diagonal lines. With no further structure, the solution to the marriage market problem is not unique.[10] Hence every point in or on the bold polytope in Figure 4.2 is a solution. It is the core.

Any such core has what is called a lattice structure. This property guarantees that there is a best solution for the men that coincides with the worst solution for the women. Conversely there will also be a best solution for the women that coincides with the worst solution for the men. Figure 4.2 labels these so called M-optimal and F-optimal points as M and F.

"Sympathetic" Solutions

The M- and F-optimal points play a key role in mechanisms that select a unique solution from among all the possible core solutions. For example, one well-known solution, "split the difference," would draw a line connecting M and F and then implement the allocation corresponding to the midpoint. Other schemes implement the F-optimal and M-optimal points. Crawford and Knoer (1981) showed that these can be implemented via an "English auction." If, for example, Sotheby's employed its usual procedures and auctioned off the men to the women, the final equilibrium would be (to a well-specified approximation) the F-optimal point. Since this is the best possible outcome for each woman there, no woman would have any incentive to manipulate the auction by misrepresenting her preferences.

The English auction is one of a class of auction schemes designed to solve the classic difficulties of nonuniqueness and manipulability. The traditional game-theoretic approach considers these difficulties to be "solved" when a mechanism for implementing the desired unique solution is found that cannot be successfully manipulated.[11] Although these are insightful solutions in the context of auctions and other asymmetric buyer-seller problems, they are less than satisfactory in the more symmetric context of monogamous marriage markets of men and women.

Note, however, that the split-the-difference solution, the English auction, and other solutions, all share a common feature: the final utility of the men is nondecreasing in the M-optimal point and nonincreasing in the F-optimal point. Because of the lattice property, this result implies that the final utility of

---

10. For markets with more than two men and two women, in general, the matching is also not unique.

11. There are several other, more sophisticated, solutions satisfying uniqueness and non-manipulability. See Roth and Sotomayor (1990) or Demange and Gale (1985).

the women is nondecreasing in the F-optimal point and nonincreasing in the M-optimal point. To indicate that the final utilities of participants on both sides of the market move in a predictable way with the M- and F-optimal points, this chapter terms implementation schemes with this property "sympathetic" implementation schemes.

Henceforth it is assumed that the actual mechanism for selecting a unique solution from the core is sympathetic. Under this assumption it is sufficient to analyze the comparative statics of changes in the M- and F-optimal points.

The Comparative Statics of "Sympathetic" Marriage Markets

The economic independence of women or men is defined as their economic ability to maintain themselves (and possibly their children) outside marriage. Changes in economic independence can occur in many ways, including increased wages; increased nonwage income via inheritance or good luck; government taxes and transfers; changes in the laws regarding marriage, divorce, alimony, and child support; or any changes in legal or social rules that promote the ability of men or women to maintain themselves outside marriage. This section assumes that such changes can be monetized. As the analysis shows, it is crucial to distinguish portable from nonportable changes. A portable increase is defined as one that is carried from the single to the married state. Nonportable changes cannot be so carried.

CASE 1: NONPORTABLE INCREASES IN WOMEN'S ECONOMIC INDEPENDENCE. Consider the core illustrated in Figure 4.2 as the baseline case. Now consider an exogenous increase in the incomes of single women of amount c. Assume this income is lost upon marriage and is therefore nonportable. This increase raises the normalized single incomes of women from 0 to $c > 0$. Since this increase is not portable into the married state, the z_{ij}s remain the same. The array of possible outputs now looks like this (with $c > 0$):

Case 1	F_0	F_1	F_2
M_0	0	c	c
M_1	0	z_{11}	z_{12}
M_2	0	z_{21}	z_{22}

Since the zs are unaltered, the feasibility conditions (equation [4.4]) and the stability conditions (equation [4.7]) remain unchanged. However, individual rationality (equation [4.5]) now requires

$$m_{11} \geq 0, \qquad f_{11} \geq c$$
$$m_{22} \geq 0, \qquad f_{22} \geq c \qquad (4.5')$$

Hence the women's individual rationality rules out allocations in the cross-hatched northeast border in Figure 4.3, reducing the core to the shaded polytope ($F'M'Q'P'$).

FIGURE 4.3 Case 1 versus baseline case

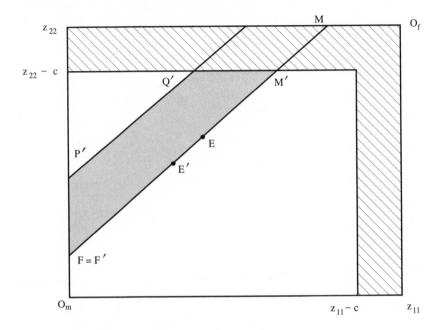

Notice that by equation (4.5′) the M-optimal point decreases from M to M′ while the F-optimal point remains at F = F′. Hence the M-optimal solution moves from M to M′ (increasing both f_{11} and f_{22} by c and thereby decreasing both m_{11} and m_{22} by c), the equal-split solution moves from E to E′ (increasing both f_{11} and f_{22} by $c/2$ and thereby decreasing m_{11} and m_{22} by $c/2$), and the F-optimal solution remains unchanged (at $m_{11} = 0$, $m_{22} = z_{21} - z_{11}$). Note that the change in final allocations under a split-the-difference solution is exactly halfway between the changes incurred under the M-optimal and F-optimal solutions. This pattern is associated with the nonportability of the increase in the women's single incomes from the unmarried to the married state.

CASE 2: PORTABLE DECREASES IN WOMEN'S ECONOMIC INDEPENDENCE. The first case considered a nonportable increase in women's independence. This second case considers a portable decrease in women's income. Again, consider the core in Figure 4.2 as the baseline case. Denote the decline in the economic independence of women as a fall in their normalized single incomes from 0 to $c < 0$. Since this decline is portable into marriage, the new total married incomes are given by

$$z_{ij}' = z_{ij} + c < z_{ij}, \qquad i,j = 1,2$$

FIGURE 4.4 Case 2 versus baseline case

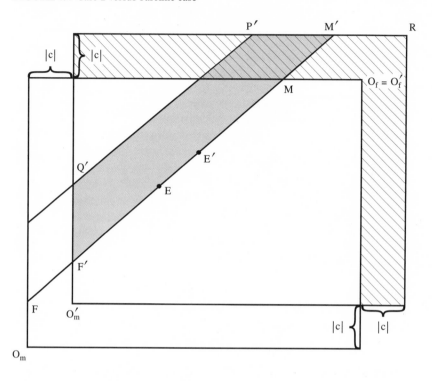

The array of possible incomes is now (with $c < 0$)

Case 2	F_0	F_1	F_2
M_0	0	c	c
M_1	0	$z_{11} + c$	$z_{12} + c$
M_2	0	$z_{21} + c$	$z_{22} + c$

As in the first example, individual rationality (equation [4.5]) becomes (4.5'), only in this case c is now a negative number. Since the women's economic loss is portable into the marriage, the feasible set shrinks from equation (4.4) to

$$m_{11} + f_{11} = z_{11} + c < z_{11}$$
$$m_{22} + f_{22} = z_{22} + c < z_{22} \tag{4.4'}$$

Figure 4.4 superimposes the core for case 2 on the baseline case of Figure 4.2. Since total married income has decreased by $|c|$ for each couple, both dimensions of the available set go down by $|c|$. Holding the F origin fixed ($O_f = O_f'$), this is shown as the translation of the M origin from O_m to O_m'. In addition, since the single incomes of women have decreased by $|c|$, the set of allocations that satisfy individual rationality now includes the hatched border along the north and east edges. If each husband drove his wife to indifference between marriage and bachelorhood, and if the stability conditions were not binding, the men could get to R in the extreme northeastern corner, where each wife would receive $c < 0$. Since the (lower bound on) stability is binding, however, the best the men can do is M', the new M-optimal point. Conversely, the best the wives can do is to get all of the marital output at F', the new F-optimal point. The case 2 core is the shaded polytope $F'M'P'Q'$. Despite the reduction in marital surpluses, it is as large as the baseline core (the bold polytope) because the loss of income to single women converts some previously unstable allocations (involving negative, normalized incomes for women as small as $c < 0$) into stable allocations. These allocations are in the intersection of the hatched border and the shaded core.

In moving from the baseline case to case 2, both the F-optimal and the M-optimal points respond to the portable decrease in women's incomes. Hence all three sympathetic marriage market equilibria respond as well. The M-optimal solution moves from M to M' (maintaining a constant distance from the M origin but moving relative to the F origin). Hence each husband suffers neither loss nor gain, while each wife absorbs the entire loss in her portable income (that is, her income declines by $|c|$). Similarly the F-optimal solution moves from F to F' (getting closer to the F origin while maintaining a constant distance from the M origin). Once again the entire loss is absorbed by the wives (each wife's income declines by $|c|$) and each husband's income remains unchanged. Finally, the split-the-difference solution moves from E to E' (closer to the F origin, but a constant distance from the M origin). Yet again, each wife absorbs the entire loss to her marriage and her husband's income remains unchanged.

Note that the M- and F-optimal solutions represent two extremes for the intrafamily distribution of income and the split-the-difference solution lies midway between. Nonetheless the response of all three sympathetic equilibria to a decrease in women's portable income is the same: the wives absorb the entire loss; their husbands remain unaffected.

CASE 3: PORTABLE INCREASES IN MEN'S ECONOMIC INDEPENDENCE IN COMBINATION WITH A DECREASE IN WOMEN'S ECONOMIC INDEPENDENCE. Suppose, as in case 2, the single incomes of all women decreased by $|c|$, where $c < 0$, and, in addition, the single incomes of all men increased by $b > 0$. Furthermore suppose both types of income changes are portable into marriage. The array of possible incomes becomes (with $b > 0$, $c < 0$)

Case 3	F_0	F_1	F_2
M_0	0	c	c
M_1	b	$z_{11} + (b + c)$	$z_{12} + (b + c)$
M_2	b	$z_{21} + (b + c)$	$z_{22} + (b + c)$

FIGURE 4.5 Case 3 versus case 2 and baseline case

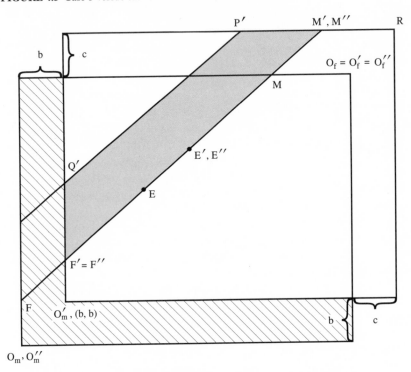

As in the last example, stability (equation [4.7]) is unchanged. Feasibility (equation [4.4]) becomes

$$m_{11} + f_{11} = z_{11} + (b + c)$$
$$m_{22} - f_{22} = z_{22} + (b + c) \tag{4.4''}$$

Finally, individual rationality (equation [4.5]) becomes

$$m_{11} \geq b, \quad f_{11} \geq c$$
$$m_{22} \geq b, \quad f_{22} \geq c \quad \text{for } b > 0, c < 0 \tag{4.5''}$$

Figure 4.5 superimposes the core of this case over that of case 2 from Figure 4.4, which, in turn, was superimposed on the core of the baseline case in Figure 4.2. (All of the labels from Figure 4.4 were carried over to Figure 4.5.) To produce a simple graph, assume that $b = |c|$. Holding the F origin fixed at $O_f'' = O_f' = O_f$, the increase in mens' incomes by b is shown as the translation of the M origin from O_m' to $O_m'' = O_m$. However, since the single incomes of men have increased by b, the set of allocations that satisfy individual rationality for the men now excludes the cross-hatched border along the south and west edges. If each wife drove her husband to indifference between marriage and bachelorhood, and if the stability conditions were not binding, wives could get only to the point (b,b), not all the way to O_m''. Since (the lower bound on) stability is binding, the best the wives can do is only $F'' = F'$, the new F-optimal point. Conversely, if each husband drove his wife to indifference between marriage and bachelorhood, and if the stability conditions were not binding, husbands could get all the way to R in the extreme northeast corner. Since (the lower bound on) stability is binding, however, the best the husbands can do is M'', the new M-optimal point. The case 3 core $F''M''P'Q'$ coincides with the case 2 core $(F'M'P'Q')$. Owing to the increase in each husband's portable income, every allocation in the case 3 core represents his gain of b over his corresponding allocation in the case 2 core.

In moving from case 2 to case 3, the M-optimal point responded to the portable increase in men's incomes: the distance between the M origin and the M-optimal point increased by (b,b) (that is, the distance from O_m'' to M'' is larger—by (b,b)—than the distance from O_m' to M'). Hence if the M-optimal solution is implemented, each husband captures the entire increase in his portable income; each wife neither gains nor loses. The distance between the F-optimal point likewise responded to the portable increase in men's incomes (that is, the distance between the M origin and the F-optimal point increased by $[b,b]$). Hence if the F-optimal solution is implemented, again each husband captures the entire increase in his portable income; each wife neither gains nor loses. Finally the case 3 split-the-difference solution is at E'', midway between M'' and F''. Comparing this with the case 2 solution at E' reveals the effect of the portable increase in men's incomes: each husband captures his entire increase and each wife neither gains nor loses. As before, the M- and F-optimal solutions represent two extremes of the intrafamily distribution of income; the split-the-difference solution lies in between. Nonetheless all three solutions respond the same way to an increase in the men's portable income: each husband captures his entire gain; the wives gain nothing.

Now the net effect of a portable increase in men's economic independence in combination with a portable decrease in women's economic independence can be seen by comparing the core and solutions in Figure 4.2 (the baseline case) with those in Figure 4.5 (case 3). Figure 4.5 illustrates case 3 when $c = -b$, and hence there is no change in family income ($z_{ij} + b + c = z_{ij}$). For any of the three sympathetic solutions considered, the net result is the same: the women lose on two counts. First they lose $|c|$ because their economic independence has declined, and then they lose b because their husband's economic independence has risen. Conversely the men gain $|c|$ and b for the same reasons. Note that even if there is a net gain in family income (that is, if $b > |c|$), women still incur a two-part loss ($-b + c < 0$) and men still receive a two-part gain ($b - c > 0$).

To sum up, all three examples illustrate the defining property of sympathetic implementation schemes: an increase (decrease) in the economic independence of one gender generally increases (decreases) and never decreases (increases) the married incomes of that gender. Distinctions between portable and nonportable changes in economic independence play a key role.

Finally, as case 3 illustrates, systematic gains in the economic independence of one gender that come at the expense of the economic independence of the other can be deceptively harmful. Although such changes may increase family income or leave it unchanged, the resulting large changes in the intra-family distribution of income will nonetheless systematically help one gender at the expense of the other. A seemingly benign increase in family income may represent a double gain to one gender, but a "double whammy" to the other.

A note on the level of generality is appropriate here. Many additional cases can be analyzed. With appropriate sign changes, gains can be converted into losses and vice versa. The roles of the men and the women can be interchanged. The gains or losses need not be the same for each member of each gender. Moreover, gains and losses could be only partially portable or super-portable (diminishing or gaining in size upon marriage). Furthermore, many of these results for the two-by-two example presented here will generalize to a marriage market with m men and n women (see Demange and Gale 1985).

Some Policy Applications

Many policy issues can be illuminated with this simple marriage market model. For example, suppose a government subsidizes single mothers and their children, but not married mothers. For simplicity, let the size of the subsidy be $c > 0$. This example fits case 1. One oft-bemoaned effect of such subsidies is the marriage disincentive represented by the reduction in the size of the core in Figure 4.3. One previously unrecognized effect of such subsidies is that (under any sympathetic implementation scheme that is less extreme than the M-optimal one) the existence of welfare payments for unmarried mothers will increase the incomes of married mothers who are potential welfare recipients. This occurs because the welfare cushion shifts the intrafamily distribution of income in the mother's favor. This effect is stronger the smaller the mother's share would be in the absence of welfare (the closer the implemented marriage market solution is to the M-optimal solution). At a minimum, the wife must capture a gain from marriage equal to her potential welfare payment.

As a second example, suppose government policies or traditions restrict the education of women, thereby making them less productive both as single individuals and as wives. For simplicity suppose that the decrease in each woman's productivity, whether single or married, is represented by $c < 0$. Then c is a portable decrease in each woman's income and the effect of this policy fits case 2. The prediction is that women's incomes are lowered both inside and outside marriage.

As a third example, take some development policies for poor rural regions that foster the development of crops for the market (such as rice) in order to raise family incomes. Sometimes such policies systematically remove land from the control of wives (who raised subsistence crops) and turn it over to their husbands to raise cash crops, often using improved technologies such as fertilizer and irrigation (see, for example, Boserup 1970 and Schultz 1989). Such examples fit case 3. Husbands gain on two counts, because they now have more resources and because their wives have less. Their wives suffer doubly. Note that compensating the wives will not help them unless that compensation is portable outside the marriage.

As a fourth example, take comparable worth, implemented in such a way as to raise women's wages without lowering men's.[12] These wage increases are portable into marriage (simplistically assuming the women do as much market work married as they would if single). This fits case 2 except that $c > 0$ replaces $c < 0$. Under any sympathetic marriage market solution, the predicted result is that the wives gain c and the husbands gain nothing. As in the previous example, family income increases but the increase is not shared between the genders.

More realistically, assume that comparable worth were implemented by paying women more and men less. Reversing the roles of women and men, this fits case 3. A similar analysis holds for affirmative action or quotas. Men would have an obvious motive for resisting a decline in their economic independence—immediate market wage and income losses. But would they still be motivated to resist if they were married to a working wife whose benefit from the policy exceeded their loss? Sympathetic solutions to marriage markets predict they would resist. After all, a husband's equilibrium share of married income is predicted to decline both because his income is down and because his wife's income is up.

As a fifth class of examples, take child-care subsidies, family allowances, or any government transfer that is targeted to benefit children. To make a clean case, assume that upon divorce mothers always obtain custody, and that upon divorce or separation the benefit is fungible. Let the size of the benefit be c and let it be received by the couple if married and by the mother if divorced. Then c is a portable increase in the woman's income, increasing both her single income and the marital surplus to be split. Accordingly (this fits case 2, except that now $c > 0$), under all three sympathetic solutions, the mother is expected to capture the entire benefit.

This fifth class of examples can be made more interesting by assuming that the subsidies are paid for by a poll tax. Moreover, suppose the amount of the subsidy is S and the poll tax is T, and that $S = 2T$ so that families neither gain nor lose income (that is, $z_{ij} + S - 2T = z_{ij}$). However, unmarried mothers gain $S - T = T$, whereas unmarried fathers lose T. This fits case 3, with $b = -c = T$,

---

12. The question of who pays for such an increase is ignored here.

except that the roles of the sexes have been interchanged. Hence it is concluded that under any of the three sympathetic marriage market solutions examined in this chapter, the tax-subsidy policy causes each husband's income to decline by $S = 2T$ and each wife's income to increase by $S = 2T$. This analysis reveals why such subsidies are often considered "women's issues."

Conclusion

As the previous section of the chapter demonstrates, certain marriage market models share a key feature with cooperative-bargaining models of family decisions: in the long run, the intrahousehold distribution of income reflects the outside opportunities of household members. These outside opportunities vary systematically with individual nonwage incomes and other variables. In the context of Nash-bargained family decisions, these other variables that parameterize shifts in these outside opportunities have been termed extrahousehold environmental parameters or EEPs. In both partial- and general-equilibrium contexts, they provide an analytical vehicle for analyzing the impact of the social and economic environment on household decisions and the intrafamily distribution of income. Moreover the complementarity of the partial-equilibrium cooperative-bargaining models with the general-equilibrium marriage market models gives rise to the conjecture that individually bargained household allocations may be aggregated in a consistent way up to a marriage market equilibrium. Although much work remains to be done, at both the theoretical and the empirical levels, and especially at their intersection, empirical evidence is emerging that EEPs may play a crucial role in the intrafamily distribution of income, especially where interest focuses on the long run.

5 Separate-Spheres Bargaining and the Marriage Market

SHELLY LUNDBERG AND ROBERT A. POLLAK

The expectation that family policies will affect distribution within marriage is implicit in much popular discussion. For example, child-care subsidies and child allowances are often regarded as women's issues. Women's groups are outspoken advocates of such programs, and women are expected to be among their primary beneficiaries. This linking of women's and children's welfare with child-based subsidies is rooted in the gender assignment of child care: mothers expect and are expected to assume primary responsibility for their children.[1] Yet the distributional implications of these policies are far from clear. Child-conditioned subsidies would certainly transfer resources to the heads of single-parent families, who are predominantly women. But what effect, if any, would such programs have on distribution between women and men in two-parent families?

Using a new model of marital bargaining, we analyze the distributional effect of such programs in two-parent families, focusing on an analytically tractable special case. We compare two child allowance schemes: in the first, a cash transfer is paid to the mother; in the second, it is paid to the father. In the event of divorce, we assume that under both schemes the mother becomes the

This chapter was first published in *Journal of Political Economy* 101:988–1010 (1993) and is reprinted with light editing with the kind permission of the *Journal of Political Economy*. The authors thank their respective spouses for their cooperation and the Rockefeller Foundation for financial support. Neither our spouses nor the Rockefeller Foundation is responsible for the views expressed here. We are grateful to the anonymous referees; to Laurie Bassi, Gary Becker, David S. Johnson, Andrew Postlewaite, Mark Rosenzweig, and Pepper Schwartz; and to seminar participants at Chicago, Georgetown, Indiana, Pittsburgh, Penn, Penn State, Texas, and Washington for useful comments.

1. As Crawford and Pollak (1989) point out, it is often asserted that mothers are primarily responsible for child care in three senses: it is mothers who find a child-care provider and make the arrangements; it is mothers who take time off from work when a child is sick or when child-care arrangements collapse; and it is mothers who "pay" child-care expenses from their discretionary incomes.

custodial parent and receives the child allowance. The comparison we propose is simpler than those involving more familiar programs such as child-care subsidies because the alternative policies we consider involve neither price effects nor tax incentive effects.

The two leading economic models of intrafamily allocation imply that these alternative child allowance schemes have identical implications for distribution in two-parent families. In the altruist model (Becker 1974a, 1981), the equilibrium is the point in the feasible consumption set that maximizes the altruist's utility; that point is independent of which parent receives the child allowance because the feasible consumption set is identical under the two child allowance schemes. In the bargaining models of Manser and Brown (1980) and McElroy and Horney (1981), the equilibrium is determined by the feasible consumption set and a threat point that is interpreted as the utility of remaining single or of getting divorced. The equilibrium is independent of which parent receives the child allowance because the feasible consumption set and the well-being of single and divorced individuals are identical under the two child allowance schemes.

Many participants in the public debate concerning actual government transfers take it for granted that intrafamily distribution will vary systematically with the control of resources. When the British child allowance system was changed in the mid-1970s to make child benefits payable in cash to the mother, it was widely regarded as a redistribution of family income from men to women and was expected to be popular with women: "Indeed so convinced did some Ministers become that a transfer of income 'from the wallet to the purse' at a time of wage restraint would be resented by male workers, that they decided at one point in 1977 to defer the whole child benefit scheme" (Brown 1984:64).

In this chapter, we propose the "separate-spheres" bargaining model, a new model of distribution in two-parent families. The separate-spheres model differs from the divorce-threat model in two ways. First, the threat point is not divorce but a noncooperative equilibrium defined in terms of traditional gender roles and gender role expectations. Second, the noncooperative equilibrium, although it is not Pareto optimal, may be the final equilibrium because of the presence of transaction costs. We show that in the separate-spheres bargaining model, cash transfer child allowance schemes that pay the mother and those that pay the father can—but need not—imply different equilibrium distributions in existing marriages. The separate-spheres model is thus not inconsistent with the view, popular among noneconomists, that distribution between women and men in two-parent families will depend on which parent receives the child allowance payment.

In the long run, the redistributive effects of child allowances depend on the feasibility of making contractual arrangements in the marriage market. The marriage market will wholly undo any redistributive effects if prospective couples can make binding, costlessly enforceable, prenuptial agreements to transfer resources within the marriage; dowry and bride-price can, under certain circumstances, be interpreted as examples of practices that facilitate such Ricardian equivalence. If binding agreements cannot be made in the marriage market—and we think that this is the relevant case for advanced, industrial societies—child allowances may have long-run distributional effects.

The analysis of alternative cash transfer child allowance schemes is analytically tractable because it does not require us to consider policies that affect prices (for example, subsidizing child care) or policies that affect the well-being of single or divorced individuals (for example, Aid to Families with Dependent Children and other welfare programs). Cash transfer schemes such as child allowances are the policies most likely to be undone in the short run by bargaining within existing marriages and in the long run by adjustments in the marriage market. The effects of other policies, such as child-care subsidies, on distribution between women and men in two-parent families are thus likely to be greater than this comparison of alternative child allowance schemes suggests.

We begin by presenting an overview of the problem of intrafamily distribution and then develop several versions of the separate-spheres bargaining model. Next we show that in the long run the marriage market can completely undo any redistribution effects of child allowances if binding, costlessly enforceable, prenuptial agreements can be made. We then consider the case in which individuals cannot make binding, costlessly enforceable agreements in the marriage market; it is shown that in this case the redistributive effects of child allowances may induce changes in the equilibrium number of marriages, as well as changes in distribution within particular marriages. The final section is a brief conclusion.

Models of Intrafamily Distribution

Economic models of household behavior have generally ignored distribution within the family. Samuelson's (1956) consensus model provided the first formal justification for this neglect. Samuelson was concerned not with explaining distribution within the family but with identifying the conditions under which consumer demand analysis could proceed without doing so. In the consensus model, each member of the family behaves as if there were a family utility function that all attempt to maximize; this assumption allows the family to be analyzed as a single unit. Because the incomes of individual family members are pooled in the joint budget, the effect of lump-sum payments (for example, property income or government transfers) is independent of which family member receives the payment. As Samuelson made clear in his original article, as a theory of distribution within the family the consensus model is a nonstarter.

The economist's standard model of distribution within the family is Becker's (1974a, 1981) altruist model. Becker postulates that the family contains one "altruistic" individual—the husband, father, patriarch, dictator— whose preferences reflect his concern for the welfare of other family members. Becker argues that the presence of one altruist who makes positive transfers to each member of the family is sufficient to induce purely selfish but rational family members to maximize family income. The resulting distribution is the one that maximizes the altruist's utility function subject to the family's resource constraint. Becker's "rotten-kid theorem" (Becker 1974b, 1981) embodies this result; Pollak (1985), Bergstrom (1989), and Johnson (1990) articulate the conditions under which the conclusion of the rotten-kid theorem holds. The source of the altruist's power in Becker's model is not his concern with the welfare of others but rather his assumed ability to confront others with take-it-or-leave-it choices; altruism in the sense of caring about the welfare of others is required only to explain why the altruist chooses a distribution that allows other members of the family a positive surplus (that is, more than their reservation levels of utility). The altruist model implies that an increase in family resources, within certain limits, will have the same effect on intrafamily distribution regardless of which spouse receives the resources. It therefore implies that a government program of child allowances would have identical effects on distribution regardless of whether the payments went to mothers or to fathers. According to both the altruist model and the consensus model, the family behaves as if it were maximizing a single utility function. This approach implies restrictions on observable outcomes that the data fail to support.[2]

Bargaining models of marriage (Manser and Brown 1980; McElroy and Horney 1981) treat marriage as a cooperative game: spouses with conflicting interests or preferences are assumed to resolve their differences in a manner prescribed by the Nash or some other explicit bargaining solution. A distinguishing feature of bargaining models is that family demand behavior depends not only on total family resources but also on the resources controlled by each spouse individually. Individual control of resources matters because bargaining outcomes depend on threat points as well as on the feasible consumption set. The threat point in a cooperative game is usually described as reflecting the outcome that would obtain in the absence of agreement. Manser and Brown (1980) and McElroy and Horney (1981) specify the threat point as the individuals' maximal levels of utility outside the family—that is, the value of divorce. The more attractive are an individual's opportunities outside the

---

2. A survey by McElroy (1981) concludes that there is little empirical support for these restrictions. Lundberg (1988) empirically rejects a simple version of the consensus model as a foundation for the labor supply behavior of husbands and wives.

family, the more strongly that individual's preferences will be reflected in the intrafamily distribution of resources.[3]

The dependence of intrafamily distribution on the well-being of divorced individuals provides a mechanism through which government policy can affect distribution within marriage in divorce-threat bargaining models. An increase in the child allowances paid to divorced mothers will increase the expected utility of divorced women and cause a reallocation of family resources in two-parent families toward goods and services more highly valued by wives. An increase in child allowances paid to all mothers would affect distribution in two-parent families through the divorce-threat effect and through an income effect. Under the assumption that, in the event of divorce, the mother gets the children and the child allowance, both husbands and wives would be indifferent between a child allowance scheme that paid mothers and one that paid fathers: an increase in child allowances paid to married mothers and a decrease in child allowances paid to married fathers creates neither divorce-threat effects nor income effects.

Although divorce may be the ultimate threat available to both spouses and is a possible destination for marriages in which bargaining has failed, it is not the only possible threat point from which bargaining could proceed.[4] Following a suggestion made by Woolley (1988), we consider a noncooperative Cournot-Nash equilibrium within marriage as an alternative threat point.[5] Within an existing marriage, a noncooperative equilibrium corresponds to a utility-maximizing strategy in which each spouse takes the other spouse's strategy as given. Under some circumstances, this equilibrium more accurately represents the outcome of marital noncooperation than does the costly and time-consuming alternative of divorce.

What distinguishes a noncooperative marriage from a pair of independently optimizing individuals? Joint consumption economies are an important source of gains to marriage, and even noncooperative family members enjoy the benefits of household public goods. If individual family members can supply public goods consumed by the entire household, then the noncooperative

---

3. As McElroy (1990) emphasizes, this dependence of household demands on the external alternatives available to individual family members is a testable implication of the bargaining framework. Empirical evidence consistent with family bargaining has been accumulating. For example, unearned income received by husbands and wives has been shown to have different effects on outcomes such as time allocation and fertility (Schultz 1990) and child health and survival (Thomas 1990).

4. We ignore the threat and the actuality of family violence, although we think that the relationship between family violence and intrafamily distribution deserves more attention. For an interesting discussion, see Tauchen, Witte, and Long (1991).

5. Because Nash's name is associated with both the cooperative and the noncooperative equilibrium concepts we use, we have tried to avoid the phrase "Nash equilibrium."

family equilibrium is analogous to the voluntary provision of public goods model analyzed by Bergstrom, Blume, and Varian (1986). As one might expect, public goods are undersupplied in this noncooperative equilibrium, and there are potential gains to cooperation. Additional gains can be expected if coordination of individual contributions is required for efficient household production. In the absence of cooperation and coordination, the effective quantity of public goods and services such as meals and child care will be less than the amounts that could be produced from the individual contributions. Specialization in the provision of such goods reduces the need for complex patterns of coordination, and traditional gender roles serve as a focal point for tacit division of responsibilities.

Specialization by gender is a pervasive aspect of family life. In the United States, though market work by married women has increased enormously in recent decades, men continue to carry most of the responsibility for earning income in two-parent families, while women continue to carry both the responsibility for and the actual work of supplying household services. Carried to extremes, the traditional division of labor and responsibilities suggests a "separate-spheres" equilibrium in the family. When husband and wife each bear the responsibility for a distinct, gender-specific set of household activities, minimal coordination is required because each spouse makes decisions within his or her own sphere, optimizing subject to the constraint of individual resources. If binding, costlessly enforceable agreements regarding transfers can be made prior to marriage, such agreements may involve a "housekeeping allowance" for the wife or "pocket money" for the husband.[6] If binding agreements cannot be made, the level of transfers may be zero, or it may be determined by custom or social norms.

In a noncooperative marriage, a division of labor based on socially recognized and sanctioned gender roles emerges without explicit bargaining. In the separate-spheres bargaining model, this voluntary contribution equilibrium is the threat point from which bargaining proceeds. Cooperative bargaining is distinguished by the ability of the players to make binding agreements within marriage.[7] The negotiation, monitoring, and enforcement of such agreements give rise to transaction costs, which may vary over husband-wife pairs. The

---

6. Pahl (1983) describes four types of financial management in husband-wife households, three of which are consistent with the "separate-spheres" equilibrium. Under the "whole-wage" system one partner, usually the wife, manages all family income and is responsible for all expenditures, except for the personal spending money of the other partner. This system is characteristic of low-income families in Britain and other European countries. Under the "allowance" system, the husband pays the wife a set amount and she is responsible for specific items of expenditure. With "independent management," separate incomes are used to finance expenditures within each partner's "sphere of responsibility." In all empirical studies cited, these three systems are together more prevalent than the fourth—"shared management."

7. Caution: We are concerned here with the ability of the spouses to make binding agreements *within* marriage. Their ability to make binding agreements *before* marriage plays a crucial role in determining long-run effects.

noncooperative default allocation avoids these costs; the voluntary contribution equilibrium is maintained by social enforcement of the obligations corresponding to generally recognized and accepted gender roles.[8] It will be optimal for couples with high transaction costs or low expected gains from cooperation to remain at the stereotypical noncooperative solution.

The distributional implications of the separate-spheres bargaining model differ from those of the divorce-threat bargaining model. As Warr (1983) and Bergstrom, Blume, and Varian (1986) have shown, the control of resources among the potential contributors to a public good in a voluntary provision model affects neither the equilibrium level of the public good nor the equilibrium utility levels of the potential contributors, provided that each potential contributor makes a strictly positive contribution. These invariance properties do not hold, however, at corner solutions. In the noncooperative, voluntary contribution equilibrium in the family, gender specialization generates corner solutions and hence the equilibrium distribution may depend not only on total family resources but also on who controls those resources.

Household Public Goods and Bargaining

We first consider distribution within a particular marriage. The preferences of the husband, h, and the wife, w, are represented by the von Neumann–Morgenstern utility functions $U^h(x_h, q_1, q_2)$ and $U^w(x_w, q_1, q_2)$, where x_h and x_w are private goods consumed by the husband and wife, and q_1 and q_2 are household public goods jointly consumed by the husband and wife. Thus we assume that interdependence in the marriage operates only through consumption of the public goods: there is no "altruism" in the sense of interdependent preferences, although it would be a straightforward extension to allow i's utility to depend directly upon j's private consumption or j's utility.[9] Cooperative solutions to the family's distribution problem have been extensively analyzed elsewhere. With Nash bargaining, the equilibrium values of x_h, x_w, q_1, and q_2 are those that maximize the product of the gains to cooperation; these gains are defined in terms of a threat point representing the utility each spouse would achieve in the absence of agreement. Figure 5.1 depicts the threat point, the feasible set, and the Nash bargaining solution in the utility space.[10] An alternative

---

8. This is, of course, a cop-out. By appealing to the social enforcement of gender roles, we beg the question of how "norms" of any type are established and maintained. Elster (1989) and Sugden (1989) discuss this issue and provide references to the literature.

9. Although child allowances may affect fertility, we ignore this complication. Instead we assume that all marriages produce the same number of children, thereby avoiding the issues of endogenous fertility and stochastic fertility.

10. Nash (1950) shows that a system of four axioms uniquely characterizes the Nash bargaining solution: Pareto optimality; invariance to linear transformations of individual von Neumann–Morgenstern utility functions; symmetry (that is, interchanging the labels on the players

FIGURE 5.1 The household Nash bargaining solution

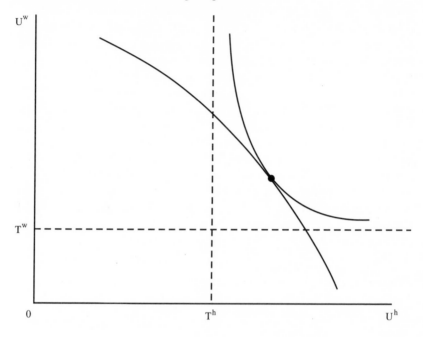

characterization of the Nash bargaining solution is as the point in the feasible set that maximizes a "social welfare function" that depends on the threat point. More precisely, the Nash social welfare function is a symmetric Cobb-Douglas function, where the origin has been translated to the threat point: $N = (u^h - T^h)(u^w - T^w)$. It follows immediately that the utility an individual receives in the Nash bargaining solution is an increasing function of the utility the individual receives at the threat point: thus, for example, an increase in the threat point utility of h and a decrease in that of w will cause an increase in the Nash bargaining solution utility of h and a decrease in that of w. We write the threat point as $[T^h(p_1, p_2, I_h, I_w), T^w(p_1, p_2, I_h, I_w)]$, where $T^i(p_1, p_2, I_h, I_w)$ is the indirect utility function, p_1 and p_2 are the relative prices of the public goods (we assume that the prices of x_h and x_w are equal and we normalize them to 1), and I_h and I_w are the exogenous incomes received by husband and wife.[11]

---

has no effect on the solution); and what Sen (1970) calls "property α." Luce and Raiffa (1957) call this property "independence of irrelevant alternatives" (except the so-called threat point), but Sen points out that this is not equivalent to Arrow's condition of that name.

    11. Instead of treating income as exogenous, we could treat wage rates as exogenous and focus on labor-leisure choices, with leisure as a private good.

To derive the demand functions for the public and private goods, we maximize the Nash social welfare function

$$N = [U^h(x_h, q_1, q_2) - T^h(p_1, p_2, I_h, I_w)][U^w(x_w, q_1, q_2) - T^w(p_1, p_2, I_h, I_w)]$$

subject to the constraint that joint expenditure equal joint income:

$$x_h + x_w + p_1 q_1 + p_2 q_2 = I_h + I_w$$

This yields the demand functions

$$x_i = g^{x_i}(p_1, p_2, I_h, I_w) \qquad i = h, w$$

$$q_k = g^{q_k}(p_1, p_2, I_h, I_w) \qquad k = 1, 2$$

Incomes received by the husband and wife enter these demand functions separately because they affect not only the feasible set but also the threat point. If the threat point depends on other parameters representing the extramarital environment, then these parameters will also enter the demand functions of two-parent households. So far we have been silent about the interpretation of the threat point: it could correspond to divorce, to violence or the threat of violence, or to a noncooperative equilibrium within marriage.

A noncooperative marital equilibrium provides an interesting alternative to divorce as a specification of the threat point. If divorce involves substantial transaction costs or can be dominated by sharing public goods within an intact but noncooperative marriage, then the voluntary contribution equilibrium offers a more plausible alternative to divorce as the threat point from which bargaining may proceed. Replacing an "external" threat point with an "internal" one and introducing transaction costs will affect final household allocation in two ways: it will influence cooperative-bargaining outcomes via the threat point for each spouse, and it may be an equilibrium allocation in marriages for which transaction costs outweigh the potential gains to cooperation. Until otherwise noted, we assume that divorce is impossible or prohibitively expensive so that the relevant threat point is the noncooperative, voluntary contribution equilibrium within marriage.

We begin with a simple Cournot equilibrium in the provision of public goods by husband and wife, assuming that socially prescribed gender roles assign primary responsibility for certain activities to the husband and others to the wife. The implications of household separate spheres are straightforward; they generate corner solutions and thus nonneutrality in the provision of public goods. We then show how these results are modified when we allow cash transfers or binding premarital agreements between husband and wife.

Suppose that the public good, q_1, falls within the husband's traditional sphere so that, in the absence of a cooperative agreement, the husband decides unilaterally on the level of q_1 consumed by the household. Similarly, suppose that q_2 falls within the wife's sphere. In a noncooperative marriage, husband

and wife decide simultaneously on the levels of q_1 and q_2 they will contribute to the household. This exclusive assignment of public goods reflects a socially sanctioned allocation of marital responsibilities and is independent of preference or productivity differences between husband and wife in a particular marriage.[12]

The husband chooses x_h and q_1 to maximize $U^h(x_h, q_1, \overline{q}_2)$ subject to $x_h + p_1 q_1 = I_h$, where $\overline{q}_2$ is the level of public good chosen by the wife. This decision leads to a set of "reaction functions,"

$$x_h = f^{x_h}(p_1, I_h, \overline{q}_2)$$
$$q_1 = f^{q_1}(p_1, I_h, \overline{q}_2)$$

Similarly the wife's demand functions for (x_w, q_2) will depend upon $\overline{q}_1$. The Cournot equilibrium is determined by the intersection of the public goods demand functions. For a simple example, consider the Klein-Rubin-Stone-Geary utility functions:

$$U^h = \alpha_h \log(x_h - x_h') + \beta_h \log(q_1 - q_{1h}') + (1 - \alpha_h - \beta_h) \log(q_2 - q_{2h}')$$
$$U^w = \alpha_w \log(x_w - x_w') + \beta_w \log(q_2 - q_{2w}') + (1 - \alpha_w - \beta_w) \log(q_1 - q_{1w}')$$

Because these utility functions are separable, the reaction functions are independent of the quantity of the public good provided by the spouse, and demands take a very simple form:

$$x_h = x_h' + \alpha_h I_h^* \qquad q_1 = q_{1h}' + \frac{\beta_h}{p_1} I_h^*$$
$$x_w = x_w' + \alpha_w I_w^* \qquad q_2 = q_{2w}' + \frac{\beta_w}{p_2} I_w^*$$

where I_h^* and I_w^* are the husband's and wife's supernumerary or discretionary expenditures, which are defined as

$$I_h^* = I_h - x_h' - p_1 q_{1h}'$$
$$I_w^* = I_w - x_w' - p_2 q_{2w}'$$

Substituting the reaction functions into the direct utility functions yields indirect utility functions of the form $V_0^h(p_1, p_2, I_h^*, I_w^*)$ and $V_0^w(p_1, p_2, I_h^*, I_w^*)$. The husband's utility depends upon the resources of his wife through his consumption of "her" public good and vice versa.

---

12. Household production models, on the other hand, explain specialization by gender as a response to pervasive and persistent differences in home and market productivities of the husband and wife in a particular marriage, while recognizing that these individual productivity differences may reflect past investments in specific human capital. Average differences in preferences or productivities may help to explain the evolution of gender roles, but individuals take gender roles and gender role expectations as given.

In the separate-spheres model with a Cournot threat point, the alternative child allowance schemes imply different household allocations: the non-cooperative equilibrium depends on the individual resources of husband and wife, and thus on which parent receives the child allowance payment. A change in child allowance policy that affects the threat point will also affect the cooperative equilibrium. Thus distribution between men and women in two-parent families can be affected by policy changes that have no effect on the relative well-being of divorced men and women.

This nonneutrality result is sensitive to our assumptions. If the model is altered by removing the separate-spheres assumption, then household allocation will be invariant to changes in the child allowance policy whenever positive contributions to each public good are made by both husband and wife. If the model is altered by allowing additional mechanisms for reallocation between spouses, such as cash transfers or binding premarital agreements, then household allocation will be invariant under some conditions. We examine these two modifications in the next version of the model, in which the wife specializes in the provision of a single household public good, q, which we describe as child services, and the husband specializes in the provision of money income, some portion of which he may transfer to his wife.

In the model with transfers, we assume that the process determining the distribution of the marital surplus occurs over two periods. In period 1, marriage contracts are made. When these contracts are made, the parties do not know the actual values of individual incomes, I_h and I_w, though the distributions from which they are drawn are common knowledge to all marriage market participants. We assume that prospective couples can make binding, costlessly enforceable, prenuptial agreements that specify a minimum transfer, t, which will be paid from husband to wife in period 2. The agreed minimum transfer cannot be contingent on future income realizations;[13] it may be voluntarily augmented by the husband in period 2, or it may be superseded by cooperative bargaining. If binding agreements are not possible, then all marriages that form will be based on a contractual transfer level of zero, although all marriage market participants recognize that voluntary supplementary transfers may be made in period 2. We discuss marriage market effects later in this chapter.

In period 2, the husband's and wife's incomes are realized and the husband may voluntarily make a supplementary transfer, $s > 0$, in order to increase his consumption of q. We suppose that the husband acts first, choosing x_h and s to maximize $U^h(x_h, q)$ subject to the budget constraint $x_h = I_h - t - s$ and the wife's reaction function $q(s)$. The wife takes the husband's supplementary transfer as given and chooses x_w and q to maximize $U^w(x_w, q)$ subject to $x_w + pq$

---

13. There will be no marital bargaining in period 2 if complete contingent contracts can be made in the marriage market.

$= I_w + t + s$, where p is the relative price of child services. Consider the case of Klein-Rubin-Stone-Geary utility:

$$U^h = \alpha_h \log(x_h - x_h') + (1 - \alpha_h) \log(q - q_h')$$
$$U^w = \alpha_w \log(x_w - x_w') + (1 - \alpha_w) \log(q - q_w')$$

where, to simplify the algebra, it is assumed that $q_h' = q_w' = q'$.[14] The discretionary expenditures of each spouse are given by

$$I_h^* = I_h - x_h'$$
$$I_w^* = I_w - x_w' - pq'$$

The supplementary transfer to the wife will be positive when

$$I_h^* - t > \alpha_h(I_h^* + I_w^*)$$

When $s > 0$,

$$x_h = x_h' + \alpha_h(I_h^* + I_w^*)$$
$$x_w = x_w' + \alpha_w(1 - \alpha_h)(I_h^* + I_w^*)$$
$$q = q' + \left[\frac{(1 - \alpha_w)(1 - \alpha_h)}{p} \right](I_h^* + I_w^*)$$

yielding indirect utility functions (and threat points) of the form $V^i(p, I_h^* + I_w^*)$. If the equilibrium is one in which positive supplementary transfers are made from husband to wife, then the value of the noncooperative solution to each spouse depends only on the total resources of the family, and not on the separate sources of income. Redistributions from husband to wife will be offset dollar for dollar by adjustments in the supplementary transfer, s.

If the realizations of I_h and I_w are such that the condition for positive supplementary transfers is not met, however, individual incomes affect the noncooperative equilibrium. If $s = 0$, the husband spends his entire uncommitted income, $I_h - t$, on his private good, x_h, and the wife allocates her total income, $I_w + t$, to her private good and child services. The utilities corresponding to this voluntary contribution equilibrium are

$$V_0^h(p, I_h^* - t, I_w^* + t) \qquad V_0^w(p, I_w^* + t)$$

In the separate-spheres bargaining model with transfers, the alternative child allowance schemes have identical effects if supplementary transfers are positive when the child allowance is paid to the mother. But if the family is at a corner solution—that is, if $s = 0$ when the child allowance is paid to the

---

14. Allowing q_h' and q_w' to differ complicates the algebra but does not substantially alter the results.

mother—then the threat point will be affected by which parent receives the payment.[15]

It is straightforward to apply the separate-spheres bargaining model in a household production framework and to allow husband and wife to have different productivities in producing the public good. With constant returns to scale and no joint production, this is equivalent to assuming that the husband can purchase the public good at a different (presumably higher) price than the wife. Ignoring coordination problems, let the total amount of child services consumed by the couple be $q = q_h + q_w$, where q_h is purchased by the husband at a price p_h and q_w is purchased by the wife at a price p_w. There are now two ways in which the husband can influence his own consumption of child services in a noncooperative household: he can influence his wife's resources through supplementary transfers and he can purchase child services directly.

Under our assumptions about the wife's utility function, the husband faces a constant "price" of purchasing the public good via supplementary transfers, namely $(1 - \alpha_w)/p_w$. Hence, except in a razor's edge case, the husband will not simultaneously make positive supplementary transfers and direct purchases of the public good but will choose the method with the lower price. If the noncooperative equilibrium is such that $q_h > 0$ and $q_w > 0$, redistribution between husband and wife will be neutral only if they face the same price for the public good. In a cooperative household, all child services will be purchased by the wife at the lower price.

We can relax our earlier assumption that divorce is impossible or prohibitively expensive and modify our analysis to recognize that, for some marriages, divorce is the relevant threat point. When both divorce and noncooperative marriage are possible outcomes, the relevant threat point will depend on the utility possibilities associated with these states and on the institutional rules governing divorce.[16] The separate-spheres model can be interpreted as the case in which the voluntary contribution marriage is Pareto superior to divorce, so that neither spouse can convincingly threaten divorce; hence, the voluntary contribution equilibrium is the relevant threat point for the bargaining game. On the other hand, if both spouses prefer divorce to any noncooperative marriage, then divorce is the relevant threat point. In general the recognition

---

15. Nonneutrality at corner solutions also occurs in Becker's altruist model, although corner solutions in the two models have different interpretations.

16. One approach would be to assume that, at the beginning of the cooperative bargaining game, both spouses recognize that if they fail to reach an agreement, they will play a noncooperative game. Institutional rules must specify the outcome of the noncooperative game when one spouse prefers the voluntary contribution equilibrium within marriage. If unilateral, no-fault divorce is permitted, then divorce is the outcome unless both parties choose a voluntary contribution marriage. If, on the other hand, the rules permit divorce only with the consent of both spouses, then a voluntary contribution marriage will eventuate unless both spouses choose divorce. The expected utility for each spouse in this noncooperative postgame is the threat point for cooperative bargaining.

that divorce is the relevant alternative for some marriages attenuates the link between child allowances and intrafamily distribution. When divorce is the threat point, the two child allowance schemes we consider have identical distributional effects.

Marriage Markets with Binding Agreements

As Becker has emphasized, the marriage market is an important determinant of intrahousehold distribution. Bargaining within a marriage is limited to the "surplus" generated by that marriage and thus depends on the alternatives available outside the marriage. If there are no information, search, or contracting problems, then a continuous distribution of preferences and traits in the population implies that distribution within marriage will be completely determined in the marriage market; there is no surplus to be bargained over in any particular marriage, because the next-best marriage is just as good. Stapleton (1990) provides a careful analysis of this extreme case.

If marriage market participants are heterogeneous, surpluses depend on the matching of men and women. Matching models (see Mortensen 1988; Roth and Sotomayor 1990) provide an analytical framework for investigating equilibrium or stable assignments of men to women in the marriage market, and such models typically possess multiple equilibria. Search costs further complicate the analysis of marriage market equilibria (see Mortensen 1982a, 1982b, 1988). Becker (1973, 1974a, 1974b, 1981) was among the first to recognize the relationship between distribution within marriage and "assortative mating" in marriage markets. Lam (1988) analyzes the effect of household public goods on marriage patterns and shows how different assumptions yield results very different from those predicted by Becker.

The noncooperative distribution of household resources described in the previous section will depend upon the value of the transfer, t, determined in the marriage market. To analyze the short-run effects of a new child allowance scheme (that is, its effect on distribution in existing marriages), it was appropriate to take the value of this transfer as predetermined. In the long run, however, new marriages will form taking the new policy into account. In this section, we show that, when prospective couples can make binding, costlessly enforceable prenuptial agreements about the minimum level of transfers, a "Ricardian equivalence" result emerges: new marriages will completely offset the effects of any change in the child allowance scheme.

In this model, a marriage contract specifies a transfer that is not contingent on the realized values of income. We denote the marriage of female i to male j by the pair (i,j) and the transfer that the male is obliged to make to the female by t_{ij}; a negative value of t_{ij} thus implies a transfer from female i to male j. We denote a marriage contract by (i,j,t_{ij}).

A marriage market structure is a set of marriage contracts: $S = \{(i,j,t_{ij})\}$. Both female i and male j evaluate a prospective marriage contract (i,j,t_{ij}) in terms of the expected utility associated with it; this utility can depend on attributes of the spouse as well as on consumption of the private good and the public good. To calculate expected utility, the expectation is taken over the joint distribution of incomes and transaction costs facing the pair (i,j). The reduced-form expected utility functions can be written as $V^i(i, j, I_{0i} + t_{ij}, I_{0j} - t_{ij})$ and $V^j(i, j, I_{0i} + t_{ij}, I_{0j} - t_{ij})$, where I_{0i} and I_{0j} are the noncontingent components of female and male income.

Child allowances can be easily introduced into the model. If a child allowance, a, is paid to the husband, then the reduced-form utility functions are $V^i(i, j, I_{0i} + t_{ij}, I_{0j} + a - t_{ij})$ and $V^j(i, j, I_{0i} + t_{ij}, I_{0j} + a - t_{ij})$. If the child allowance is paid to the wife, then the reduced-form utility functions are $V^i(i, j, I_{0i} + a + t_{ij}^*, I_{0j} - t_{ij}^*)$, and $V^j(i, j, I_{0i} + a + t_{ij}^*, I_{0j} - t_{ij}^*)$, where t_{ij}^* is the transfer from the husband to the wife when the wife receives the child allowance.

In the long run the marriage market can undo any short-run distributional effects achieved by paying child allowances to wives rather than to husbands. That is, the set of equilibrium marriage market structures is independent of the child allowance scheme. When the child allowance is paid to wives rather than to husbands, the marriage market structure with the same pairing of women and men, but with transfers from men to women reduced by the amount of the child allowance, is an equilibrium. With binding transfers, therefore, the distributional effect of a policy changing the recipient of child allowances will persist only within marriages in existence at the time of the policy change. For subsequent generations of marriages, adjustments in prenuptial transfers will exactly offset the shift in child allowances. This Ricardian equivalence result, of course, depends on the assumption that prospective couples in the marriage market can make binding, costlessly enforceable agreements.

Marriage Markets without Binding Agreements

Even without binding agreements, the requirements of equilibrium in the marriage market can generate substantial differences between the short-run and the long-run effects of child allowances. In this section, we focus on a simple special case to illustrate the range of long-run outcomes that are consistent with this model. We assume that all individuals live as adults for two periods. In the first period everyone participates in the marriage market. Those who do not marry in the first period remain unmarried in the second period. Those who marry in the first period remain married in the second period; divorce is impossible or prohibitively costly. We assume that the only differences among individuals are differences in the utility associated with remaining unmarried: all men have identical (nonstochastic) incomes, and all women have identical (nonstochastic) incomes. Distribution within marriage is determined by bargaining, and since divorce is ruled out, the threat point is a noncooperative marriage. We assume that the representative marriage is at a corner solution with respect to supplementary transfers, so that a change from the child allowance scheme that pays fathers to the scheme that pays mothers will increase the utility of married women and decrease the utility of married men.

Under our assumptions that all women are identical except in the utility of remaining unmarried, and that all men are identical except in the utility of remaining unmarried, the utilities associated with a particular marriage—say (i,j)—are independent of i and j. Individuals contemplating marriage can compare the utility of the representative marriage with the utility of remaining unmarried. Since all marriages are identical, the only function of the marriage market is to determine which individuals marry and which individuals remain unmarried.

To analyze equilibrium in the marriage market, we introduce a function $G^w(U^w)$ showing the number of women for whom the utility of being unmarried is less than or equal to the utility of being married, U^w; $G^h(U^h)$ is the corresponding function for men. The value of the function $G^w(U^w)$ is, of course, the number of women willing to marry when the utility of married women is U^w.

Instead of focusing on just two child allowance schemes—one paying fathers and the other paying mothers—we can consider a continuum of child allowance schemes in which a portion of the child allowance is paid to mothers and the remainder to fathers. We denote the child allowance payment to mothers by γa and the payment to fathers by $(1 - \gamma)a$. Thus if $\gamma = 0$ the entire child allowance, a, is paid to the father; if $\gamma = \frac{1}{2}$ the child allowance is divided equally between the parents; and if $\gamma = 1$ the entire child allowance is paid to the mother.[17]

We now use γ to reparameterize the "willingness to marry" functions, $G^w(U^w)$ and $G^h(U^h)$. Because U^w is an increasing function of γ, we can define a new function: $G^{*w}(\gamma)$ by $G^{*w}(\gamma) = G^w(U^w(\gamma))$; $G^{*w}(\cdot)$ is an increasing function of γ (more precisely, a nondecreasing function of γ). Similarly, $G^{*h}(\cdot)$ is a decreasing (more precisely, nonincreasing) function of γ. The number of marriages corresponding to various values of γ is given by $N = \min\{G^{*w}(\gamma), G^{*h}(\gamma)\}$.

There are three interesting cases, illustrated in Figure 5.2A–C, distinguished by whether women or men are in short supply in the marriage market at various values of γ. In case A, $G^{*w}(\cdot)$ is less than $G^{*h}(\cdot)$ for all γ in the interval $[0,1]$, so that more men than women wish to marry. A change from the child allowance scheme that pays fathers to one that pays mothers will increase

---

17. Values of γ outside the interval $[0,1]$ correspond to imposing a lump-sum tax on one spouse and paying the child allowance plus the lump-sum tax to the other spouse. To avoid invoking lump-sum taxes, we confine ourselves to values of γ in the interval $[0,1]$.

FIGURE 5.2 The marriage market and division of the child allowance

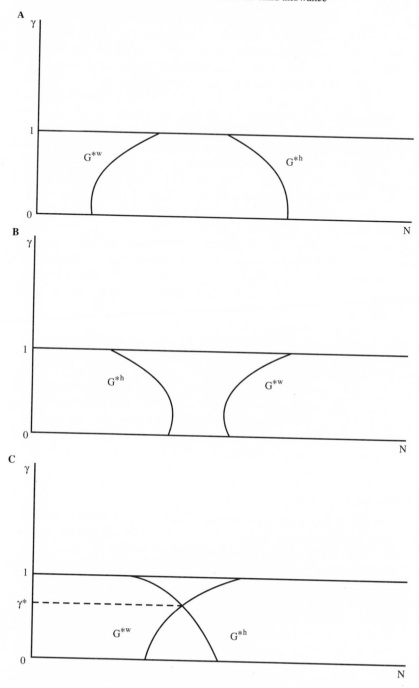

the utility of married women and decrease the utility of married men; such a change will also increase the number of marriages, because the number of women willing to marry is the binding constraint under both child allowance schemes. Individuals who were unmarried under the old scheme and marry under the new scheme experience a welfare gain.

In case B, $G^{*h}(\cdot)$ is less than $G^{*w}(\cdot)$ for all γ in the interval $[0,1]$. In this case the number of men willing to marry is the binding constraint at both endpoints of the interval. Shifting the child allowance payment toward mothers will increase the utility of married women and decrease the utility of married men; such a shift will also decrease the number of marriages. Individuals who were married under the old scheme but remain unmarried under the new scheme will experience a welfare loss.

In case C, the curves $G^{*h}(\cdot)$ and $G^{*w}(\cdot)$ intersect at some value γ^* in the interval $[0,1]$. There is, however, no mechanism to drive γ to γ^* because individuals cannot make binding agreements in the marriage market. In case C, the effect on the number of marriages of a change from the child allowance scheme that pays fathers to the one that pays mothers is indeterminate: as we have drawn the curves, the number of marriages is the same under both child allowance schemes.

This section has analyzed long-run implications for distribution between spouses when binding agreements cannot be made in the marriage market in a very restrictive special case. Even when all individuals of the same gender are perfect substitutes in the marriage market and differ only in the reservation utility for marriage, the range of possible outcomes is very wide. This suggests to us the impossibility of obtaining strong general results. Although there is much to be said for models that allow additional heterogeneity among individuals and hence assortative mating, such models are likely to be consistent with an even wider range of possible outcomes.

Conclusion

In this chapter we have introduced the separate-spheres bargaining model, a new model of distribution within marriage. To compare the separate-spheres model with the leading economic models of distribution within marriage—Becker's altruist model and the Manser-Brown/McElroy-Horney divorce-threat bargaining model—we have emphasized the distributional implications of alternative child allowance schemes that differ only in their treatment of two-parent families. Under one scheme payments go to the father; under the other they go to the mother; under both schemes, in the event of divorce, the mother gets the children and the child allowance. In the altruist model and the divorce-threat bargaining model, these alternative child allowance schemes imply identical distributions between mothers and fathers in two-parent families. In the separate-spheres bargaining model, these schemes can imply different distributions.

The separate-spheres bargaining model, like the divorce-threat bargaining model, views marriage as a cooperative game. The separate-spheres model differs from the divorce-threat model in its specification of the threat point. In the separate-spheres model, the threat point is a noncooperative equilibrium within marriage defined in terms of traditional gender roles and gender role expectations. Because the child allowance schemes can imply different noncooperative equilibria, they can imply different distributions in two-parent families.

Any redistribution between women and men resulting from the choice of one child allowance scheme rather than the other may be transitory. If binding, costlessly enforceable prenuptial agreements can be used to specify transfers within marriage, then the marriage market will undo any redistribution. If, on the other hand, binding prenuptial agreements are impossible, then the choice of one child allowance scheme rather than the other can have long-run effects on distribution in two-parent families. We show, however, that even without binding agreements, the requirements of equilibrium in the marriage market can generate long-run results that differ substantially from short-run results.

Bargaining models of marriage have almost invariably treated marriage as a cooperative game, and the separate-spheres bargaining model follows this tradition. Recent advances in noncooperative bargaining theory provide an alternative approach: specifying the bargaining process as a sequence of moves and a corresponding information structure, and analyzing it as a game in extensive form. Rubinstein (1982) analyzes a bargaining game in which the players take turns making offers and shows that a class of alternating offer games have unique, subgame perfect equilibria. Binmore, Rubinstein, and Wolinsky (1986) show that the Nash bargaining solution, a standard axiomatic solution concept for cooperative games, can be reinterpreted as the solution to a noncooperative alternating offer game if the threat point is suitably interpreted. On the basis of these results, we might reinterpret the Nash bargaining solution to our separate-spheres bargaining model as the solution to a specific noncooperative bargaining game.[18]

We have two reservations regarding this approach. First, we doubt that marriage is best formulated as an alternating offer game. Solutions to extensive-form games are sensitive to the details of their specifications, and this particular extensive-form game does not seem to capture the essential features of marital bargaining. Second, we have doubts about whether marriage is best formulated as a noncooperative game: cooperative game theory may provide a

---

18. Kanbur and Haddad (1994) apply the results of Binmore, Rubinstein, and Wolinsky (1986) to the analysis of intrahousehold allocation.

more fruitful framework for analyzing distribution between spouses. Discussing cooperative games, Shubik (1989:103) writes as follows: "The game in extensive form provides a process account of the detail of individual moves and information structure; the tree structure often employed in its description enables the researcher to keep track of the full history of any play of the game. This is useful for the analysis of reasonably well-structured formal process models where the beginning, end and sequencing of moves is well-defined, but is generally not so useful to describe complex, loosely structured social interaction." It is difficult to think of many better examples of a "complex, loosely structured social interaction" than marriage.

6 Separate Spheres and the Conjugal Contract: Understanding the Impact of Gender-Biased Development

MICHAEL R. CARTER AND ELIZABETH G. KATZ

Economic development can extend new opportunities unevenly to members of households based on their gender. How important is the gender bias of development, and, in particular, of development strategies explicitly induced by public policy? To answer this question, and in order to understand whether, when, and how gender bias matters, the complex interplay of the individual and mutual interests, expectations, and activities that characterize the household must be understood.[1]

Among economists, the best-known model of household resource allocation is Becker's (1981) household-welfare-function model, which relies on notions of altruism to aggregate preferences of individuals within the household into a single decisionmaking logic (sometimes called the "common preferences" or "unitary" model). Yet qualitative studies of household behavior from other social science disciplines suggest that although altruism plays some role in household labor supply and consumer demand decisions, gender-based norms, divisions, and conflicts are equally, if not more, important in the

This work is part of a project on the socioeconomic impact of nontraditional agricultural export growth in Guatemala, which has been generously supported by grants from the Tinker Foundation, the University of Wisconsin (MUCIA), the Inter-American Foundation, the John D. and Catherine T. MacArthur Scholars Program at the University of Wisconsin–Madison, the Land Tenure Center, and the U.S. Agency for International Development. None of the views expressed here should be attributed to either employing or supporting organizations. The authors also thank the reviewers of this volume for their thoughtful and insightful comments on the work.

1. In the agricultural sector, providing incentives for the introduction of new crops is a common policy prescription for raising rural incomes, and, in the case of export crops, generating foreign exchange. In a study of the impact of such policies on the intrahousehold allocation of labor and expenditures in the highlands of Guatemala, for example, Katz (1994, 1995) finds a pronounced gender bias in the distribution of the costs and benefits of agricultural diversification, a bias that largely manifests itself in a series of complex transactions and negotiations within peasant households. Similarly, International Food Policy Research Institute (IFPRI) studies in five developing countries found that gender-specific phenomena such as control over income substantially altered the impact of cash cropping on nutritional outcomes.

determination of household resource allocation (Hochschild 1990; Wolf 1990). This latter view states that the household is better conceived as consisting of separate, gendered spheres of decisionmaking and activity that are related to one another by a "conjugal contract"—the terms under which household members exchange goods, incomes, and services among themselves (Whitehead 1981).

Both the common preferences and conjugal contract views of the household can imply the existence of intrahousehold patterns of inequality that may evolve over time. However, the conjugal contract theory developed here suggests that intrahousehold inequality is relevant for policy analysis precisely because its pattern is mutable, economically endogenous, and shaped by gender bias in development and development policy. Specifically the conjugal contract model allows us to explore

1. whether and how the adoption of a new economic opportunity depends on its gender bias;
2. whether gender-biased development can fundamentally alter the intra-household terms of exchange implicit in the conjugal contract; and
3. whether and how the gender bias of a new economic opportunity will affect intrahousehold expenditure and welfare patterns.[2]

This chapter explores these questions by putting forward a model of the household economy composed of separate gender-specific spheres of economic activity and resource allocation linked by a conjugal contract. While building on other critiques that have challenged the unitary model's assumption of unified household preferences, the conjugal contract model also modifies the assumption—characteristic of both the unitary model and many of its critics—that the various sources of household income are pooled into a single fund from which household members draw in order to obtain goods. Research in developing countries (for example, Dwyer and Bruce [1988]) has shown that household budgeting patterns vary widely, with full income pooling being the exception rather than the rule. Income itself, and not just the goods and services it can buy, is most appropriately seen in many cultural contexts as the private property of the individual who earns it, although it may be subject to the claims of other household members.

The Conjugal Contract Model: Autonomy and Interdependence in the Household Economy

The alternatives to the conjugal contract model that are prevalent in the literature include the unitary model; the cooperative-bargaining model, suggested by McElroy and Horney (1981) and Horney and McElroy (1988); and Chiappori's (1992) Pareto-efficient model.

---

2. The unitary model also allows this.

To varying degrees, the following issues distinguish and drive these four models of intrahousehold resource allocation:

1. Individualism of preferences. Can the preferences of household members be aggregated to the level of the household (that is, is a household utility or social welfare function appropriate)?
2. Interdependence within the household economy. What are the bases for interdependence and cooperation within the household economy? Interdependence can be generated by conventional consumption externalities (caring about one's partner's consumption); jointly consumed intrahousehold public goods; and labor market imperfections that make family labor relatively more productive than hired labor.
3. Property rights, information, and autonomy within the household. Do "property rights" (broadly defined) and information costs give individuals autonomous control over their income, or is all income pooled as "marital property"? Without pooling, intrahousehold transfers of labor power and income—the conjugal contract—become relevant as a way of dealing with interdependence in the household.
4. Exit options. What is the nature of the individual's alternative to participation in the household economy? The individual's alternative or exit option is ultimately a social as well as an economic phenomenon.
5. Voice within the household. How are individual preferences mediated? In particular, is it a one-sided or a dictatorial process, or do all individuals enjoy "voice"—the right and ability to bargain?

The four models of the household economy can be distinguished along these five dimensions. In the unitary model, individual preference heterogeneity and autonomous control over income are not important. McElroy and Horney's model differs from the unitary model because preferences—but not budget constraints—are individualized.[3] Chiappori's model allows for both individualistic preferences and autonomous income control, but without any form of interdependence among household members. The conjugal contract model to be developed here characterizes the household economy as a site of independent preferences and resource allocation decisions bound together by various forms of interdependence—what Sen (1990) calls "cooperative conflict." The conjugal contract model also considers the ways in which the social construction of patriarchy is reflected in the alternative or "exit" options individuals have to the household economy, as well as the determination of the degree of

---

3. The cooperative-bargaining model's reformulation of the household economy has a major impact on the analysis and interpretation of inequality and specialization within the household. For example, changes in intrahousehold resource allocation induced by relative price shifts do not necessarily appear as a noncontentious response to a new price set in order to maximize collective well-being. Instead price shifts and other phenomena can generate shifts in bargaining power and the relative weight of each individual's preferences in the final decision.

"voice" that individuals have to bargain with over the terms of the conjugal contract.

The Simple Conjugal Contract Model of the Household Economy

In the conjugal contract model, individuals are relatively autonomous in the allocation of their resources, and resource allocation decisions are linked through the mutual need for each other's contributions to the production of a public good (z) produced through a simple household production process. Formally, a simple version of the conjugal contract model can be represented as shown in equation (6.1):

$$\max_{x_f,\; \tilde{l}_f^z,\; l_f^w} U_f(x_f, z \mid \Theta) \qquad\qquad \max_{x_m,\; \tilde{l}_m^z,\; l_m^w} U_m(x_m, z \mid \Theta)$$

$$\text{s.t.} \qquad\qquad\qquad\qquad \text{s.t.}$$

$$p_f x_f \le w_f\, l_f^w + \Theta \qquad\qquad p_m x_m \le w_m\, l_m^w - \Theta$$

$$z = a_z(\tilde{l}_f^z + \hat{l}_m^z) \qquad\qquad z = a_z(\hat{l}_f^z + \tilde{l}_m^z)$$

$$\tilde{l}_f^z + l_f^w \le L_f \qquad\qquad \tilde{l}_m^z + l_m^w \le L_m \qquad\qquad (6.1)$$

where each household member's utility (U_f, U_m) is a function of a private good (x_f, x_m) and z and is conditional upon the level of the net income transfer that makes up the conjugal contract (Θ). Each person is constrained in her or his purchase of x by the income she or he can earn by supplying labor to the market at a gender-specific, parametric wage rate (w_f, w_m), net of whatever income transfers she or he receives from her or his partner. The Z good is produced using inputs of time according to a linear production technology, $z = a_z l_z$, where l_z is simply the sum of male and female time allocated to Z-good production ($\tilde{l}_f^z + \tilde{l}_m^z$). Here, $\hat{l}_m^z$ represents the man's Z-good labor supply contributions anticipated by the woman, and $\hat{l}_f^z$ represents the woman's contributions anticipated by the man.[4]

Simultaneous solution of the choice variables in the constrained maximization problem in equation (6.1) can be modeled as a two-person, strictly competitive game of complete information, which means that no coordination is required for the two household members to choose equilibrium strategies (Friedman 1986:31–32). Each person solves his or her optimization problem,

---

4. The specification of autonomous intrahousehold subeconomies, or separate spheres, in equation (6.1) is, in part, a statement about property rights and information. To the extent that individuals are considered to exercise exclusive rights over the income they earn, or to the extent that asymmetric information lets individuals hide what they earn, there is no reason to assume automatic income pooling. Note that asymmetric information can also give individuals autonomy over their resource allocation decisions. Direct bargains over such allocations would be enforceable only at some cost. For example, the amount of labor time and effort devoted by an individual to household Z-good production may not be directly observable by one's partner, meaning that the individual's time allocation is relatively autonomous and subject only to indirect control.

treating the partner's behavior as fixed at some expected level. For each individual, this noncooperative optimization behavior results in a set of conditional demand and supply functions that depend on expectations or conjectures about the partner's behavior. These functions can be viewed as "best-reply mappings"—that is, they give the optimal resource allocation for one individual, given the behavior of the partner. Equilibrium (for a given net income transfer) is then found by the simultaneous solution of each player's conditional supply and demand functions.

For each individual (f,m), the maximization problem in equation (6.1) can be rewritten as a Lagrangian function after using the time constraint to substitute out for l_k^w. For the woman, the Lagrangian will appear as

$$\mathcal{L}_f = U_f(x_f, a_z(\hat{l}_m + \check{l}_f)) + \lambda_f(w_f(L_f - \check{l}_f) + \Theta - p_f x_f) \tag{6.2}$$

where λ_f is the shadow price of female-controlled income. Assuming interior solutions, the first-order necessary conditions can be written as

$$\lambda_f = \frac{\partial U_f / \partial x_f}{p_f} \tag{6.3a}$$

$$(\partial U_f / \partial z)a_z = \lambda_f w_f \tag{6.3b}$$

$$w_f(L_f - \check{l}_f) + \Theta - p_f x_f = 0 \tag{6.3c}$$

Condition (6.3b) indicates that the woman will allocate labor to Z-good production until the utility-valued marginal returns to that labor ($[\partial U_f / \partial z]a_z$) just equal the opportunity cost of labor (w_f) marked up by the shadow price of her own cash income (λ_f). For a woman with relatively little cash income and low levels of consumption of x_f such that the marginal utility of $x_f(\partial U_f / \partial x_f)$ is high, condition (6.3a) shows that the value of λ_f will be high. This supports a tendency to supply relatively little of her labor to the intrahousehold public Z good, in order to allocate time to her own income-earning activities, even if w_f is low. Note that positive income transfers to the woman will boost her consumption levels, reduce $\partial U_f / \partial x_f$, lower the shadow price of own-income, and thereby alter labor allocation in favor of Z-good production. Thus intrahousehold income transfers effectively operate as inducements to modify individuals' autonomous time allocation decisions. In contrast the unitary and cooperative bargaining models use only a single, household-level shadow price of (pooled) income to value the use of time in home versus market activities, thereby guaranteeing that the trade-off between income and leisure is equalized between partners (barring corner solutions).[5]

---

5. Because of full income pooling in the cooperative-bargaining models, the household achieves a conventional "tangency rationality," equating the marginal rates of substitutions between all pairs of goods (as judged by the bargained preferences) to the relative prices of those goods. Labor time is always allocated according to a comparative advantage rationality, once the decision to cooperate has been made.

FIGURE 6.1 Equilibrium Z-good labor supply (transfer level fixed at $\bar{\Theta}$)

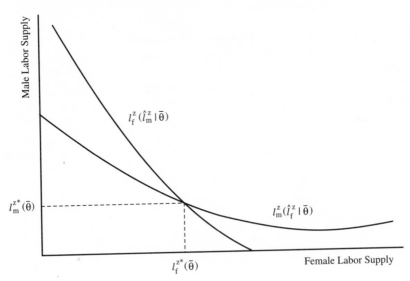

Depending on conjectures about the behavior of the other individual in the household, solution of the system of equations (6.3a–c) defines "best-response" or conditional demand and supply functions:

$$x_k^c = x_k^c(\hat{l}_j^z \mid \Theta) \qquad (6.4a)$$

and

$$l_k^{zc} = l_k^{zc}(\hat{l}_j^z \mid \Theta) \qquad (6.4b)$$

where $\hat{l}_j$ represents individual k's conjecture about the behavior of partner j. If each individual (myopically) treats the partner's behavior as fixed and non-responsive to changes in his or her own behavior, the special case of a Nash-noncooperative equilibrium is defined as

$$x_k^*(\Theta) = x_k^c(l_j^{z*}(\Theta) \mid \Theta) \qquad (6.5)$$

$$l_k^{z*}(\Theta) = l_k^{zc}(l_j^{z*}(\Theta) \mid \Theta)$$

Note that this equilibrium is stable in the sense that there is no incentive for deviation from the equilibrium. Each individual's equilibrium behavior is the best response to the equilibrium behavior of the partner. For the sake of clarity, denote the equilibrium values given by equation (6.5) as the conditional

FIGURE 6.2 Conjugal contract and Z-good labor supply

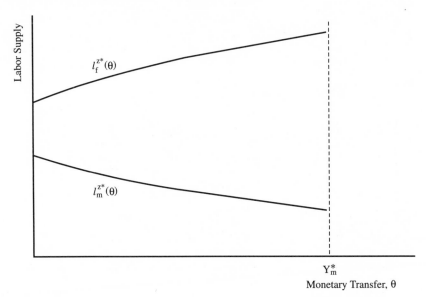

equilibrium values, to emphasize their dependence on Θ. Figure 6.1 illustrates equilibrium Z-good labor supply for the male and female household members.[6]

As the net intrahousehold transfer income varies, the conditional equilibrium values given in equation (6.5) will also vary. Figure 6.2 shows the impact of increasing levels of Θ on the amount of male and female supply of labor to Z-good production, assuming males and females have identical preference structures and that the male wage rate exceeds the female rate. Starting at a position of zero income transfer, increases in Θ (male to female income transfers) indirectly induce greater female supply of labor to Z-good production under fairly general assumptions. As discussed in the previous section, higher values of Θ reduce the λ_f markup the woman applies to her own earnings, thereby indirectly increasing her Z-good labor supply. Male supply of labor to Z-good production will correspondingly decrease.

Building on Figure 6.2, Figure 6.3 shows the impact of Θ on conditional indirect male and female utility defined by the maximization problem in equation (6.1) and the conditional equilibrium values in equation (6.5). Denoting these indirect utility functions as $V_f^e(\Theta)$ and $V_m^e(\Theta)$, Figure 6.3 shows that

---

6. See Katz (1992) for comparative static analysis of this equilibrium, which illustrates the impact of a rise in male wages on labor allocation.

FIGURE 6.3 Conjugal contract and intrahousehold welfare

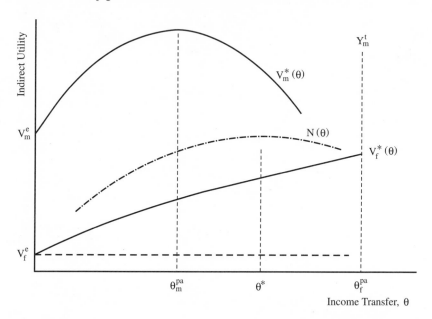

female indirect utility will be strictly increasing in Θ.[7] Male indirect utility, $V_m^e(\Theta)$, will initially increase in Θ (reflecting the gains from cooperation within the household). Eventually, $V_m^e(\Theta)$ will decrease in Θ as the male-to-female transfers approach total male income, $Y_m^*(\Theta)$.

Intrahousehold resource allocation and welfare depend, in part, on the transfer level Θ. Figure 6.3 portrays the potential gains available to each partner from these intrahousehold income transfers. The values of Θ denoted Θ_f^{pa} and Θ_m^{pa} illustrate those intrahousehold income transfer levels that would respectively maximize female and male indirect utility. The flexibility of Θ will determine the agility with which the household deals with the interdependencies between the autonomous intrahousehold economies. Note, however, that unlike models in which a comparative advantage–based labor allocation can be achieved separately from consumption allocation decisions, the transfers required to induce labor supply response in the conjugal contract model precommit income to a particular expenditure pattern. The following section develops an approach to the determination of Θ, or more generally, the conjugal contract, which reflects the interplay of economic logic and the social forces that construct the degree of patriarchy.

---

7. The notation indicating the dependence of indirect utility on wages, prices, and other external factors is suppressed.

Exit, Voice, Patriarchy, and the Determination of the Conjugal Contract

The ability to have "voice" in the determination of the conjugal contract and the nature and strength of "exit" options from the conjugal contract are what shape the process by which the equilibrium Θ is determined. As fundamentally social constructions, both voice and exit reflect a complex of attitudes, mores, and opportunities exogenous to the household that can be labeled the "degree of patriarchy." Although patriarchy is largely exogenous to the household, it is precisely its mutability within the development process that underlies the importance of intrahousehold models that emphasize that individual preferences cannot be uniquely aggregated.

"Voice" within the household refers to the degree to which both partners can influence, or bargain over, the determination of Θ. A strongly patriarchal social structure would be one in which women have no voice—that is, they would have no socially recognized right to bargain over the conjugal contract.[8] In such a world, determination of the conjugal contract could be represented as a principal-agent process, with one partner (say, the man) acting as the principal, selecting the value of Θ to maximize his well-being, and subject only to a "competitiveness constraint" to keep his partner present in the household. Within less patriarchal social structures, which grant women voice, determination of the conjugal contract could be modeled as a bargaining process.

As for the exit condition, this might be given by the indirect utility the individual could gain by dissolving and leaving the household (McElroy and Horney 1981). For women, in particular, the feasibility and strength of this indirect utility option outside the household depend on social attitudes toward and opportunities open to them. Alternatively exit from the conjugal contract could take the form of noncooperation within the household. In Jones (1983: 122) noncooperation takes the form of "no transfer of income . . . between husband and wife, although each continues to be responsible for their particular household maintenance expenditures." Lundberg and Pollak (Chapter 5, this volume) suggest "a division of labor based on socially recognized and sanctioned gender roles." Here noncooperation within the household is represented by a zero net income transfer; that is, partners continue to allocate their labor between home and market, but without the mediating influence of Θ.[9] In terms of Figure 6.3, the noncooperation exit constraint would be given by V_f^e, that is, by the level of V_f at the point of its intersection with the vertical axis. The dashed line in Figure 6.3 extends this exit constraint horizontally across the graph. When $V_f^*(\Theta = 0)$ is the relevant exit constraint and there is strong patriarchy (no female voice), the maximizing male principal would not be

---

8. But note that, as modeled here, such women still have their sphere of autonomous economy defined by property rights and guarded by asymmetric information.

9. Katz (1992) expands this notion of noncooperation to include zero transfers of land and income-generating labor time as well as income.

bound by the exit constraint and would simply select his individually preferred level of Θ, Θ_m^{pa}.[10] Alternatively, a Nash-cooperative bargaining concept gives the following model for the determination of the conjugal contract:

$$\max_{\Theta} N = \left[V_f^*(\Theta) - V_f^e \right]\left[V_m^*(\Theta) - V_m^e \right]$$

s.t.

$$\Theta \leq Y_m^*(\Theta)$$
$$V_f^*(\Theta) \geq V_f^e$$
$$V_m^*(\Theta) \geq V_m^e \tag{6.6}$$

where V_f^e and V_m^e, respectively, are the exit indirect utilities for female and male members of the household. Again the notation indicating dependence on prices and other external factors is suppressed. The inequality restriction on Θ simply reflects the fact that the male-to-female monetary transfers cannot exceed (male) monetary income $Y_m(\Theta)$. Note that if it were assumed that all household resource allocation decisions could be bargained and enforced, then there would be no individual autonomy, and the problem in equation (6.6) could be reduced to McElroy and Horney's model. Property rights over and information about income are thus key factors that distinguish the conjugal contract and cooperative-bargaining models.

The first-order condition for this problem is simply

$$(\partial V_f^*/\partial\Theta)G_m + (\partial V_m^*/\partial\Theta)G_f \geq 0 \tag{6.7}$$

where $G_m = [V_m^*(\Theta) - V_m^e]$ is the male gain from the bargain and G_f is the female gain from the bargain. An interior solution to this problem requires that $\partial V_f^*/\partial\Theta$ and $\partial V_m^*/\partial\Theta$ take different signs, since the G_k terms must be nonnegative. As discussed earlier and shown in Figure 6.3, this condition is met for large values of Θ. More straightforwardly, allowing for women's "voice" in the bargaining process will necessarily move the equilibrium value of Θ to the right of the "no-voice," or principal-agent transfer value Θ_m^{pa} shown in Figure 6.3. The cooperatively bargained transfer value would be a point such as Θ^*, which corresponds to the maximum of the Nash-bargaining objective, $N(\Theta)$, illustrated in Figure 6.3.

The following section employs this model of the conjugal contract to examine the impact of gender-biased development on intrahousehold resource allocation and welfare.

---

10. Note that in this instance information costs and property rights over income allow the woman to achieve utility above her reservation level, despite the fact that she has no voice with which to bargain.

Gender-Biased Development and Intrahousehold Allocation and
Welfare in the Conjugal Contract Model

Consider an increase in w_m, the male wage rate. Working back through the autonomous intrahousehold maximization problems and equilibrium conditions reveals that such an increase in the market value of male time shifts down male supply of labor to Z goods (the $l_m^{z*}(\Theta)$ curve in Figure 6.2). For any given Θ, equilibrium female supply of labor to Z-goods production ($l_f^{z*}(\Theta)$) would shift up in response to the diminished male Z-good labor supply.

However, with fixed Θ, male labor supply response would be less elastic than in unitary and income-bargaining models, because there is a limit to women's willingness to reallocate their labor time away from income-generating activities without some sort of compensation. Thus failure to renegotiate the conjugal contract following the wage increase would dampen response to the new opportunity.

Note also that the higher male wage increases the male's indirect utility exit constraint while leaving unchanged the female exit opportunity. Let V_{m0}^e denote the male exit indirect utility prior to the wage increase, and let V_{m1}^e denote the same measure after the wage increase. Female exit utility remains fixed at V_f^e. Assuming that the cooperative bargaining problem given in equation (6.6) determines the equilibrium Θ, the new conjugal contract will be determined by maximization of the following objective expression:

$$[V_f^*(\Theta) - V_f^e][V_m^*(\Theta) - V_{m1}^e] \tag{6.8}$$

which, by adding and subtracting V_{m0}^e, can be rewritten as

$$[V_f^*(\Theta) - V_f^e][(V_m^*(\Theta) - V_{m0}^e) + (V_{m0}^e - V_{m1}^e)]$$

or

$$[(V_f^*(\Theta) - V_f^e)(V_m^*(\Theta) - V_{m0}^e)] + [(V_f^*(\Theta) - V_f^e)(V_{m0}^e - V_{m1}^e)] \tag{6.8'}$$

The first term in square brackets in expression (6.8′) generates the reallocation effect of the wage increase on the conjugal contract. The second term generates the bargaining power effect. The reallocation effect refers to the redistribution of household resources that occurs to take advantage of a new economic opportunity, holding bargaining power constant—that is, the effect predicted by the unitary model. Here, however, this intrahousehold resource reallocation is modified by whatever shifts in relative bargaining power may have been brought about by the introduction of the new opportunity: in the case of a male wage increase, the male's bargaining power will be enhanced in such a way as to shift the benefits of the wage increase to him, as manifested, for example, in an expenditure pattern more consistent with his individual preferences.

A Conjugal Contract Model of the Peasant Household Economy

Applying the conjugal contract model to a rural, developing-country setting requires recognition of at least two distinguishing features of peasant households. First, there tend to exist well-defined gender-specific responsibilities for the different categories of expenditures made by the household; thus it is possible to know what types of goods a person is likely to acquire within his or her budget. Second, in the peasant household the interdependence of the resource contributions of household members to both Z-good production and income-generating activities is even more pronounced than in economic contexts in which the sites of production and consumption are more highly specialized. That is, the material basis for intrahousehold exchange is greatly expanded by the fact that peasant households draw extensively on their own land and labor with limited mediation from external, often imperfect, markets.[11]

Modifying the model presented in equation (6.1) to incorporate the material bases for cooperation in a stylized peasant household yields

$$\max_{\tilde{l}_f^z,\, l_f^s,\, x_f,\, l_f^h} U_f(x_f, x_m, z \mid \hat{\tilde{l}}_m, \Theta^m, \Theta^l)$$

s.t.

$$p_f x_f \le Y_f + \Theta^m$$

$$Y_f = Q_f[(l_f^s - \Theta^l + \gamma l_f^h), T_f] - w l_f^h$$

$$z = z[x_f, x_m, (\hat{\tilde{l}}_m + \tilde{l}_f^z)]$$

$$\tilde{l}_f^z + l_f^s \le L_f$$

$$l_f^s \ge \Theta^l$$

$$\max_{\tilde{l}_m^z,\, l_m^s,\, x_m,\, l_m^h} U_m(x_f, x_m, z \mid \hat{\tilde{l}}_f, \Theta^m, \Theta^l)$$

s.t.

$$p_m x_m \le Y_m - \Theta^m$$

$$Y_m = Q_m[(l_m^s + \Theta^l + \gamma l_m^h), T_m] - w l_m^h$$

$$z = z[x_f, x_m, (\hat{\tilde{l}}_f + \tilde{l}_m^z)]$$

$$\tilde{l}_m^z + l_m^s \le L_m$$

$$l_m^s \ge -\Theta^l \qquad (6.9)$$

where the transfers that make up the conjugal contract are defined as net male-to-female monetary transfers:

$$\Theta^m = (\Theta_m^y + \Theta_m^p + \Theta_m^r) - (\Theta_f^y + \Theta_f^p + \Theta_f^r)$$

and net female-to-male labor transfers:[12]

---

11. Jones's (1983) adaptation of the cooperative-bargaining model to a West African context incorporated these two distinguishing features—gender-specific expenditure responsibilities and direct labor exchange for income-generating activities—of the peasant household. Jones's empirical observation of the reluctance of women to transfer labor to high-return, male-controlled agricultural projects contradicts the joint income maximization rationality of the cooperative-bargaining model. By disaggregating the budget constraint, the conjugal contract model deals with Jones's anomalous observation. Why should women necessarily allocate their unremunerated labor time to male-controlled rice production when they have no guarantee of receiving any of that income for their own expenditure responsibilities? Although the notion of a conjugal contract does not analytically preclude a woman from working on her husband's more highly remunerated crops, it does explicitly link this decision to an expectation regarding her own level of intrahousehold compensation for this work.

12. Transfers of land among household members may also play an important role in establishing the basis for interdependence and cooperation in the household; such transfers are

$$\Theta^l = \Theta^l_f - \Theta^l_m$$

The components that make up the net monetary transfer are transfers from earned income (Θ^y_m and Θ^y_f), transfers from unearned property income (Θ^p_m and Θ^p_f), and transfers from remittance income (Θ_m and Θ_f). Although the fungibility of money makes these transfers perfect substitutes for each other in this model, households may, in practice, separately account for monetary transfers based on their source. Similarly, in this model, male and female labor times perfectly substitute for each other and can be aggregated into the single net-labor-transfer measure. But if timing and seasonality matter, it is entirely possible that positive amounts of female-to-male (Θ_m) and male-to-female (Θ_f) labor transfers could be observed. Finally denote the ratio Θ^m/Θ^l as the intrahousehold terms of exchange. The transfer parameters that make up the conjugal contract are set by a bargaining or a principal-agent problem.

In equation (6.9), each household member's allocational decisions result from a maximization of utility, defined over one's own goods as well as one's partner's, and over joint Z goods that are produced in the home, using labor and (some) purchased commodities. As in Jones (1983), female (male) goods should be interpreted as goods for which the woman (man) has primary responsibility to purchase, and not necessarily as "private goods" that only one individual consumes.[13] Individuals thus care directly about commodities purchased by their partners, as well as caring about them indirectly to the extent that the purchased commodities assist in the production of the jointly consumed Z good. Note that choice variable l^s_k is the labor supplied to all household income-generating activities, so that $l^s_f - \Theta^l$ is the amount of labor a woman supplies to activities the income from which she controls.[14]

Male and female monetary incomes are produced according to the two strictly concave (diminishing returns) production technologies, Q_m and Q_f, which depend on inputs of efficiency labor and a fixed asset, T (perhaps land). These production functions are most easily thought of as representing agricultural production processes, but they are general enough to represent an array of activities ranging from agriculture to petty commerce to supply of labor to a

---

certainly empirically observable in a number of cultural contexts. For simplicity's sake, however, intrahousehold land transfers are abstracted from this discussion.

13. Among the Massa in northern Cameroon, for example, women are responsible for food purchases and men for cattle purchases (Jones 1983). In the central highlands of Guatemala, typical male expenditures are for agricultural inputs and equipment, land, and prestige items, whereas women tend to spend their money on food, small animals, and domestic goods (Katz 1995).

14. Because of the consumption interdependence in this specification (for example, males care directly about commodities purchased by women), individuals might independently transfer resources from their sphere to that of the spouse (for example, men might independently transfer income to women). However, notation indicating choice of transfers is suppressed on the assumption that the bargained Θs always require a higher level of transfer than that which would be undertaken independently.

market in which employment probability (or search costs) diminishes (increases) with the amount of labor supplied (Carter and Kalfayan 1989). Household male and female labor is considered a perfect substitute in efficiency labor terms, whereas hired labor time, l_k^h, has a lesser productivity than household labor, as shown by the efficiency labor discount factor, γ $(0 < \gamma < 1)$. This specification of hired labor conforms to the notion that hired wage labor will tend to be less productive per hour than labor provided by family members, who have some interest in the residual income generated by the production process. In addition, family labor may be subject to a set of disciplinary controls that are not legitimately employed against hired labor.

This specification of the income-generating process, and ultimately the vision of the labor market on which it is based, create a strong material basis for cooperation within the peasant household economy. However, as the next section will indicate, the ability of the peasant farm to exploit its comparative advantage in cheap labor will ultimately depend on its ability to mobilize its household labor. Indeed some analysts (Friedmann 1980; Bennholdt-Thomsen 1988; Reinhardt 1988) have noted that the competitiveness of peasant family farming is ultimately a reflection of patriarchy in the sense that it relies on the mobilization and exploitation of cheap family labor. According to such a view, as certain tenets of patriarchy are challenged at a societal level—here understood as the social legitimation of female bargaining voice and extrahousehold exit opportunities—the hyperproductivity and competitiveness of peasant family farms are diminished accordingly.

Resource Reallocation and Renegotiation of the Conjugal Contract in the Peasant Household following Gender-Biased Development

Although more empirically compelling than the earlier specification, the complex interdependencies of the peasant household erase the simplicity that made relatively sharp comparative static results possible. Nonetheless, using the basic mode of analysis developed earlier, it is possible to characterize generally the nature of reallocation and renegotiation in the conjugal contract model.

Consider an increase in monetary returns to the male production function, Q_m. Such a change could occur for a variety of reasons, including extension programming, cooperative enterprise, or farming contracts that target either men or crops traditionally contained in the male sphere of activity. The discussion that follows assumes that (marginal) returns to labor are sufficiently high in Q_m and that male land stock is sufficiently large that the man desires to supplement his efforts with spousal labor, hired labor, or both.

In the unitary and cooperative-bargaining models, such a development would lead to a reallocation of labor time based on comparative advantage, with the woman, for instance, shifting time from her activities to her husband's. Allocation of the increase in pooled family income would be a separable issue, subsequently undertaken in accord with the nature of common household or bargained preferences. In the conjugal contract model, no reallocation of female labor time to the Q_m will occur without renegotiation of the conjugal contract.[15] Separability between labor allocation and the determination of the consumption bundle breaks down. Female labor will only be shifted to male agricultural production by renegotiating the conjugal contract in a way that elicits female labor by precommitting funds, via a monetary transfer, to the female expenditure sphere.

Following the increased returns to the male activity, the woman has muted incentives to reallocate her time to an activity that generates income controlled by the male, income that will be allocated to commodities in his sphere. The man is, of course, anxious to circumvent the imperfections in the labor market and employ family labor that is cheap in efficiency wage terms. Indeed, to the extent that female labor is mobilized at the expense of reduced earnings in the female sphere, the male has muted incentives to worry about the opportunity cost of additional female labor. However, in the absence of changes in the conjugal contract necessary to bring forth additional female labor, the man will reallocate his labor time away from any Z-good production and toward the now more remunerative commercial activity. Reduction in l_m^z will lead the woman to increase l_f^z, her Z-good labor time, compensatorily and reduce her labor supply to income-earning activities, l_f^s, diminishing her monetary earnings, Q_f, given the fixed Θ^l. The net effect of these first-round reallocations is to leave the woman more tightly income constrained than before, with a higher shadow value of own-income—λ_f.

Thus two countervailing changes are induced by the increased returns to the male activity: the man's incentive to mobilize family labor increases and the woman imputes an even higher shadow value to her own income. Renegotiation of the conjugal contract confronts direct and indirect coordination problems. Increased female labor supply to the male activity can be negotiated directly. But the male-to-female income transfer needed to compensate for the labor supply increase has indirect effects. As in the simple model given earlier, the monetary transfer, via its effect on λ_f, influences the allocation of the woman's time between her income-earning activities (Q_f) and Z-good production.

To summarize, the conjugal contract model proposes a way to analyze the reallocation of household resources following a new economic opportunity. It suggests an array of factors that may condition the elasticity of the household response to the new economic opportunity. Finally the model implies that a

---

15. Strictly speaking, if consumption externalities were strong enough, or if Z-good production were highly dependent on male-purchased commodities, it would be possible for the woman to allocate labor beyond that contractually required to the male activity. The discussion that follows will ignore this possibility and assume that the conjugal contract always binds female and male behavior.

change in the intrahousehold terms of exchange is a preliminary indicator of the intrahousehold distribution of the gains of the new opportunity.[16]

Conclusions and Policy Implications

The conjugal contract model is intended to capture in a formal way the internal complexity of the household economy. In the context of a peasant economy, the exploration of the balance between individual preferences, income control, and labor and expenditure responsibilities, on the one hand, and resource exchange reciprocity, on the other, has largely taken place in fields other than economics, and it has not been systematically incorporated into the design and assessment of economic development initiatives. The model developed in this chapter has sought to characterize households as simultaneously sites of conflict and cooperation, of autonomy and interdependence, and to analyze the way in which they respond to changes in their economic environment in light of this internal richness of material relations.

Perhaps the central methodological contribution of the model is its recognition of the key mediating role of resource exchanges that occur within the household. These internal exchanges play two important roles in the household economy. First, expectations regarding the level and type of exchanges determine each household member's decisions about how to allocate labor time and income among competing uses. Second, changes in exogenous economic parameters, such as prices and wages, are absorbed by the household in part via their effects on the relative claims that individual household members have on one another's resources. Although previous economic models of the household have allowed for the differential impact of economic change on household members, conceptualizing this impact in terms of an alteration in the intrahousehold terms of exchange is quite new.

Such a model has several implications for economic policy. The model encourages the prior careful identification of gender-based spheres of economic activity, including remunerated and unremunerated labor, as well as expenditure responsibilities where these are well defined. Such prior identification allows policymakers to better predict whether the intervention they are considering—a price subsidy, for example, or the introduction of a new agricultural technology—will have a more direct effect on men or women. Second,

---

16. Katz (1995), for example, finds that adoption of male-biased export crops in Guatemala flattens the intrahousehold terms of exchange between male cash and female labor transfers. Women in export-crop households work longer in their husbands' fields, gain little in the way of increased monetary transfers, continue to devote undiminished amounts of labor time to market activities to earn their own income, and are relieved from unpaid domestic labor only insofar as they can tap into their older daughters' labor time. The study also finds that export crop income is more likely to be spent on items in the male expenditure sphere, such as land and agricultural equipment, and less likely to be spent on "female" goods such as food and household items.

economic policy design must recognize the types of resource exchanges that occur within the boundaries of the household and the way in which these exchanges mediate the household's collective response to policy initiatives and the distribution of the costs and benefits of such initiatives. For example, although increasing opportunities for male agriculturalists may sound like an unambiguously positive development strategy, when intrahousehold resource transfers are taken into account, enhancing men's economic opportunities may have the effect of increasing male claims on female resources such as land and labor, while decreasing female claims on male resources such as income, with further implications for collective household welfare if expenditure responsibilities are taken into account. By recognizing the central role of the "conjugal contract" in the determination of household behavior and welfare, policies could be designed to enhance productivity and well-being without contributing to intrahousehold inequality, and perhaps even alleviating it.

7 Endowments and Assets: The Anthropology of Wealth and the Economics of Intrahousehold Allocation

JANE I. GUYER

Four related themes in this volume deserve further comment: the need for interdisciplinary collaboration between economics and anthropology with respect to household and gender issues, the emergence of "assets" as a possible theme for common attention, the current divergence of approach to that theme, and the shared problem of generating adequate data on it. In this chapter I examine each discipline separately and then consider the problems each faces in addressing the concerns and analytical terms of the other. It should be said at the outset that my vantage point is that of anthropology, which inevitably affords a limited view of economics. This chapter discusses the potential connections and problems only as they present themselves from the household literature. There may well be other methods within the broader repertoire of the discipline for addressing some of the issues raised here. If so, their import into household studies would clearly strengthen both disciplines, so shortcomings in this rendition of economics in fact represent not only this author's own limited knowledge of current work but also new frontiers to explore in the study of intrahousehold dynamics.

The first theme to address is the need, expressed in many of the chapters in this volume, for more interdisciplinary work, in particular, between economists and anthropologists. At the same time, there is a sense that collaboration is particularly difficult. Although the two disciplines may be studying similar phenomena—for example, households and gender relations in non-Western economies—the chasms between them are wide and the bridges fragile. This is the case even though each discipline contains varying theoretical paradigms (neoclassical, neo-Marxist, public choice theory, postmodernism, and so forth), some of which create conditions more conducive to interdisciplinary connection than others. Some of the intellectual bases for disciplinary differences in the field of household studies will be briefly illuminated in this chapter.

Second, in the very recent past the economics and anthropology of households have appeared to be edging toward a new convergence of concern around the nature and use of assets, particularly by populations that are conventionally thought of as "poor." Much of this convergence is implicit and constitutes the logical next step beyond this volume on intrahousehold allocation. However, this convergence could profitably be more strongly connected to both the "anthropology of wealth" and the "economics of saving and insurance." Neither of these two literatures is yet strongly represented in intrahousehold thinking, which is focused—in both economics and anthropology—on the units and processes of decisionmaking about material needs.

Third, many of the assets of the poor are intrinsically and necessarily polyvalent, particularly in the absence of formal-sector financial institutions; that is, people with few goods are likely to prefer to invest in, and maintain, goods that have multiple uses. But this observation may be differently approached by anthropology and economics. Anthropology has been directly concerned with the polysemic (multimeaning) character of cultural elements and social practices. It attempts to describe and explain how elements form configurations, and how, into what, and under what conditions meanings can be transformable. Economics, in contrast, rarely deals with configurations and transformations. At this level, however, the disciplinary difference is not totally intractable. It can be bridged by the application of different analyses to the same data; "consumption" items can be regrouped and reanalyzed as both consumption and investment.

The more profound problem is that differences of analytical instruments are linked to diverging assumptions about the nature of the dynamic processes studied. Sociocultural anthropology has become oriented toward understanding the social and cultural dynamics of configurations such as assets (their creation or destruction and delegitimation) and their transformations through the rules for convertibility. Most chapters in this volume, in contrast, work from the methodological individualism of decisionmaking theory, in which decisions are made, given an exogenous endowment structure. Often these endowments are viewed as static; these models use a single-period time horizon in which assets are treated as exogenous (with the exception of human capital investment, to be discussed separately). Even the economic models that are dynamic (namely those relevant to discussions of the intertemporality of insurance and savings) are focused, it appears, not on the history of asset creation and transformation in society and culture, but on the cyclical and structural processes of asset management by decisionmakers over life cycles, across periods of crisis, or in relation to the predictable risks of seasonal production. In brief, anthropological dynamics deal with nominal variables, socially composed, over historical time, and economic dynamics in household models tend to deal with continuous variables, individually managed, over cyclical time. These are two different endeavors, albeit with strong potential for complementarity.

In many respects, the concern with gender finds fuller play in the study of asset creation than it does in the study of asset management, because the differences in consumption "preferences" between men and women can often most plausibly be traced to profoundly different asset endowment and control. Feminist advocacy has everywhere focused precisely on improving women's access to and control of assets, especially as new kinds of assets are created. It is, however, obvious that study of both the nature and the management of assets should be part of an economics of gender.

Finally, whatever the temporal frame in which one works (seasonal, life cyclical, historical), economists and anthropologists have similar problems of data availability and interpretation. It may well be here, in the research design problems of studying dynamics over time, that interdisciplinary discussions about "new methodologies" may be most profoundly beneficial to both disciplines.

Disciplinary Bases

To an anthropologist's eye, there appears to be a substantive gap in intrahousehold economic studies that almost exactly matches the theoretical branch of economic anthropology's greatest strength, namely the study of "wealth." Although concepts such as "endowment" and "human capital" increasingly enter into economic analysis, the explanations of the phenomena that make up these categories are comparatively limited (see, for example, Thomas 1991). One gets hardly any tangible sense of the florescent abundance of items considered to be "wealth" that appears in ethnography. To a significant degree and in spite of being largely devoted to populations conventionally understood as "poor," anthropology has devoted some of its most acute analytical thinking, over at least 80 years, to wealth and value creation, rather than poverty and scarce resources. The elaboration of theories of different social and cultural systems stresses phenomena that are powerfully and self-consciously present, rather than those that are comparatively—and perhaps, unconsciously, to the people themselves—absent or scarce.

The chapters by economists on intrahousehold allocation in this volume manifest a distinct and generally endorsed movement toward incorporating a more complex set of personal endowments into the analysis of poor households. There will remain unbridgeable barriers between the theoretical "central tendencies" in the two disciplines, but this newly introduced topic of assets does constitute a kind of narrows: from a bedrock of comparable strength in each discipline, it offers one promising connection by a fairly short route.

The Anthropology of Wealth

The anthropological emphasis on wealth is foundational to the discipline. Some of the greatest landmarks in this discipline's history have been devoted to the study of the creation and valuation of items for which use had to be sought at the level of social function, so relatively impractical did they seem. Malinowski (1922) went so far as to compare the famous kula shell valuables—so powerfully emotive that they were laid on the breast of a dying man to give comfort and joy—with the British crown jewels. Mauss (1925) created an entire social theory and, ultimately for him, a political morality on the basis of his study of The Gift, that is, of exchanges of goods imbued with power and value by virtue of their capacity to create relationships rather than by their use in (literal) consumption.

The development of the study of exchange and valuation from these seminal works has taken place within anthropology almost completely independently of the discipline of economics, thanks, at least in part, to the polemic stance these "founding fathers" took against the tendency of economics to universalize what they saw as particular—and Western—modes of rationality. By now the literature on value and exchange constitutes one of the largest and most challenging within anthropology. Five very recent contributions are mentioned, none of which is deeply indebted to economic theory. Thomas (1991) has traced out in detail the processes by which novel Western goods were incorporated into the economies of the South Seas in the eighteenth and nineteenth centuries. Humphrey and Hugh-Jones (1992) have examined the social incidence and history of barter. Weiner (1992) critiques the theory of reciprocity and develops the concept of "inalienable possessions." Guyer (1993) has reexamined the Africanist concept of "wealth in people" whereby the ultimate goal of material wealth has been seen as the transformation of goods into rights in people. Ferguson (1988, 1992) has questioned an ordinal scale ("ranking") approach to wealth and poverty, arguing that "the extent to which one form of wealth is transformable into another is an empirical question" (1992:59).

The topics of production and consumption that have animated household economics (Becker 1981; Sen 1985b; Chayanov 1986) come very late into the history of economic anthropology, and largely as a product of the development philosophies of the post-1960 world and political-economic theory. Oscar Lewis's famous book (1959), subtitled in part *The Culture of Poverty,* was a departure from past tradition and highly controversial within the discipline. Anthropological studies of production took great stimulation from debates about the European peasantry (see, for example, Brenner [1985] on production and exchange), and then from the historical importance of market demand for goods (see, for example, Thirsk 1978). Within the classic, ahistorical, anthropology of non-Western cultures and societies, the study of consumption had already been stimulated by symbolic and structural analysis (see, for example, Levi-Strauss 1969 and Goody 1982), but the analysis was performed in terms of classifications, exchangeability, and relative status, rather than quantitative variables such as calorie consumption or indexes of welfare. The conceptual frameworks themselves militated against studying the kind of variable that would define standards of living as distinct from ways of life. Even when theoretical work devoted to commodities and consumption began to be written in the mid-1980s (Appadurai 1986; Rutz and Orlove 1989), it was self-consciously innovative in its terminology compared with the older tradition, and its "homing instinct" remained oriented toward wealth, value, aspiration, and inspiration. Faced with poor populations who, in spite of their poverty, finance temples, go on pilgrimages, donate resources to causes, purchase arms to engage in "peasant wars" (see Wolf 1969), and so on, anthropology has found its older literature on value on the whole more illuminating than the newer economic approaches to production and consumption. In fact, the apparent stubborn reluctance to move from "values" to "prices" and from qualitative to quantitative attention to the "quality of life" has earned some angry exasperation from heavily studied groups such as Native Americans. It may be that the convergence of anthropology and economics around household issues has been too short and too partial for this history and these intradisciplinary backward linkages to be apparent to economists.

The Economics of Households

With this background in mind, it is striking how much of household economics is concerned with production and consumption, and how little with wealth for its own sake (rather than as a means to achieve a desired level of consumption). As Haddad and Kanbur (1990:867) write, "the object of interest is the well-being of individuals, which is measured by some agreed standard (consumption, nutrition, and so forth)." Putting aside for the moment the issue of differential wealth in the conventional sense (for sample- and class-stratification of unitary households), it is one of the most interesting innovations of the collective household models that they have highlighted the importance of differential wealth control within the household and what determines that control, that is, phenomena variously designated as "endowments" (Pitt and Lavy 1992), "extra environmental parameters" (McElroy 1990), "public goods" (Lundberg and Pollak, Chapter 5, this volume), and "human capital" (Pitt and Lavy 1992).

Two achievements result. First, in substantive terms, the intrahousehold studies implicitly recognize that even poor households and poor people are units invested with value as well as being consumption units; otherwise, the complex distribution of their collective and individual "endowments" could not make such major differences to patterns of consumption. Poor people do not just have values in the sense of preferences, given by culture and expressed in market choices; they also control different "things" with different values (or powers) relevant to consumption decisions. Second, in terms of the logic of analysis, wealth ("endowments," "capital") now enters into the equation as an active element in economic processes that influences the process of decision-making, rather than entering into empirical analysis as only a passive indicator of the characteristics of population categories.

Parallel to the question of why poverty came so late into anthropology is the question of how wealth came so late into household analysis. Though

Becker (1965) contends that a household "is truly a small factory," with "capital goods, raw materials, and labor," this model has been applied mainly in its production and consumption modes; capital goods were given far less attention in household analysis than was labor. One possibility is that the major populations for whom household studies and the theory of consumer choice were developed did not really own assets—if the concept of assets is understood in the narrow sense of the term for capitalist economies—until the advent of new developments in consumer credit in midcentury. Small-scale capital has always fit rather awkwardly, both theoretically and politically, into capitalist dynamics.

Housing as a lower-middle-class asset is an example. In a fascinating review of British housing policy, Daunton (1990) points out that petty bourgeois families of the nineteenth century saved throughout their working lives to invest in a house for the rental market, since this could provide a regular and reliable income for men in retirement or in case of disability, and for women, whose class position and associated social symbolism allowed them very limited access to the labor market, especially in old age or widowhood. The ownership of a house, apart from the one in which a family lived, was therefore a major economic and social asset for that segment of the population. Daunton points out, however, that these owners of "house capital" were in an untenable political situation in the early twentieth century, allied for some purposes with the conservative (rural) landed interests and for others with the progressive (urban) industrial interests. Over a period of decades, they largely lost out, to be replaced by the ideal of the owner-occupier, supported financially by bank mortgages and building societies. Assets that were petty and nonproductive by capitalist standards fell out of the political configuration. Thus this category of "capital" has possibly always been analytically difficult, just as it has been politically ambiguous.

For those recognized as poor, the issue of assets was made more or less irrelevant as welfare systems took over much older criteria of eligibility that presumed the beneficiaries to be propertyless. In the United States, asset holding is generally incompatible with receipt of benefits, and there is some moral outrage when recipients try to develop small asset portfolios (the "welfare Cadillac"); hence, perhaps, the limited development of the idea of assets in the poor and lower middle classes. The theoretical concomitant of the low political profile of small capital is that, in systemic terms, it is not really investment (in the sense of being devoted to production), but neither is it only consumption (in the sense of being used up).

One might argue (and a sociocultural anthropologist certainly would) that, in fact, the poor have a special need for small-scale assets, for example, the single big-ticket item that can be pawned when necessary to float consumption over a bad patch but can also be displayed to validate reputation in good times, or the network of solid relationships that can be tapped for remittance income and hand-me-down clothing, and for information about jobs and bargains. The more fragile regular income sources are, the greater the importance of valuables that lend themselves to multiple uses, including leverage of short-run credit and income infusions. It is only marginally flippant to endorse the advice that, in an era of women's low status relative to financial and labor force access, "Diamonds (really) are a girl's best friend": you can wear them (for status validation or to attract a new male patron), pawn them, save them against price rises, loan them (thereby investing in social relations [Berry 1989]), endow them to a daughter, or, in extremity, sell them. A fur coat and a Cadillac are even more polyvalent, since the first keeps you warm and the second gets you from place to place, although both suffer from the deterioration of classic consumer items; unlike diamonds, they are not "forever."

In countries with limited state and banking institutions to fill some of these demands, the case for looking at assets is still stronger than it is in other contexts. The house of a Nigerian *mai gida* (head of household) is the basis of his business; he runs a major interregional trading system or international money-changing enterprise from his lodging chambers, storage rooms, and front porch (Cohen 1969). And his "investment in social relations"—as Berry (1989) develops this idea in order to extend the concept of investment—is a constant outlay that creates, reaffirms, and extends the reputation and trust on which the entire enterprise rests. The poorest landless laborer may develop a portfolio of assets, and lack of any such investments is a sign not just of poverty, but of total destitution.

The chapters in this volume, and other recently published works that use collective household models, begin to incorporate assets as an active component in household processes. McElroy's bargaining model locates the "threat point" for collective solutions in accordance with "extrahousehold environmental parameters" that may include individual and collective rights under divorce laws, the tax code, the welfare structure, and even kinship practices according to which a wife may have the right to return to her parents' house in case of separation (1990:566, 571). Schultz (1990) and Thomas (1991) both focus on the importance of individually owned "non-earned income," which "has a distinct association with the family's labor supply and reproductive behavior" (Schultz 1990:623). The sociological concept of "endowment" is used and extended to apply to personal biological characteristics such as individual susceptibility to illness (Pitt and Lavy 1992).

This direction of thinking could clearly be related to the study of savings and insurance (see Alderman and Paxson 1992), since some—at least—of these "endowments" implicitly relate to the logic of income smoothing. The problem with this particular "marriage" of literatures appears to be that the savings-insurance literature is written largely in terms of the unitary, rather than the collective, household. The most important "endowments" for the intrahousehold models are precisely those that, in effect, "insure" particular elements (such as the wife's economic viability, irrespective of the fate of the marriage) rather than the continuity of the unit as a whole. In other words, exactly who is insured in Modigliani's life cycle theory of savings is a critical question (Besley 1993), since it is ultimately individuals and not households that have life cycles.

In summary, assets are becoming an important component of intrahousehold models. A dynamic approach to investment, however, seems to be embedded in a branch of economics that still uses the unitary household model. Neither approach takes the substantive and historical approach to assets—their creation, maintenance, and polyvalent transformations—that is embedded in sociocultural anthropology. Both of them, however, seem to be moving in on the same set of phenomena.

Before moving on to the potential conjunctures, it is worth noting that certain works in political science address the investment rules and preferences of kin and community groups (but not yet disaggregated households, as far as I know, and usually not in a historical context), with a view to explaining the role of local capital in political dynamics (see, for example, Bates 1990).

Anthropology-Economics Interfaces

Economics

The potential link from a focus on assets to the anthropology of value can be clearly recognized: in collective models, differential wealth access and control is no longer a simple variable for classifying households prior to the analysis, but a complex, gendered variable that crosses the threshold of the household and enters the analysis. The next step is more difficult, however. Owing to the demands of model-building for short-run decisions, endowments are viewed as exogenous. None of the households or individuals analyzed in the chapters in this volume is seen as systematically saving up to buy land or a house, maintaining clientage ties, purchasing gold jewelry, bribing officials, or storing cloth or enamel bowls for a dowry, unless these transactions figure as "consumption" of housing, household furnishings, clothing, and business expenses. In these models, people may have property, reputation, and social insurance as endowments before the bargaining begins, but they do not yet seem to be actively working at or investing in them, except as human capital in the form of educated and healthy children. These chapters endow people and households with assets, but they do not show people investing in them: maintaining, increasing, scheming, and planning. Admittedly these temporal processes are difficult to document because of the lack of panel data and so on. But part of the problem—a point to which this chapter will keep returning—lies in both the incomplete nature of the intrahousehold model's embrace of assets and investment and the intrinsic ambiguity of these goods at any one point in time, especially in poor populations.

The first issue can be pinpointed through a brief comment on Thomas's (Chapter 9, this volume) analysis of the data for 38,000 urban households in Brazil. Taking the sample as a whole, nonlabor income is an important income source. Forty-three percent of male heads of households and 23 percent of female heads report some nonlabor income. For male heads, nonlabor income sources make up 25 percent of their income; for female heads, they account for 40 percent, although the absolute level of nonlabor income for women is only 26 percent of that for men. In general, then, these are people with some level of assets, both financial and social (pensions, social security), even if one restricts the notion of assets to the conventional definition and thereby does not include "investment in social relations," which, in this case, would surely include ceremonial expenditures. On the expenditure-consumption side, "investment" figures as expenditures on education, health, and recreation, construed as "human capital." The interesting implication, then, is that the less well-endowed, poorer partner (the wife) is performing a disproportionate amount of the total investment of the household as a unit.

Once the idea of investment has been brought in, one is not simply in the realm of gendered consumer "preferences" to account for this odd finding. One logical inference to draw would be that the woman is trying to increase the value of her own asset endowment (in the broadest, nonconventional meaning of assets or endowment), that she is trying to raise the level of her (inferior) asset control. Perhaps a woman is investing because she is so relatively asset poor, compared with a man (that is, the lower the assets, the greater the marginal propensity to invest). Or she may be following a gender-specific compensatory strategy: since key assets that ensure lifetime income smoothing are male specific (pensions and social security, for example), she needs to cover the same long-term needs through other instruments, such as human capital investment in healthy and educated children. Or alternatively—and to raise the cooperative instance of Sen's "cooperative conflict"—there may be a total household investment portfolio, implicit in the gender division of expenditure, such that members of poor families maximize and then place in complementarity each individual member's access to whatever they can best invest in, given external social, structural, and labor market constraints. These asset dynamics, in the broadest sense of the concept, are not clear, unless investment is more broadly considered. The link must be forged between women's endowment and women's investment, between men's endowment and men's investment, and between the dynamics of the two in collective activities. To explore these issues, one would need to know what other kinds of investment might be undertaken, particularly by men, that are perhaps hidden by having been construed—as "health" and "education" also could be, if one did not coin the term "human capital"—simply as consumption "expenditures."

Economic modeling faces three problems, not all of them tractable within a decisionmaking frame of analysis: (1) the intrinsically multifaceted nature of small-scale assets, which has already been mentioned; (2) the processual aspect of their formation, both exogenous and endogenous; and (3) the great likelihood that the processes of asset creation are locally and historically specific.

THE MULTIFACETED NATURE OF SMALL-SCALE ASSETS. Small-scale assets veer unnervingly between "investment," "consumption," and "prestige" expenditures, precisely because—as has been claimed many times for many different theoretical purposes—families are not, in fact, factories, if only for the reason that they tend intransigently to resist going totally out of business in the face of adverse conditions. The marriage may break up, but the parenthood of at least one party does not. And the claims that kin who were once co-members of the same household can make on each other, regardless of residence, can be lifelong and realizable under a vast variety of conditions. McElroy's (1990:566) possibility of a woman's returning to her parents' house is an extraenvironmental parameter to her at that time, but it may depend on her investment in her parents' current or future welfare. It is precisely their multi-faceted nature, which is the result of layers of "investment" over the long term, that gives these relationships the status of parameters. In social terms, they are emphatically not "givens" but "creations," often resulting from extraordinary diligence and cultivation. Declaring total family bankruptcy, á la the factory model, is social suicide. People's interests lie in creating and maintaining at least some goods and some relationships that are multipurpose, that can veer from investment to consumption to status signifiers as needed.

Conceptually, this is home territory for anthropologists. The intrinsically polysemic (multiple-meaning) character of "things of value"—people's punctilious attention to creating and recreating those meanings and selectively substituting one meaning for another in differing situations—has been a terrain of enquiry since Levi-Strauss's (1949) early work on structures of exchange and Richards's (1956) study of people's understandings of the symbolism in female initiation rituals.

The challenge to household studies is to define more clearly the space into which things of value (in anthropological terms) and small-scale investments in assets (in economic terms) could be imported explicitly. The incorporation of investment into intrahousehold models has already been carried out to the greatest degree with respect to children's nutrition and health. The multifaceted nature of children as consumption and as assets has already been acknowledged. Schultz's (1990) analysis of the ways in which fertility and remittance income by children are connected in Thailand demonstrates the investment facet of a mother's interest in her children and shows how different an interpretation can be given to "consumption" (the demand for children) if it is looked at as an investment in future income sources.

Intrahousehold analyses, by showing that the gender and generational control of such endowments matters, have created the space to extend this kind of analysis beyond children and health. For example, Hausa women buy small livestock (Hill 1972). Like Monroe's diamonds, they are portable, loanable, and savable and resist depreciation. They can also be given away to create patronage ties, set loose on gardens to provide manure, eaten for Muslim festival meals, or sold for cash. At any one moment, they are potentially all of these: gift, savings, investment, consumption. Historically, their absolute importance and the relative relevance of their various potentials may wax and wane with the politics of marriage and the state of the economy: the incidence of divorce, the ease with which a woman is able to return home, the presence of own or fostered children to tend them, the levels of religious consumption, the vicissitudes of women's incomes and alternative expenditures.

INVESTMENT AS A PROCESS. The nature of investment in endowments by individuals and families as a process does seem to be problematic for econometric analysis, since variables must be unambiguously either exogenous or endogenous to the decisionmaking process. However, people may create conditions for themselves through endogenous processes of resource allocation that will incrementally alter the "threat point." With a view of asset formation as a process, the threat point becomes variable over time. In anthropological terms, people are at one and the same time embedding their decisions in both short- and long-term frameworks, in which present consumption or expenditure decisions express, confirm, or create a potential claim over the longer term. The optimal solution meets both sets of expectations and predictions.

Moreover, ordinary people's ordinary strategies must extend into time frames beyond the individual life cycle, either through basic philosophies of existence or through realpolitik. Most really critical social and cultural assets fall into this long-term category. Kula valuables, massive gold earrings, caches of cloth, sacred amulets, and so on are not primarily intended to bring about income smoothing over the life cycle or the seasons, even if they can be adapted to fulfill that function. They are relevant to reproduction over much longer time frames: in some cases, the cycles of age grades; in others, the succession of alternate generations; in yet others, the rebirth of individual souls; and in some currently critically important cases, the continuous preservation of material symbols of an ethnic historical identity in an increasingly unstable world (temples, libraries, ritual positions, ethnic festivals). It may be that household economics cannot easily address this level of "investment," even if rather large amounts of resources are involved, since the investment breaches the tight logical assumptions of life-cyclical dynamics and is undertaken in terms of collectivities much larger than households. But if investment as an intrahousehold process—as distinct from endowment as an exogenous state of being—is to be broadened to at least some other goods and services, the expectations and forecasting (the time frames) that are intrinsic to the cultural analysis of social value necessarily become part of the economic analysis.

A fully anthropological approach would embrace this extension. It is axiomatic to anthropology that assets are imbued with their value through social and cultural processes much larger than the household or family, extending over much longer time frames than the life cycle. Since the sociocultural anthropology of the past 25 years is an anthropology that has been increasingly focused on dynamics and history (valuation rather than values, cultural construction rather than the structure of culture), the study of assets would become the study not only of the assets themselves, or of asset management (in the life-cyclical sense), but of asset creation (in the active, historical sense). Both policies and popular processes create assets. Policies can define things as assets and set up conditions of access and use. Asset creation is something governments and banks, often together and in concert, can do and are doing all the time. This is one area in which gender has probably been more important than in any other context, namely in the struggle to ensure equal access to economic and social assets as they are created and reworked, and to define women's claims and controls with respect to assets that have been (as Strathern [1988] would put it) "jointly authored" with men.

LOCAL AND HISTORICAL SPECIFICITY. The third problem, that of local and historical specificity, follows logically from the previous one. Even in highly formalized economies, there are popular processes of asset formation. This topic may, then, lead down what must seem to be an inexorably slippery slope toward cultural specificity for economics, a discipline that tends to be formal in method. In particular cultural contexts, different goods and qualities are considered to be assets. Under honor systems, a wife's seclusion within the home and the sexual modesty of daughters are family assets: they cost, they bring returns, and, under unstable and competitive political conditions, they can become highly vulnerable to theft (rape). In parts of Africa, a woman's capacity to work outside the home is a family asset: it elicits marriage payments and commands health expenditure, and it brings returns. Not only are personal and collective assets valued externally to the household, but the goods themselves often originate and are stored, accessed, and passed on beyond household boundaries. This means that intrahousehold processes relative to assets are necessarily extrahousehold processes as well, contingent on the wider society (see Guyer and Peters 1987).

For analysis of formal-sector assets, however, the conceptual problem may be much less problematic than cultural anthropology insists, simply because the processes and models used by policymakers throughout the world in the late twentieth century now owe something to a common, collective, and internationalized tradition of governance. Since policymaking is explicitly about the mobilization of parts of that repertoire in new contexts, it may be that it is here—in addition to its more familiar terrain of popular asset creation— that anthropology could make a stronger contribution than it has made so far: by addressing the full range of ways in which policies that originate in this internationalized collective repertoire have created and destroyed assets and defined or undermined gendered access and control, and by studying the ways in which formal and popular processes have influenced one another.

Anthropology

At this point a classic barrier is faced, namely the long-term reluctance (bordering on intransigence) at the theoretical centers of anthropology to import a capitalist vocabulary—investment, capital, and so on—into the analysis of noncapitalist systems. Since this chapter is oriented toward economics rather than anthropology, and since other chapters to come summarize well a productive kind of interdisciplinary engagement, only one or two additional points need be made here. First of all, it is worth noting that one of the points of contention in the new literature on "commodities" in anthropology is a new version of the same, much older question, namely whether the concept of "commodities," originating as it does in the theory of capitalism, can be lifted out of the full-fledged capitalist context at all (see Guyer [1993] for a brief summary). Present thinking seems to be generally somewhat more open than it has been. Hart (1982) suggests that "commodity" can legitimately bridge the noncapitalist-capitalist divide, as long as some key subcategories of commodity types are recognized. Appadurai (1986), and many archaeologists, simply use the term "commodity" whenever something is sold. Political economists of otherwise somewhat different theoretical convictions apply capitalist vocabulary without any of the elaborate self-scrutiny that characterizes certain kinds of current anthropology: Bates (1990) applies the concepts of capital, investment, and risk to African household and kinship strategies that clearly lie outside capitalist dynamics; Berry (1989) applies the concept of investment to social relations. Cultural anthropologists, in contrast, either remain much more skeptical and avoid the capitalist terminology altogether (using instead wealth, valuables, authorship, redistribution, and so on) or else demote the analytical content of these terms and use them as simple descriptive words, without any necessary theoretical implications.

Although there is still a great deal to be gained from the classic culturalist view that every system is built from its own premises, the fact is that all peoples now deal to some degree with formal-sector assets of the kind developed within capitalist contexts: either with their increasingly defined and regulated presence or their policy-driven absence. And sociocultural anthropologists frequently work in capitalist economies and societies, which are now varied enough to be subject to comparative cultural analysis. The ideas of capital and investment are used by people themselves. In the situation in which capitalism is now plural (capitalisms), in which many of the capitalist institutions have been selectively domesticated in different contexts, and in which continuities with the local precapitalist past seem quite striking, the methodological assumptions of classic cultural anthropology (variety, cultural premises, locally specific innovation) can be adapted quite readily to the study of capitalism itself.

Conclusion

There may be a limit to the elasticity of collective decisionmaking models to take on fully all the implications of "endowment" as an anthropologist would see them, including long temporal frames of investment and the historical-political process of asset creation and destruction. And there are certainly limits to cultural anthropology's enthusiasm to embrace the calculative, means-end implications of the concept of investment when it comes to multifaceted valuables with polysemic characteristics and multiple temporal referents. But by incorporating investment more boldly and broadly, the interface between complementary types of study could be strengthened, as it should be, in order to appreciate fully the social and cultural creativity of everyday life among poor populations.

The study of small-scale assets necessarily involves social, cultural, and policy analysis in a dynamic framework. It builds in the study of differentiation and control within and beyond households and families. It opens household analysis in economics a little more widely to other branches of anthropology, branches that nevertheless deeply inform some of the gender and kinship analyses with which household economists are more familiar. And it would possibly open the anthropology of value a little more widely to the economics and economic history of those assets and investments that make up the repertoire of options in the—now very substantially shared—capitalist traditions of modern policymaking.

PART II

Measuring the Outcomes of Intrahousehold Resource Allocation

8 Testing Competing Models of Intrahousehold Allocation

JOHN HODDINOTT, HAROLD ALDERMAN, AND
LAWRENCE HADDAD

The chapters by Pitt, Chiappori, McElroy, Lundberg and Pollak, and Carter and Katz develop the two aspects of intrahousehold distribution that are the focus of this book: the determinants of allocations among individuals and the decisionmaking process that leads to these allocations. The purpose of this chapter is to assess empirical tests of the underlying models of household decisionmaking. A comprehensive review of all the empirical evidence on intrahousehold resource allocation in developing countries is not attempted here; such a review would constitute a book in itself. Thorough summaries of this literature include Behrman and Deolalikar (1988), Behrman (1990, 1996), Strauss and Beegle (1995), and Strauss and Thomas (1995). Some, though by no means all, of the studies that these reviews cover depend critically on the assumptions underlying the unitary model. The objective in this chapter is to review tests of those underlying assumptions.

Direct Testing of the Unitary Model

Are Incomes Pooled?

The unitary model assumes that all income sources within the household are pooled. This implies that the identity of the individual earning income has no effect on household demand for goods and leisure, except through the wage (price) effect on the substitution of leisure and commodities. However, the view that income is not pooled within the household has figured prominently in sociological and anthropological studies. Other arrangements that households adopt include systems in which one person manages all finances and expenditures except for personal spending money; a "spheres of responsibility" system in which, for example, a husband gives his wife a set amount for purchasing specified commodities; and an "independent management" system in which each individual has his or her own income and is responsible for certain expenditures, and neither has access to all household funds (Pahl 1983). A consequence, though perhaps not a surprising one, is that differential control of income translates into different patterns of expenditures. It is widely perceived that men spend a higher share of their income on goods for their personal consumption than do women. Alcohol, cigarettes, status consumer goods, and even "female companionship" have been noted. In contrast, women are believed to be more likely to purchase goods for children and for general household consumption. Guyer (1980) is particularly noted for this observation, although a number of other researchers have commented on the phenomenon as well.[1]

This proposition has been tested in a number of settings. Von Braun (1988) finds a positive relationship between the proportion of cereals produced under women's control and household consumption of calories in Gambian households. Garcia (1990) finds that raising the share of income accruing to wives in Philippine households increased acquisition of calories and protein. However, by using women's income as a regressor, both studies implicitly make the strong assumption that labor supply decisions are exogenous. If this is incorrect, there will be a correlation between the explanatory variable—women's income—and the error term that incorporates factors influencing labor supply decisions. Thus the parameter estimates in these studies may be biased.

Since these studies do not distinguish the impact of individual prices (wages) from income control, they do not constitute a strict test of the income pooling hypothesis. Suppose an exogenous change occurs that, by raising women's wages, induces an increase in women's labor market participation. In the unitary model, any change in expenditures may reflect cross-price effects of wages. The reallocation of members' time may lead women to purchase maize flour rather than grind maize themselves. Although the cooperative bargaining model does not rule out such changes, it also predicts that women may renegotiate the gains from marriage on the basis of this new (or enhanced) earning opportunity. Thus changes in wages could alter the distribution of income within the household or change a woman's potential earnings should the marriage dissolve. This could affect the pattern of household expenditures. Thus the same outcome is predicted by both approaches.

Similarly one may have a unitary household in which the correlation between women's cash income and acquisition of certain goods reflects differences in purchasing productivities. If women are working as traders in the marketplace, the household may economize on transaction costs if women purchase food in the market (and the man's income is used to purchase other goods). It is difficult to distinguish this household from one in which an increase in women's earnings outside the household changes expenditure patterns because it raises the woman's bargaining power (either because her threat

---

1. See, for instance, Kumar (1979), Tripp (1981), Pahl (1983), and Engle (1993), as well as the studies cited in Dwyer and Bruce (1988) and Bruce (1989a).

point is higher or because her perceived contribution within the household has increased). This is a problem of "observational equivalence"—the phenomena observed by these studies can be explained by either the unitary or the collective model. For this reason, economists have sought additional means of gaining insights into household behavior.

Hoddinott and Haddad (1995) partly control for this possibility in their study of expenditures in Côte d'Ivoire. Using Ulph's (1988) noncooperative model as a guide, they use two-stage least squares estimation with budget shares and women's predicted cash share of household income being treated as jointly endogenous. They assume that certain variables—such as the proportion of landholdings operated by women, women's share of household business capital, and the ratio of women's to men's education—will influence women's share of cash income, but not expenditure shares, directly. They find that doubling women's share of cash income within Ivorian households raises the budget share of food and lowers the budget shares of alcohol and cigarettes. These results are conditional on their identifying restrictions. However, their results are robust to changes in functional form, are reflected in reduced-form estimates, and concur with budget shares obtained from an examination of single-sex households.

Haddad and Hoddinott (1994b) use the same framework in analyzing child health in rural Côte d'Ivoire. Using fixed-effects estimation to control for household-level unobservables, they find that increasing women's share of cash income raises boys' health anthropometric status relative to girls'. The explanation of this finding draws on two separate strands of the intrahousehold literature. The first, as outlined in Behrman, Pollak, and Taubman (1982), emphasizes that allocation of resources among children reflects both equity and efficiency considerations. Here, equity concerns take the form of a desire to equalize health outcomes across genders—specifically to compensate boys for their poorer initial health endowment. Efficiency concerns manifest themselves in that because sons are a form of old age support, investing in them produces a higher return. Second, for women's income to have greater impact, different adults must also see different gender-specific returns to such investments, or weigh equity concerns differently, or both.

Another means of formally testing the pooling assumption has been the use of gender-specific nonlabor or nonearned income. (Direct tests of this assumption, using labor income, are problematic because of the endogeneity of income.) Provided that this is independent of labor choices, Schultz (1990: 601–602) notes that "The challenge to the neoclassical model of household demand arises if nonearned income of different family members is observed to affect differently the household's allocation of resources. If nonearned income (or ownership of the underlying asset) influences family demand behavior differently depending on who in the family controls the income (or owns the asset), then the preferences for that demand must differ across individuals and such families must not completely pool nonearned income."

An example is given by Thomas (1990). Drawing on survey data from Brazil, he examines the differential impact of nonlabor income in the hands of men and women. Thomas rejects income pooling in the demand for per capita caloric and protein intakes, fertility, child survival, and weight-for-height for children less than 8 years old. The results for child survival are particularly powerful—the increase in the probability of child survival is 20 times larger with a marginal increase in female earnings than with a comparable increase in male earnings.

Thomas's (1990) results could be interpreted as providing a further test of the cooperative, collective approach. Such a claim must be made cautiously, as nonlabor income may be conditional on being in a particular state. For example, individuals may be receiving unearned income in the form of sick benefits because they are temporarily ill. Such income cannot be considered a pure threat-point shifter. Similarly some unearned income (such as dowry) may be conditional on being married; it too cannot be considered a threat-point shifter. Distinguishing between such possibilities is central to Thomas's contribution to this volume (Chapter 9). He tests whether these results are robust to treating nonlabor income as an aggregate or using only asset income. Under both definitions, income in the hands of women is associated with a larger increase in the share of the household budget devoted to human capital and leisure.

Schultz (1990) finds that unearned income has a significant effect on women's labor supply. "This pattern is clearest in the case of Thai women, where the own nonearned income effect on participation is six times as large as that of their spouse's nonearned income. The preponderant sign of all the labor supply effects of transfer and property income is negative, as anticipated." However, he also finds that women's transfer income is positively and significantly related to fertility, whereas women's property income has no such effect. He notes (1990:623) that "the connection between transfer income and fertility may reflect the reverse causation to that hypothesized here, where women with more children to support are more likely to receive transfers from family and other groups in society."

Horney and McElroy (1988) examine data from a 1967 sample of American married men and women, residing in households in which both partners worked. They disaggregate nonlabor income into transfer (pensions, veteran's payments, workmen's compensation, other disability payments, and Aid to Families with Dependent Children) and business (business, farm, rental, and interest) income. Transfer income is of particular interest because a number of its components (such as disability and veteran's payments) are independent of marital status. They find limited evidence that male and female nonlabor income has a differential impact on the leisure choice of males (male transfer income reduces male labor supply), but not on that of females or a composite consumption commodity.[2]

---

2. They attribute the weakness of their results to difficulties in obtaining complete information on rights to unearned income within the household.

A number of recent income-based studies derive a set of testable restrictions requiring only the assumption that household decisions are Pareto efficient. As Chiappori (Chapter 3, this volume) provides a detailed discussion of this approach, only a brief summary is provided here.

Browning et al. (1994) develop the idea that certain goods within the household are exclusive—that is, they are consumed by only one person. They show that this concept can be used to recover the household's sharing rule. They use expenditure data from childless Canadian couples who work full time. Using women's clothing as an exclusive good, they recover the sharing rule parameters. They also compare a sample of couples and two subsamples of singles: the unitary restrictions are rejected for the former, but not for the latter. This would be the case if the rejections were due to a sharing process negotiated between family members.

Bourguignon, Browning, and Chiappori (1994) construct a general model that encompasses the unitary and collective frameworks as special cases. This approach generates two hypotheses: (1) if income is not pooled, the coefficients for male and female income in an expenditure equation should be significantly different from each other; and (2) the existence of a cooperative model requires that certain restrictions be placed on the coefficients of total household- and individual-level incomes. Using French data consisting of married couples working full time with no children or one child, income pooling is rejected, but the cooperative approach is not rejected.

Browning and Chiappori (1995), analyzing data on consumption, find that Slutsky symmetry is rejected for couples, but not for singles, whereas the collective generalization of symmetry is not rejected for couples. Thomas and Chen (1994) apply this model to data from Taiwan. They strongly reject the unitary model; that is, the distribution of both individual total (instrumented) and individual nonlabor income affects budget shares.

The concept of exclusive goods that allows for identification of sharing rules in Chiappori (Chapter 3, this volume) is also employed by Deaton (1989, 1995) to study how consumption patterns are affected by the demographic composition of households. This outlay-equivalency methodology tests whether parents reduce expenditures on adult goods more severely in the presence of an extra (young) girl than for an extra (young) boy and thus is a means of studying which decisions are made, more than the actual process of decisionmaking. Nevertheless, a natural extension could complement the evidence on income pooling. This extension would test whether the reduction in expenditure on adult *male* goods is equal to the reduction in expenditure on adult *female* goods in the presence of an additional boy or girl. To date, no such test has been performed.

Finally, an additional perspective on income pooling is found in a study of informal credit programs in Bangladesh (Pitt and Khandker 1994). This study (which is further discussed later in this chapter) finds that credit affects household education and consumption choices differently if it is obtained by women rather than men. As the study employs a fixed-effect methodology that treats the availability of credit much as an experiment, it is able to control for the fact that credit choices reflect household preferences.

Studies of Labor Supply

Although leisure is conceptually similar to other commodities, it is recognized as an exclusive good, even in the context of unitary models of households. Thus the literature on labor supply provides a number of alternative approaches to testing models of intrahousehold allocation. In a unitary model, cross-substitution wage effects must be equal—"the effect of an income-compensated increase in the husband's wage on the wife's labor supply must be identical to the effect of an income-compensated increase in the wife's wage on the husband's labor supply" (Lundberg 1988:225). However, evidence presented in Ashenfelter and Heckman (1974), Killingsworth (1983), and Alderman and Sahn (1993) rejects the equality of these effects. Using panel data to control for unobserved fixed effects, Lundberg (1988) rejects the hypothesis that the husband and wife's labor supply is jointly determined, as predicted by the unitary model. Similarly Fortin and Lacroix (1993) estimate a general model of labor supply in which both the unitary and the collective framework can be tested as special cases. Using data from Canada, they find that, although the unitary restrictions are strongly rejected, the collective are not.

Furthermore, there exist a variety of studies that support the claim that labor is not pooled within the household. Jones's (1983, 1986) study of rice cultivation in north Cameroon provides several results of interest:

- Women supply a suboptimal amount of labor to their husbands' rice fields, preferring to spend time working on their own sorghum plots. A profit-maximizing household would increase the amount of women's labor supplied to rice production.

- Women receive compensation, in cash and kind, for labor they provide to their husbands. This amount rose as more labor was supplied. In addition, senior wives in polygamous households and women whose husbands still owed bride-price received higher levels of compensation. As Jones (1983: 1053) notes about the husband, "He can ill-afford to dispute his wife's right to compensation since he needs the additional income he receives from his wife's labor on a second rice field."

- The level of compensation paid is less than the market wage: "One might wonder why women continue to work for their husbands if they are compensated at a rate much lower than what they could earn working as hired labor. The answer is that, in principle, married women are expected to work on their husbands' fields if they are not working on their own. If they refuse to work on their husbands' fields, they risk a beating" (Jones 1986:111).

Udry (1996) develops a series of tests on the efficiency of the nonpooling of labor, as well as other agricultural inputs, in farm production in rural Burkina Faso. He finds that relative to Pareto-efficient allocations, too little labor and other inputs are used on plots controlled by women. Reallocating the factor usage on women's plots could increase output by as much as 20 percent. Although methodologically different from most studies in the literature, Jones's and Udry's results are not isolated examples.[3] More general discussions of this literature include Roberts (1979), Guyer (1981), Gladwin and McMillan (1989), Whitehead (1990a), Kabeer (1991), Quisumbing (1994a), and Dey Abbas (Chapter 15, this volume). Udry's study (and to a degree, Jones's as well) challenges much of the intrahousehold literature as it rejects Pareto efficiency in production, rather than addressing the question of allocation conditional on an assumed efficient use of resources in income generation. From a policy standpoint, the message of most of these studies vis-à-vis the issue of labor pooling within the household is succinctly summarized by Whitehead (1990a: 452): "More than one study has identified women's refusal to perform the family labor that the project had planned for or demanded of them as contributing to the failure of the development project."

Indirect Tests of the Unitary Model

Are Households and Families Characterized by Altruism?

As discussed by McElroy (Chapter 4, this volume), though there exist a number of rationales for the assumption of a single household welfare function, Becker's "rotten-kid theorem" is the most persuasive. It relies on the assumption of an altruistic head. Though altruism undoubtedly plays a role in many households, its universality is open to question.

There is considerable evidence that domestic violence is prevalent in both developed and developing countries (Levinson 1989). This issue might appear tangential to issues of household modeling, but that is not the case. Violence clearly refutes the altruism justification for the unitary household model (though it is consistent with a dictatorial head). As already noted, Jones (1986) relates that respondents claimed that the threat of being beaten influenced their labor allocation.

Altonji, Hayashi, and Kotlikoff (1992) test whether income is pooled across generations. They note that "if parents and children are altruistically linked, their consumption will be based on a collective budget constraint, and the distribution of consumption between parents and children will be independent

---

3. Other case studies documenting conflict, compulsion, and negotiation over women's labor allocation include Conti (1979), Haugerud (1982), Koenig (1982), Burfisher and Horenstein (1985), Spiro (1985), McMillan (1987), Babalola and Dennis (1988), Carney (1988a), Funk (1988), Ongaro (1988), and Leach (1991).

of the distribution of their incomes." Drawing on panel data from the United States, they reject this hypothesis. They find that the resource position of a particular family member—as measured by total income, nonlabor income, home equity, or wage rates—influences the consumption of that member. The study is fairly robust to alternative measures of income and to dynamic and fixed-effect formulations. Although it is still possible that the rejection of altruism is due to a definition of the functional family that is different from that used by the household, the study provides a convincing rejection of a polar case of intergenerational altruism.

A related framework also appears to refute the notion that altruism justifies the existence of a single welfare function. In the context of inter-generational transfers, the unitary model implies that benefactors have no incentive to behave strategically—that is, to manipulate intentionally the be-havior of the recipient. In other words, kids—even rotten ones—do not attempt to raise their consumption at the expense of others, because an altruistic benefactor will automatically reduce the size of the transfers made to them. This hypothesis is testable. If Becker's model holds, evidence should not be found of benefactors behaving strategically, for example using bequests to obtain attention or monetary transfers from their offspring. Behrman (1996) discusses the literature on transfers and bequests in detail. Empirical studies from developing countries include Lucas and Stark (1985) and Hoddinott (1992a). Both of these studies find that parents behave strategically; increased holdings of inheritable assets lead to higher monetary transfers from non-resident members in Botswana (Lucas and Stark) and from sons who anticipate receiving an inheritance in western Kenya (Hoddinott). Cox and Jimenez (1992) investigate whether social security payments "crowd out" private trans-fers from younger to older generations. They find some evidence of crowding out in that these transfers would have been about 20 percent higher without social security benefits. However, this displacement is significantly less than that predicted by purely altruistic motives.

The Significance of Extrahousehold Environmental Parameters

A few recent studies use extrahousehold environmental parameters (EEPs) to support collective models. Although such studies do not generally set up formal restrictions to falsify unitary models, given that EEPs have an explicit role in some collective models, they provide additional indirect sup-port for such models. In principle, differences in EEPs can be used as a natural experiment to test predictions of household models, although in the absence of randomized experiments, the question of the exogeneity of the environmental differences must be addressed. As an illustration, consider Rao and Greene's (1993) analysis of the impact of bargaining on fertility in Brazil. This study is sensitive to the possible endogeneity of individual choices and thus concen-trates on regional-level variables as the main evidence for bargaining over fertility choices. They find a negative relationship between fertility and the ratio of males aged 25–29 to females aged 15–19 in the region. One, although not the only, reasonable interpretation of this result takes it as an indication of the availability of alternative spouses. As this ratio increases, women have a greater chance of remarrying, hence a greater ability to bargain for the smaller families they prefer. Regions that have a lower average preference for fertility, however, will also have higher male-female ratios (owing to the age gap in the measure). Thus variations in regional preferences may also contribute to their finding; the suggestive results may not be completely free of simultaneity bias.

Though Pitt and Khandker (1994) do not explicitly refer to the collective literature, their results are consistent with shifts in EEPs influencing intra-household distribution. They observe that communities where a credit program is in place have a higher demand for schooling than other communities. Although EEPs may be one possible explanation for this difference, it could also be due to different expected returns mediated by economic impacts of credit or to preexisting differences between communities for which they did not fully control.

In a related vein, several studies indicate that EEPs affect domestic violence. In a case study, Erchak (1984) found little spouse abuse in rural Liberia, where neighbors quickly interfered in domestic disputes. In contrast, in urban areas of Liberia, where external intervention was less prevalent, the incidence of abuse was higher. Rao (1994) uses data on domestic violence in India to explain differences in household investment in nutrition. He shows that food purchases are influenced by the probability of violence. Moreover, he also finds that EEPs may determine the probability of violence. Tauchen, Witte, and Long (1991) present further evidence that community factors, including access to public assistance and places of refuge (such as the ability to seek shelter with family and friends), reduce domestic violence.[4]

Limitations to Empirical Tests of Intrahousehold Models

Central to many of the empirical studies that test alternative models of intrafamily or intrahousehold allocation are tests of whether the impact of women's income differs from that of men's income. Despite the range of evidence

---

4. Hoddinott (1996) presents some preliminary findings based on changes in EEPs over time using data from Canada. This study examines the impact on female rates of suicide of changes to provincial legislation dealing with the partition of estates upon divorce. In all provinces save Quebec, these laws were altered during the period 1975–79, going from a system under which wives' share of estates was effectively determined by their husbands to one under which household wealth was, with some minor variants, divided equally between partners. Drawing on data from Quebec, Ontario, and British Columbia, and controlling for provincial economic and demographic characteristics, Hoddinott finds evidence of a structural break in the trend of female suicide; in all provinces except Quebec, it falls sharply in the post-1975 period. Male rates of suicide are unaffected by this change.

acquired, there are legitimate econometric issues on which challenges to the interpretation of the results can be based. As already noted, it is widely recognized that observed wage income is an inappropriate variable for testing models of intrafamily allocation, since that income reflects household choices about nonmarket activities as well as the allocation of leisure within the household. In studies in which this question is addressed via instrumenting women's income, as in the work by Haddad and Hoddinott, the issue becomes that of the appropriateness of the identifying conditions. Thus nonlabor income (transfers and pensions as well as returns on assets) is offered as an exogenous measure of resource control. Furthermore, to be a credible candidate to test models dependent on a threat point, the nonlabor income must not be contingent on remaining in a marriage.

However, as noted by Schultz, certain forms of transfer income may be endogenous. For example, women with more children may receive larger transfers from other family members. Nonlabor income from assets or in the form of pensions may be considered endogenous in a life cycle context if it originates from previous labor participation rather than, say, inheritance or dowries.[5] Any current unobserved differences in tastes and productivity may also have been present in the past and thus have influenced asset accumulation. This issue is widely recognized: Behrman (1996) provides an extensive discussion of endowments in the context of unitary models. Both Pitt and Thomas (Chapters 2 and 9, this volume) indicate how such unobserved differences could affect econometric results. Yet many studies of income pooling ignore these, effectively testing a compound hypothesis that these are unimportant and that pooling does not occur.

Since it is difficult to assign ownership to one individual, asset income may also not be assignable. Interviewers responsible for obtaining the data used in subsequent econometric tests, however, may make assignment on a nonrandom basis to avoid either omissions or double counting; often joint asset income is assigned to a male. Similarly, if control over resources is enhanced by concealing income, both female and male respondents may have an incentive to underreport income. Moreover, asset income is subject to measurement errors that may differ by type of asset and may indirectly be systematically correlated with other household characteristics. Even in the absence of endogeneity, measurement error that differs by source of income can generate spurious patterns of differences in expenditures by income source, that is, increase the chance of a false rejection of pooling restrictions.

In this context, Thomas's results (Chapter 9, this volume) are roughly consistent with larger errors in measurement for male nonlabor income than for female. That said, errors in variables cannot explain the difference in patterns

---

5. Even these forms of transfer income have been challenged as unlikely to provide unbiased instruments because of intergenerational links of unobserved productivities.

toward daughters and sons found by Thomas (1994). Although that result may be explained by reverse causality—mothers with daughters chose to work or invest differently than those with sons—this explanation strains credibility. The reverse-causality interpretation is further undermined by the household fixed-effects model in Thomas (1994).

Furthermore, rejecting pooling is not the same as accepting an alternative model. Various tenable bargaining and sharing models can generate conditions under which income pooling is rejected, EEPs contribute to consumption patterns, or both. Thus there is a particular appeal in the approach taken by Chiappori since, if one good is assignable, a sharing rule can be derived for the entire decision process. Although this approach is in contrast to the greater structure that must be imposed in order to recover the details—if not necessarily the flavor—of the bargaining process, it nevertheless does offer a means of distinguishing between alternative models. However, the consumption of many goods of interest to policymakers, such as child health, cannot be unambiguously assigned to one household member. This is a further limitation of this approach. Assignability of goods is particularly difficult in household-equivalency models, since the consumption of adult goods may not be separable from fertility choices (Strauss and Beegle 1995).

Commodity demand models also generally reject the restriction of weak separability of leisure and goods (Browning and Meghir 1991; Alderman and Sahn 1993). Although both commodity and labor allocations are used to test models of intrafamily decisions, few commodity models have addressed the potential bias from ignoring labor supply. Moreover, one study that explicitly tests restriction implied by a Nash bargaining model (Horney and McElroy 1988) is limited as it poses a demand system in which leisure and commodity demand are separable.

In addition to having testable single-equation restriction on income and, in some cases, cross-equation restriction on commodity substitution, collective models may offer testable restriction regarding the impact of EEPs on demand. These are particularly interesting as they may suggest policy measures that can achieve reallocation toward, say, children's consumption. As with testing of income pooling, however, testing of restrictions on the impact of EEP faces econometric challenges and data limitations. EEPs are unlikely to vary much in cross-sectional data sets. Where variation may be found—over time or across regions—regional differences in tastes or the impact of community unobservables may be credible alternative explanations for the patterns observed. These would provide alternative explanations for findings such as those in Rao and Greene's analysis of bargaining over fertility in Brazil.

The work of Browning et al. (1994) is based on a sample restricted to childless couples working full time. It could be plausibly argued that their results are biased by the selectivity processes that generate such a sample. For example, issues relating to pooling of resources in such couples might differ from those in households in which children are present. They avoid issues relating to the endogeneity of income by an appeal to economic and legal conditions that make the assumption of fixed labor supply plausible. In turn, this approach illustrates the possibility that specific tests of bargaining and sharing will depend on economic, social, cultural, and legal structures that differ significantly in developing countries. In many countries, households are larger, more apt to contain more than one adult of the same gender and generation, and more likely to contain three generations than French or Canadian households. Similarly, separation and reformation of households owing to migration and child fostering will affect allocation processes differently in different contexts. The fact that cultures differ is not, of course, a direct limitation of their analysis of French or Canadian consumers, but rather a caveat that reiterates the need to perform a range of studies before generalities can be drawn. The findings of Thomas and Chen (1994) are valuable in that they suggest that the Pareto-efficient model extends beyond the conditions found in developed countries.

For many purposes, studies of household resource allocation take the household structure as predetermined. Yet, clearly, the formation and dissolution of households—or even seasonal separations owing to labor migration—are central to any questions of intrafamily allocation. Central to McElroy's contribution to this volume is the contention that the phenomena that shift threat points in Nash cooperative bargaining models also affect the gains from marriage realized in a marriage market. This situation allows for a number of empirical applications of bargaining models to fertility and marriage. However, it also means that it is extremely difficult to model household formation simultaneously with budget allocations conditional on household structure. Thus the comparisons between the demands of married individuals and those of divorced individuals offered by McElroy (1990) are difficult to implement because of an inability to account for selectivity into particular marital states.

The issue of whether family structure can be regarded as predetermined is also relevant to tests using data across generations. For example, Bernheim, Shleifer, and Summers (1985) and Hoddinott (1992b) assume that the number of children, their education, and earnings are exogenous. Yet child quality and quantity is the outcome of parental decisionmaking, and this feature may affect their results.

A final caveat is appropriate. One can expect a bias in any comparative review of the literature in that it is more likely that studies that report rejections of the unitary model will be submitted for publication and, given that, more likely that they will be accepted for publication. This tendency has been termed "publication bias" and has been shown to apply to a number of—and perhaps all—scientific disciplines (Begg and Berlin 1988).

Conclusion

We recognize that not all the studies discussed in this chapter are ideal. Particularly problematic are the endogeneity of incomes, the neglect of unobserved endowments, and the assumption—also held by many applications of the unitary model—that household formation and sometimes composition can be regarded as predetermined. Other studies are very region-specific or are based on relatively small samples. This said, it remains difficult to imagine that econometric difficulties singly or jointly can account for all the rejections of income pooling and all the evidence supporting various collective models. This conclusion, together with the policy costs of rejecting the collective approach when it holds (discussed in Chapter 17), leads to the argument that the evidence may be taken as shifting the burden of proof. The assumption that the unitary approach is sufficient to account for all aspects of household resource allocation must be defended rather than maintained.

The objective of this chapter has been to review empirical tests of the assumptions underlying the unitary approach and those that have been proposed in support of various collective models. This has been done primarily to provide a context for the chapters presented in this section of the book, and partly to fill what is perceived to be a gap in the literature. It could be inferred from this review that the modeling of intrahousehold allocation is a question of using either a unitary or a collective approach. Such an interpretation is wrong. As stressed in Chapter 1, the unitary approach offers both a valuable set of tools for examining the rationale underlying distribution within the household and the means for linking several aspects of these within a single analytical framework. This argument is more modest: that the evidence suggests that such an approach is not sufficient to account for all aspects of intrahousehold resource allocation. It should be stressed that there is a need for much further work in this area. This issue is pursued further in Chapter 17, but it is worth outlining some directions for future work here. They include more sophisticated tests of the income-pooling hypothesis, modeling labor allocation in the context of agricultural production, examining processes of household formation and dissolution, and work of an interdisciplinary nature. A number of contributions in this volume—such as those of Guyer, Thomas, and Gittelsohn and Mookherji—begin to address these issues.

9 Incomes, Expenditures, and Health Outcomes: Evidence on Intrahousehold Resource Allocation

DUNCAN THOMAS

Although the traditional (unitary) model of the household is simple, it is hard to overstate its contribution to the understanding of economic and social behavior. Whether or not it is an adequate description of household choices is fundamentally an empirical question—the answer to which likely depends on the specific application. There has, however, been little empirical testing of the model.

In this chapter I provide some evidence on this question, drawing on survey data from Brazil. Whether observed consumption and investment patterns are sensitive to differences in the distribution of income between men and women is determined in the context of household demand for commodities, nutrition, and health. Such sensitivity would be prima facie evidence against the traditional model of the household, which assumes that household decisions are unaffected by shifting resources from one member to another within a household. Rejection of the traditional model has obvious implications for public policy. It suggests, for example, that policies that result in more resources in the hands of women will have different effects on household choices than policies that generate income for men.

Previous chapters have described the theoretical models underlying the analyses presented here. In this chapter the empirical strategy adopted is outlined first, followed by a description of the data. Empirical results are presented in three sections. We examine shares of the household budget spent on a series of commodities first and then consider household nutrient demands. These outcomes are measured at the household level. The third section focuses on indicators that can be assigned to individuals within the household, namely child anthropometrics, which are measures of health and nutritional status. Special attention is paid to the role of measurement error and unobserved heterogeneity, and robust tests are developed that exploit comparisons of income effects among siblings in the same household. The robustness of the results to variation in the definition of the household unit is also explored.

142

The evidence suggests that treating the household as a homogeneous unit is not consistent with the data. Placing more resources in the hands of women results in greater spending on human capital goods and nutrients and a bigger positive effect on child nutritional status.

Model

This section begins with a simple static model of household behavior in which household welfare in any period, W, depends on the utility of each household member, m $(= 1, \ldots, M)$. In turn each individual's utility function, U_m, depends on the commodity consumption of all household members, $X_{im}(i = 1, \ldots, G,$ goods), as well as the consumption of leisure by each individual in the household, $l_1, \ldots, l_M$. In addition, utility is affected by a vector of home-produced goods, $\theta_{1M}, \ldots, \theta_{HM}$, which will include, for example, the health, nutrition, and education of each household member. A set of observed individual- and household-specific characteristics, μ, may affect tastes and therefore utility, $U_m(X, l, \theta; \mu, \omega)$, and ω captures unobserved heterogeneity.

The household welfare function is akin to a Bergson-Samuelson social welfare function and aggregates the individual felicity functions:

$$W = W[U_1(X, l, \theta; \mu, \omega), \ldots, U_M(X, l, \theta; \mu, \omega)] \qquad (9.1)$$

This is maximized subject to a production function for each element of θ and a household budget constraint. The production functions are specified in general terms:

$$\theta = \theta(\kappa, \mu; \upsilon) \qquad (9.2)$$

where κ are inputs, some of which are purchased in the market and some of which are not; this vector of inputs thus includes some elements of the consumption vector, X.[1] Outputs, θ, may depend on individual and household characteristics, μ, such as the age and gender of the person and the education of the parents. Individual and family unobserved heterogeneity is represented by υ. The household budget constraint is

$$pX = \Sigma_m [w_m (T - l_m) + y_m] \qquad (9.3)$$

where the vector p is the set of prices of all goods in $X;$ all household members are assumed to face parametric commodity prices. The price of time for each individual is w_m, so that individual's total income is given by the value of earned income, $w_m(T - l_m)$, together with nonlabor income, y_m. Household income is simply the sum of all individuals' incomes.

---

1. Without loss of generality, κ is allowed to include purchased inputs that are not valued in and of themselves, in which case those elements of X are given zero weight in the utility function (9.1).

Solving the maximization problem given by equations (9.1)–(9.3), there is a household demand for each element of the commodity vector, X, and each element of θ. Denoting the vector $\{X, \theta\}$ by Ω for notational ease,

$$\Omega_i = g(p, w, y_1, \ldots, y_M, \mu, \varepsilon) \tag{9.4}$$

Thus, under the assumptions of this collective (or "individualistic") model of household decisionmaking, the commodity consumption, health, and nutrition of household members (among other demands) depend on all prices (p), wages (w), household characteristics (μ), *individual* nonlabor incomes ($y_1, \ldots, y_M$), and unobserved heterogeneity (ε). This specification is quite general and underlies the models discussed in the previous chapters.

In contrast to these collective models, the traditional economic model of the household assumes either that all household members have common preferences (in which case U_m is identical for $m = 1, \ldots, M$ in equation [9.1]) or that one member dictates all allocation decisions (in which case the aggregator function, $W(\cdot)$, assigns a zero weight to all but that member's utility function). Under these assumptions, the demand functions (equation [9.4]) depend not on individual nonlabor incomes but on their sum:

$$\Omega_i = g(p, w, \Sigma_m y_m, \mu, \varepsilon) \tag{9.5}$$

Clearly, if all members are altruistic,[2] household demand will depend on total household nonlabor income; the (perfect) altruism, common preference, and dictatorial models are, therefore, observationally equivalent, at least in terms of their predictions for the impact of individual income on household commodity demand.

This observation suggests a very simple empirical test of the model of common preferences against the more general collective models. Under the assumptions of the "traditional" economic model, household members may be treated as if they pool all their incomes, in which case the distribution of resources within the household should have no impact on the allocation of those resources. That is, observed consumption and investment patterns should be unaffected by shifting the control of income from, say, men to women. This is a key prediction of the common preference model, not shared by any of the more general models that permit heterogeneity in preferences of household members. Maintaining that nonlabor income is exogenous, the prediction of the common preference model will be tested by determining whether nonlabor income attributed to a man in the household has the same impact on demands as nonlabor income attributed to a woman in the household.

---

2. If only some members of the household are altruistic, then the preferences of the altruist(s) must dominate: in essence, he or she must behave as a dictator (Manser and Brown 1980).

Typically nonlabor income represents only a small fraction of total resources available to a household for consumption and investment. Furthermore nonlabor income is unlikely to be measured without error. In addition, drawing on the intuition of a bargaining framework, which suggests that bargaining power depends on the resources that one would control if the household were to break up, nonlabor income is an error-ridden proxy for control over those resources. The next step, then, is to examine the impact on demand of the total income of each individual, Y_m:

$$X_i = g(p, Y_1, \ldots, Y_M, \mu, \xi) \tag{9.6}$$

where $Y_m = w_m(T - l_m) + y_m$ and ξ represents unobserved heterogeneity. Several studies of household resource allocation examine the impact of male and female income on a variety of outcomes (for a review see Blumberg 1988). Since each household member's utility depends on consumption of his or her own leisure, and possibly that of other members, it may be inappropriate in this model to assume that labor supply $(T - l_m)$ is exogenous and thus treat total income as predetermined. Intuitively household members are likely to negotiate over the allocation of resources to goods, X, home production, θ, *and* leisure, l, *simultaneously.*

Under the maintained assumption that current nonlabor income is exogenous, it is unaffected by current choices and so is a valid instrument for total income. This is a strong assumption, and so the results of experiments with alternative identification assumptions will also be discussed. Given a set of instruments, it is possible to determine whether the distribution of total income within the household affects household demand and investment patterns. As with nonlabor income, the equality of the impact of (instrumented) total income in the hands of different individuals on outcomes, Ω_i, will be tested.

Rejection of equality of income effects in equation (9.4) or (9.6) says nothing about the appropriate alternative model. This work may be viewed, then, as a precursor to testing these alternative models of household resource allocation. Although the aim of the chapter is modest, testing a simple hypothesis is a useful exercise, because even this task presents several empirical problems.[3]

The trickiest problem probably lies in the measurement of resources under the control of an individual. If, in the survey, the reported assignment of income to one individual or another within the family is random (or if everything is perceived as being de facto jointly owned) then the equality of income effects should not be rejected and the traditional economic model of common preferences is the appropriate empirical model. In a sense, then, rejection of

---

3. For recent tests that seek to discriminate between bargaining models and models that only assume that household allocations are Pareto efficient, see Bourguignon et al. (1993), Browning et al. (1994), Thomas and Chen (1994), and Browning and Chiappori (1995).

equality is a strong result. Different income effects may, however, simply reflect differences in the extent of measurement error. Furthermore, the assumption that nonlabor income is predetermined may not be innocuous, since it reflects past labor supply behavior. In a dynamic framework, nonlabor income is appropriately treated as endogenous.

These concerns will be addressed in three ways. The first is an experiment using only asset income, which is less closely tied to recent labor supply choices than all nonlabor income—although even asset income is not exogenous in a dynamic model of household choices.

Second is a test of whether differences in income effects reflect heterogeneity in the composition of nonlabor income. This amounts to testing whether the effect on demands of asset income is equal to the effect of nonasset income. Since it is unlikely that asset and nonasset income will share the same measurement error, it is expected that such error would result in rejection of this equality.

The third set of experiments focuses on child anthropometric outcomes and compares the impact of maternal and paternal income on child height and weight. If a father's income (say) has a greater effect on his son than on his daughter, then it is reasonable to conclude that fathers prefer sons to daughters. However, mothers may also prefer sons to daughters, in which case maternal income effects will be larger on sons. If this observation is true, the results are consistent with both the common preference model and the more general collective models. However, if maternal income affects the health of daughters more than that of sons, then the evidence indicates that preferences of mothers and fathers do differ and that the control over resources within the household does affect allocation decisions. The common preference model would be rejected. By placing the spotlight on the difference between the effect of paternal income on sons relative to daughters, on the one hand, and the effect of maternal income on sons relative to daughters, on the other, a "difference-indifference"–type estimator is constructed that is robust to measurement error and also to fairly general forms of unobserved heterogeneity. To see why, consider measurement error. For a particular parent, measurement error in income is common across all children, and so it will have the same impact on sons and daughters: it is thus possible to calculate unbiased estimates of the *differential* effect of income on sons relative to daughters. It is the difference between mothers and fathers in these differential income effects that is at the center of the test. A similar argument holds for other sources of unobserved heterogeneity, such as tastes for work, as long as they are not correlated with the gender of the child. This assumption rules out, for example, women choosing to work because they have a son rather than a daughter. This is, it seems, about as close as one is likely to get to a "natural experiment" in this context.

Data

The Estudo Nacional da Despesa Familiar (ENDEF) is a large-scale household budget survey carried out by the Instituto Brasileiro de Geografia e Estatistica (IBGE) from August 1974 through August 1975. Some 55,000 households were included in a budget survey that gathered information on income in addition to household expenditures. Each member of the household was asked about his or her own labor supply, earnings, and nonlabor income.

It is not obvious how to attribute income from family enterprises to individuals within the household; in this survey all income was attributed to the "household head." This is a problem particularly in the rural sector, where many families operate farms; in the urban sector, however, unpaid family workers account for less than 5 percent of all workers in the survey. The study sample is therefore restricted to the approximately 38,000 urban households in the survey, and the focus is on the incomes of the head and spouse; they will be referred to as the male and female heads. About 18 percent of all the households in the survey are headed by single females, whereas 6 percent are headed by single males. There are both a male and a female head in the remaining three-quarters of households.

The distribution of income within the household is reported in Table 9.1. On average, household income is about Cr$27,000 per month[4] and, of that, three-quarters is attributed to the male head. This share is stable across the distribution of household per capita expenditure (PCE). Essentially every male head reports at least some income, and the average male receives about Cr$28,000 per month. Just under 50 percent of female heads report some income, and among these women average monthly income is Cr$8,700, which is only one-third of the average male income.

About one-quarter of total household income is derived from nonlabor sources, and positive nonlabor income is reported by somewhat less than one-half (43 percent) of all male heads and nearly one-quarter (23 percent) of all female heads in the survey. On average, male heads report about Cr$6,500[5] in nonlabor income, which makes up about a quarter of their total income. The share of nonlabor income in the total income of men tends to rise as PCE rises. In contrast, for women the share of income from nonlabor sources is constant across the distribution of PCE, accounting for about 40 percent of total income. The average female head reports about Cr$1,700 in nonlabor income.

---

4. Household income is defined here as the income of the male and female heads. Other income is ignored throughout. Inflation was approximately 35 percent per year during the survey, so all incomes and expenditures were converted to real values using monthly deflators provided by IBGE.

5. This is computed by dividing Cr$5,302 by 0.81, the proportion of households with a male head.

TABLE 9.1 Distribution of income within the household by total, labor, and nonlabor incomes: means and standard errors

	Mean for All Households (Cr$)	Percent of Households Reporting Income	Mean Income Conditional on Reporting Some Income (Cr$)
Total income	27,006	98.3	27,467
	(390)		(396)
Labor income	20,097	84.7	23,715
	(259)		(302)
Nonlabor income	6,909	52.5	6,909
	(232)		(302)
Asset income	1,883	14.8	12,722
	(76)		(500)
Nonasset income	5,026	40.9	12,289
	(189)		(457)
Male head			
Percent of households	81.9		
Total income	23,020	99.0	28,407
	(382)		(465)
Labor income	17,718	89.2	24,239
	(258)		(338)
Nonlabor income	5,302	43.1	15,029
	(225)		(629)
Asset income	1,300	14.5	10,925
	(74)		(603)
Nonasset income	4,002	35.0	13,924
	(184)		(629)
Female head			
Percent of households	93.5		
Total income	3,986	49.1	8,676
	(84)		(154)
Labor income	2,379	35.8	7,111
	(40)		(110)
Nonlabor income	1,606	23.1	7,456
	(59)		(264)
Asset income	531	7.0	8,045
	(20)		(638)
Nonasset income	1,075	13.1	8,819
	(49)		(389)

NOTE: Figures within parentheses are standard errors.

Income is notoriously difficult to measure well in household surveys, and it is quite likely that income from nonlabor sources is subject to considerable measurement error. ENDEF, however, was a comprehensive and intensive survey, with each household visited on a daily basis for a week by the same enumerator. There is some evidence that enumerators were able to elicit additional information later in the week as households came to view them as less alien (Vasconcellos 1983). The survey took considerable care in the collection of income data, in particular nonlabor income, which was broken down into six categories: income from rents and physical assets, financial assets, pensions, social security and workers compensation, gifts, and other irregular income. Pension benefits and social security are likely to be related to previous labor supply choices, and so the impact of asset income on household commodity demands will be examined separately. Although this asset income may be a cleaner measure of nonlabor income, it too potentially reflects previous earnings and savings behavior. This is a tough problem to crack, at least with a single cross section of data. Indeed even information on bequests or dowries—as suggested by, for example, Schultz (1990)—may not be predetermined in the context of these models of household behavioral choices.

Among the survey respondents, 14 percent of men and 7 percent of women reported some asset income. Such income accounts for a very small fraction (7 percent) of total household income, although among those who report any asset income, the amounts are certainly not trivial. Experiments with the effects of asset income on commodity demand can be seen as checks on the robustness of the results based on the broader measure of nonlabor income.

Empirical Results

In order to assess whether redistributing income within a household affects household consumption and investment patterns, the equality of the impact of male and female incomes on a series of household demands, Ω_i, is tested. The first set of results focuses on shares of the household budget allocated to a series of commodities, whereas the second set examines the demand for nutrients. These outcomes are all measured at the household level and so are not assignable to particular individuals (or groups within the household) without making strong assumptions. In the third set of results, the impact of parental income on child nutritional status, measured at the individual level, is considered. Sample summary statistics are reported in Table 9.2.

Since the empirical specifications, and level of observation, differ across these three sets of outcomes, they are each discussed separately. Throughout

TABLE 9.2 Sample summary statistics

	Mean	Standard Error	Percent Greater Than Zero
Expenditure shares			
Food	40.88	0.090	98
Meals out	4.24	0.048	41
Housing	18.53	0.061	100
Human capital	6.77	0.035	94
Education	1.89	0.016	62
Health and medical	3.43	0.025	84
Household services	1.45	0.015	60
Leisure	3.93	0.029	81
Ceremonies	1.49	0.017	56
Recreation	2.44	0.022	71
Household goods	7.79	0.037	99
Adult goods	13.10	0.044	99
Nutrient intakes			
ln (calorie intake)	7.61	0.001	...
ln (protein intake)	6.44	0.002	...
Child anthropometrics (Z scores)			
Height-for-age	−0.97	0.010	...
Boys	−1.01	0.014	...
Girls	−0.93	0.014	...
Weight-for-age	−0.01	0.008	...
Boys	−0.04	0.012	...
Girls	0.02	0.012	...
Household characteristics			
Fraction with male head	0.818	0.002	...
Fraction with female head	0.935	0.001	...
Education of male head			
Fraction literate	0.36	0.002	...
Fraction completed elementary education	0.20	0.002	...
Fraction completed secondary education	0.15	0.002	...
Education of female head			
Fraction literate	0.39	0.002	...
Fraction completed elementary education	0.22	0.002	...
Fraction completed secondary education	0.13	0.002	...
Household composition			
ln (household size)	1.38	0.003	...
Males aged 0–4/household size	0.059	0.001	...
Females aged 0–4/household size	0.057	0.001	...
Males aged 5–9/household size	0.051	0.001	...
Females aged 5–9/household size	0.051	0.001	...
Males aged 10–14/household size	0.049	0.001	...
Females aged 10–14/household size	0.050	0.001	...

TABLE 9.2 (*continued*)

	Mean	Standard Error	Percent Greater Than Zero
Household characteristics (*continued*)			
Household composition (*continued*)			
Males aged 15–54/household size	0.262	0.001	. . .
Females aged 15–54/household size	0.291	0.001	. . .
Males aged >54/household size	0.052	0.001	. . .
Females aged >54/household size	0.129	0.001	. . .
Price aggregate for community characteristics ln (prices)			
Cereals	0.057	0.001	. . .
Tubers	0.025	0.001	. . .
Sugar	−0.055	0.001	. . .
Beans	0.042	0.001	. . .
Fruits and vegetables	0.024	0.001	. . .
Meat and fish	0.043	0.001	. . .
Dairy	−0.001	0.001	. . .
Fats	−0.015	0.001	. . .
Oils	−0.017	0.001	. . .
Housing	0.683	0.003	. . .
Fuel/transport	−0.050	0.001	. . .
Clothing	0.173	0.001	. . .
Personal hygiene	0.020	0.001	. . .

NOTE: . . ., not applicable.

the chapter, only income effects are reported, although the regressions include additional controls as described in each section.[6]

Demand Functions

This section begins with commodity consumption and estimates a series of expenditure share demand functions. ENDEF reports expenditures for more than 300 different goods over a variable recall period, ranging from a week for commonly consumed foods to a year for infrequently purchased goods such as

---

6. According to Lagrange multiplier tests (Breusch and Pagan 1980), the assumption of homoskedastic errors is rejected in all the regressions. Variance covariance matrices are thus estimated by the infinitesimal jackknife (Jaeckel [1972]; also called the influence function estimator [Hampel 1974] and attributed to White [1980]), which is consistent in the presence of heteroskedasticity. In very large samples, it may make good sense to adopt a size of test that trades off Type I and Type II errors. The Schwarz (1978) proposal, which will asymptotically pick the model that is a posteriori most probable, is followed here. For a χ^2 test statistic, the critical value is the logarithm of the sample size multiplied by the number of restrictions, r.

durables and semidurables. Since a large fraction of households do not purchase many of these goods, estimating demand functions at this level of disaggregation would entail addressing the auxiliary problem of the decision to purchase (Wales and Woodland 1983; Lee and Pitt 1986; see Deaton 1986 for a discussion). The focus, therefore, is on a set of aggregates (and subaggregates) for which at least most households report nonzero expenditures.

Housing expenditures are either reported by or imputed for all urban households in the survey; they account for almost one-fifth of the budget of the average household. Food, which is also purchased by virtually every household during the survey week, accounts for 40 percent of the budget. According to the anthropological literature, women in Brazil tend to have control over food in the home (Neuhouser 1989); whether this carries over to food purchased outside the home is not clear. Demand for the latter, therefore, is examined separately (although food is purchased outside the home by only 40 percent of households and such purchases account for about 4 percent of the budget).

If adult clothing could be separated for men and women, it could be termed an "assignable good" and used to identify the household income sharing rule (see Bourguignon et al. [1993] and Browning et al. [1994], who examine the demand for these goods among others). In ENDEF, however, it is not possible to separate clothing expenditures unambiguously along gender lines. Alcohol, tobacco, and clothing and footwear have traditionally been treated as "adult goods" in the equivalence-scale literature; they have been examined both separately and as an aggregate here. The results for the aggregate carry through to the three commodities separately. In the interests of brevity, only the aggregate case is reported.

The demand for health services (including medical expenditures) and expenditures on education (including tuition payments, transport to school, school uniforms, and items needed at school such as books) are examined. Household services (many of which are domestic services, but labor around the home and charges for items such as the telephone are also included) are grouped with health and education as a "human capital" aggregate. Almost all households purchase at least some of these human capital goods, which account for just under 7 percent of the budget of the average household. Each of these subaggregates is examined separately as well as together.

Expenditures on books, magazines, clubs, and other recreation items, in addition to expenditures on ceremonies (birthdays, baptisms, weddings, and funerals), are grouped together in the leisure aggregate, which accounts for about 4 percent of the budget of the average household. The final category discussed here is household equipment, which includes expenditures on linens, furniture, electrical equipment, and other semidurables. Almost every household spends something on these goods; they account for nearly 8 percent of the total budget. The remaining 10 percent of the budget is accounted for by other commodities not reported here.

Each household in the survey reports both the value and the quantity of goods consumed, and so it is possible to compute a household-specific price for each commodity purchased. Since variation in these prices may reflect measurement error and heterogeneity in quality choices, it is not appropriate to treat household-level prices as exogenous (Deaton 1988). Instead market average price indexes for 12 commodity groups[7] are included, as are state and month controls to account for other unobserved heterogeneity in the community environment.

The demand functions depend not only on income and prices but also on a set of household characteristics, μ. In principle, the price vector includes individual wages that should be treated as endogenous and needs to account for the choice to work in the labor market. To keep the model simple, the determinants of the price of time, in particular the education of the male and female head, are included. In addition controls for the presence of a male and female head are included in μ. To pick up scale effects of demand, (the logarithm of) household size is added to the covariates, and to permit variation in the effects of different household compositions, μ includes the proportion of household members in each of five gender-specific age groups.[8] To control for community heterogeneity and seasons, the regressions include month dummies and state dummies.

The impact of nonlabor income on household budget shares is reported in Table 9.3. The two-stage least-squares estimates, using total individual income (treated as endogenous), are also reported. In each case, the estimated income effects (evaluated at the mean)—based on a model that includes quadratics in the income of the senior male and female in the household, along with interactions between them—are reported.[9] χ^2 statistics for joint significance of all three covariates are reported below each income effect. The third column of

---

7. It is not obvious how to define market boundaries, at least from an empirical perspective. Using prices on 135 homogeneous commodities (such as black beans, mulatto beans, green corn, and corn flour), median prices were computed for each of 23 states, distinguishing metropolitan from nonmetropolitan areas. These median prices were then aggregated into Tornquist price indexes based on the shares of the budget spent on that good in each market:

$$\ln p_{GM} = \Sigma_{g \in G} \tfrac{1}{2}(w_{gm} + w_g \cdot)(\ln p_{gm} + \ln p_g \cdot)$$

where g represents goods within the Gth commodity group, $\cdot$ represents national averages, and w_{gm} is the share of expenditure on good g in market m. Price indexes are included for 12 commodity groups: cereals, tubers, beans, fruits and vegetables, meat and fish, dairy products, fats, oils, housing, fuel and transport, clothing, and personal care items. (See Thomas, Strauss, and Barbosa [1991] for details.)

8. The household age groups are children aged 0–4, 5–9, and 10–14 years and adults aged 15–54 and older than 54. One group (older females) must be dropped, leaving nine composition categories.

9. Linear models are rejected by the data. Experiments with more flexible polynomial models indicate that cubic terms (and additional interactions) do not significantly improve the explanatory power of the regressions.

TABLE 9.3 Effects of male and female income on budget shares: quadratic model with interactions, effects evaluated at mean

Shares	Nonlabor Income Ordinary Least Squares (OLS)			Total Income Two-Stage Least Squares (2SLS)		
	Female	Male	Ratio	Female	Male	Ratio
Food	−246.08	−60.06	4.10	−261.10	−66.90	3.90
	(305.39)	(128.30)	(143.78)	(269.45)	(61.31)	(115.95)
Meals out	−63.44	−7.82	8.12	−66.63	−9.22	7.23
	(105.85)	(50.95)	(74.03)	(126.04)	(45.30)	(90.29)
Housing	72.43	12.77	5.67	76.10	13.79	5.52
	(32.50)	(14.28)	(21.79)	(31.89)	(10.83)	(21.60)
Human capital	86.79	18.25	4.76	91.69	21.01	4.36
	(146.65)	(78.20)	(103.84)	(64.87)	(4.14)	(30.06)
Education	18.45	2.92	6.31	19.44	3.39	5.74
	(36.72)	(9.06)	(22.32)	(36.34)	(9.55)	(22.84)
Health	22.29	6.44	3.46	23.89	7.94	3.01
	(29.51)	(36.53)	(23.49)	(30.08)	(36.59)	(25.00)
Household services	46.05	8.89	5.18	48.45	9.72	4.98
	(145.47)	(75.10)	(85.49)	(143.16)	(47.19)	(93.51)
Leisure	58.58	16.06	3.65	62.20	17.10	3.64
	(58.71)	(64.61)	(40.60)	(61.23)	(41.99)	(45.72)
Ceremonies	19.80	0.71	27.90	20.66	1.31	15.76
	(28.44)	(11.80)	(26.11)	(29.48)	(14.63)	(26.75)
Recreation	38.79	15.35	2.53	41.55	15.79	2.63
	(37.75)	(63.64)	(28.94)	(37.93)	(35.53)	(29.09)
Household goods	12.22	1.86	6.56	13.15	2.74	4.80
	(7.56)	(7.55)	(6.08)	(7.71)	(7.63)	(6.31)
Adult goods	−17.57	−11.21	1.57	−18.77	−11.50	1.63
	(29.23)	(38.59)	(1.90)	(31.49)	(26.81)	(2.25)

NOTES: There are 38,799 observations in the sample. Income effects are evaluated at mean; χ^2 tests for joint significance of income covariates are below the estimates. Ratios of female to male income effects are in the third column of each panel; χ^2 test statistics for equality of male and female effects are in parentheses below the ratios. All tests are based on heteroskedasticity-consistent estimates of standard errors. By the Schwarz criterion, the critical value for χ^2s is 31.7. All incomes are measured in millions of crusados. In addition to quadratics in male and female income, and interactions between them, regressions include controls for existence of male and female head, their education (three dummies each—literate, completed elementary school, completed secondary school or more), ln household size, proportions of members in nine age-gender groups, ln prices, and month and state dummies. Instruments for (2SLS) estimates are quadratics and interactions in male and female nonlabor income. Human capital goods are education, health, and household services. Education includes tuition, uniforms, and other schooling expenses. Health includes medications, prescriptions, and medical care expenses. Household services include domestic services, labor around the home, and utilities such as telephones. Leisure expenditures include those on ceremonies (baptisms, birthdays, and weddings) and recreation (books, magazines, clubs, and sports fees). Household goods are linens, furniture, and other household semidurables. Adult goods are alcohol, tobacco, and clothing.

each panel reports the ratio of the female to male income effects and the χ^2 test for equality of these income effects (or, equivalently, for the ratio of effects being equal to unity). According to the Schwarz criterion, the critical value for the χ^2 tests is 31.7.

IMPACT OF NONLABOR INCOME.   Additional nonlabor income in the hands of women increases the budget share spent on housing, education, household services, recreation, and possibly health. More nonlabor income in the hands of men raises the budget share spent on health, household services, and leisure. For all these goods, however, the income effects are larger for women than for men by a factor of between 3 and 5: the differences are significant for the human capital aggregate (education, health, and, in particular, household services) and also for the leisure aggregate (ceremonies and recreation). The household services subaggregate comprises largely payments for domestic services, labor in the home, and utilities such as telephones; these are likely to be substitutes for the time of the female head. Education and recreation expenditures might be viewed as investments in human capital and are directed mostly toward children; health expenditures may also be viewed as investments in human capital. Some shares must also decline, and it turns out that food shares (both at home and out of the home) decline with income (for both men and women), with the decline being larger for a marginal crusado in the hands of a woman.

But not all estimated income effects differ between men and women. There is no evidence, for example, that rearranging the distribution of (nonlabor) income within the household will have any (significant) impact on the shares spent on housing and household goods, both of which are presumably like "public" goods to household members. In addition, estimated effects of income in the hands of men and women are essentially the same for those goods that are traditionally treated as adult goods, namely alcohol, tobacco, and clothing (taken separately or together).[10]

ROBUSTNESS OF RESULTS.   Since a large fraction of the survey respondents report no nonlabor income, it may be that the estimated income effects largely reflect heterogeneity between those who do have nonlabor income and those who do not. Therefore, the same regressions have been reestimated, but included are a pair of indicator functions for whether the male or female head reports any nonlabor income. Conditional on reporting some nonlabor income, the estimated income effects do *not* change dramatically and are significantly different for men and women in the case of human capital and leisure goods, as well as food (consumed at home).

---

10. Testing for male and female clothing (to the extent they can be identified in these data) did not indicate any significant differences in the impact of male or female nonlabor income on their purchase.

As an additional check on the robustness of these results, nonlabor income has been defined more narrowly to include only asset income. Because fewer than 15 percent of households report any asset income, its effect on the demands for commodities that are not purchased by (almost) all households will be difficult to estimate. It turns out that, qualitatively, the results are in line with those based on the broader definition of income: additional asset income in the hands of women, rather than men, is associated with larger budget shares spent on human capital and leisure goods, higher nutrient intakes, and lower food shares. These differences are, however, significant only for food (consumed at home and away), whereas the differences in income effects on human capital border on being significant.

Differences in the impact on demand of asset and all other nonlabor income (nonasset income) have also been tested: their effects are in general not significantly different from each other; this is true for both men and women. This finding implies that the differences in the effects of male and female income cannot be attributed to differences in the composition of nonlabor income, to the extent that heterogeneity in composition is captured by this dichotomy. (See Thomas [1992] for details of these robustness checks.)

EFFECTS OF TOTAL INDIVIDUAL INCOME. The focus thus far has been on nonlabor income. Would household consumption patterns change if *total* income were to be redistributed from men to women? The second panel of Table 9.3 reports the results of estimating the demand functions with quadratics in male and female total income along with an interaction. The instruments include male and female nonlabor income, their quadratics, and interactions.

Raising the income of women will tend to increase budget shares spent on housing, education, health, household services, and recreation; if additional income is in the hands of men, then budget shares spent on health, household services, and recreation will increase. As was the case with nonlabor income, the budget shares rise more if additional income is put in the hands of women. Taken together, the estimated male and female income effects are different for both the human capital and leisure aggregates.

Additional income has a negative impact on adult goods—but the effect is the same independent of the gender of the person to whom the income is attributed. The share of the budget spent on food (consumed at home and away) also declines with income; this decline is significantly greater if additional income is in the hands of women rather than men.

The results for total (labor and nonlabor) income are, therefore, remarkably similar to those that examine the impact of only nonlabor income. Furthermore the results for total income are also robust to the inclusion of a dummy for whether or not the individual reported any income (also treated as endogenous, with dummies for the reporting of nonlabor income as the instruments). Once again permitting more flexibility in the income responses (by including cubics in male and female income) does not change the thrust of these conclusions.

All the demand functions have included dummies for the education of the male and female heads in order to control for heterogeneity in tastes as well as the price of time. If household consumption is affected by education *only* through its impact on earnings and thus income, then education may be excluded from the demand functions and can be considered, under these strong assumptions, a valid instrument for total income. This model is, therefore, overidentified. It turns out that, once again, relative to men, income in the hands of women is associated with larger increases in the share of the budget spent on human capital goods and leisure, and these differences are significant in all cases except housing. In this model, more income under the control of women is associated with higher shares spent on adult goods, but lower shares if the income is under the control of men. This difference is significant and is the *only* instance of significantly different income effects on the demand for adult goods. Budget shares for food (consumed at home and away) decline with income, and this decline is significantly faster for women.

In sum, there is evidence that additional income in the hands of women is associated with significantly higher budget shares spent on human capital goods (education, health, and household services) as well as on leisure goods and lower shares spent on food. This is true for both the ordinary least squares estimates that use nonlabor income and the two-stage least squares total income estimates. The results appear to be quite robust.

Demand for Nutrients

It is a straightforward procedure to generalize the demand model given previously to include the consumption of not just foods but also the nutrients they provide. Thus the impact of income on the demand for calories and protein is also examined. In ENDEF, total household consumption of nutrients was measured by weighing the food consumed at each meal (taking care to account for any wastage or leftovers) during the course of a week. These data were then converted to nutrient intakes using tables compiled by the Food and Agriculture Organization of the United Nations. The presence of every person at each meal was reported, and so per capita intakes of each nutrient can be calculated for each household, taking account of the presence of both household members and visitors. The survey is very intrusive—the enumerator weighs food prepared at home for seven days—but not so intrusive that every respondent is followed on his or her daily travels. Thus no information is reported about meals eaten away from home. It is assumed that the nutrient content of these meals is, on average, the same as that for meals eaten at home.[11] On average, daily per capita intakes amount to 2,100 calories and 70 grams of protein.

---

11. Forty percent of households report eating some food away from home. On average about 4 percent of the budget is spent on these meals, which account for only 10 percent of the total food budget.

TABLE 9.4 Effects of male and female income on nutrient demand: quadratic model with interactions, effects evaluated at mean

Nutrient Intakes	Nonlabor Income Ordinary Least Squares (OLS)			Total Income Two-Stage Least Squares (2SLS)		
	Female	Male	Ratio	Female	Male	Ratio
ln (calories per capita)	1.60	0.14	11.08	1.68	0.18	9.40
	(69.64)	(16.13)	(52.88)	(69.57)	(17.68)	(53.44)
ln (protein per capita)	3.47	0.59	5.91	3.66	0.69	5.32
	(207.85)	(72.83)	(119.47)	(201.22)	(66.88)	(130.19)

NOTES: There are 38,799 observations in the sample. χ^2 tests for joint significance of income covariates are in parentheses below the estimates. Ratios of female to male income effects are in the third column of each panel; χ^2 test statistics for equality of male and female effects are in parentheses below the ratios. By the Schwarz criterion, the critical value for χ^2s is 31.7.

The empirical model for nutrient demands is identical to that used in the previous section, except that the logarithms of nutrients are used as the dependent variables. Table 9.4 presents the estimated effects of nonlabor income and total income.

In the previous section, it was shown that, consistent with Engel's law, food shares decline with income. Food expenditures, however, increase, and the rate of increase depends on the distribution of income within the household. At the mean, for example, additional income in the hands of a woman is associated with about a 3 percent increase in food expenditures, whereas this effect is about 0.6 percent for men (and these differences are significant). Furthermore, as income (of men or women) is increased, the per capita consumption of both calories and protein increases. As with food expenditures, the marginal effect of additional income in the hands of women is significantly larger than the impact of an increase in male income. This is true for both nonlabor and total income. For calories, the income effects differ by a factor of between 9 and 11; for proteins, the ratio is between 5 and 6.

Higher nutrient intakes are likely to be associated with improved nutrition (at least in Brazil), and so these results suggest that women tend to allocate resources under their control toward foods that are associated with better health of household members. In the next section, this hypothesis is tested directly by estimating the effect of individual parental income on child anthropometric outcomes.

Child Anthropometrics

Among nutritionists, child height-for-age is considered to be a long-run measure of nutritional status and weight-for-height, a shorter-run indicator

(Waterlow et al. 1977). Parental education and, to a lesser extent, household income typically have a significant positive impact on both anthropometric outcomes, even after controlling for genetic endowment (Horton 1986; Behrman and Deolalikar 1988; Thomas, Strauss, and Henriques 1990). Child height is standardized by comparing it with the height of well-nourished children of the same age and gender in a reference population. The United States is used as the reference (National Center for Health Statistics 1976). In the regressions, height is expressed as a Z score (by removing the median and dividing by the standard deviation in the reference population). The height of the average urban child is almost one Z score below the U.S. standard. Weight, conditional on height, is similarly standardized: in contrast with the longer-run nutritional indicator, Brazilian children are on average only slightly lighter, given height, than their U.S. counterparts (see Table 9.2).

Because the analysis of anthropometric data is restricted to children less than 8 years old, relatively younger (and poorer) households are included in this level of data. Average income is about 20 percent lower than that in the sample used in the last two sections. Nonlabor income accounts for a smaller proportion of total income (17 percent), the father controls relatively more (80 percent), and the proportions of mothers and fathers reporting any income from nonwage sources are slightly smaller (14 percent and 34 percent, respectively).

The effects of parental income on anthropometric outcomes are reported in Table 9.5. Because the hypothesis that the income effects are linear is not rejected, only the linear terms are reported. In addition to income, the regressions include controls for the presence of parents, their education and state of residence, and the age and gender of the child.

In the previous two sections, it was found that as income attributed to women rose, expenditure shares on health, education, and nutrient intakes increased faster than when additional income accrued to men. The results here show that the same pattern carries through to child health. As household resources rise, child weight-for-height and height-for-age also increase; the rate of increase, however, is faster if the income is in the hands of the mother. The magnitude of the difference is substantial—around a factor of 8 for weight-for-height and half that for height-for-age—and it is significant in the case of weight-for-height. All these results are true for both nonlabor income and total income. Apparently, relative to paternal income, additional maternal income is associated not only with higher budget shares spent on health and education, as well as higher nutrient intakes, but also with improved child nutrition outcomes.

Role of Measurement Error

Thus far the fact that income may be measured with error (and nonlabor income may be endogenous) has been ignored. It is possible that all the results discussed previously may simply reflect differences in the extent of measurement

TABLE 9.5 Effects of male and female income on child anthropometric outcomes: linear model

	Nonlabor Income Ordinary Least Squares (OLS)			Total Income Two-Stage Least Squares (2SLS)		
	Female	Male	Difference	Female	Male	Difference
All children						
Z score						
Weight-for-height	0.0357	0.0045	0.0312	0.0329	0.0040	0.0289
	(3.2)	(2.2)	(2.7)	(3.2)	(2.1)	(2.8)
Height-for-age	0.0276	0.0065	0.0211	0.0255	0.0058	0.0197
	(2.3)	(2.8)	(1.7)	(2.3)	(2.8)	(1.7)
Gender-specific results						
Z score of weight-for-height						
Sons	0.0217	0.0081	0.0136	0.0204	0.0112	0.0092
	(1.8)	(2.8)	(1.1)	(2.5)	(5.0)	(1.3)
Daughters	0.1254	0.0007	0.1247	0.1172	0.0039	0.1133
	(4.2)	(0.2)	(4.1)	(4.2)	(0.1)	(4.7)
Differences	−0.1036	0.0074	0.1100	−0.0968	0.0073	−0.1041
	(3.2)	(1.8)	(3.4)	(3.2)	(1.9)	(3.3)
Z score of height-for-age						
Sons	0.0223	0.0079	0.0144	0.0206	0.0073	0.0133
	(1.7)	(2.4)	(1.0)	(2.9)	(6.0)	(1.4)
Daughters	0.0639	0.0051	0.0588	0.0590	0.0043	0.0547
	(2.0)	(1.6)	(1.8)	(1.9)	(1.5)	(1.8)
Differences	−0.0416	0.0028	−0.0444	−0.0384	0.0030	−0.0414
	(1.2)	(0.6)	(1.2)	(1.2)	(0.7)	(1.2)

NOTES: There are 26,538 observations in weight-for-height regressions and 26,670 in height-for-age regressions. *t*-Statistics are given in parentheses below income effects. F-statistics for equality of income effects appear below the ratios. In addition to parental income, regressions include presence of parents, their education, state of residence, and age and gender of the child.

error in male and female income (see Thomas [1990] for a discussion and some tests). For example, if the variance of male income is larger than that of female income, assuming that the extent of measurement error is proportional to the variance, estimates of male income effects would be expected to be biased downward more than those of female income effects. The evidence is consistent with this view: estimated female income effects are absolutely larger than the estimates for male income. However, the differences in the estimated income effects are very large for several outcomes and suggest measurement error that is 5 to 10 times larger for male income relative to female income. This possibility does not seem especially plausible.

To address concerns about measurement error directly, the estimated income effects on brothers and sisters are compared. As discussed previously, measurement error in parental income should not be related in any systematic manner to the characteristics of the children, including their gender. The lower panel of Table 9.5 presents income effects separately for sons and daughters.

For sons and daughters, maternal income effects are larger than paternal income effects, and the differences, given in the third column of each panel, are greater than zero. As discussed earlier, however, these differences may reflect measurement error in income or some other source of unobserved heterogeneity. Thus the impact of each parent's income on sons and daughters is compared next.

If the parent does not take gender into account when allocating resources to his or her children, income effects should be the same on sons and daughters. They are not. For example, maternal income has a significant impact on the weight-for-height of sons, but the impact on daughters is between five and six times larger. Mother's income also has a bigger effect on the height of daughters relative to sons. The difference in these income effects on sons and daughters is significant in the case of weight-for-height. Paternal income, on the other hand, has no impact on the anthropometric outcomes of daughters, yet it is associated with significantly higher height and weight-for-height of sons. But these differences are only marginally significant.

The fact that maternal income has a greater effect on daughters relative to sons, and paternal income has a greater effect on the health of sons, is prima facie evidence against the common preference model. To test explicitly whether the differential effects are significant, Table 9.5 reports the "difference-indifference" estimates in the bottom right corner of each block. For example, in the case of weight-for-height and total income, the 2SLS estimate is -0.1041 with a t-statistic of 3.3. The common preference model is unambiguously rejected; it is hard to resurrect the model by appealing to an argument based on measurement error.

These results are robust to the inclusion of household fixed effects, which amounts to comparing brothers with sisters. Similar results hold for the effect of parental education on child anthropometry: maternal education has a larger effect on the daughter relative to the son, whereas paternal education effects are larger on the son. (For more detail and further results, see Thomas [1994].) Finally, Thomas, Schoeni, and Strauss (1995) compare parental income effects on the educational attainment of sons and daughters, using a different survey from Brazil. They also reject the common preference model.

Intact Households and Two-Income Households

Table 9.6 reports estimates of all the demand functions based on subsamples of the data. The first sample is restricted to those households with both a male and a female present. (This reduces the sample by about a quarter in the

TABLE 9.6 Restricted samples: effects of income on demand, two-stage least squares, nonlabor income as instrument

	Households with Intact Couples as Male and Female Heads			Both Male and Female Heads Report Some Income		
	Female	Male	Ratio	Female	Male	Ratio
Shares						
Food	−188.35	−65.05	2.90	−210.35	−127.15	1.65
	(99.39)	(60.11)	(36.52)	(61.68)	(198.11)	(11.20)
Meals out	−20.43	−7.60	2.69	−37.77	−20.85	1.81
	(22.37)	(35.77)	(36.94)	(39.09)	(35.87)	(49.16)
Housing	80.76	13.66	5.91	133.14	25.46	5.23
	(12.02)	(10.95)	(7.40)	(22.40)	(15.87)	(22.07)
Human capital	86.76	20.41	4.25	88.52	42.15	2.10
	(34.90)	(30.10)	(30.09)	(31.57)	(49.63)	(6.54)
Education	4.61	3.48	1.33	2.10	4.71	0.44
	(14.01)	(6.74)	(8.79)	(14.75)	(7.38)	(8.93)
Health	22.54	8.02	2.81	22.60	19.35	1.17
	(11.85)	(23.46)	(18.90)	(13.73)	(20.04)	(17.01)
Household services	59.61	8.91	6.69	63.83	18.09	3.53
	(57.43)	(28.95)	(40.70)	(39.38)	(43.71)	(15.71)
Leisure	48.65	16.05	3.03	46.40	37.83	1.23
	(18.81)	(24.15)	(22.35)	(16.24)	(34.82)	(6.09)
Ceremonies	20.24	1.14	17.79	25.03	2.55	9.80
	(6.38)	(9.16)	(6.78)	(3.83)	(2.84)	(2.58)
Recreation	28.41	14.92	1.90	21.37	35.28	0.61
	(17.39)	(26.52)	(21.35)	(13.99)	(41.66)	(6.51)
Household goods	−10.15	3.30	−3.07	−26.18	2.86	−9.15
	(8.71)	(3.86)	(9.03)	(9.38)	(1.16)	(6.11)
Adult goods	−39.14	−10.51	3.72	−61.24	−27.11	2.26
	(15.24)	(20.40)	(5.05)	(14.75)	(23.80)	(4.36)
Nutrient intakes						
ln (calories per capita)	0.78	0.19	4.13	1.10	0.42	2.59
	(2.15)	(1.04)	(15.56)	(6.52)	(8.93)	(3.49)
ln (protein per capita)	2.48	0.68	3.67	3.65	1.16	3.14
	(2.31)	(0.90)	(20.21)	(37.45)	(39.73)	(10.71)
Child anthropometrics						
Weight-for-height	0.0237	0.0041	5.78	0.0269	0.0127	2.11
	(2.13)	(2.14)	(2.78)	(1.01)	(0.40)	(0.61)
Height-for-age	0.0255	0.0058	4.44	0.0032	0.0061	0.52
	(2.28)	(2.81)	(2.77)	(0.14)	(2.91)	(0.02)

NOTES: For shares and nutrient intakes, χ^2 test statistics are given in parentheses below estimated effects at mean (quadratic model) and below the ratios. There are 29,273 households in the sample of intact couples; the critical value of χ^2 for equality of effects is 30.9. There are 11,119 households in the sample of income recipients; the critical value of χ^2 is 27.9. For child anthropometrics, the t-statistic is given below the estimated effect (linear model) and the F-statistic is given below the ratios. There are 24,696 children in the sample of intact couples and 8,696 in the sample of income recipients.

share and nutrient demand functions and by about 10 percent in the sample of younger households, with at least one child less than eight used in the child anthropometric analyses.) The essential results are generally robust to this exclusion, although only those income effects on human capital (especially household services) and food shares (in and out of the home) remain significantly different for men and women (under the Schwarz criterion) in the case of the demand functions. The results for both child weight-for-height and height-for-age are also robust to the restriction.

The results are substantially different, however, if the sample is restricted to those households in which both the male and female heads report some income. Differences in the effects of income in the hands of men and women tend to be smaller and so the ratios of income effects are closer to one. For most shares this reflects (absolutely) larger effects of male income. In fact income effects are not significantly different for any of the commodities except food eaten away from the home (which accounts for less than 5 percent of the total budget). Furthermore the effects of male and female income on child anthropometrics are no longer significantly different, and the only significant income effect is that of the father on child height-for-age.

These results do not, however, have an unambiguous interpretation. It is not at all clear how to model the sample selection where attention is restricted only to those households in which both the male and female head report some income. It seems inappropriate, and certainly not in the spirit of the model described previously, to treat this characteristic as exogenous rather than the outcome of choices. What the evidence does indicate is that if attention is restricted to this subsample of households, then modeling their decisions as if the head and spouse share common preferences is consistent with the data. For all other households, however, the common preference model is apparently not appropriate. This suggests that the key to understanding household resource allocation may lie in a better understanding of household composition patterns along with labor supply decisions.

Conclusions

Most economic models treat the household as a black box. This chapter has attempted to delve into that box by examining household consumption and investment patterns. The impact of income has been analyzed, distinguishing income attributed to women from that attributed to men. Under a model of common preferences of all household members, dictatorial decisionmaking or (perfect) altruism, the distribution of income within the household should have no impact on demand. Using household survey data from Brazil, this model has been tested with both nonlabor income, which is assumed to be exogenous, and total (labor and nonlabor) income.

Under both definitions, this model is rejected. Income in the hands of women is associated with a larger increase in the share of the household budget devoted to human capital (household services, health, and education) and leisure goods (recreation and ceremonies). The proportion of the budget spent on food (consumed at home and away) declines more if the income is in the hands of women, although food composition also changes, with nutrient intakes rising faster as women's income increases. It appears that, as income under the control of women rises, more is spent on health- and nutrition-related expenses. The evidence on child health outcomes is consistent with this interpretation: maternal income has a significantly larger effect on the weight-for-height and height-for-age of children than paternal income.

All of these results may be explained either by differences in errors of measurement of male and female incomes or by unobserved heterogeneity. However, maternal income effects are significantly larger on daughters relative to sons—and paternal income effects are larger on sons. Thus it is difficult to explain these gender-specific results with an argument based on measurement error or unobserved heterogeneity, because their effects should be the same across sons and daughters.

When analysis is restricted to only those couples in which both members have some income, there is little evidence that income in the hands of men and women has significantly different effects on consumption and investment patterns. This is not, however, generally true. Rather, the evidence suggests that an economic model of the household that treats it as a single unified unit is not consistent with the data used here, at least when all households are examined. This does not mean that the unitary model is not useful: on the contrary, the economics and social science literatures have been substantially enriched by the insights provided by the model.

10 The Application of Anthropological Methods to the Study of Intrahousehold Resource Allocation

JOEL GITTELSOHN AND SANGEETA MOOKHERJI

The study of intrahousehold resource allocation is neither easy nor straight-forward. Much intrahousehold resource allocation occurs behind closed doors. Although behavior is usually measured through the use of recall methods, resource allocation is made up of many day-to-day activities; these mundane events prove challenging for individuals to recall accurately. Moreover, certain aspects may be considered private or sensitive information and therefore not amenable to investigation using traditional survey methods. Finally, intra-household resource allocation may be highly variable, with different patterns being observed within cultures and subcultural groups.

In this chapter we explore methods of examining intrahousehold resource allocation using conceptual frameworks, data collection techniques, and modes of analysis drawn from anthropology. We begin by aligning useful approaches found in the anthropological toolbox, and we then move to specific examples of situations in which these methods can be applied, including improvements in survey design, insight into appropriate community interventions, measurement of activity, and monitoring of change.

The Anthropological Toolbox

Traditionally the anthropologist's tools have been classified into two categories: quantitative and qualitative methods (Table 10.1). Quantitative methods are the primary mode of data collection for many social scientists. They are usually structured forms of data collection through which identical data are collected for a large number of randomly selected respondents. This information can be used to systematically describe communities, households, and individuals and to measure outcomes.

It is useful to describe (briefly) qualitative research, one of the hallmarks of anthropological inquiry, in order to distinguish it from quantitative research. Qualitative methods encompass both a set of techniques and an approach for conducting research. The techniques of qualitative research include key

TABLE 10.1 The anthropological toolbox

Characteristics of Communities, Households, and Individuals	What Goes on Inside People's Heads	What Goes on Inside People's Households	Outcome Measures
Surveys Direct observation	Key informant interviewing Focus groups Systematic data collection (free lists, pile sorts, triads, ranking, rating)	Participant observation Direct observation (unstructured and structured) Key informant interviewing (narrative accounts of past behavior)	Surveys

informant interviewing, different forms of systematic data collection (free lists, pile sorts, triads, ranking, rating), focus groups (and other group techniques), and the direct observation of behavior. The relatively open-ended nature and textual orientation of these techniques make them ideal for exploring beliefs and behaviors from the point of view of the people being studied.

Key informant interviews involve a series of repeated in-depth interviews with a small number of purposively selected "expert" informants. These are built around open-ended questions and emphasize building rapport and trust. This technique has many applications, but it is especially useful for determining the language of discourse surrounding a particular topic area, including those culturally defined categories (domains) of key importance from the local perspective.

Free listing is a structured data collection technique in which an informant is asked to list all the different items in a particular cultural domain (for example, all possible illnesses of children). These are tabulated to obtain a list of more "cognizant" items. Pile sorting is a structured data collection technique that elicits indigenous categories and groupings of domain items by asking informants to group a set of domain items either "freely" (according to what they think is important) or according to some predetermined criteria. Triad sorting is often used as an alternative to pile sorting, which can prove difficult for illiterate informants. In triad sorting, informants are presented with groups of three domain items at a time and are asked to identify the item that does not belong or is the most different for all possible triad combinations of items. Ranking requires informants to order domain items along a dimension determined by either the investigator or the informants, for example, "order household members according to relative respect and authority." No two items may share the same rank position. Rating requires respondents to order items along a predetermined and set number of steps, for instance, along a three-step continuum of low, medium, and high respect.

Focus groups are guided discussions within small groups of 6 to 12 people. Topical guides are utilized by a skilled moderator who stimulates discussions around areas of interest.

Direct observation provides records of actual behavior (as opposed to recalled behavior), including actions, conversations, and physical descriptions. Exact procedures and appropriate applications of these and other techniques have been described in a large number of books and articles (Pelto and Pelto 1978; Spradley 1979; Bernard et al. 1986; Scrimshaw and Hurtado 1987; Werner and Schoepfle 1987; Bernard 1988; Whyte 1991; Crabtree and Miller 1992; Gilgun, Daly, and Handell 1992; Morse 1992).

The qualitative research approach embodies four key concepts: flexibility, iteration, triangulation, and creation of context (Gittelsohn 1996). Flexibility requires that data collection methods be continually refined and modified throughout the research process, in order to explore new dimensions as they arise; instruments are not rigidly defined and implemented. Iteration, a concept closely linked to flexibility, refers to a process in which research topics are explored with increasing refinement and focus in successive stages of the data collection. Triangulation involves the use of several different data collection methods to address the same key research questions (Jick 1979). In addition, triangulation can help capture a more holistic, contextual portrayal of the beliefs or behaviors under study (Peshkin 1988).

Applications of Anthropological Methods to the Study of Intrahousehold Resource Allocation

The integration of qualitative and quantitative methods has led to the development of several approaches by anthropologists for examining intrahousehold resource allocation. These include the following:

1. identifying local concepts and terms related to resource allocation and learning their meaning from the insider's point of view;
2. exploring local perspectives on grouping and organizing household members and/or actual resources that are being allocated;
3. identifying local systems for the differential valuation of individuals and methods for measuring the impact of these systems;
4. directly observing resource allocation within the household;
5. modeling resource decisionmaking within the household; and
6. exploring change and determinants of change in intrahousehold allocation of resources.

The following sections address these approaches in turn, giving some background and offering suggestions for appropriate anthropological research methods.

Identifying Local Concepts and Terms

Anthropologists define two different ways of looking at human beliefs and behaviors: etically and emically. The concepts of "etic" and "emic" were first used by the linguist Kenneth Pike (1956) to describe language, and they were applied by Goodenough (1956) to other areas of culture. Although there is some debate about how the two terms should be applied, "etic" is used here to refer to the interpretation of human beliefs and behaviors from the outsider's (that is, the investigator's) perspective, whereas "emic" refers to the interpretation of beliefs and behaviors from the insider's (that is, the native's) point of view. Both perspectives are critical for the study of intrahousehold resource allocation. As Messer (1990:58–59) observes, "the native's emic household constructs and his/her cultural values, including gender ideologies, that lead to or limit options in residence, work, and resource distribution patterns, are as important for predicting project outcomes as are the social scientist's etic definitions."

As a first step in developing an understanding of what people consider meaningful, anthropologists concern themselves with language. Different languages create and express different realities and categorize experience in different ways.

The concept of the household is a good example of the discrepancy between etic and emic definitions. Local concepts of "household" often differ significantly from those of an outsider. Rogers (1990:9) notes that "any fixed definition of household can create arbitrary and possibly misleading distinctions." The set of etically derived terms developed by social scientists (for example, education, social status, and economic status) can rarely be directly applied to particular cultural contexts. Even within the discipline of anthropology, definitions of household are by no means standardized (Messer 1983). Bohannan (1963) classifies the household by the most fundamental kinship relationship it contains. Bender (1967:496) also observes that families are defined primarily in terms of kinship and that they are "kinship groups that must be defined strictly in terms of kinship relationships," but he goes on to define the household simply as a residence group that carries out domestic functions. Netting (1984:xxii) considers households as "a fundamental social unit . . . a primary arena for the expression of age and sex roles, kinship, socialization, and economic cooperation where the very stuff of culture is mediated and transformed into action."

From work in a variety of cultural settings, it appears that although households contain one or (usually) more features (coresidence, joint production, shared consumption, and kinship links), no particular single feature or combination of these features constitutes a universal definition of the household. The only definite point that can be made is that the concept of the household will vary from culture to culture and probably within cultures as well.

FIGURE 10.1 Nepali terminology and the concept of "household"

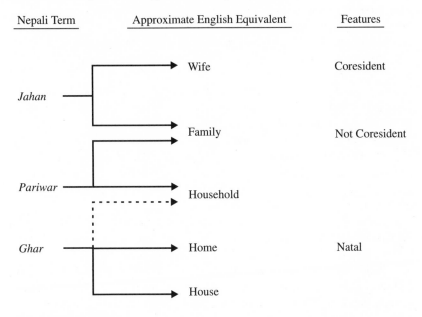

Nepali Term	Approximate English Equivalent	Features

SOURCE: Gittelsohn (1989).

Figure 10.1 illustrates this principle in the case of Nepal. In Nepali, at least three overlapping terms are commonly used to refer to the household, as etically defined: *jahan, pariwar,* and *ghar.* (There is undoubtedly a great deal of regional variation in the way these terms are applied within Nepal.) The term *pariwar* is commonly used to refer to a group of people, usually related through kinship ties, who live together and jointly produce and consume resources. However, *pariwar* is also used to refer to family who are not coresident within the same household but who still maintain kinship links to a joint household. The term *ghar* usually refers to the natal home of the individual, though it can also refer to the place where a group of people are currently living together and sharing resources. (It is also used to refer to dwellings in general.) *Jahan* can be used to indicate family (usually coresident), and it also serves as an endearing form of address for one's wife. Any effort to collect primary data on intrahousehold resource allocation in Nepal would have to take the emic meanings of these terms into account. Responses will vary according to the term used; for example, to a wife and mother *ghar* may indicate "natal home," a place with which she may not have had contact since her marriage. The particular term used may or may not be perceived to include absent members who either transfer resources into or receive transfers out of the household.

Another important concept that can vary according to the use of either emic or etic perspectives is the term "resource." In the literature on intrahousehold resource allocation, resources are of several key types: food, health care, labor supply, education, and material goods. In-depth investigation of the intrahousehold allocation of etically derived resource types usually reveals that these broad classifications poorly represent emic categories. For instance, health care may not be a clearly defined resource for allocation. Local people often have "styles" of health-seeking behavior that are differentially allocated to household members (for example, whether one should seek treatment for mild illnesses or wait to get treatment for serious illnesses) (Graham and Larme 1992). Many cultures distinguish at least two main types of food: a staple food (or foods) and side dishes (including condiments) that accompany them. These two types of food are subjected to different allocation patterns, often along gender, class, and age lines.

Some work in Nepal indicates very different patterns of distribution for the main staple foods (*daalbhat* or *roti*) versus side dishes and condiments (*taarkharis, achars, ghiu,* and so forth) (Gittelsohn 1989). Staple foods in most households were allocated in a fairly egalitarian manner, with individuals consuming as much as they wanted. However, special side dishes were frequently distributed only, or in relatively greater quantities, to favored household members, such as adult males. Local emic perceptions of "resources," therefore, can greatly affect actual allocation patterns and must be explored.

The term "allocation" also deserves attention. Allocation implies that one or more persons control distribution of food, health care, or other resources. In the case of food consumption, serving can be considered an "allocative" component of the intrahousehold allocation of food. But individuals often acquire food from household stores in a variety of different ways, including begging, stealing, and sharing. Should the concept of allocation incorporate these kinds of behaviors? More importantly, how do local people describe these patterns of acquisition?

The following methods can be used to explore emic perceptions and concepts affecting intrahousehold resource allocation:

1. Preliminary exploration through key informant interviewing can identify and determine the use of local terms and concepts relevant to the study of intrahousehold resource allocation. Some key terms to identify would include "household" or its nearest equivalent(s) and "resource types" (broken down into emically meaningful terms). Some possible key informant question formats would be the following: "What is the word for the place where a person and his or her spouse and children live together?" "What is the word for the group of people who eat together from the same pot/hearth/kitchen?" "What is the difference between a staple food and a side dish?"

2. Free listing may be employed to elicit lists of items within prominent conceptual domains generated through key informant interviewing (Weller and Romney 1988). For instance, a useful early free list question might be one of the following: "What are all the different side dishes that people eat here in the community?" "Within the household, what are all the different ways in which children get food?"

Exploring Local Perspectives on Resources Being Allocated

Understanding indigenous systems of classifying terms is important for several reasons. Indigenous models or systems of grouping elements are part of the underlying set of "rules" for intrahousehold resource allocation in a given cultural context.

In The Gambia, qualitative research was conducted on infant feeding in order to develop culturally acceptable weaning foods (Samba and Gittelsohn 1991). After identifying a list of foods commonly given to young children, mothers were asked to group pile sort cards (with small packets of the foods attached) according to their own choice. The results were analyzed using the ANTHROPAC computer program, and a multidimensional scale (MDS) was produced (Figure 10.2). Items that are physically proximate on the MDS were more likely to be sorted together in the same pile and were seen as similar by mothers. In Figure 10.2, foods for children are grouped on the left, with breast milk isolated from the other foods. Pap (*hondeh*), porridge or rice and groundnuts (*tigansombi*), and millet porridge (*bundunyeche*) were first described as "given to children" and then as "they are the same thing" by informants. Fish, meat, and sauce made from green leaves (*jamboo*) are distant from the other foods. Most mothers remarked that these foods "do not go together" with the other foods. This figure gives a useful approximation of how likely, in the local system, mothers are to add one of these distant foods to the weaning pap—information of particular interest to nutrition intervention projects. More generally, understanding how people think about and categorize their resources is a necessary precursor to understanding allocation patterns.

Anthropological methods useful in the examination of local grouping systems of key concepts and terms relating to intrahousehold resource allocation include the following:

1. Using key informant interviews to define cultural or semantic domains for key concepts as described by key informants in their own language (Spradley 1979; Weller and Romney 1988). These include terms for different categories of household members and resources, and subtypes of these categories.
2. Conducting free listing on randomly selected adult respondents ($N = $ 15–20) and asking them to name all the different kinds of people who will live together in the same household (terms determined from the previous

FIGURE 10.2 Multidimensional scale of pile sort data: foods commonly given to weaning-age children in Kulari village, The Gambia (*N* = 11 mothers)

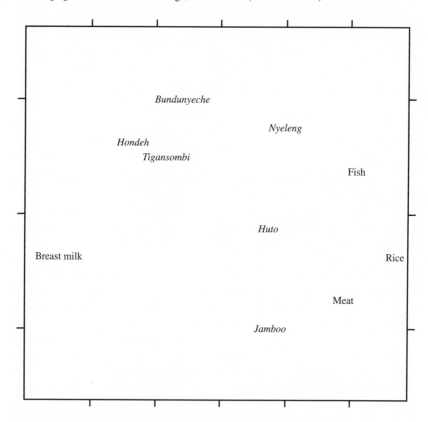

SOURCE: Samba and Gittelsohn (1991).

NOTE: Local terms are defined as follows: *bundunyeche,* porridge with groundnut sauce; *hondeh,* thick porridge or pap made with cereal flour; *huto,* boiled cereal grains with pounded raw groundnuts, dried fish, onions, or oil; *jamboo,* sauce of green leaves; *nyeleng,* steamed millet or sorghum grains; *tigansombi,* porridge or pounded rice and raw groundnuts.

step). This process should provide an extensive list of different types of people: husband, wife, grandfather, infant, and so forth.

3. After tabulating the results of the free list, selecting the subset of the most commonly mentioned household members and preparing a set of cards, each representing one household member. Have at least 10 respondents do pile sorts, placing associated cards together in one stack, to see how local people group different types of household members.

4. Repeating the process using local terms for different resources to determine local perspectives on grouping of these resources.

Identifying Local Systems for the Differential Valuation of Individuals

What is the impact of these cognitive elements on patterns of intra-household resource allocation? One approach is to emphasize the perceived present and future economic contribution of an individual (Gross and Underwood 1971; Chen, Huq, and D'Souza 1981; Katona-Apte 1983; Kumar 1983). However, individuals can be valued socially, religiously, and in many other ways apart from their economic contributions. In most developing countries, for instance, the elderly receive special access to food resources, although they may no longer be significant contributors to the household economy. In Nepal, the economic-benefit hypothesis would lead us to predict favoritism of boys, who remain with the household and become its main supporters during their adult years; however, no differences were observed in terms of favoritism between young girls and boys (Gittelsohn 1989). Thus understanding local systems for valuing individuals can be an important tool for predicting patterns and the outcomes of intrahousehold resource allocation and for predicting how changes in determinants of the valuation system might affect intrahousehold resource allocation.

The following methods can be used to explore the differential valuation of individuals:

1. Use key informant interviewing to identify main patterns and concepts associated with the valuation of individuals.
2. Using the same set of cards developed previously for looking at links between different types of household members, have another group of respondents order the cards by relative "importance" of the individual (or some similar cultural term, identified through key informant interviews). Obtain detailed qualitative explanations of these rankings.
3. Experiment with variations on the ranking technique to explore valuation systems that may affect resources, for example, food serving order or the likelihood of being taken to the clinic (for minor and serious illnesses).

Directly Observing Resource Allocation within the Household

Probably the most powerful method utilized by anthropologists for measuring actual behavior is direct observation. A number of recent reviews of the use of direct observation techniques have been published (Mulder and Caro 1985; Bentley et al. 1994). Observation techniques employed by social scientists range from unstructured data collection formats, such as participant observation and unstructured focused observation, to highly structured formats, such as spot-check observations (Paolisso and Regmi 1992) and ratings of observed features in the environment (for example, level of sanitation). Participant observation and unstructured focused observation provide a more subjective record of human behavior, whereas structured observations rely on the use of precoded behavioral categories and produce a quantifiable record that is amenable to statistical analysis. Natural variability in behavior and reactivity to the observer's presence are two factors that must be considered when conducting direct observation studies. The former refers to the problem of inferring behavior patterns from a limited number of observations, whereas reactivity refers to the concern that subjects might alter their behavior during an observation owing to the presence of the observer. Neither of these problems is simple to solve (Altman 1973; Mulder and Caro 1985; Martin and Bateson 1986; Bernard 1988). Preliminary observations of a small sample of households can provide information about when subjects cease to react to the observer (the reactivity threshold); more importantly, the nature of the subjects' behavioral variation should be noted during this process (Bentley et al. 1994).

Observational techniques such as continuous monitoring studies are well suited to the acquisition of information on public behavior. They can also be extended to other aspects of intrahousehold resource allocation (Stanton and Clemens 1987; Bentley et al. 1991a, 1991b; Gittelsohn 1991; Kaiser and Dewey 1991). These may focus on people (a target child), on locations (the kitchen), on events (the meal), or on some combination thereof. Observational methods are likely to be most productive for assessing resource allocation processes that occur relatively frequently (typically at least once per day), such as food preparation, consumption, and daily work activities. The allocation of other household resources is more difficult to observe because of its relative infrequency: people eat every day but may receive a new set of clothes only once a year.

Direct observational techniques useful in measuring intrahousehold resource allocation include the following:

1. Determining the relative frequency of occurrence of the type of resource allocation of interest through direct, unstructured focused observations in a small sample of households. This initial step presumes identification of important emic subcategories of resource types through previous key informant interviews.

2. Generating a list of potential key allocative behaviors through literature review, interviews with key informants, and unstructured observation of a sample of households. In the case of food, these might include encouraging an individual to eat, refusing to serve particular foods, or ignoring someone's request for food.

3. Identifying actors, locations, times, and events associated with the key allocative behaviors to permit effective targeting of observations.

4. Selecting an appropriate type of structured observation to conduct continuous monitoring, spot checks, or observation through a ratings checklist (see Bentley et al. [1994] for guidelines).

Modeling Resource Decisionmaking within the Household

A number of different systems have been proposed for describing the decisionmaking process (Acharya and Bennett 1983; Gladwin 1989). Decisionmaking is sometimes modeled on individuals alone, but it is also described as the result of interactions between household members (Piwoz and Viteri 1985). These interactions may take different forms, including negotiation, suggestion, and disagreement. Of course, a simple decision may merely involve an individual mentally reaffirming his perceptions about what constitutes appropriate behavior. In the "simple" day-to-day decisions of everyday life, this mental reaffirmation of the "rules" may be the only determinant of a particular allocative behavior. A woman serving food at dinner may give a larger share to her sons than to her daughters without going through any type of formal decisionmaking process. On the other hand, long-term goals such as saving for an upcoming wedding or preparing for a festival period can also affect apparently "simple" daily allocative decisions.

Anthropological methods can assist in developing decisionmaking models within the household by gathering data on the process of making decisions. Although a great deal of decision modeling is based on measuring outcomes, qualitative methods can be used to gather verbal data on the perceptions and values that help to produce these outcomes, as well as provide in-depth reporting (narratives) of past decisionmaking episodes. A method for developing decisionmaking models (from Gladwin 1989) is briefly outlined below:

1. Beginning with local emic categories for a key resource(s), and on the basis of participant observation and unstructured focused observations, identify those individuals in households most likely to be the primary allocators of a resource. These are those individuals who actually distribute the resource to the end receiver. In the case of food, this would be the food server.
2. Use iterative interviews with key informants (who should be the primary allocators) to develop a preliminary ethnographic decision-tree model. This takes the form of a "tree" with a series of yes-no questions arranged in a hierarchy.
3. Test this decision-tree model by having a different set of informants (also primary allocators) narrate their past decisions regarding allocation of the resource. Record errors (deviations) and revise the model if errors are numerous.

Exploring Determinants of Change in Intrahousehold Allocation of Resources

Neither households nor their internal patterns of distribution are static (Rogers 1990). Changes in household composition can have a profound effect on patterns of intrahousehold resource allocation. Research on intrahousehold food allocation in rural Nepal shows that meals at which the male head of household was present contained many more side dishes and condiments and were much more likely to contain elements of preferential food allocation (Gittelsohn 1989). Leonard's (1991) work in the Peruvian Andes indicates that the effects of seasonal changes in food availability were mitigated by changes in food allocation that favored young, nutritionally vulnerable children.

Anthropological methods for examining change and determinants of change in intrahousehold resource allocation include the following:

1. Ask small groups of informants to illustrate time and/or seasonal changes using locally available materials. On a single scale of seasons, men are asked to indicate the relative amount of time spent on different activities. This can be compared with a similar record of work patterns diagrammed by a group of women. Other patterns relating to allocative behavior, such as food availability by season, can also be investigated in this manner.

2. Using the local terms for resources and different household members (determined by the processes described earlier), select a unit of time for study. Relevant time units can be identified through key informant interviews. It may turn out, for example, that there are specific festival seasons that determine alternative patterns of resource allocation.

3. Sample several households within the community and conduct direct observations of the allocation of the resource(s) of concern. These observations should be conducted on different days of the week in the same household (if interested in weekly changes) or during different seasons (if interested in seasonal changes).

4. Analyze these data to detect differences in allocative patterns (for example, more food consumed in a more egalitarian manner on weekends). Cross-check observed changes in allocative behavior with key informants.

Discussion and Conclusions

One objective of this chapter has been to describe ways in which qualitative research can lay the foundation for more valid, reliable, and meaningful quantitative research. The use of ethnographic research methods for developing structured quantitative data collection instruments is gaining popularity (Coreil et al. 1989). However, no qualitative researcher likes to think that the sole purpose of his or her work is to lay the trail for the "real" research—the quantitative research. The other great strength of qualitative research lies in its ability to provide independent inputs into intervention design and implementation.

Typically, researchers are interested both in the policy implications of intrahousehold resource allocation and in developing effective interventions.

Interventions must be effective within household contexts. All too frequently, interventions fail because they did not address issues of time management, division of labor by sex, or some other relevant sociocultural feature that could be anticipated through in-depth qualitative research.

At the same time, limitations in using anthropological methods to investigate intrahousehold resource allocation should also be noted. Typically, qualitative information has not been incorporated effectively into predictive models; merging qualitative data into models of intrahousehold behavior for the purpose of predicting specific patterns of food allocation, for example, is an area in which more effort is needed. Qualitative research and, in particular, direct observation tend to be very time- and labor-intensive; efforts to make these data collection methods time- and cost-efficient are essential. In addition, more work is required to determine how qualitative data can be directly incorporated into the design of interventions seeking to modify intrahousehold resource allocation patterns.

It could be argued that health and nutritional status outcomes in individuals are cost-effective indicators of intrahousehold resource allocation patterns, so why look at intrahousehold behavior? However, in the long run, these indicators may not provide sufficient information for the development of effective interventions because the allocation functions inside the "black box" are either overlooked or inadequately described. The community, household, and individual characteristics that influence people's beliefs, attitudes, systems of valuation, and decisionmaking and determine behaviors are all critical proximate determinants of health outcomes.

Anthropological research can assist in the effective design, targeting, and evaluation of interventions in several ways. It aids in the design of interventions by identifying, describing, and working within local cultural models. Targeting of resources can also be improved using anthropological research. Knowledge of intrahousehold processes can permit interventions to target particular beliefs and behaviors as well as particular individuals. In the case of food allocation, at least three levels of behavior affect food intake: food selection at the household level, allocation within the household, and individual food preferences that determine consumption patterns. Anthropological research can indicate which of these levels is most amenable to change and offer insight on how to promote that change. Qualitative methods can also assist in effectively identifying vulnerable household members who should be targeted by the intervention.

Anthropological methods can be used to evaluate the effect of intrahousehold resource allocation patterns on health interventions. An intensive observational study of intrahousehold food allocation has been conducted to trace the flow of a supplemental food (Nutriatol, a vitamin A–rich gruel) through the household in Guatemala (Solomons and Barrows 1991). Researchers found that serving of Nutriatol was characterized by a distinct age and sex bias, with smaller children being discriminated against. In most households, Nutriatol was considered a "medicine" and rarely given to small children. This is an example of an intervention evaluation that occurs inside households, and of a result that would not have been obvious in an examination of outcomes only.

Although advances continue to be made in the case of anthropological methods to investigate intrahousehold resource allocation, there are still many gaps. In particular, anthropologists have not been successful in modeling intrahousehold behavior for the purpose of predicting patterns of allocation, or in incorporating qualitative data directly into these models. This is an area in which collaboration between anthropologists and economists may be particularly fruitful.

11 Inequality in the Intrafamily Distribution of Food: The Dilemma of Defining an Individual's "Fair Share"

HOWARTH E. BOUIS AND CHRISTINE L. PEÑA

If all individuals required identical amounts of nutrients regardless of age, gender, physiology, and activity pattern, and if all individuals had identical taste preferences and knowledge of their nutritional requirements, it would be relatively simple to measure inequality in the intrahousehold distribution of foods. That is, if all of these conditions were to hold, favoritism in the allocation of a particular food or nutrient reasonably could be determined using the following expression:

$$\frac{X_i \Big/ \sum_{i=1}^{n} X_i}{1/n}$$

where

n = the number of household members,

X_i = consumption by the ith household member of food or nutrient X,

and $\sum_{i=1}^{n} X_i$ = total household consumption of food or nutrient X.

In this example, $1/n$ may be interpreted as the index of an individual's "fair share" of household consumption.

Precisely because none of the foregoing conditions ever hold, it has proven difficult to define an empirically acceptable index (denominator). Most attempts to do so have used calorie intakes in the numerator, correcting each X_i by an individual-specific factor, say a_i, which corrects for differences in calorie requirements due to age, gender, weight, pregnancy or lactation, and activity patterns, depending on data availability (that is, nutrient intakes are expressed as adult equivalents).

As discussed later in this chapter, this generally is considered to be an unsatisfactory solution in that (1) recommended calorie intakes for these various criteria are still the subject of considerable debate, (2) some critical information (for example, activity patterns) is difficult to measure, and (3) once all relevant criteria are accurately taken into account, calorie adequacy in theory measures whether an individual is in energy balance (possibly at below average weight), which is not necessarily a measure of relative welfare.[1] Nevertheless, use of calorie intakes has the advantage that individuals know, to some extent, when their requirements are not being met (they experience hunger), and avoiding hunger is widely presumed to be of high priority to most individuals.[2]

We argue in this chapter that it is reasonable to assume that necessities are more equitably distributed within households than are luxuries. Therefore, calorie intake (a necessity) is a rather insensitive (and so inadequate) empirical measure of inequality, compared with consumption of foods with higher income elasticities (for example, nonstaple foods). However, this particular property of relative equity makes it a good candidate for use as an index to replace $1/n$ in the expression given earlier in deriving an alternative expression for measuring inequality in the intrahousehold allocation of food. This expression is then used to identify favoritism or discrimination in the intrahousehold distribution of food for a sample of rural households in Bukidnon, a southern province in the Philippines, and to examine various factors that influence the intrahousehold distribution of food.

In the following section we review the existing literature on intrahousehold distribution of food, focusing on the measure(s) of discrimination used. Next, food consumption patterns for the Bukidnon population at the household level are described, in particular how food consumption patterns change with increases in income. This provides an intuitive basis for presenting the proposed alternative indicator(s) of inequality. The next section applies the methodology to the Philippine data, which are disaggregated by nonstaple food groups and type of nutrient intake. Both a descriptive analysis and regression results are presented. This section is followed by concluding remarks.

---

1. In theory, if the calorie adequacy ratio is correctly measured and is chronically below 1.0, an adult is in deficit energy balance and will lose weight, with the opposite result if the calorie adequacy ratio is chronically above 1.0. Thus, other things being equal, an "overweight" adult may be eating more than an "underweight" adult but would have a calorie adequacy ratio lower than that of the underweight adult if the overweight adult were currently losing weight and the underweight adult were currently gaining weight. If both had stable weights, then both adults would have calorie adequacy ratios of 1.0. For children, in theory, calorie adequacy ratios measure energy intakes required to maintain "normal" growth, given the child's observed weight.

2. This similarity of preference for hunger satiation across cultures may be contrasted with the utility associated with any specific food or food group. A food may be highly prized in some societies and disliked in others. The awareness of shortfalls in consumption of calories (hunger) may be contrasted with, say, deficiencies in vitamin A or iron intakes.

Identifying Discrimination: Methodological Issues

Most studies of the intrafamily distribution of food rely either on anthro-pometric indicators such as weight-for-age and height-for-age, standardized by measurements from a healthy reference population, or measurements of diet adequacy, which assess the degree to which the nutrient intakes of individuals meet established requirements.[3] Both approaches pose problems. First, the use of anthropometry assumes that low weights and heights are primarily the result of poor nutrition. However, substandard growth can be attributed to factors other than undernourishment, such as unsanitary living conditions and in-adequate health care (Haaga and Mason 1987; Osmani 1990). Second, the reference population that serves as the basis for the "desired" physical measure-ments is assumed to be biologically representative of the population being studied (Ross 1992). Third, the anthropometric approach cannot take into account reduc-tion in levels of activity—another result of poor nutrition (Osmani 1990).

When evaluating the adequacy of energy intakes, it is important to control for differences in energy needs between individuals. However, a major prob-lem in comparing intake with requirements by age and gender is the lack of consistency in estimating requirements; such estimation processes are "contro-versial and undergoing constant revision" (Chen, Huq, and D'Souza 1981:61). Controversy exists in selecting which factors influencing energy needs should be incorporated into the calculation of recommended daily allowances (RDAs) and which factors can be safely ignored (Randolph et al. 1991). For example, failure to account for differences in activity patterns could result in a conclu-sion that some individuals are overnourished when, in fact, they are consuming the extra calories necessary to sustain themselves while doing heavy manual labor. As a result of variations in concepts of needs and adequacy criteria, as well as kinds of foods consumed in different cultures and countries, recommended RDAs in 41 countries differ substantially (Harriss 1990; Wheeler 1991).

Moreover, as mentioned in the previous section, even if no controversy existed as to how RDAs are to be calculated, in theory these RDAs for adults would measure intakes required to remain in energy balance. Thus it is possible that highly favored, higher-weight individuals would appear to be no better off than highly disfavored, lower-weight individuals, if both groups were in en-ergy balance. In fact, if disfavored individuals were in the process of gaining

---

3. See Haddad et al. (1995) for a comprehensive review of approaches and findings. Refer to Farmer and Tiefenthaler (1995) for an analytical approach to interpreting the findings of intrahousehold food distribution studies. Their work deals with a number of fairness concepts from the perspective of parents that may lead to different food allocation outcomes. They point out that although the focus has been on investment strategies (Rosenzweig and Schultz 1982) such that parents allocate more resources to children who can contribute more to family income, parents may also decide to give more food to the child with the greatest nutritional need, or they may distribute food equally regardless of need.

weight, their higher calorie adequacy ratios might make them appear to be better off than favored individuals.

A Measure of an Individual's "Fair Share" of Food

Food Consumption Patterns at the Household Level

In order to provide an intuitive basis for an alternative measure of discrimination in intrahousehold food distribution, it is instructive to examine how food consumption patterns change at the household level as income increases. Table 11.1 presents per capita food expenditures, price paid per kilogram, and per capita kilogram consumption by expenditure quintile for 11 food groups in the rural Philippines. The data were collected from four rounds of interviews at four-month intervals, using 24-hour dietary recall information.[4] Note that, at the margin, as income and food expenditures increase, consumers buy beverages, dairy products, legumes, and meats in large quantities. Combined expenditures for primary food staples (corn and rice) and vegetables increase with income, but the percentage increases are far smaller than those for the other food groups.

Table 11.2 disaggregates per capita calorie intakes by the same 11 food groups. Calorie consumption from corn and rice combined is nearly constant across expenditure quintiles. As income increases, marginal increases in calorie intakes come from nonstaple sources. At very low levels of income, food consumption choices are driven by the need for inexpensive sources of energy (corn and rice) and variety (vegetables). Even for this low-income population, marginal utilities derived from additional energy and variety apparently have diminished to the point that taste considerations for individual foods influence consumption decisions at the margin as income increases.[5] (In particular, desire exists for more beverages, dairy products, and meats in the diet.)

Identifying Discrimination: An Alternative Measure

The data in Tables 11.1 and 11.2 on food expenditures and calorie intakes can be used to illustrate the derivation of the proposed formula for measuring inequality in intrahousehold food distribution. Suppose that the data in these

---

4. These food-recall data are used because they provide a more accurate reflection of actual food intakes than do food expenditures (Bouis and Haddad 1992). These households were surveyed during 1984 and 1985. A wide range of data was collected, including information on landholdings, income sources, expenditure patterns, food intakes, time allocation, and heights and weights. The analysis to follow utilizes data from 448 households, which were present for all survey rounds, in particular the 24-hour recalls of individual food intakes conducted in each round. See Bouis and Haddad (1990) for a more detailed description of the survey site and data collection methodology and Bouis, Haddad, and Kennedy (1992) for a discussion of how the 24-hour recalls of food intakes were conducted.

5. See Bouis (1996) for a more comprehensive discussion of this point.

TABLE 11.1 Food expenditures, food prices, and kilograms consumed, by expenditure quintile and food group

| Food Group | Expenditure Quintile | | | | | | Quintile 5/ Quintile 1 | Quintile 4/ Quintile 2 |
	1	2	3	4	5	All		
Food expenditures (pesos per capita per week)								
Corn	9.05	9.35	8.86	8.46	4.26	8.00	0.47	0.90
Rice	2.12	3.58	4.52	4.48	9.61	4.86	4.53	1.25
Beverages	0.26	1.76	4.23	6.83	9.83	4.58	37.81	3.88
Dairy products	0.05	0.07	0.14	0.24	1.26	0.35	25.20	3.43
Fruits	0.18	0.16	0.26	0.30	0.33	0.25	1.83	1.88
Meats	6.51	8.18	10.03	14.75	20.40	11.97	3.13	1.80
Green leafy vegetables	1.51	1.58	2.14	1.85	1.66	1.75	1.10	1.17
Legumes	0.18	0.33	0.37	0.49	0.99	0.47	5.50	1.48
Other vegetables	1.04	1.20	1.32	1.87	2.01	1.49	1.93	1.56
Cooking ingredients	1.98	3.12	3.34	4.63	4.62	3.54	2.33	1.48
Other foods	1.60	2.08	2.05	2.97	4.48	2.64	2.80	1.43
All	24.50	31.41	37.29	46.88	59.46	39.90	2.43	1.49
Food prices (pesos per kilogram)								
Corn	4.41	4.52	4.50	4.49	4.50	4.48	1.02	0.99
Rice	5.72	5.97	5.80	5.67	5.64	5.74	0.99	0.95
Beverages	82.42	65.22	105.26	112.78	110.81	102.62	1.34	1.73
Dairy products	37.76	45.70	36.93	41.95	43.77	42.44	1.16	0.92
Fruits	4.69	3.67	3.79	4.44	6.05	4.60	1.29	1.21
Meats	20.33	21.27	22.14	23.13	23.76	22.26	1.17	1.09
Green leafy vegetables	11.54	10.81	11.51	11.27	11.23	11.28	0.97	1.04
Legumes	9.40	12.70	12.03	11.03	12.35	11.77	1.31	0.87
Other vegetables	4.52	4.07	4.57	4.55	4.69	4.49	1.04	1.12
Cooking ingredients	15.25	17.46	17.68	19.31	19.22	17.84	1.26	1.11
Other foods	3.42	4.67	3.68	5.57	7.52	5.15	2.20	1.19
All	6.12	6.73	7.40	8.39	10.15	7.76	1.66	1.25
Kilograms (per capita per week)								
Corn	2.09	2.07	1.97	1.91	0.96	1.80	0.46	0.92
Rice	0.37	0.60	0.79	0.79	1.72	0.85	4.65	1.32
Beverages	0.01	0.04	0.06	0.08	0.22	0.08	22.00	2.00
Dairy products	0.00	0.00	0.00	0.01	0.03	0.01	23.07	5.00
Fruits	0.05	0.06	0.07	0.08	0.05	0.06	1.00	1.33
Meats	0.32	0.43	0.47	0.70	0.86	0.55	2.69	1.63
Green leafy vegetables	0.16	0.16	0.20	0.20	0.17	0.18	1.06	1.25
Legumes	0.02	0.03	0.04	0.05	0.08	0.04	4.00	1.67
Other vegetables	0.24	0.34	0.28	0.43	0.45	0.35	1.88	1.26
Cooking ingredients	0.12	0.14	0.17	0.22	0.22	0.17	1.83	1.57
Other foods	0.73	0.82	0.95	0.98	1.03	0.90	1.41	1.20
All	4.11	4.68	5.00	5.43	5.79	5.00	1.41	1.16

SOURCE: International Food Policy Research Institute/Research Institute for Mindanao Culture Survey, 1984/85.

NOTE: Food prices are taken from the food expenditure survey; food quantities are taken from the 24-hour recall of food intakes; food expenditures are computed from these quantity and price data.

TABLE 11.2 Calorie intakes per adult equivalent and calories purchased per peso of expenditure, by expenditure quintile and food group

Food Group	Expenditure Quintile					Quintile 5– Quintile 1
	1	2	3	4	5	
Calorie intakes[a]						
Corn	1,501	1,469	1,372	1,317	659	−842
Rice	252	388	511	489	1,111	+859
Beverages	2	6	11	15	33	+ 31
Dairy products	1	1	3	4	19	+ 18
Fruits	5	8	9	7	6	+ 1
Meats	77	98	109	149	218	+141
Green leafy vegetables	15	14	17	17	15	0
Legumes	10	19	22	25	46	+ 36
Other vegetables	15	21	18	25	24	+ 9
Cooking ingredients	61	81	97	143	178	+117
Other foods	150	163	191	207	253	+103
Corn and rice	1,753	1,857	1,883	1,806	1,770	+ 17
All others	336	411	478	592	791	+455
All	2,089	2,268	2,361	2,398	2,561	+472
Calories purchased (per peso)[b]						
Corn	872	846	858	858	847	. . .
Rice	570	563	582	570	604	. . .
Beverages	126	80	102	67	71	. . .
Dairy products	121	83	115	91	94	. . .
Fruits	350	265	334	224	164	. . .
Meats	71	69	63	61	56	. . .
Green leafy vegetables	61	61	58	60	55	. . .
Legumes	474	346	358	321	304	. . .
Other vegetables	117	122	102	99	80	. . .
Cooking ingredients	145	171	180	214	268	. . .
Other foods	612	511	553	474	418	. . .
All	492	441	414	344	286	. . .

SOURCE: International Food Policy Research Institute/Research Institute for Mindanao Culture Survey, 1984/85.

NOTE: . . ., not important or easily interpretable.

[a]Calories are computed from the 24-hour recall survey.

[b]Calorie information is taken from the 24-hour recall survey; price information is taken from the food expenditure survey.

two tables, presented by expenditure quintile, represent, instead, individual food consumption information for a five-member household in which food consumption is highly skewed. That is, this hypothetical household spends 40 pesos per capita per week for food, on average, with 60 pesos being spent on the most highly favored member and only 25 pesos being spent on the least favored member.

Assume that, given this distribution of total expenditures (designated, say, by household member 5, who is the recognized decisionmaker), each individual member is allowed the freedom to allocate her own total food expenditure as she wishes among various individual foods. Whatever food allocation decisions are subsequently made by individual members might be termed Pareto optimal, in the sense that whatever allocation each chooses maximizes her own individual utility without affecting the utility of other household members.

Assuming that the preferences of these individuals reflect those of the Philippine sample population (and, by extension, other poor populations as well), household member 5 will choose a diet that is beverage-, dairy-, and meat-intensive relative to household member 1, whose diet will be relatively staple-intensive. Member 1 will not choose to spend her 25 pesos in the same proportion on individual foods as household member 5, simply because satisfying hunger will take precedence over the tastes of more preferred foods. These allocation outcomes can be modeled in terms of a lexicographic utility function (Encarnacion 1990), in which satiation of hunger is given top priority, or in terms of a marginal utility curve that is quite steep (relative to marginal utility curves for other goods or characteristics) up to a certain level of satiation and then abruptly levels off as if "kinked." It is the cruel decisionmaker, indeed, who will not allow individual household members to satisfy hunger first (to the extent possible within a given individual's budget constraint) before satisfying other wants.

The linking of the assumptions of individual Pareto optimality (as just defined) and the primal desire for hunger satiation leads to a conclusion that among the most equitably distributed commodities within households will be those that can least expensively satiate hunger. Consequently, hunger satiation (which will be highly correlated with staple food consumption, calorie intakes, and body weights) will be one of the *least* sensitive empirical indicators of discrimination in the intrahousehold distribution of resources. Foods, nutrients, or even nonfoods with high income elasticities should provide much more sensitive measures of such discrimination.

The measure of inequality in the intrahousehold distribution of food presented here uses a presumption of *relative* equality in hunger satiation across individual household members as the basis for calculating an index for what would be an individual's "fair share" in the consumption of nonstaple foods. This measure is given by

$$R_i = \frac{X_i \Big/ \sum_{i=1}^{n} X_i}{C_i \Big/ \sum_{i=1}^{n} C_i}$$

where

X_i = consumption by individual i of food or nutrient X, where X_i is
　　　measured in kilograms, units of a nutrient, or total expenditures;

C_i = calorie intake of individual i;

$\displaystyle\sum_{i=1}^{n} X_i$ 　 = total household consumption of X; and

$\displaystyle\sum_{i=1}^{n} C_i$ 　 = total household calorie intake.

The denominator is the proportion of total household calories that an individual consumes. It takes account of interindividual differences (within a specific household) in metabolic rates, heights, activity patterns, and physiological status (pregnancy, breast-feeding), so that persons who require more calories than other family members to satiate hunger for these reasons receive a higher proportion of household calories.[6]

The numerator is the individual proportion out of total household consumption of any specific food or nutrient. For favored persons in a family, the ratios of food share to energy share (FS/ES) will be greater than 1.0 for "preferred" foods (foods with relatively high income elasticities).

Empirical Application and Analysis

Descriptive Analysis

The Philippine data described earlier are used to calculate FS/ES ratios for nine food groups. Mean individual food intakes, based on 24-hour recalls by mothers across four rounds, were used to minimize intraindividual variations in food consumption (USDA 1986; Behrman 1988a). The results are graphed in Figure 11.1. The ratios shown in Figure 11.1 and the ratios used in the regression analysis use kilogram shares in the numerator.

---

6. However, there are some economies of scale in calories needed for maintaining body weights. Other things being equal, an adult weighing 10 percent more requires fewer than 10 percent more calories to maintain that weight; returns to scale for young children are more nearly constant (FAO/WHO/UNU 1985; see Bouis [1994] for a discussion). Thus some downward revision of adult calorie proportions may be advisable relative to child proportions.

Figure 11.1 indicates that preschoolers are highly favored in the intra-household distribution of food.[7] For six out of nine food groups (the exceptions are legumes and vegetables), preschoolers have among the highest ratios. Generally, the opposite is true for parents, who have among the lowest ratios for most of the food groups, although among the highest ratios for legumes and vegetables. By contrast, using calorie adequacy ratios unadjusted for individual weights or activity patterns for this same population, Bouis and Haddad (1990) concluded that adults were favored in the intrahousehold distribution of food.

FS/ES ratios for sons and daughters 6–19 years old typically fall between the preschooler and adult ratios. Not unexpectedly, ratios for younger children in this age range look somewhat similar to those of their even younger siblings, and ratios of older adolescents look somewhat similar to those of their parents. Adolescents receive among the highest shares of legumes and other vegetables and the lowest shares of cooking ingredients, beverages, meats, and dairy products.

The intrahousehold distribution of dairy products is particularly skewed in favor of preschoolers; the distribution of meats is relatively even. Above the age of 14, female ratios tend to be higher than male ratios for several food groups, particularly fruits and vegetables, although this does not come out as statistically significant in regression analysis.

Does inequality in food distribution translate into unequal nutrient distribution? This is addressed by calculating FS/ES nutrient ratios for all five age groups. Results are presented in Figure 11.2.

A comparison of Figure 11.2 with Figure 11.1 suggests that the distribution of nutrients is more equal than the distribution of foods. This is explained by the interaction of two patterns: (1) each age-gender group has a high FS/ES ratio for at least one food group and (2) nutrients are relatively well distributed across food groups. For example, parental shares of dairy products and cooking ingredients are relatively low, but parental shares are high for green, leafy vegetables, which are rich in several micronutrients.

Protein, iron, niacin, riboflavin, and thiamine are remarkably evenly distributed, although this is coincidental, as it is unlikely that respondents were aware of the nutrient content, other than calories, of the foods being consumed. The high ratios for calcium and retinol for preschoolers are a consequence of their high dairy and meat shares. The higher ratios for vitamins A and C for adults (in particular for mothers) are a consequence of their high green, leafy vegetable and fruit shares.

It is very important to note that equity in FS/ES nutrient shares does not in any way take into account nutrient requirements. For example, iron requirements

---

7. All breast-feeding children were excluded from the calculations and analyses.

FIGURE 11.1 Deviations from 1.0 of proportions of nonstaples over proportions of calories, by food group and type of household member

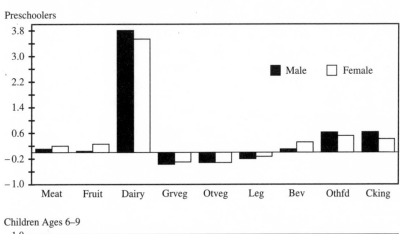

Preschoolers

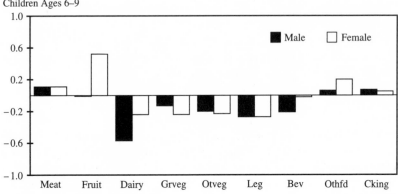

Children Ages 6–9

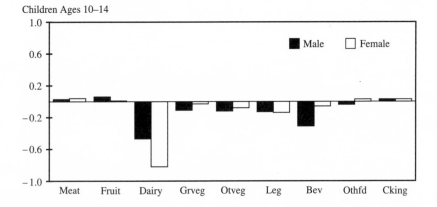

Children Ages 10–14

FIGURE 11.1 (*continued*)

Children Ages 15–19

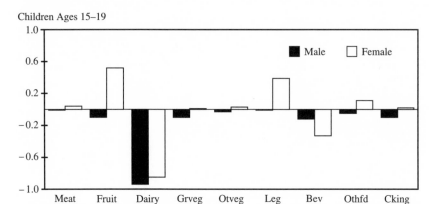

Parents

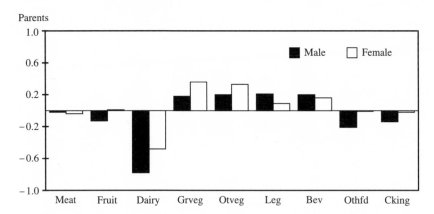

SOURCE: International Food Policy Research Institute/Research Institute for Mindanao Culture Survey, 1984/85.

NOTE: Abbreviations are as follows: Grveg, green, leafy vegetables; Otveg, other vegetables; Leg, legumes; Bev, beverages; Othfd, other foods; Cking, cooking ingredients.

for adolescent girls and adult women are approximately twice as high as those for their male counterparts. For this population, iron adequacy is twice as high for fathers as for mothers.

Regression Analysis

Do particular household or individual characteristics influence the intra-household distribution of food? To address this question, regressions were run with access to resources (proxied by the value of household assets), parental education, nutritional knowledge of the mother, age, gender, and household

FIGURE 11.2 Deviations from 1.0 of proportions of nutrient intakes over proportions of calorie intakes, by type of nutrient and household member

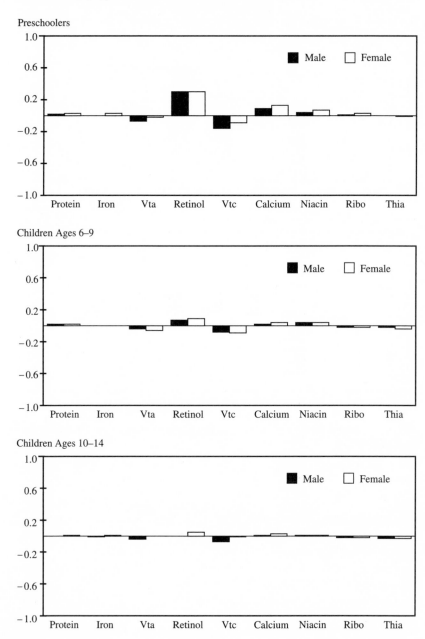

Preschoolers

Children Ages 6–9

Children Ages 10–14

FIGURE 11.2 (*continued*)

Children Ages 15–19

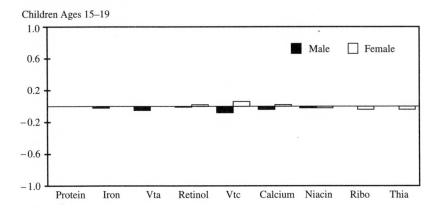

Parents

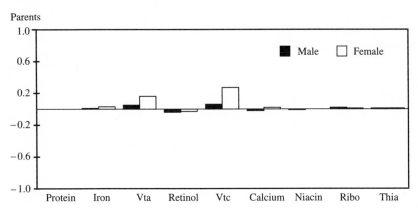

SOURCE: International Food Policy Research Institute/Research Institute for Mindanao Culture Survey, 1984/85.

NOTE: Abbreviations are as follows: Vta, vitamin A; Vtc, vitamin C; Ribo, riboflavin; Thia, thiamine.

size as regressors and the FS/ES ratio for each food group as the dependent variable.[8] The sample was divided into four groups: fathers, mothers, preschoolers, and older children and adolescents (the 6- to 19-year-old age group). Separate ordinary least squares regressions were run for each group. Details of these results are available from the authors upon request.

---

8. All of these regressors are treated as exogenous in the short-run allocation of household resources. This approach permits use of ordinary least squares. The value of household assets is positively correlated with household income and per capita expenditures.

The only evidence that asset value has an effect on redistribution of food among types of household members is the positive effect on the share of dairy products for preschoolers and older children. (Dairy products have a very high income elasticity, one that is highly skewed in favor of preschoolers even at low asset values.) In the Philippine setting, it may be that parents from asset-poor households would like to provide children with more dairy products but are inclined to express their favoritism more fully toward children (inequality rises) only at higher levels of absolute food consumption for all household members associated with greater value of asset holdings.

There is no evidence that a mother's years in school affect redistribution of food among types of household members. However, greater nutritional knowledge of mothers is associated with less vegetable consumption among preschoolers and older children and greater vegetable consumption for the parents. Years in school for the father are associated positively with increases in his own consumption of meats, vegetables, and beverages. This is at the cost of the meat and beverage consumption of preschoolers and the vegetable consumption of older children.

Larger household size appears to result in some loss of status for older children, who eat relatively less meat and dairy products (high income elasticity) and more vegetables (low income elasticity). Possibly these older children receive less parental attention and are forced to fend for themselves more. Fathers in large households receive proportionately more vegetables. The vegetable shares of preschoolers decline.

Shares of vegetables increase with age and shares of cooking ingredients decline with age throughout childhood and adolescence. All gender dummy variables are statistically insignificant for children. However, in combined mother-father samples, the gender dummy variable for mothers was positive and significant for vegetables, fruits, cooking ingredients, and other foods.

Conclusions

A new measure of inequality in intrahousehold distribution of food has been proposed, based on a presumption that satiation of hunger (energy consumption) is more equitably distributed among household members relative to other foods and nutrients. A related presumption is that where favoritism or discrimination occurs it will be manifested more strongly in terms of how nonstaple foods (in particular, those that have high income elasticities) are distributed.

Application of this measure of inequality to a Philippine data set indicates that preschoolers are favored in the intrahousehold distribution of food, a conclusion different from that reached by comparing only energy adequacy levels, both uncorrected (Bouis and Haddad 1990) and corrected for individual weights and activity patterns (Haddad, Kanbur, and Bouis 1992a), as well as results obtained by Peña (1996) using actual cost of daily diet less cost of diet if only the cheapest calorie source (corn) had been consumed. Even though preschoolers have diets preferable (in a nonnutrient sense) to those of other age and gender groups, the latter are compensated by greater proportions of less-preferred foods. Consequently, nutrients were relatively evenly distributed among various age and gender groups. However, it is again stressed that equity in nutrient shares does not imply equity relative to individual requirements.

Most previous food-based studies of inequality have used energy intakes, which are highly correlated with staple food consumption, as a basis for measuring "fairness" in the intrahousehold distribution of resources. This chapter argues that calorie intakes are a poor indicator of inequality in that necessities can be expected to be more fairly distributed than luxuries.

12 Gender Bias in Intrahousehold Nutrition in South India: Unpacking Households and the Policy Process

BARBARA HARRISS-WHITE

Public policy discourse has placed increasing confidence in the capacity of states to target individuals (Drèze and Sen 1989; World Bank 1990). This process of agenda formation has been accompanied by the development of theoretical models of the internal economic and power relations of households (see Pitt, Chapter 2, and Bruce and Lloyd, Chapter 13, this volume). At the same time, budgets for state welfare (especially for health, education, food, and antipoverty policy) have been on the decline in real per capita terms in many underdeveloped countries. Targeting is, therefore, increasingly invoked as the means of delivery of such welfare and development policies. These political and theoretical developments are likely to be no historical coincidence.

If the demand for more individual-specific welfare data is a fairly recent phenomenon, the generation of certain kinds of empirical data (including nutrition information) about individual household members has a long and distinguished academic history.

This chapter is concerned with the sensitivity of policy recommendations to statistical methodologies employed in analysis—particularly when the analysis is of individual-level data. Specifically, I deconstruct, compare, and contrast the analytical means whereby five studies using the same Indian database on the nutrition of individuals have given rise to different policy-relevant conclusions and recommendations. One of these studies is my own, and I try to apply the same critical standards to my methods as to those of others. Though the purpose is simple, the discussion is less so. In particular, it highlights the issue of the contrast between deductive and inductive approaches to policy-relevant analysis. The chapter is ordered so as to systematize the presentation of the substantive results of each study in the order in which the studies first appeared (irrespective of their final publication dates), before drawing out general issues and methodological comparisons and contrasts.

Measuring Individual Nutrition within the Household

Individual nutrition is measured in three different ways. One, clinical signs and symptoms, will not concern us here (see Harriss 1991). The others, nutrients consumption and anthropometric status, are both extremely hard to measure accurately and to interpret.

Nutrients consumption is considered an input into health production functions (see Behrman 1988b), although one nutrient, energy, is a key dietary constraint and is usually correlated with the other nutrients. To measure nutrients consumption, it is necessary to have (seasonal) on-site observations of "normal" food consumption behavior over a stipulated period of time. Feast days and fast days (of special interest to anthropologists studying the symbolic content of food) are regarded by nutritionists as abnormal elements of the food cycle. Food allocations may be assessed by recall (typically over 24 hours, and preferably for seasonal sets of 24 hours). The method may involve direct weighing before consumption or the copying by the researcher of portions (raw or cooked) using standardized estimates of the weights of known volumes. Error may creep in through omissions (snacking, meals taken out of the household, breast milk, extraordinary food events) and commissions (in the conversion factors between raw and cooked ingredients, in the measurement of portions, in the classification of ingredients, in digestibility). There is widely alleged to be a trade-off between efforts to obtain high precision and modifications to behavior on account of being observed (Abdullah 1983).

Finally, the "adequacy" of nutrients consumption is interpreted in relation to estimates of needs that are controversial (Pacey and Payne 1984). Nutrients requirements are based on averages estimated for populations, usually corrected for body weight, sex, activity, age, and certain physiological states such as pregnancy and lactation. Requirements at the individual level are difficult to assess owing to substantial interindividual variability. Thus nutrients requirements based on averages for populations are abused by the user if applied to individuals. For example, half of a normally distributed population will have a less than average calorie (or any other nutrient) "requirement." The controversial notion of metabolic adaptation (the concept that the human body may have the capacity benignly to regulate the efficiency with which energy is metabolized over a range of intakes) casts further doubt over the analytical value of the "requirement." And the notion of a requirement must be distinguished from that of a recommended daily allowance (RDA), which is set somewhere (usually two standard deviations) above average to account for people whose requirement exceeds the average, except in the case of energy, for which the average is used.

Anthropometric status indicators are the "health product" in a health production function approach to the household. Weight, height, and age are all surprisingly hard to measure accurately, and by themselves they cannot tell us if there is failure in the equity of household food distribution, because they are the summary outcome of the interaction between food intake and infection. Infections within the first 24 months have consequences for height trajectories, in particular growth deviations, which are now thought to be irreversible (Payne 1994).

Heights and weights must be compared with standards to improve their interpretation. Local standards that are disaggregated by gender and derived from populations in which there is gender bias will lead to underestimates of gender bias. Height deficits relative to standards are often interpreted as indicators of chronic disadvantage, though they may be more accurately attributed to disadvantage in infancy. Weight deficits in relation to height or age are interpreted as signifying more acute conditions. However, states of deficit are not of global significance; the same degree of deficit does not necessarily imply the same risk levels across different ethnic groups (Pacey and Payne 1984).

The ICRISAT Database

The data collected under the auspices of the International Crops Research Institute for the Semi-Arid Tropics (ICRISAT) cover some 1,200 individuals of all ages (except wholly breast-fed babies) from 240 households in six villages from four agroclimatically different regions of the semi-arid tropics of India. Forty households were selected in each village. Ten households were randomly selected from each class: agricultural labor and small, medium, and large cultivator classes. Village-level differences in agrarian structure mean that the sampling fraction varies in every stratum.

The data on food intake (24-hour recall), anthropometric status, and clinical signs and symptoms were obtained over an unexceptional time period, spaced approximately every 3–4 months, over a time span of 16 months between September 1976 and January 1978. The accuracy of these data was improved by using standardized cooking and storage containers. Dietary data were converted into values for 10 nutrients. Whole-household anthropometric data and clinical symptoms were also collected by a nutritionally and medically trained medical team (Ryan et al. 1984:6–16, 25). ICRISAT has subsequently and generously made publicly available these data, which have been used in various policy-relevant ways. After discussing the original research, I will examine the four later studies of the ICRISAT data.

Ryan et al. (1984)

ICRISAT's original research did not set out (as did later research) to test a deductive theoretical model, or indeed any specific hypotheses about intrahousehold allocation. Its concern with individual nutrition was addressed to three practical and general issues relevant to the conduct and objectives of agricultural research. The first was the most specifically formulated: to test the correctness of the decision to prioritize yield stability at the expense of protein quality as a plant breeding objective (a decision made in the light of metabolic research showing that dietary energy was the limiting nutritional factor for health). The second goal was to examine the effects of the extreme seasonality of the semi-arid tropics on nutritional status (in the light of evidence showing the conjuncture of morbidity, vital reproductive events, low food stocks and consumption, and maximum energy expenditure, particularly among the poor [Chambers, Longhurst, and Pacey 1981; Lipton 1983]). The third objective was to explain individual nutritional status, at different aggregative scales relevant to policy emphases on production or distribution, as a function of agroclimatic region, socioeconomic status, household characteristics, and individual demographic detail.

With regard to the first objective, the research confirmed that proteins or essential amino acids were not the limiting nutrients in semi-arid tropical diets (Ryan et al. 1984:25–26), thereby vindicating the research priorities of breeders. It is the second and third objectives that are more relevant to subsequent work on intrahousehold allocation. Seasonal analysis used nutrient data aggregated into lean (mostly monsoon) and surplus (hot or cold, but dry) seasons based on the agricultural calendar and disaggregated variously by village, by age group (1–12 years, 13–18 years, and above), and by gender. These groups were also repooled in a variety of ways. The key finding with respect to seasonality was that little relationship was found between energy intake and village-specific agricultural seasons. It was concluded that nutritional seasonality in the semi-arid tropics was not so marked that the increased human energy requirements of high-yielding variety dryland crops would have deleterious effects on welfare. Moreover, there was no marked seasonal effect on the nutrient intakes of children. The 13- to 18-year-old age group experienced most "seasonal deprivation" of both protein and energy (relative to other age-sex groups), regardless of gender.

The characteristics of villages were found to be major determinants of the nutritional status of their inhabitants, but in ways that are counterintuitive. The ICRISAT study suggests that the more risky the agroclimatic and socioeconomic setting of a village, the less likely are the chances of finding individuals with hard-core energy deficiencies that linger across the seasons, but no explanation was offered for this result and interpretation.

With respect to the determinants of individual nutrient intakes, regression analyses were undertaken on 938 children under 12 years of age. Region and season were represented by dummy variables. Socioeconomic status was measured by farm size, income, and caste. Household features comprised the educational status of the mother and family size, and demographic status was characterized by age, sex, and clinical nutritional morbidity. The results are very interesting for what they have been taken to imply about intrahousehold allocation:

1. "There were no significant differences between boys and girls in the intake of these 10 nutrients" (38). Nor did birth order affect discrimination. Caste also had no effect on individual nutrition.
2. A "novel finding" was that carefully collected data on income "fails to explain nutrients consumption" (30).
3. Of statistical significance were the village dummies. "These primarily reflected differences in agroclimate and socioeconomic characteristics" (36); household size ("quantity and quality are substitutes in the context of household decisions" [36]); and land size (though the report expresses doubt over whether farm size is a "cause" or a "correlate reflecting one or more logically prior unmeasured factors" [30]).[1]

Regression analysis of anthropometric measures for children under 12 revealed that intervillage variation and household size were the only significant influences on weight-for-height. For a subset of children under seven years of age (with weight-for-age as the dependent variable), gender was not a significant variable, although birth order and village were. Weight-for-age declined 3 percent for each increase in birth order. The average weights in one village were 21 percent less than those in another in the same state. No explanation was offered for these phenomena. The authors state that "there are many more influences on the nutritional well-being of preschool children as measured by anthropometric indicators than we were able to specify in our equations" (53). It was later concluded using one case study as an example that "poor sanitation, hygiene, and public health infrastructure are most likely responsible for why our findings on energy and nutrients intake are often incongruent with results based on anthropometry" (Walker and Ryan 1990: 269).

Policy implications included the controversial one that individual malnutrition and undernutrition could not be addressed by the targeting of certain income groups; more positively, Ryan et al. suggest the targeting of households (irrespective of income) with characteristics such as larger size, assetlessness, and maternal illiteracy in "certain villages."

This study has been discussed at some length because it was the first and the referent research using the data.

Behrman and Deolalikar (1989)

Behrman and Deolalikar (1989) estimated a log-linear, reduced-form regression demand model on 1,786 individual-season observations averaged for lean and surplus seasons to test the hypotheses that demand for nutrition (calories and protein consumption) or health status (weight-for-height) de-

---

1. Later ICRISAT work draws a different conclusion, however: "In general, the most important personal characteristic in explaining the variation in energy and nutrients intake across individuals was age" (Walker and Ryan 1990:284).

pends upon the environment (value of assets, landholding status [an income proxy], and season); genetic endowment (age and sex); and relative prices, specifically those of inputs (labor) and outputs (three staple foods: sorghum, rice, and pulses). Calorie and protein consumption were expressed as proportions of sex-specific RDAs. Weight-for-height was standardized by modified and sex-specific Harvard standards.

The results of this study were somewhat different from those of Ryan et al. (1984). Nutrients consumption was found to be significantly affected by prices, particularly that of protein in the lean season. The only intrahousehold gender discrimination in nutrients consumption (calories and protein) was against males. The response of anthropometric status to prices was less dependent on seasons. Further disaggregation by landholding status revealed that small cultivators operating less than 7 hectares had higher food price protein (calorie) elasticities than did larger cultivators (Behrman and Deolalikar 1989: 70), a result that the authors concluded was due to "greater dependence on product and labor markets" (76).

The conclusions for policy stressed (1) the usefulness of taking into account that seasonal differences in demand for nutrients were affected by prices, particularly for small cultivators (which underlies an appeal for better integration of local food and financial markets into regional and national markets); and (2) that the consumption-price responsiveness in the lean season means that "the more vulnerable children are likely to be particularly exposed to malnutrition risk when food is scarcest" (78).

The published study, however, did not disaggregate between adults and children. These conclusions were further qualified by the authors by their acknowledgment of multicollinearity associated with the limited price variation in the data and conditional on their choice of functional forms (77).

Behrman (1988b)

Although the weak antimale bias in the ICRISAT set had been established (though not explained) in the two previous studies, Behrman embarked on a separate and very interesting modeling exercise testing antifemale bias. Noting that the earlier absence of gender bias or of seasonal discrimination could be masked by the "genetic-related endowments (including gender)" (Behrman 1988b:33), he explored the distinction between gender preference per se, on the one hand, and the maximization of total returns to labor in gendered labor markets, on the other. The ICRISAT data were used to test an innovative allocation model that distinguished between the position and the convexity of parental indifference curves between the health outcomes of pairs of children within the household. The convexity of the parental indifference curves described the aversion to inequality in health-related outcomes among their children. The position of the indifference curves around the 45-degree ray described the extent of parental preferences for equal health outcomes between children.

Estimation proceeded by comparing health outcomes (weight-for-height, weight, triceps skinfold thickness, and mid-upper-arm circumference) for pairs of children in terms of each nutrient (calories, beta carotene, riboflavin, vitamin C, and calcium). Investments in nutrients were made subject to budget constraints (with prices fixed and identical for all children) and subject to genetic and environmental factors (such as the gender composition of children of a household, gender differences in susceptibility to disease, and the valuation of labor market success). The health production function required in this model is assumed to have diminishing marginal returns to nutrients (37).

The validity of the assumptions underlying this model must be evaluated, even though this chapter is not primarily a critique of method per se but a comparison of the results of method. Health (measured as anthropometric status) is assumed to be produced simultaneously by nutrients. Behrman does not use weight-for-age, which would be the most appropriate indicator, because the functional form has to be independent of age and only in the case of twins (or children from different reproductive subunits within one joint family) will it be possible for children in this sample to be the same age. In actual fact, the functional form will vary with age. It seems to be assumed that the relationship between the percent of RDA and the anthropometric outcome is not age-dependent. The effects, for instance, on the indicator of anthropometric status of transferring a given quantity of nutrients between a mainly breast-fed child of 6 months and one of 36 months are extremely different. The impact on health of nutrient deficits in relation to RDAs will vary according to age. Moreover, it is assumed that a somewhat arbitrary subset of 5 of ICRISAT's 10 measured nutrients are "critical nutrients" (43).[2]

The model was run on lean- and surplus-season mean anthropometric and nutrient intake data for children under 13 years of age in that subset of households with more than one child. There were 390 pairs of data for lean seasons and 379 for surplus seasons. Weight proved the most important health indicator in the lean season, as it behaved in statistically significant and expected ways. In the same way, for the surplus season, weight-for-height replaced weight as the most significant health-outcome indicator.

The results show significant variation in the preference parameters between seasons. In the lean season, there is weak inequality aversion: "some parental concern with distribution" (47). In contrast, in the surplus season, parents behave in a compensating way and distribute nutrients to favor less well-endowed children, irrespective of gender (47–48). As for "unequal con-

---

2. The five nutrients are calories, beta carotene, riboflavin, vitamin C, and calcium. They were selected because they are the nutrients said to be critical by Ryan et al. (1984). Ryan et al. (1984:57) actually conclude that these nutrients, including two B vitamins, were those in which villagers were "mostly deficient," and Behrman and Deolalikar (1989) had themselves earlier shown the arguably equally "critical" seasonal changes in price elasticities of protein, which was excluded from Behrman (1988b).

cern" or male-gender preference, although there is no significant relationship in the surplus season, in the lean season parents weight a given health-related outcome (that is, anthropometric score) for their boys about 5 percent more than for their girls. This is not an egregious parental bias. It is concluded that promale gender bias is greatest when food supplies are tightest.

A further regression analysis of lean-season gender bias, using an array of available household characteristics, reveals "somewhat surprisingly" that land-holding "above some minimum level" does not affect promale bias, but caste and the educational level of the household head do (50). Boys are most favored in the lowest castes (for reasons not given) and boys are most favored in the lean season by most educated household heads (though actually, of course, by their wives).

The policy conclusions from Behrman's study are derived from these last results and are aimed at policy-oriented research as well as, implicitly, at the monitoring and targeting aspects of the policy process. The weak promale bias, identified here as occurring in the lean season, is "probably not just a response to differential expected labor market returns to nutrient investments in boys versus those in girls" (52). In addition, feeding behavior tends to compensate nutritionally disadvantaged household members in the surplus season. The nutritionally vulnerable are low-caste female children under lean season condi-tions when they may be "close to or even below the margin for survival" (52). Policy-oriented research should be seasonally disaggregated.

Behrman and Deolalikar (1990)

Here Behrman and Deolalikar estimate a series of reduced-form log-linear demand models on 1,264 individual observations (this time, annual averages of lean and surplus seasons) of the intakes of seven nutrients. Their objectives are not only to estimate price and income elasticities of demand for individual nutrients by individuals within households, but also to assess sys-tematically the impacts of unobserved fixed effects, nested in aggregation at the individual, household, and village level, and to distinguish the effects of current and permanent income on intrahousehold nutrients allocation. The selective availability of income data series constrained the analysis to half the villages. As previously, nutrients were expressed as proportions of sex-specific RDAs. Prices of labor and of food staples were village-specific annual aver-ages. Individuals were pooled for analysis across agrarian class and village in groups of men, women, boys, and girls (Behrman and Deolalikar 1990), though the crucial age thresholds were not published.

The results of this thorough research proved hard to summarize. For adult males, 60 percent of the food price elasticities for the seven nutrients were significant, those for nonstaples being higher than those for staples. Only 7 percent of these elasticities were significant for boys. Elasticities for women and girls tended to be lower (a quarter of them being significant for both women and girls).

From a policy perspective, the authors stress that although this study shows no gender discrimination in nutrient levels or in nutrient intake variances, it revealed gender-specific adjustment to "changes" (in fact to spatial variations) in food prices. Despite their data's averaging of lean- and surplus-season observations and despite the cross-sectional nature of this study, they infer that women and girls are penalized (and rewarded) more in scarcity (and glut) than are men and boys.

For the other two objectives, Behrman and Deolalikar not only confirm the initial finding by Ryan et al. (1984) that current income does not determine nutrient intakes, but also find deflated permanent income of no significance. Last, though Ryan et al. (1984) had introduced (but not explained) village-level characteristics as factors affecting nutrient intakes, Behrman and Deolalikar here not only confirm this phenomenon as an unobserved "fixed effect," which they. attribute to infrastructure (677, 681, 693), but also confirm the importance of fixed effects at the household and individual levels (though the latter did not apply to the most important single nutrient: calories). Elasticities computed without these controls will thus be a "misleading base for policy formulation" (692).

Harriss (1990)

Harriss took the ICRISAT data as case study material in synthesizing Indian evidence for intrahousehold calorie allocations. A method developed for 24 other Indian studies of nutrient allocation was applied. For each household, a relative intake (RI) of each individual in relation to that of the household head was computed:

$$RI = \frac{\text{Intake of individual}}{\text{Intake of household head}}$$

A second index adjusted for age and sex was then derived from Indian Council of Medical Research (ICMR) norms for recommended intakes (based on age, sex, and physiological status, but not body size or activity level): a "recommended relative intake" (RRI) index:[3]

$$RRI = \frac{\text{Recommended intake of individual}}{\text{Recommended intake of household head}}$$

---

3. The controversial assumption underlying this method is that humans are fixed-efficiency machines and incapable of metabolic, physiological, or behavioral adaptations to variations in energy supply. This problem was discussed in Harriss (1990:376–378). The approach used here is a default option awaiting operationalizable evidence on adaptation. If adaptive responses are ever modeled, they are likely to show that this approach overestimates discrimination, but by how much is not yet known. The ICMR-recommended intake estimates are among the most carefully determined and most regularly revised. "They indicate that the female adult needs 85 percent of the male's energy intake. Comparison with Western norms and recent empirical research (which suggest, respectively, that adult females need 27 and 32 percent less than men) open up the possibility that the Indian norms err on the side of generosity to women. In which case, using them as a standard will tend to lead to overestimation of anti-female discrimination" (Harriss 1990:378).

For each individual, the RI was then expressed as a proportion of the RRI to obtain an index of relative intake (IRI):

$$IRI = \frac{RI}{RRI}$$

An IRI of 1.0 means that the individual's share relative to that of the household head was the same as the share under optimal conditions recommended by the ICMR. A value greater than 1.0 means that the share was greater than the norm and a value less than 1.0, that the share was less, a state that was interpreted as indicating discrimination. The IRI cannot be used to make inferences about absolute intakes.

The disaggregated data were used to ascertain whether intrahousehold allocations varied according to class position and changed under conditions of scarcity. From demand-based theories attempting to explain the Indian sex ratio's regional and social distribution, it could be hypothesized that female shares would be fairer under conditions in which women participate in the wage-labor market and in which their economic status would, as a result, be relatively higher than that of comparable nonparticipants. Fairest female shares were expected to be found in the landless laboring classes, and the greatest protection of females' shares was expected to be found under scarcity conditions in this class too, for the same reason (Harriss 1989b).

This method hit some rocks. First, the actual head of each household was not identified in the data set. The referent for RIs and RRIs was initially taken to be the largest calorie consumer who is male; but this person is often a teenager, with an absolute intake in excess of the recommended intake for adult males! Social and economic power and decisionmaking responsibility will almost certainly not reside in this character. Eventually, the head of household was taken to be the male aged 20–40 with the largest calorie consumption, recognizing that this choice was arbitrary.

Second, the variation between the two surplus seasons exceeded in magnitude any other seasonal difference, including any difference between a surplus and a lean season. The agricultural seasons in these rather widely scattered villages are not coterminous. Furthermore, agricultural production seasons are not nutritional seasons, probably because dietary energy can be obtained from farm and (via trade) nonfarm production, from employment in the farm and nonfarm economy, from stocks, and indirectly from loans and other exchanges. The study confined its data to the extreme maximum and minimum energy supply to each household out of the four rounds of data and regardless of how these readings had fallen under ICRISAT's seasonal classification. Therefore, allocation was examined under relative gluts and scarcity.

Owing to limited research resources, only four of the six ICRISAT villages were studied. The 160 households were grouped by four villages; by four land-size classes; by three age groups (using physiologically relevant disaggregations: under 10, 11–19, and 20 years and over); and by the two sex groups.

The IRIs for each group in glut and scarcity were then tested for significance by *t*-tests (96 of them). A further 96 tests were applied to experimental aggregations of agrarian classes and size groups in order to increase cell sizes.

Out of the total 192 *t*-tests, only 14 were significant at the 5 percent level and only 2 were significant at the 1 percent level.[4]

The results showed complex village- and class-specific patterns of age and sex bias in allocation. These were so idiosyncratic as to defy any generalization.

Among landless labor, significant scarcity adjustments favored adolescent females at the expense of young boys and girls in two villages. In one village, scarcity conditions led to the favoring of young children of both sexes at the expense of adult women. In another village, there were no significant adjustments in sharing practices.

Among the most landed classes, scarcity conditions penalized all females under 20 and favored adult men in one village. In another, all children were penalized to the benefit of adult men. In a third, adolescent females were favored at the expense of adult men. In a fourth, there were no significant adjustments. In the other studies considered here, the use of agricultural rather than food-supply seasons masks contradictory village- and class-specific nutritional experiences in both "lean" and "surplus" seasons.

The implication for policy was much clearer. Direct and remedial welfare intervention (such as that advocated and carefully justified by Drèze and Sen [1989]) must be researched, planned, and implemented at the individual village level, such is the degree of intervillage variation. This is easier said than done. "The age and gender impact of discrimination, its social and seasonal incidence and severity all vary regionally at levels which are below those at which the policy process of agenda formation, authorization and resource mobilization and allocation normally operate. It is most unlikely that this situation would be changed by further research" (Harriss 1991:409–410).

Commentary

These five pieces of work using one database have produced conflicting results for policy:

1. Ryan et al. (1984) found neither seasonality nor gender bias nor consistent relationships with income with respect to individual anthropometric indexes or nutrient intakes.
2. Behrman and Deolalikar (1989) allowed for more seasonality and found that protein consumption varies seasonally in expected ways according to prices. They also found antimale bias in nutrient allocation, though not in anthropometric status. Using holding size as an income proxy, their re-

---

4. There is a major problem of small cell sizes with ICRISAT's database.

search reported significantly greater nutrient-price elasticities among smaller cultivators.

3. Behrman's (1988b) model showed weak but statistically significant lean-season pro–male child bias and anti–female child bias. But landholding status was not a significant determinant of allocative practice.

4. Behrman and Deolalikar (1990) discovered gender and age differences in nutrients adjustments to intervillage price variations, but, because this implied for them a profemale bias in glut seasons, they were cautious about terming this behavior discrimination.

5. Harriss (1990) found village- and class-specific patterns of age and sex bias coexisting with absence of bias and significant, complex, and countervailing village-specific adjustments to nutritional scarcities.

These discrepancies arise because of differences in the subsets of data selected, in the type of classifications made, and in the analytical methods employed (see Table 12.1). Careful specification of the problem for research is a necessary precondition for measurement. Just as there is a difference between modeling what is seen and seeing what is modeled, there is also a world of difference between the testing of a model by disproof and making sense of an existing database. The original sample selection of villages and households was for purposes other than the description and explanation of individual nutrition. It was to look at representative conditions of dryland agricultural production (Walker and Ryan 1990:9–24).[5] So the type and size of the samples mean that the possibility of nontrivial intervillage variation in the explanation for individual nutrition was not seriously contemplated prior to or during the period of field survey. Modeling what is seen with respect to intrahousehold nutrients is in its infancy.

In the same way, the collection of data may involve a more or less conscious selection between the competing theories and models of other disciplines. In the case considered here, data collection has, from the beginning, assumed a nutritional model of human energy metabolism as a fixed-efficiency machine and has not allowed for the investigation of seasonal or individual nutrient allocations under conditions of metabolic, physiological, and behavioral adaptation (Payne and Lipton 1994).

Individualistic Classification of Data

Some of the divergences in results are the product of individualistic classification and the exclusion of data. Taking the case of individualistic classifications

---

5. Two further comments on field method are relevant. First, a common problem is that a prioristic research procedure with a piloted but precoded questionnaire does not generally allow room for maneuver if initial hypotheses generate unanticipated results. Second, a hierarchical structure of personnel for data collection is known to run risks of greater measurement errors (if only because of investigator bias and multiple transcription) than alternative structures, such as one in which the final analyst does the fieldwork, although this places serious constraints upon scale.

TABLE 12.1 Individualism in research on gender and seasonal biases in nutrition using ICRISAT data

		Source			
Data	Ryan et al. (1984)	Behrman and Deolalikar (1989)	Behrman (1988b)	Behrman and Deolalikar (1990)	Harriss (1990)
Number of cases	1,200 people	1,768 observations	390 child pairs (lean seasons); 379 child pairs (surplus seasons)	1,264 observations	2,400 observations
Households	240	240	Not specified	120	160
Villages	6	6	6	3	4
Nutrients	10	2	5	7	1
Anthropometric indicators	6	1	4	. . .	. . .
Age groups (years)	1–12, 13–18, >18	1–15	<13	Men, women, boys, girls	<10, 11–19, >20
Seasons	Each of two lean and two surplus	Averages for lean and surplus seasons	Averages for lean and surplus seasons	Lean and surplus averaged for each year	Nutritionally extreme observations—minimum and maximum calories per household
Subsets analyzed	Individuals, children <12 (M,F), children <5 (M,F)	Individuals (M,F)	Children <13 (M,F)	Men, women, boys, girls	Households: three age groups as above

Other variables	Agrarian class Income Caste Household size Household composition	Land Prices for: M,F labor, sorghum, rice, pulses	Labor (M,F) Caste Education Household composition	Income Land Caste Labor (M,F) Price for rice, grain, sorghum, milk Age and education of household head Household size Household composition Village population	Holding size
Results					
Seasonality in nutrient intake	No	Yes	Yes	...	Yes[a]
Variations according to income/land class	No	Yes	No	No	Yes
Antifemale gender bias	No	No	Yes, in lean seasons	Yes, in adjustments	Yes
Age bias	Yes	...	...	Yes	Yes

NOTE: . . ., not applicable.

[a]All results (a) village-specific; (b) coexisting with absence of relationships.

of children, for example, Ryan et al. (1984) classify children into a set aged 1–12 years and a subset aged 1–6 years. In Behrman and Deolalikar (1989), they are 1–15; in Behrman (1988b), they are under 13; and in Behrman and Deolalikar (1990), their age is not mentioned. In Harriss (1990), children are under 10 years old. Behrman and Deolalikar obscure the teenage category important in Ryan et al. (1984) and in Harriss (1990). Methodology may necessitate data exclusion. Behrman (1988b), for instance, has to exclude any household without pairs of children under 13 years of age.

Seasonality

Seasonality was an important parameter in four studies, but the implication that agricultural seasonality implied seasonality in food supply was accepted in all but one. Despite cautions in Ryan et al. (1984), no interannual seasonal variation was modeled in Behrman and Deolalikar (1989) and in Behrman (1988b). In Harriss (1990), the analysis was confined to data for the rounds of minimum and maximum nutrient availabilities to each individual household, quite irrespective of how these rounds were classified, since "lean" had been discovered not to correspond with minimum nor "surplus" with maximum. Energy balances, so crucial to studies of seasonality in nutrition, were out of the scope of the field study and were not estimated by ICRISAT. All of the studies subsequently had to assume that energy expenditure could be held seasonally constant and was "moderate" (therefore not needing special accommodation), which is probably unrealistic.

Nutrients Studied

The range of results is also a product of selectivity in the deployment of nutrients. Ryan et al. (1984) meticulously analyzed 10 nutrients and five anthropometric measures combined into six indicators and attempted to interpret the complicated nutrient-specific patterns. Behrman and Deolalikar (1989) looked at two nutrients (calories and protein) and one health status indicator (weight-for-height); Behrman (1988b) looked at five nutrients (excluding protein) and four anthropometric indicators; Behrman and Deolalikar (1990) looked at seven nutrients; Harriss (1990) looked at calories alone. Nutrients intakes were analyzed as absolute values in the research reported here of Ryan et al. (1984), as proportions of RDAs in Behrman and Deolalikar (1989, 1990) and Behrman (1988b), and as proportions of male household head's consumption in Harriss (1990). The use of RDAs introduces further possible measurement error into the analysis, since RDAs are in any case not known to the same precision for all nutrients. Walker and Ryan (1990:267–269) is a useful reference both for a representative discussion of deprivation using RDAs and for a conclusion diametrically opposed to that of ICRISAT's earlier study. Whereas Ryan et al. (1984) stressed intervillage variation as being crucial in explaining variation in individual nutrient intakes, Walker and Ryan (1990:278–279) concluded that as a result of partitioning the sums of squares of nutrients expressed as proportions of RDAs, "interhousehold variation was the dominant contributor [50 percent] to the total variation in energy and nutrient intakes; next in importance was intrahousehold variation [33 percent] and intervillage variation contributed only one-sixth." Behrman and Deolalikar (1990:677) find village size significant for 46 percent of the nutrient elasticities calculated, about which they write: "our results underscore the importance of village infrastructure for nutritional improvements," although village size is more likely to be a product of local agricultural productivity (the causal relation then reversed) and village infrastructure is well known to depend on remoteness or distance from towns (von Oppen, Rao, and Rao 1985).

Stratification of Households by Size of Landholding

Differences in results may also be generated by differences in the aggregation of data. Behrman disaggregated by size of holding (though the empirical groupings were not specified) and found that size of holding did not affect the promale bias identified in his model. Behrman and Deolalikar (1989) disaggregated using a 7-hectare cutoff and found significantly greater seasonal adjustments in price elasticities of consumption among "small" rather than large cultivators. Harriss (1990) found not only class variation in age-sex allocative bias and in adjustments between gluts and scarcity, but also intervillage variation in these phenomena. Ryan et al. (1984:58–59) concluded that the "agroclimatic and socioeconomic characteristics of the villages and regions" were the most important determinant of low individual intakes in the households of small farmers and landless laborers. Harriss took the landholding size classes of Ryan et al., which varied from village to village and were radically different from those of Behrman and Deolalikar (1989).

Analytical Groups of Individuals

Ryan et al. (1984) and Behrman and Deolalikar (1989) used data on individuals measured in the field within households but analyzed in aggregated age bands (and sometimes age-sex bands). In contrast, Behrman (1988b) and Harriss (1990) empirically examined intrahousehold allocations. Behrman compared those households containing pairs of children, and Harriss calculated individual discrimination within each individual household, then averaged these indexes by age, sex, land-size class, and village. It is not possible to judge the relative roles of research method, data classification (especially aggregation), and data selection (and exclusion) in the array of results. But it is clear that development economics does not insist on replicability prior to offering policy advice.

Empirical Conclusions

Conclusions in all but Behrman's study run counter to orthodoxy: the intrahousehold bias, if it exists at all, is found to be against male children by Ryan et al. (1984) and against males by Behrman and Deolalikar (1989), whereas Behrman and Deolalikar (1990) report a bias oscillating against and toward females according to supplies. In Harriss (1990), some scarcity bias is significantly antichildren of whatever sex, some anti–adult male, and some antifemale of whatever age! All the unexpected results proved impossible to explain. Age bias rather than gender bias was also found by Ryan et al., teenagers being most vulnerable. This was also impossible to explain.

In the absence of hard evidence for a specific interpretation of empirical results, appeal is made to residual factors for which there are no data to buttress speculation. Ryan et al. (1984), for instance, speculate on the lack of influence of income on nutrition as follows: children may be protected from income fluctuations; the range of incomes is low; the intrahousehold control over income may be a more important determinant of nutrition than income per se, but it is not known. The problem of intervillage variation was certainly recognized by Ryan et al., but it had to be explained by referring in great detail to the characteristics of one village as an example. Harriss (1990:397–398) struggles without conspicuous success to use village agroecology and labor relations to explain age-sex patterns of sharing and adjustment in shares specific to holding class and village. Behrman and Deolalikar (1990) load the variable of village population with many unmeasured characteristics.

Policy Conclusions

Although the publication of these results has been phased in time and although it is unlikely that a policymaker in the field of public health and food would have read them all, in a scenario under which such a policymaker were presented with the results of these five studies, she or he would be right to be intervention-averse.

Not only is the policy advice contradictory, it also suffers from vagueness and triviality, despite—or perhaps because of—the specificity of many of the substantive results. "Policy relevance" may be used to justify research (and its funding) in the first instance, but in practice "policy" tends to be residualized and often smacks of tokenism. Facts do not speak for themselves and need values (and assumptions) for their interpretation. One of Behrman and Deolalikar's (1989) policy recommendations is a plea for improved private market integration (by means unspecified), but the factual evidence on class-specific price elasticities of nutrients consumption would equally well support a plea for price stabilization (by state intervention). From their later results,

Behrman and Deolalikar (1990:692–693) conclude that "The food price results have important implications for the food subsidy policies that many less-developed countries pursue in order to improve the nutrient intake of the poor. Our results suggest that subsidies on foods other than inferior ones (e.g. sorghum or cassava [*sic*]) actually can reduce individual nutrient intakes on the average in households and particularly for males." In these five studies, cavalier assumptions are made about state delivery capacity. It is equally clear that there is no quick fix for policy. There are general appeals for targeting, but by village in Ryan et al. (1984) and Harriss (1990); less confidently by holding size class, family size, and maternal educational status in Ryan et al.; and by caste, season, gender, and education of the male household head in Behrman (1988b).

Yet the questions of what is to be targeted, by what means, and at what expense are unaddressed. Furthermore, the means whereby what is here an inadequately defined part of the process of policymaking and implementation might be shifted to the village level, given village-specific needs, is also unaddressed. In order to answer these entirely legitimate questions, another kind of research on the policy process would need to be carried out.

It is outside the scope of this chapter to consider in detail how this can be done. The standard approach involves a rigorous consideration of the (social) costs and benefits of alternatives. But it has been pointed out from a number of empirical examples (Clay and Schaffer 1984) that here, too, the assumptions determine the outcomes, and the entire process of implementation is residualized. If "policy is what policy does," some different approaches may be useful. The policy process is fruitfully conceptualized as three sets of activities that occur simultaneously. One is the process of agenda formation, in which present, actual actions and future, possible actions by the state are identified and prioritized in various ways (rhetorically, in terms of budgetary allocations, and so forth). Statements of advisability and of intention (as found in planning documents and in the remarks addressed to policy concerns and appended to technical research papers) are politically located in this phase. But a great deal of other political activity competes with science at this point. The second activity has been called proceduralization and refers to the making of laws or informal rules (which carry sanctions on their breaching but are not necessarily legally binding). By means of these rules, agendas may be translated into material action. Comparative analysis of agendas and procedures (and, further, of the legal adjudication of apparent breaches of procedure) demonstrates slippage (Sections 3 and 4 in Ghai, Luckham, and Snyder 1987). Last, there is the complicated process of state allocation of resources and of peoples' access to them. Here again much slippage is to be found (Harriss 1991). Allocation and access have been less well researched than agenda. Procedure is hardly addressed in social science. Agenda is studied, but it is less often analyzed historically and critically as a problem.

At the very least, it is evident that the research discussed here is aimed as a technical input to agenda formation. Both the ideology of "policy relevance" that informs these technical inputs and the fate of the kind of policy advice discussed here ought to be as valid as areas for research as intrahousehold allocation per se. And every bit as difficult. Not only do households need unpacking, so does the policy process.

13 Finding the Ties That Bind: Beyond Headship and Household

JUDITH BRUCE AND CYNTHIA B. LLOYD

In this chapter, the literature dealing with households and headship is reviewed to lay the foundations for a new research and policy focus on the family. Specifically, it is argued that the family is a more important resource allocation arena to understand than is the household, at least when it comes to designing public policy for improving child welfare in developing countries. In addition, it is argued that the gender of the household head has proved to be a useful window of convenience into the workings of the family and household, but it has provided an incomplete picture. In this chapter we provide a reason for going beyond headship and household to the design of data collection instruments that focus on the real interest—family survival strategies and intrafamily resource allocation as they affect child welfare. In the first half of the chapter we assess recent literature on female-headed and -maintained families and newly available data on the family circumstances and living arrangements of women and children to answer three broad questions with important implications for research and policy: What is the operational meaning of headship? Is the household concept a useful guide for understanding the family relationships that determine children's welfare? Is the household a sufficient context for understanding women's economic roles and vulnerabilities? In the second half of the chapter we draw lessons from these conclusions for both population and economic development policy. A case is built for a new research focus on the family that transcends the physical and temporal boundaries of the household, and for a policy focus that inquires into meaningful family relationships. The specification and support of parenting roles—

We acknowledge the helpful comments of Lawrence Haddad, Susan Greenhalgh, Robert Heidel, and Linda Edwards. We owe an intellectual debt to many members of the Population Council/International Center for Research on Women Advisory Group on Family Structure, Women's Economic Contribution, and Poverty. We note, in particular, Mayra Buvinic, Sonalde Desai, Anastasia Gage-Brandon, Sandra Rosenhouse, Patrice Engle, Nancy Folbre, Beatrice Rogers, and Jacques van der Gaag.

particularly fathering roles—in fulfilling the social and economic needs of children are emphasized.

Households and Families: What Has Been Learned?

Coresidential arrangements and family relationships form the context within which resource sharing and exchange among individuals take place. Households are the institutions within which the researcher usually studies these interpersonal transactions at the micro level. Because residentially distinct households are relatively easy to identify in most settings, they provide efficient units within which to study people's domestic lives and assess their relative welfare. In the short run, it is reasonable to assume that the members of any particular household are bound together by ties of mutual interest that surpass the possibilities for sharing and support available in alternative living arrangements. However, not all resources of household members are fully shared, and households rarely contain within them a closed circle of interpersonal transactions.[1] The maintenance of networks of mutual obligation and support between kin does not require coresidence or even physical proximity (Stone 1977; Thadani 1978). Most household members are likely to have family members residing outside the household with whom they have long-term economic connections. Thus a view of intrafamily connections and resource flows—particularly important when considering children's well-being—requires looking beyond the immediate residential household. In the discussion that follows, a family is defined as a group of individuals related by blood or marriage and a household as a group of individuals living together and sharing meals.

Headship: A Window into the Household?

The designation of a household member as its "head" is commonly used in censuses and surveys to identify a "reference person" to whom individuals are linked and by whom they are counted and their characteristics recorded. The head is not usually defined by any objective criteria (the possible exception is duration of residence) but instead by the subjective criterion that he or she is so designated by other household members. Among the attributes commonly assigned to the head are that he or she carries primary economic responsibility, functions as the primary decisionmaking authority, or is the

---

1. The degree to which such a closed circle of transactions does not exist is likely to vary cross-culturally. To take an extreme example, an in-depth anthropological study of a residential neighborhood in Accra, Ghana, concluded that most production as well as key consumption activities occurred outside the household, that household members usually performed these activities separately, that sexual activity more often occurred between men and women from different households rather than from the same household, and that most children had primary relationships of socialization with adults living in other households (Sanjek 1982).

most respected person. There is a tendency in many cultures for household members to name the oldest male affiliated with the household as its head, even when he is no longer economically active or even in regular residence. Thus the meaning of headship is far from standard, and its social meaning is likely to vary cross-culturally as well as among members of the same household.

A comparison of households according to the sex of the head has often been used as a means of learning indirectly about the relative roles of men and women in household production and resource allocation. A key analytic dilemma in studying the differences between male- and female-headed households, however, is the asymmetry of their structure. A household labeled male-headed almost invariably has one or more females present, including the spouse of the male head. A female-headed household, on the other hand, is most often a male-absent household. In comparing these two household types, the analytical problems implied by this asymmetry are dealt with not just once but at every point in the research and in interpreting the findings for policy. In the discussion that follows, the focus is on the relative household responsibility and authority of male and female heads and the consequent implications for allocation of resources in these two household types.

In developing countries, where much production occurs outside the market sector, it is often difficult to evaluate the relative economic roles of household members. In male-headed households, where men and women are coresident and often work side-by-side in family farms and businesses, a comparison of their earnings will confirm the economic advantage of the male head. The male advantage stems from two sources: the male typically earns more for the same effort, and he is awarded control over the cash collectively generated because of his position of authority (and sometimes the explicit biases of a development policy). According to Sen (1990:130), such joint economic activities often create "systematic biases in the perception of who is 'producing' what and 'earning' what" within the household.

An alternative approach to the analysis of relative economic contributions is a comparison of work effort between household types, or the proportion of total household work hours contributed by male and female heads. Lloyd and Gage-Brandon (1993b), in a comparison of the relative work hours of men and women in Ghana, showed that, controlling for other relevant factors, household heads (men or women) work longer hours, on average, in the market than other adult household members. This finding confirms that heads do carry extra responsibility in the household. Furthermore, they found that female heads work significantly longer hours, on average, than male heads when domestic work was taken into consideration, corroborating findings by Rosenhouse (1989) for Peru. However, comparisons of the share of total household work contributed by male and female heads in these two studies revealed that female heads are much more likely to be primary workers[2] in the household than male heads, who often share significant work responsibility with at least one other member. Indeed, in 30 percent of male-headed households in Ghana, the spouse of the head was identified as a "main worker." In Peru, 40 percent of the households in which the primary worker was a woman were actually reported to be "male-headed."

There is little information on the relative decisionmaking responsibility of male and female heads, but data on relative economic responsibility suggest that the authority structure in female-headed households may be more cohesive because of the absence of adult male members (Dwyer and Bruce 1988). Male-headed households and multigenerational households tend to be larger and to have more earners, so the potential for conflict is much greater (Doan and Bisharat 1990). In Ghana, household members were asked who was best informed about different activities within the household, such as agriculture and livestock tending, nonfarm business, and food purchasing. In male-headed households, the spouse of the head was named as the best informed about nonfarm business in 52 percent of the cases and about food purchases in 69 percent of the cases (Haddad 1990). In female-headed households, the female head was almost always declared the most knowledgeable in all areas of household activity. Although knowledge is not synonymous with control, it is certainly a precondition. Such evidence supports the view that authority is more fully vested in one person in female-headed households and more variably distributed in male-headed households. Thus, with regard to both productive work effort and degree of authority, women who are named household heads appear more likely to fulfill the range of assumed roles of head than men so named for the very reason that female heads rarely live with other adults who could compete for such roles.

Evidence is growing that the internal distribution of resources in female-headed households is more child-oriented than in male-headed households. This evidence is derived from comparisons of the overall pattern of household consumption, the types of food purchased and consumed by members of male- and female-headed households, and differences in children's school enrollment. One hypothesis is that women can implement their priorities more easily and hence redirect resources more efficiently to children when they are fully in charge of the household. For example, recent evidence from Jamaica indicates that female-headed households consume foods of higher nutritional quality and spend a larger share of their income on child goods and a significantly smaller share on alcohol (Horton and Miller 1989). Selective evidence of the longer-term impact on children of these expenditure differences between male- and female-headed households is primarily derived from data on child nutritional

---

2. The primary worker is defined as the household member with the greatest share of the household's total hours of market work.

status. Despite lower household incomes, a smaller percentage of children in some types of female-headed households in Kenya and Malawi are moderately to severely malnourished than in male-headed households (Kennedy and Peters 1992). Furthermore, when households with similar resources are compared in seven Sub-Saharan African countries, children in female-headed households have higher school enrollment and completion rates than children in male-headed households (Lloyd and Blanc 1996).

Observed differences in child welfare and in expenditure patterns by headship status provide an indirect way of assessing the implications for the household of women's greater access to and control over household income. Several careful empirical studies of the distribution of income and expenditures within the household provide direct evidence for the contrasting expenditure priorities of men and women and support the hypothesis that women in a variety of household types—including male-headed—are more child-oriented in their expenditures. Hoddinott and Haddad (1991), using household expenditure data from Côte d'Ivoire, show that a doubling of the income under women's control would lead to a 2 percent rise in the budget share going to food and a dramatic decline in the budget share going to alcohol (−26 percent) and cigarettes (−14 percent). Using household budget data from Brazil, the analysis by Thomas (Chapter 9, this volume) confirms that additional income in the hands of women leads to a greater share of the household budget going to human capital goods as well as higher per capita calorie and protein intake. Finally, in a sample of periurban children in Guatemala, Engle (1993) has estimated that the attainment of an additional half a standard deviation in a child's weight-for-height would require US$11.40 per month if earned by the mother and US$166 per month if earned by the father. Based on the same Guatemalan data, Engle (1991) also found that the higher the share of total household income earned by a child's mother, the higher the child's nutritional status.

Children's Living Arrangements: The Ties That Bind

The data on children's well-being in female-headed households suggest that female stewardship of resources is especially beneficial to children. Data more descriptive of intrahousehold processes, such as those analyzed by Thomas (Chapter 9, this volume) and Engle (1993), further suggest a differential propensity on the part of mothers and fathers to spend on children. As these intrahousehold data are less easy to come by than the more commonly available headship data, an important research and policy goal has been to assess the value of headship information as a means of identifying the family links through which child welfare is determined. Do headship and related household structure data accurately direct us to the resource base of children? An unspoken assumption in linking child welfare to the characteristics of the head is the notion that the head somehow acts, because of biological links, on behalf of the

TABLE 13.1 Percent of children living away from mothers, by age

Area/Country	Total	Age (years)		
		0–4	5–9	10–14
Sub-Saharan Africa				
Botswana	27.6	18.7	32.2	33.7
Burundi	4.8	1.2	6.4	9.5
Ghana	15.2	4.2	18.2	29.4
Kenya	6.8	2.8	7.7	11.4
Liberia	25.3	11.2	33.0	40.9
Mali	10.5	3.6	13.5	17.8
Senegal	13.6	5.7	16.3	24.0
Zimbabwe	14.3	6.8	15.9	22.8
Asia and North Africa				
Indonesia	3.7	1.5	3.3	6.5
Morocco	2.8	0.9	2.6	5.7
Sri Lanka	2.7	1.2	2.9	4.2
Thailand	7.0	4.0	6.5	10.4
Tunisia	0.5	0.2	0.4	0.9
Latin America and Caribbean				
Brazil	4.0	2.6	4.3	5.7
Colombia	6.0	2.8	6.3	9.6
Dominican Republic	12.4	6.6	12.9	18.8
Ecuador	3.7	1.5	3.6	6.6
Peru	3.5	1.3	3.1	6.5
Trinidad and Tobago	5.7	3.3	5.7	9.1

SOURCE: Lloyd and Desai (1992).

children and the household. Implicit in much child welfare research is the assumption that the household head is the biological parent of the children residing in the household. But are children who reside in male-headed households residing with both parents? Are children who reside in female-headed households residing with their mother?

In most countries of North Africa, Asia, and Latin America, all but a few percent of children under the age of five years reside with their mothers (Table 13.1). In Sub-Saharan Africa, the proportions of younger children living apart from their mother can be higher—for example, 11 percent in Liberia and 19 percent in Botswana. As children age, the proportions living away rise in all regions, but only in Africa do they represent a substantial minority of children. For mothers with partners who have limited resources, sending a child to another household may enhance the child's access to resources or minimize the disadvantages for children still coresident with the mothers. Lloyd and Desai's (1992) analysis of children's living arrangements showed that the probability that a child will be fostered away from its mother is significantly greater when the mother has no residential spouse or partner and when there is competition from younger siblings.[3] Thus under such circumstances a child may be transferred from a "poor" female-headed household to a presumptively richer male-headed household. Yet it is not clear that the child is advantaged by such a move, as neither of the child's biological parents is the household head; hence, neither of the child's most immediate protectors or supporters is in the strongest position to direct resources to that child. If an unexamined conclusion were to be drawn from the data about this child, it would be that he or she is in a male-headed household living with both parents when, in fact, this child is living with neither parent. A recent analysis from Ghana indicates that although 71 percent of school-age children live in male-headed households, 42 percent of school-age children are not coresiding with their fathers.[4]

Furthermore, living in a female-headed household is not synonymous with living in a mother-headed household. Table 13.2 presents data from 17 developing countries that show the proportion of childhood years lived in mother-headed households and in households headed by other women, often grandmothers.[5] Although mother-headed households represent the majority of female-headed households in most countries (except in Senegal, Sri Lanka, and Thailand), between 5 and 10 percent of children's lives in seven of the countries shown here are spent in households headed by women who are not their mothers.

Finally, a child's consumption and human capital investment prospects are determined not only by whether living arrangements permit one or both parents to direct resources to him or her, but also by the number of siblings (both resident and nonresident) with whom he or she is competing. If either parent has had children with one or more other partners, the number of "same-mother" siblings a child has will differ from the number of "same-father" siblings (Lloyd and Gage-Brandon 1993a). Extramarital childbearing, divorce, remarriage, and polygamy are all factors leading to this result. Data rarely allow a glimpse of the potential importance of the presence of half- and step-siblings to parental investments in children. One problem is that fathers may be reluctant to acknowledge all their children, if they no longer have any

---

3. This analysis included seven Sub-Saharan African countries as well as Thailand and the Dominican Republic; in all of these countries, significant numbers of children live apart from their mothers.

4. Lloyd and Gage (1995) and special tabulations from the Ghana Living Standards Measurement Survey in 1987/88.

5. These are synthetic cohort estimates calculated by adding age-specific proportions of children living in households that are mother-headed, other female-headed, and male-headed for single years of age from 0 to 15 and then dividing by 15. The effect is to standardize for differences in children's age distribution for comparisons across countries.

TABLE 13.2 Percent of a child's years spent in female-headed households, by household type

Area/Country	Headed by Mother	Headed by Other Female	Mother-Headed as a Percentage of Female-Headed Households
Sub-Saharan Africa			
Botswana	31	18	63
Burundi	8	4	67
Ghana	21	12	64
Kenya	18	5	78
Liberia	10	9	53
Mali	4	1	80
Senegal	2	6	25
Zimbabwe	29	7	81
Asia and North Africa			
Indonesia	3	3	50
Morocco	7	2	78
Sri Lanka	5	7	42
Thailand	7	9	44
Tunisia	5	1	83
Latin America and Caribbean			
Colombia	8	5	62
Dominican Republic	15	2	88
Ecuador	6	3	67
Trinidad and Tobago	5	1	83

SOURCE: Calculated from Tables 4–6 in Lloyd and Desai (1992).

links with the child's mother. In Ghana, school-aged children have roughly two more "same-father" siblings, on average, than "same-mother" siblings. A child with more "same-father" siblings than "same-mother" siblings inevitably has a smaller proportional claim on the father's resources than on the mother's (Lloyd and Gage-Brandon 1993a).[6]

Women's Living Arrangements: Is There a Safe Place?

Women's commitment to and need for the family have traditionally been much greater than men's because basic economic survival and the acquisition of valid social roles have been difficult for women to achieve outside marriage

---

6. These estimates are based on the reports of all men and women in the household about children residing in the household as well as outside. The study was limited to siblings under the age of 30.

and childbearing. Yet families, even traditional extended ones, do not always provide women with reliable economic protection. As the proportion of female-maintained households rises over time (Bruce, Lloyd, and Leonard 1995), the likelihood that a woman will become the principal economic support for her family, at least for some portion of her life cycle, increases as well. Knowledge or fear concerning the likelihood of becoming a widow or losing the economic support of a spouse has been shown to influence women's fertility choices in high-mortality settings such as Bangladesh (Cain 1986). The risk of widowhood is just one of the factors leading to women's living without partners and to female headship in developing countries. Other factors, many of which may be growing in importance, include migration (of both men and women), unpartnered (usually adolescent) fertility, marital instability, and the competing sexual relations of one partner or the other. Women's awareness of these possibilities provides them with an important motivation for achieving some control over resources even when living with an economically active spouse.

A comparison of data on the likelihood of marital disruption in very different settings in the developing world reveals a not inconsequential likelihood that a married women will experience the death of a husband or divorce or separation by her mid-40s (Bruce, Lloyd, and Leonard 1995).[7] The proportion ranges from roughly one-quarter of women in Asia and North Africa to roughly one-third in Latin America and the Caribbean and Sub-Saharan Africa. Although some of these women form new unions, those having children from earlier partnerships are no longer residentially linked with the fathers of these children.

Women's insecurity arises not only from the instability of male-female partnerships and their own circumscribed access to labor markets but also centrally from their motherhood status. For many women becoming a mother is a greater disposing factor to poverty than gender alone. The economic implications of uncommitted or unstable male-female relationships are greatly magnified when the loss of a partner jeopardizes not only a woman's livelihood but also her dependent children's access to support. Thus the father's economic relationship with the children is very much part of the economic portfolio of a woman who is a mother.

Other factors besides marital status and motherhood are likely to be important in determining the extent of a mother's financial responsibility for her children. When husbands and wives live apart because of job migration or customary residential arrangements, the contribution of fathers to the support of the household is likely to diminish. Polygamy also increases a mother's financial responsibility for her own children.

---

7. Unfortunately, results beyond age 49 cannot be seen because the Demographic Health Survey data were restricted to women of reproductive age.

Finally, the economic fate of women more than men, and of female-headed households more than male-headed households, is determined by extra-household relationships. Family members live together within households, but it is important to recognize that family relationships often transcend the geographical boundaries of the household (Lloyd 1995). Family relationships are fluid, and the implications of this—at least in the economic sense—are probably more crucial for women than for men. Some female-headed households are not only well off compared with male-headed households, but even better off because of a particularly important extrahousehold economic link—that of remittances (Kennedy and Peters 1992; Lloyd and Gage-Brandon 1993b). Other female-headed households have limited resources and no extended support systems. Indeed the very poorest of mother-child groupings are unlikely to be found in the residentially distinct female-headed category; owing to their disadvantaged circumstances, they are often incorporated into larger, and male-headed, households (Buvinic et al. 1992). The wealth or poverty of mothers and their children is determined to an important degree by whether fathers, regardless of marital or residential arrangements, contribute economically to their children. Given women's limited economic power relative to men, a noncontributing father in any household type is among the most severe welfare risks mothers and children face.

Where to Go from Here?

In developing research and policy implications from the points outlined in the previous section, the focus is on two policy arenas: (1) population and family planning and (2) economic development. In both arenas, rather lopsided and ill-founded views of the family have been central. In the case of family planning and population programs, data collection procedures track offspring through their links with the biological mother without a trace of interest in the father. The development paradigm, on the other hand, centers all of its attention and expectations on the head of the household, implicitly male and presumably a dutiful parent. Analysis in this chapter suggests that population and development policies would be more effective if they were founded on a more balanced and empirically based view of family demography, of male and female roles in households and as parents, and of intrafamily sharing.

In the discussion that follows, attention is centered on a subject of importance to both population and development policy—the parent-child relationship. This was selected from the many family relationships under strain because the parent-child link seems to be the one that should be best protected and whose rupture carries the most grievous consequences. To be more specific, it is owed this special attention on the basis of three criteria: (1) its stability over time, (2) the intrinsic vulnerability of one of its members, and (3) its potential for long-term productivity gains. Many other family relationships, such as those between spouses and between adult children and their parents, will frame and influence the parent-child relationship. Indeed an interest in women's well-being is served by this focus to the extent that a woman's own poverty is traceable to the biased attention to women only as mothers and the societal neglect of fathers' roles and responsibilities.

There is good precedent for focusing on children. National governments and international agencies repeatedly call for investments in children, such as mandatory school attendance and invigorated efforts to ensure child survival and extend primary health care. Population policy's version of child-centered language suggests that families would be better off if couples invested more fully in each child—a truism popularly expressed as "smaller families are happier families." Indeed it is key to the fertility decline that children become more costly to parents. But in fact not much real thought has been given to intrahousehold processes in framing these policies. In the discussion that follows, three directions are suggested for future research and policy efforts that would promote equity between men and women, encourage productivity, and promote investments in children based on a better understanding of family processes: (1) the articulation of culturally appropriate children's rights, (2) the further specification of and support for fathers' social and economic responsibilities to children, and (3) equity for women as individuals in the labor market.

Children's Rights

The time has come to broaden this policy purview beyond the mother-child link and to focus on something bigger and more important—the rights of children as individuals. Regardless of the potential devotion of mothers, there is general consensus among social scientists and practitioners that children are entitled to a fair share of the social and economic resources of both of their biological (or culturally ascribed) parents.[8] "Who pays for the kids?" should become an explicit and fundamental issue of development policy (Folbre 1994).

Identifying effective policies and programs to entitle children will be as challenging in developing countries as it continues to be in industrialized countries. As a start, programs that deal with children should establish expectations for the participation of both mothers and fathers and systematically portray this in media, outreach, and program design. If the root of discrimination against girls is sexual inequality in the wider society, such programs should challenge those ideologies held by parents about girls that may seem to justify their neglect.

---

8. Some societies define parenthood more broadly. However, we believe that the role of grandparents, aunts, uncles, and other normatively ascribed parent surrogates will begin to diminish as social mobility and economic pressure tend to decrease family size and homogenize family concepts. With time, a more uniform, cross-cultural definition of parental responsibility is expected to emerge.

Parental migration presents a particular challenge to the full attainment of children's rights. As mentioned previously, parents typically migrate in search of work to help their families. Yet relatively little is known about how parental migration affects children's well-being and their prospects over time. As the long-term value of outmigration to sending countries is increasingly questioned (Papademetriou and Martin 1991), more information about the long-run returns to sending families is needed. Some receiving-country migration policies differentiate between the rights of fathers and mothers to bring in children (Lim 1990). It is important to assess policies that, though established with hard-currency considerations in mind, may have unexpected returns to the custodial parent and children. For example, seasonal workers from Jamaica in the United States are paid the majority of their wage in Jamaica. In the Philippines, when shipping crews are contracted for, the contractor must pay 70 percent or more of the sailor's wage to a designated person or family in the Philippines. Do such policies increase the possibility that absent fathers will provide economic support for children?

Finally, regarding the issue of child maintenance, explicit costs and economic expectations must be assigned to those who bear children, and penalties must be imposed on those who try to avoid their responsibilities.

Effective definition of policy in this area will require further research on children's residential arrangements and access to parental and other family support in different cultures and countries and on the consequences for children of different types of parenting arrangements. Much more needs to be known about the relationship between parents' residential and marital arrangements and their children's claim on their resources. More also needs to be known about how the number and sex of a child's siblings (including half- and stepsiblings) are likely to affect his or her opportunities. Finally, further research is needed to identify the sources of inequality in parental investment in children according to their gender, circumstances of birth, living arrangements, and whether or not the child's birth was wanted.

Support for the Father's Role

There is no compelling reason why the father-child link is any less important than the mother-child link. At the level of program, policy, and social debate, the value of the father's role, expectations of fathers and incentives for "good" fathering, and sanctions for "poor" fathering must be defined. Without these efforts and in light of the changeable marital and residential arrangements of parents, it is likely that an increasing proportion of children in developing countries with inadequate access to their fathers' economic and emotional resources—a trend only too familiar in the industrialized countries—will be observed.

Most of this policy interest in children has been channeled through mothers, as if they were the sole solution to the need for generating additional income and rendering appropriate child care. A U.S. study on race, family structure, and changing poverty among children (Eggebeen and Lichter 1991) found that, without the significant increases in the labor force participation of mothers that occurred between 1960 and 1980, the rise in the proportion of children living in poverty in the 1980s would have been even greater than it actually was. Though there may be more to learn about what women can do to restructure their time or redirect their income to benefit children, it is unlikely that there is nearly as much room to maneuver here as there is with respect to fathers' behavior, time investments, and income use vis-à-vis children. Lack of interest in the topic is reflected in how little is known about fathers' roles in supporting their children. Time budget data show that fathers' total work time (market and domestic) increases less than mothers' with the arrival of each additional child (Boulier 1977; Fried and Settergren 1986).

On the matter of behavior and social support, a parallel lacuna in concern about the father's role is found. A study of the effects of maternal mortality on children in Southern Africa illustrates the point (Defense for Children International–USA 1991). Because only mothers were provided with information on their children's nutritional needs at the time of delivery, fathers had no sense of their parental responsibilities in the event of the mother's death. As a result of inadequate child care arrangements and the provision of insufficient money for food, the children's health and nutrition suffered. Nonetheless, because people did not see a child's nutrition as a father's responsibility, people in the community did not expect any more of the father. Engle (1990) recounts the results of a recent study in Nigeria, which found that 35 percent of men whose children were hospitalized for malnutrition attributed this to problems in mothering and the home environment, rather than to food sufficiency (in which they have a role) (Ojofeitimi and Adelekan 1984).

Finally, there is a good side of this story to tell. A few studies indicate an association between the father's commitment to the family and the child's well-being. For example, Engle (1993) found that in Guatemala, the proportion of the father's income devoted to the family, more than the absolute amount of his income directed to the family, was associated with the child's welfare as measured by weight-for-height. If a father's interactive time with children increased during the early years, so might his propensity to support children should a marriage fail or should he migrate.

In order to devise policies that attract more men into the business of caring for their children, one must observe how a father constructs his parenting role. Does he define his responsibility as one that flows through his relationship to the child's mother, as Furstenberg and Cherlin (1991) suggest for some fathers in the United States? Is it heavily conditioned by the circumstances of the child's conception, the existence of other sexual relation-ships, the continuing rapport between the parents, his coresidence with the child, or the child's gender? When does the father view his relationship to the child as permanent and one of obligation?

Economic Equity for Women

Nothing in the research reviewed in this chapter suggests to us that women in developing countries will be under less pressure to contribute substantially to the well-being of themselves and others in the coming decades. It is clear from all the information about how households and families operate and the volatility of partnerships that there is no one on whom the adult woman or mother can rely absolutely except herself. The available information on changing family structures, female headship, and maintenance of families argues for an intensified effort to increase the hourly return on women's work effort.

In past generations and in subsistence economies, a mother may have been able to obtain acceptable outcomes for herself and her children by growing and processing more food for home consumption and gathering fuel from longer distances, among other efforts. But increasingly, to enter the modern economy, women and their dependents require cash for school fees, transportation, and the purchase of modern medicine, and food of adequate nutritional quality.

In the 1970s and 1980s, investigators often used a "full income" concept[9] to give a clearer picture of the tremendous resourcefulness and hard work of the poor in garnering resources for survival. If such exercises continue to be useful in thinking about the total sum of effort in making up an economy, and particularly in reevaluating women's contributions, it works against poor people, and especially women, when this attributed value is mistaken for purchasing power. The fact that so many impoverished women are producing reasonable livelihoods for dependents—though not necessarily for themselves—has distracted us from the question of how economic growth and adequate investment in human capital can best be achieved. More balanced attention to men's and women's roles, realistically viewing *both* as producers *and* reproducers—as workers and parents—will provide a better basis for evaluat-ing the adequacy of income or quality of life. If gender equity is to be achieved in development policies, men and women should be able to produce their fair share of a basic standard of living for themselves and their dependents through relatively comparable work efforts and time expenditures.

---

9. Full income is defined as income earned for hours worked for pay plus imputed income from nonmarket hours of work (assumed to be equal to the hours in the day remaining after allowing for necessary hours for sleep) plus unearned income.

Current policies encumber women's livelihoods in two respects: they do not accommodate women's special family responsibilities and they tie women's access to resources, including labor markets, to marital or sexual relationships with men or to their fertility status. In the formal labor market, maternity leave provisions and child-care arrangements are the exception rather than the rule; in the informal sector and the domestic arena, the lack of infrastructure and of complementary productive inputs (such as land of adequate quality and appropriate capital equipment) keeps women's productivity low and reduces the time and energy available for their children (Desai and Jain 1994). Another source of women's economic inequality derives from the law and traditional practice. When women are treated as legal juniors in family law and economic policy, their access to family-based productive resources is prejudiced. With the mounting evidence of shifting family arrangements, diminishing coresidence of spouses, and women's growing economic responsibility for children, there is no plausible basis for policies that limit women's economic access based on marital or fertility status. The requirement of a husband's (father's or son's) consent for women's access to credit, market activity, migration for work, or asset ownership is as unproductive as it is offensive. Women's access to a fair share of marital property on the occasion of divorce or death of a spouse is as necessary to their survival as it is fair. There is little systematic information about the specific legal, administrative, and social barriers to women's rights and economic independence that remain codified in regulations and customary practice. A more systematic analysis of the ways in which presumptions about women's family roles inhibit their access to vital resources is called for.

The removal of gender bias from economic policy must include removing explicit and implicit constraints on women based on family or reproductive roles. A test of women's unencumbered access should be: "Can a celibate, childless woman own property?" "Can a pregnant, unmarried woman hold a job?" Though women will always be economic assets to their households and families, this dividend to society arises from the more fundamental recognition that women as individuals have rights to livelihoods on their own behalf.

Conclusions

This analysis of the operational meanings of headship and household in defining both the economic contributions and vulnerabilities of women and their implications for the children they support points up the important economic contribution that women make in all types of households and families, regardless of their headship status. Owing to the complexity and flux in family types, women's marital status and living arrangements provide an insufficient framework for studying their economic vulnerability and often project a false picture of either economic security or poverty. By extension, children's welfare is less conditioned by their parents' marital status than current policies and normative approaches would have us believe. The wealth or poverty of mothers and their children is determined to an important degree by whether fathers, regardless of marital or residential arrangements, contribute economically to their children, not by the family's normatively ascribed headship or household type. Indeed household living arrangements are the outcome of family survival strategies and, as such, are more likely to be the consequence of underlying economic circumstances than a determining factor in those circumstances (Lloyd 1995). The convenient assumption made by most economists that headship is exogenous has come under increasing scrutiny. Handa (1995) reports that modeling the endogeneity of female headship is possible. In particular, Handa finds that outside opportunities or extraenvironmental parameters associated with bargaining models of the household and family influence the formation of female-headed households in Jamaica.

The likelihood of increases in the extent of family separation due to the widening search for livelihoods, as well as the destructive forces of civil unrest, famine, and war, lends urgency to the pursuit of new research and policy initiatives that focus on the links between men and women, parents and children, both within and between households. The structure of existing data on households must not blind researchers to the full complexity of the family as they seek to learn more about intrafamily connections and resource flows and design policies that will strengthen these connections—particularly the neglected father-child link. For example, the collection of new data on mothers and children, as it is typically carried out in fertility, family planning, and child health surveys, must incorporate ways to link children to their biological fathers, even if they reside outside the household, as well as to gather more information from men about their childbearing and -rearing roles. Even in the absence of full information, however, certain principles and priorities are clear: the recognition of children's right to a fair share of both parents' social and economic resources, the importance of fathers to their children's well-being and future development, and women's economic equity, achieved under circumstances that are sensitive to unencumbered family roles.

PART III

The Policy Relevance of Intrahousehold Resource Allocation

14 Family Resources and Gender Differences in Human Capital Investments: The Demand for Children's Medical Care in Pakistan

HAROLD ALDERMAN AND PAUL GERTLER

Using a model of human capital investment, we examine in this chapter how gender differences in human capital allocations vary across families with different levels of resources. Differences in rates of such investment by gender have been documented extensively for South Asia and occasionally for Latin America and Sub-Saharan Africa.[1] We show theoretically that, under the same conditions that would lead to higher investments in sons, the demand for daughters' human capital will be more income and price elastic. Moreover, we find that the difference in the price elasticities falls as family resources rise. Poorer families invest less in daughters relative to sons, and the difference in the level of discrimination between wealthier and poorer families grows as the price of human capital rises. These results imply that policies designed to alleviate poverty and raise incomes will also reduce gender discrimination, especially among the poor. In addition, increases in the prices of education, medical care, and nutrition not only exaggerate the promale bias but also exaggerate the bias proportionally more within poorer families. These policy implications are independent of whether the reason for discrimination is due to market incentives or preferences.

There is substantial empirical support for these hypotheses in the literature on the demand for medical care, education, and nutrition in developing countries. For example, DeTray (1988) finds the demand for girls' schooling to be more income elastic than that for boys in Malaysia. Schultz (1985) finds girls' school enrollment rates to be more price and income elastic in an aggregate cross-national analysis, whereas Behrman (1988b) finds the proson bias in nutrition allocation to be greatest during the "lean" season in rural India. Similarly Garg and Morduch (1997) find that gender discrimination in nutrition among siblings in Ghana is apparent mainly among low-income households. As household resources increase, these patterns disappear. In this

---

1. A partial list of studies that document gender differences in human capital includes Boserup (1970), Rosenzweig and Schultz (1982), Sen and Sengupta (1983), Bardhan (1984), Schultz (1985), Behrman (1988b, 1990), Subramanian and Deaton (1990), Svedberg (1990), and Thomas (1994).

chapter we test these hypotheses, drawing on data on the demand for children's medical care in rural Pakistan. The results presented here are consistent with the predictions of the model used.

A Gender-Specific Model of Human Capital Investment

In this section a two-period model is constructed in order to investigate gender differences in the absolute level of investment in human capital as well as in the income and price elasticities of investment. An important feature of the model is that its predictions hold whether the reason for discrimination is due to market incentives or parental preferences. By contrast many existing studies have focused on the question of whether gender differences reflect preference orderings or investment opportunities. Dyson and Moore (1983), for example, use regional patterns of gender differences in child mortality rates to argue that they arise from kinship systems, among other factors. This claim is endorsed by Das Gupta (1987). The hypothesis essentially shows a preference for males for their direct contribution to household utility. In contrast Boserup (1970) and Rosenzweig and Schultz (1982) as well as Bardhan (1984) propose a model in which differences in allocation reflect differences in expected returns to investments. In such a model, there need not be a preference for males per se, but only a desire to maximize the level of expected lifetime total consumption. Behrman and Deolalikar (1995) show that wage rates in Indonesia do not indicate that lower returns to investment are a plausible explanation for differences in schooling. Behrman (1988b) finds evidence to support a combination of the two hypotheses.

Many models of human capital investments have been formulated in terms of a single household utility function. However, even if collective approaches account for the process of allocation of household resources, it is still necessary to explain why a household member chooses to invest more in one gender than the other. For example, Thomas (1994) finds evidence for differential investments in daughters and sons by mothers as compared to fathers. It is unclear whether this finding reflects differential returns to investments (including the propensity of the child to remit to the parent) or preferences per se. The model presented here—or a similar one that explains difference in perceived returns to improvements in girls' human capital relative to boys'— must hold for at least one adult in the household for bargaining to affect gender-specific investments.[2]

Assumptions

Consider a world in which parents work in the first period and retire in the second period. Consumption in the first period is income less that which is

---

2. Thus, using a variant of the principle of Occam's razor, this study does not set up a bargaining model since distinguishable predictions that can be analyzed with the data are not apparent.

invested in the human capital of children, whereas consumption in the second period depends on the wealth of the children, which, in turn, depends on their human capital.[3] Parents value their own consumption and their children's wealth. Thus there are both investment and consumption motives for human capital investments. In their human capital investment decisions, parents must trade off their present consumption against their future consumption and their children's wealth.

To focus on gender differences, the family is assumed to have two children, one of each sex. Market incentives are introduced by allowing both the return to children's human capital and children's remittance rates to differ by gender. Preference differences can also be introduced by allowing the marginal utility of children's human capital to differ by gender.

Formally let the parents' lifetime utility function be

$$U = F(C_1) + G(C_2, W_b, W_g) \tag{14.1}$$

where

C_1 = consumption in period 1,
C_2 = consumption in period 2,
W_b = the wealth of the male child, and
W_g = the wealth of the female child.

If parents do not explicitly prefer one gender to the other, it is assumed that $\partial G/\partial W_b = \partial G/\partial W_g$ and $\partial^2 G/\partial W_b \partial W_b = \partial G^2/\partial W_g \partial W_g$ when $W_b = W_g$.

Parents' consumption in the second period is generated by transfers from their children. It is assumed that the amount of resources remitted to parents is proportional to each child's wealth. Formally parents' second-period consumption is

$$C_2 = \beta W_b + \tau W_g \tag{14.2}$$

where β is the rate of transfer per unit wealth from the male child and τ is the rate of transfer per unit wealth from the female child. The relative magnitudes of male and female remittance rates partly depend on cultural patterns of intergenerational transfers. As noted by Rosenzweig and Schultz (1982), τ may be negative, for example when parents must provide large dowries in order for their daughters to marry.

Children's wealth depends on their human capital in the following manner:

$$W_b = bH_b \tag{14.3}$$

and

$$W_g = gH_g \tag{14.4}$$

---

3. The model can be expanded to overlapping generations, most simply by defining parental income as net of transfers to the previous generation.

where b and g are the respective monetary returns to investment in human capital.

Finally, the model is closed by specifying the family's budget constraint:

$$P(H_b + H_g) + C_1 = Y \tag{14.5}$$

where P is the price of human capital and Y is parental income. Parents divide this income between current consumption and investment in their children's human capital.

Equilibrium

Parents choose H_b and H_g to maximize utility subject to the budget constraint and their children's remittance function. (It is assumed that remittances are deterministic.) By substituting equations (14.2)–(14.5) into equation (14.1), the following maximization problem is derived:

$$\max H_b, H_g = F[Y - P(H_b + H_g)] + G[(\beta b H_b + \tau g H_g), b H_b, g H_g] \tag{14.6}$$

The first-order conditions are

$$\frac{\partial E}{\partial C_1}P = \frac{\partial G}{\partial C_2}\beta b + \frac{\partial G}{\partial W_b}b \tag{14.7}$$

and

$$\frac{\partial F}{\partial C_1}P = \frac{\partial G}{\partial C_2}\tau g + \frac{\partial G}{\partial W_g}g \tag{14.8}$$

Conditions (14.7) and (14.8) imply that parents invest in their children's human capital to the point that the marginal cost in terms of consumption today equals the marginal benefit tomorrow. These marginal benefits are equal to the marginal utility of second-period consumption multiplied by the remittance rate per unit of human capital, plus the utility the parents derive from a marginal increase in the children's human capital.

Now turn to the implications of the model for the allocation of resources between genders. Consider the case in which the market return to boys' human capital is greater than the return to girls' human capital ($b > g$), as in Rosenzweig and Schultz (1982). This implies that families invest more in boys' human capital than in girls' human capital. A similar conclusion is derived when boys' rates of remittance are larger (that is, $\beta > \tau$) or if parents are concerned more with sons' wealth than with daughters' wealth ($\partial G/\partial W_b > \partial G/\partial W_g$).

The left-hand sides of equations (14.7) and (14.8)—marginal cost—are identical. Hence parents invest in the human capital of boys and girls up to the point at which the marginal benefit of boys' human capital equals the marginal benefit of girls' human capital:

$$\frac{\partial G}{\partial C_2}\beta b + \frac{\partial G}{\partial W_b}b = \frac{\partial G}{\partial C_2}\tau g + \frac{\partial G}{\partial W_g}g \qquad (14.9)$$

If $b > g$, the left-hand side of equation (14.9) will be greater than the right-hand side when evaluated at the same level of human capital. Since the marginal benefit functions are decreasing in H, equation (14.9) is satisfied at a point at which $H_b > H_g$. When $\beta > \tau$ or when $\partial G/\partial W_b > \partial G/\partial W_g$, the marginal benefit from a boy's human capital will also be greater than the marginal benefit from a girl's human capital at the same value of H. By a similar argument, investment in a boy's human capital will exceed that in a girl's.

Comparative Statics

How does the allocation of human capital change in response to increases in the price of human capital and in family wealth? Results show that the conditions that led to higher investment in a boy's human capital will also imply higher price and income elasticities of investment in a girl's human capital.

Beginning with price elasticities, a price rise increases the marginal cost of human capital investment—that is, the left-hand sides of equations (14.7) and (14.8). The assumption that $b > g$ implies that the change in H_g that restores the condition in equation (14.8) for each level of H_b is larger than the change in H_b that satisfies equation (14.7) for each level of H_g following a price change. That is, the demand for a girl's human capital is more price elastic than the demand for a boy's human capital.

Alternatively stated, when $b > g$, the marginal benefit from a boy's human capital decreases faster with H than does that from a girl's human capital. Hence the adjustment necessary to restore equilibrium is less with boys than with girls. This finding implies smaller absolute values for price elasticities. It is not a statement about second derivatives, but about the product of the parameters in equations (14.3) and (14.4) multiplied by the first derivatives of the second term on the right in equation (14.1). Similarly, the demand for a girl's human capital is more price elastic than the demand for a boy's human capital when $\beta > \tau$.

The situation is more complex when $\partial G/\partial W_b > \partial G/\partial W_g$. Under that condition, the assumptions outlined previously are insufficient to determine the relative magnitude of the price elasticities. With the plausible assumption, however, that $\partial G^2/\partial W_b\partial W_b > \partial G^2/\partial W_g\partial W_g$, relative magnitudes of the price elasticities similar to the two earlier conditions will be expected.

By a similar argument, the same conditions imply that the demand for a girl's human capital is more income elastic than the demand for a boy's human capital. An increase in income affects the first-order conditions through the marginal cost of human capital investment—the left-hand sides of equations (14.7) and (14.8). The increase lowers the marginal utility of current consumption and therefore lowers marginal cost. This fall in marginal cost is analogous to a reduction in price. Therefore an increase in income leads to a greater increase in the investment in human capital for girls than for boys.

Finally, the model implies that the price elasticity of demand falls with income and that a girl's price elasticity falls faster with income than a boy's. An increase in income lowers the marginal utility of current consumption and, therefore, the marginal cost of human capital. This result implies that a rise in price represents a larger increase in marginal cost at lower levels of income than at higher levels of income. Hence increased prices will generate larger reductions in human capital investment among families with lower incomes than among families with higher incomes. Put another way, differences in gender price elasticities diminish with income.

Evidence from the Demand for Medical Care in Pakistan

In this section, the hypotheses concerning gender differences in price and income elasticities of investment in human capital are tested by examining the provision of medical care to children in rural Pakistan. Sathar (1987) notes that postneonatal mortality rates for girls in Pakistan are 15 percent above those for boys; the discrepancy is greater for daughters that are born after another girl. Indeed Pakistan has the highest ratio of males to females in the world. The ratio over all age groups in 1981 was 1.1 males for every female (Krotki 1986). Similarly, enrollment rates at all levels of schooling indicate a predominance of investment in the schooling of boys over girls.

In addition to a preference for sons, other factors may also contribute to gender discrimination. For example, participation in the wage labor force is low among women. Direct economic contribution of women to the natal household is limited not only by these employment patterns but also by the tendency of women to leave the household, and often the village, at marriage. This cultural norm contrasts with the tendency for sons to remain in an extended family structure.

These separate reasons for gender differences have the same implication for behavior in the model. Accordingly no attempt is made to identify their relative contribution, but instead the focus is placed on the degree of income and price responsiveness in health investment decisions.

In the empirical framework, utility depends on children's health and on the consumption of goods other than medical care. Only primary curative aspects of health investment are considered.[4] If a child experiences an illness, the family must decide whether or not to seek medical care and from which care provider. The benefit from consuming medical care is an improvement in

---

4. That is, the theoretical model is tested by looking at investment conditional on illness rather than the full range of investment in human capital to which it may apply.

children's health, and the cost of medical care is a reduction in the family's consumption of other goods and services. There are some potential limitations to testing the model by looking at investment conditional on illness rather than the full range of investment in human capital. These price responses that are estimated may be considered short-run elasticities and will differ from long-run elasticities if the probability of illness is responsive to price. Thus the estimates here are likely to be lower bounds to the long-run estimates. Dow (1995) presents one empirical investigation that finds that the difference between long- and short-run responses is not large and, moreover, that there is no sample selection bias using a sample conditional on illness.

The demand for a particular alternative is the probability that it yields the highest utility among the alternatives. Gertler, Locay, and Sanderson (1987) show that income can influence the choice of provider only if the conditional utility function allows for a nonconstant marginal rate of substitution of health consumption. One functional form that satisfies this condition is the semi-quadratic, in which utility is linear in health and quadratic in consumption.

Specifically, let the conditional utility function for the non–self-care alternatives be

$$U_j = \alpha_0 H_j + \alpha_1(Y - P_j) + \alpha_2(Y - P_j)^2 + \varepsilon_j \qquad (14.10)$$

where H denotes expected outcome; Y, income; and P_j, the cost of health care from the jth provider. ε_j is a zero mean random taste disturbance with finite variance and is uncorrelated across families and alternatives. Under the alternative of self-care, $P_0 = 0$, implying that the conditional utility function reduces to

$$U_0 = \alpha_0 H_0 + \alpha_1 Y + \alpha_2 Y^2 + \varepsilon_0 \qquad (14.11)$$

for the self-care alternative.

Estimation is based on the ordering of the utility of these different alternatives. This implies that the parameters in equations (14.10) and (14.11) are identified only when the values of expected health and consumption differ across the alternatives; if the contributions of either expected health or consumption to utility are constant across alternatives, they cannot influence which alternative is chosen.

In practice, specification of the demand across alternatives is based on the difference in the utility of each alternative from that of self-care. Expanding the quadratic term in equation (14.10) and taking the difference between equations (14.11) and (14.10) gives

$$U_j - U_0 = \alpha_0(H_j - H_0) - \alpha_1 P_j - 2\alpha_2 Y P_j + \alpha_2 P_j^2 + \varepsilon_j - \varepsilon_0 \qquad (14.12)$$

Note that the difference includes terms in price and price squared, allowing for declining (or increasing) price responsiveness. Income enters only in the interaction with price. One can test whether the parameter for the interaction differs from zero and whether it differs from the parameter for the quadratic price term. This latter test indicates if the relation of income and price is an artifact of the functional form. In particular, the model requires that the estimated coefficient for YP is twice that estimated for P^2.[5]

The remaining issue in the specification is the measurement of the efficacy (quality) of each alternative. The quality of health care provider j is defined as the difference between expected health outcome from the jth provider and that of self-care:

$$Q_j = H_j - H_0 \qquad (14.13)$$

Substituting into the conditional utility function (14.10) yields:

$$U_j = \alpha_0(H_0 + Q_j) + \alpha_1(Y - P_j) + \alpha_2(Y - P_j)^2 + \varepsilon_j \qquad (14.14)$$

Since Q_0 has been normalized to 0, the conditional utility function in equation (14.14) for the self-care alternative reduces to

$$U_0 = \alpha_0 H_0 + \alpha_1 Y + \alpha_2 Y^2 + \varepsilon_0 \qquad (14.15)$$

The $\alpha_0 H_0$ term appears in all the conditional utility functions. Since only differences in utility influence preference ordering, this term can be ignored.

Quality, Q_j, is not directly observable. This problem is solved by letting Q_j be a parametric function of its observable determinants. The quality of provider j's care is the expected improvement in health (marginal product) over the expected level of health that would occur from self-treatment. This is a function of characteristics of the health care provider (including distance) as well as family characteristics such as health status and ability to implement the recommended treatment. For example, the expected improvement in health from hospital care relative to self-care may be increasing in education, since families with higher education may be better able to implement recommended treatment plans.

Similarly, the marginal utility of the health of a child may depend on how many children there are in the household. In general, the value of health may vary with demographic characteristics such as age, sex, education, and family composition.

Thus basic determinants of both the quality household production function and the marginal utility of quality are demographic variables. Pollak and Wachter (1975) argue that the separate effects of demographic variables in the household production function and in the marginal utility of quality generally cannot be identified. Therefore, a reduced-form model of the utility from quality is specified. Formally, let the utility from quality be given by

---

5. This hypothesis was not rejected.

$$\alpha_0 Q_j = \varepsilon_{0j} + \beta_{1j}X + \beta_{2j}Z_j + \eta_j \tag{14.16}$$

where X is a vector of demographic variables, Z_j provides specific characteristics that do not directly enter the budget constraint, and n_j is a zero mean random disturbance with finite variance.

To make the specification as general as possible, let the coefficients in equation (14.16) vary by alternative. Allowing for different intercepts permits the baseline quality to vary by type of provider, and having different slope coefficients allows the provider's productivity relative to self-care to vary with family characteristics such as age, education, and severity of illness. The alternative specific intercept is important in this model because it allows the quality to vary across provider types.

Since $Q_0 = 0$, the utility from quality simplifies to $\alpha_0 Q_0 = 0$ for the self-care alternative. As mentioned, the coefficients in equation (14.16) are interpreted relative to the self-care alternative. The normalization sets the unobserved portion of quality in the self-care alternative, η_0, to zero.

Substitution of equation (14.16) into the conditional utility function (14.10) yields

$$U_j = V_j + \eta_j + \varepsilon_j \tag{14.17}$$

where

$$V_j = \alpha_0\beta_{0j} + \alpha_0\beta_{1j}X + \alpha_0\alpha_{2j}Z_j + \alpha_1(Y - P_j) + \alpha_2(Y - P_j)^2 \tag{14.18}$$

The intercept and coefficients on the demographic variables vary by alternative, whereas the coefficients on the economic variables are constant across alternatives.

The final step is the specification of the stochastic distribution. Many studies of the demand for medical care in developing countries have assumed that these take on a multinomial logit (MNL) form. The MNL suffers from the independence of irrelevant alternatives assumption (McFadden 1981). This assumption is equivalent to assuming that the stochastic portions of the conditional utility functions are uncorrelated across alternatives, and it imposes the restriction that the cross-price elasticities are the same across alternatives. A computationally feasible generalization of the MNL is the nested multinomial logit (NMNL). The NMNL allows for correlation across subgroups of alternatives and, therefore, nonconstant, cross-price elasticities across subgroups.

The stochastic assumptions here group the non–self-care alternatives together. The η_js imply that the non–self-care alternatives may be correlated with each other, but not with the self-care alternative. Therefore, the self-care demand function (that is, the probability of choosing self-care) is

$$\pi_0 = \frac{\exp(V_0)}{\exp(V_0) + [\Sigma_{j \neq 0} \exp(V_j / \sigma)]^\sigma} \tag{14.19}$$

and the probability of choosing a traditional healer, doctor, pharmacist, or clinic is

$$\pi_j = \frac{[1 - \pi_0][\exp(V_j / \sigma)]}{\Sigma_{j \neq 0} \exp(V_j / \sigma)} \tag{14.20}$$

where σ is a coefficient of dissimilarity between the non–self-care and the self-care conditional utility functions introduced by the η_js and the V_js given in equation (14.17).

McFadden (1981) shows that σ must be between zero and one for the model to be consistent with utility maximization. When σ is less than one, the error terms in the utility functions of the non–self-care alternatives are corre-lated. This result implies that families view the non–self-care alternatives as closer substitutes with other care than with self-care. When $\sigma = 1$, all of the alternatives are viewed as equally close substitutes and the NMNL reduces to an MNL.

Own-price effects enter the demand function via the numerator in equa-tion (14.20). Cross-price effects enter via the denominators in equations (14.19) and (14.20). When σ is less than one, the cross-price elasticities of the non–self-care alternatives are higher than the cross-price elasticities of the self-care alternative.

A further refinement, typically not reported in other studies, is in the treatment of cases for which the household reports that a type of provider is not available. Failure to modify the likelihood function for those cases in which the household choice is limited by nonavailability may have a nontrivial impact on estimated relative utilities. The likelihood function is modified by excluding the unavailable options from the denominators of equations (14.19) and (14.20). The numerators are automatically excluded from these options since an unavailable option is never chosen.

Data

The data for this study come from a 1986 survey of households residing in five low-income districts throughout Pakistan (Alderman and Garcia 1993). Female enumerators interviewed female household members and recorded data on illness by type and associated medical care use during the preceding two weeks for each child five years of age or under. Also recorded were the availability, costs, and distances of medical services, in addition to socioeco-nomic characteristics of the household. Moreover, information was collected on assets to predict household incomes, which were used as a measure of permanent income. Table 14.1 reports descriptive statistics.

The sample is conditional on acute morbidity, with trauma, surgery, and chronic illness being excluded. Since the observations are of individuals, not

TABLE 14.1 Descriptive statistics of data used in this analysis

Variable	Female children		Male children	
	Mean	Standard Deviation	Mean	Standard Deviation
Annual household income per capita (rupees)	2,464	918	2,512	965
Siani price (rupees)	14.29	13.32	15.49	13.46
Government clinic price (rupees)	19.89	13.34	20.32	13.91
Pharmacist price (rupees)	15.45	8.40	15.69	8.84
Doctor price (rupees)	35.21	9.09	35.53	9.15
Siani travel time (minutes)	42.03	46.01	46.00	48.25
Government clinic travel time (minutes)	116.88	101.65	112.04	100.22
Pharmacist travel time (minutes)	71.96	46.64	70.50	47.46
Doctor travel time (minutes)	58.56	39.36	53.75	37.50
Siani waiting time (minutes)	21.63	22.46	23.96	23.51
Government clinic waiting time (minutes)	67.42	51.49	64.65	51.09
Pharmacist waiting time (minutes)	32.97	25.52	32.94	25.45
Doctor waiting time (minutes)	31.34	12.29	29.76	11.20
Household size	10.61	5.29	10.55	5.01
Age (years)	2.31	1.56	2.21	1.52
Mother's education (= 1 if some)	0.07	. . .	0.05	. . .
Days ill	3.80	4.18	4.10	4.82
Diarrhea = 1	0.68	. . .	0.66	. . .
Cough = 1	0.06	. . .	0.06	. . .
Flu = 1	0.10	. . .	0.10	. . .
Fever = 1	0.47	. . .	0.47	. . .
Height/age	79.40	27.59	80.71	24.77
Go to *siani* = 1	0.13	. . .	0.11	. . .
Go to government clinic = 1	0.10	. . .	0.09	. . .
Go to pharmacist = 1	0.05	. . .	0.04	. . .
Go to doctor = 1	0.43	. . .	0.47	. . .
Know of *siani* = 1	0.94	. . .	0.92	. . .
Know of government clinic = 1	0.95	. . .	0.97	. . .
Know of pharmacist = 1	0.56	. . .	0.55	. . .
Know of doctor = 1	0.96	. . .	0.96	. . .
Sample size	1,649		1,781	

SOURCE: International Food Policy Research Institute survey of five districts in Pakistan, 1986–91.

NOTES: *Siani* refers to a traditional healer.
   . . ., not applicable.

households, larger households have a greater weight in the sample than would be the case in the household-based sample. This explains the large value for average household size.

Four provider alternatives in addition to self-care were identified: (1) private physicians, (2) pharmacists, (3) government clinics, and (4) traditional healers (*sianis*). Private medical care predominates in this sample, as well as elsewhere in Pakistan. The 43 percent of cases taken to private doctors observed in the sample is consistent with the 41 percent of all cases (including adult illnesses and surgery) observed in urban Pakistan (Pakistan 1987). Costs per visit are relatively low, in part due to the nature of childhood illnesses, but are of an expected relative magnitude.

Consumption net of medical care, consumption squared, and the determinants of the utility from quality must be specified for each alternative. Consumption is computed as monthly family income less the price of consultation. Monthly family income is measured by predicted total income, including the value of home production. The price of each alternative is the median reported price in each region. Consumption and consumption squared are measured in per capita terms.

Pitt and Rosenzweig (1985) provide evidence that family income depends on the health status of children through the influence on the labor supply behavior of mothers. The instrumental variables procedure corrects for possible simultaneity bias (Alderman and Garcia 1993). Measures of family assets—including irrigated and rainfed area owned, orchards, volume of livestock, vehicles and other machinery—serve as the identifying variables. The instrumenting equations also include such variables as household composition and the number of males and females with primary, secondary, and postsecondary education. The instrumenting equations allow for separate parameters for each district to accommodate different resource bases and returns to assets.

The data include the child's age in months, a dichotomous variable indicating whether the child had diarrhea, a set of mutually exclusive dichotomous variables indicating whether the child had various illness symptoms, the duration of the illness, and, as a measure of overall nutritional status, the child's height-for-age as a percentage of the international standard. In addition, the level of the mother's education and the size of the household were included.

Measures for travel and waiting times by provider are available. In a fully specified model, the corresponding time prices would enter the budget constraint and be part of the total price of medical care. There are two reasons why this approach is not feasible here: (1) the value of the time of the person would need to be known to compute the time price, and (2) there would need to be an identifiable person who takes the child for medical care. Although the survey attempted to obtain information on the family member who usually accompanied the child to the caregiver, most households indicated that the responsibility was joint. Hence no value for time could be accurately ascribed to the visits observed. Moreover, the value of time is difficult to compute for women. Although the labor force participation of adult women was between 30 and 40 percent in this sample, depending on the season, few women worked in the wage sector.

By treating time costs outside the monetary budget constraint, the coefficients of time are allowed to pick up any travel costs. It is implicitly assumed that time costs do not reduce expenditures but rather come at the expense of leisure. Thus travel time enters the conditional utility functions as a separate argument.

Results

Specification

The provider choice model was estimated separately for males and females. The hypothesis that the two samples could be pooled into a single model was rejected at the .01 significance level in a likelihood ratio test. Coefficients were estimated separately by gender and are presented in Table 14.2. The standard errors were computed by applying the formula developed in Duncan (1987) to correct for the potential bias introduced through instrumenting for family incomes.

The values of σ in both models are between zero and one and are significantly different from both these numbers. This outcome indicates that the NMNL is preferred to the MNL, implying that households view the professional choices as closer substitutes for each other than for the self-care alternative.

The coefficients on the consumption and consumption squared terms are significantly different from zero, implying that the conditional utility function is concave in consumption. Prices enter through these terms, and it is the variation in prices that identifies these parameters. Price effects are negative over the relevant income range, and the price effects diminish with income. In addition, the negative coefficient on consumption squared indicates that families with more resources are more likely to seek medical care to treat their child's illness.

The coefficients on travel and waiting time are negative and significantly different from zero. The results are consistent with results from other countries such as Côte d'Ivoire (Dor, Gertler, and van der Gaag 1987) and Peru (Gertler, Locay, and Sanderson 1987).

Older boys received care more often, whereas care is age neutral in the model for girls. Children with more serious illnesses tended to receive more care in both models. Mother's education did not affect health care choice. This finding is plausible given the low level of education and lack of variation in the sample.

TABLE 14.2 NMNL model of medical care provider choice, estimate coefficients, and *t*-statistics

	Female children		Male children	
Variable	Coefficient	*t*-Statistic	Coefficient	*t*-Statistic
Consumption	0.162	2.83	0.126	2.39
Consumption squared[a]	−0.148	2.71	−0.091	1.66
ln (travel time)	−0.209	2.85	−0.201	2.84
ln (waiting time)	−0.211	2.32	−0.326	2.69
Sigma	0.545	3.29	0.629	3.43
Siani				
Constant	2.350	5.88	3.050	6.03
Household size	−0.028	1.58	−0.022	1.22
Age	0.076	1.65	−0.035	0.63
Mother's education	0.062	0.19	−0.258	0.58
Days ill	0.168	8.75	0.221	9.71
Diarrhea	−0.706	4.96	−0.823	5.35
Cough	−1.655	5.22	−1.700	5.44
Flu	−1.573	6.16	−1.910	6.79
Fever	−1.905	9.93	−1.854	9.08
Height-for-age	0.003	1.18	−0.003	1.12
Government clinic				
Constant	2.956	5.96	2.928	5.46
Household size	−0.013	0.85	0.008	0.48
Age	0.110	2.07	0.039	0.71
Mother's education	−0.074	0.22	0.025	0.07
Days ill	0.174	8.91	1.217	9.01
Diarrhea	−0.808	4.32	−0.871	4.83
Cough	−1.830	5.36	−1.829	5.03
Flu	−1.785	6.26	−1.662	5.55
Fever	−1.629	7.91	−1.430	6.86
Height-for-age	−0.003	1.09	−0.005	−1.43
Pharmacist				
Constant	2.886	5.22	2.689	4.54
Household size	−0.043	1.71	0.007	0.30
Age	0.009	0.14	−0.037	0.50
Mother's education	−0.345	0.70	0.012	0.03
Days ill	0.165	5.10	0.266	13.75
Diarrhea	−0.788	4.09	−1.205	5.15
Cough	−1.247	2.75	−1.310	2.91
Flu	−0.942	2.36	−1.116	2.70
Fever	−1.116	3.78	−1.376	4.57
Height-for-age	−0.004	1.37	−0.008	1.75
Doctor				
Constant	3.762	5.77	4.124	5.62
Household size	−0.004	0.32	−0.016	0.99
Age	0.080	1.84	0.062	1.37
Mother's education	0.214	0.76	0.027	0.08
Days ill	0.201	15.28	0.256	15.88
Diarrhea	−0.824	5.57	−0.922	6.74
Cough	−1.819	6.03	−2.203	7.63
Flu	−1.973	7.54	−1.718	6.99
Fever	−1.575	9.30	−1.458	8.69
Height-for-age	−0.003	1.27	−0.004	1.46
Sample size	1,649		1,732	
Log likelihood	1,795.29		1,859.51	

NOTE: *Siani* refers to a traditional healer.
[a]Coefficients reflect scaling of consumption by dividing it by 10,000.

Gender Differences

Owing to the nonlinear nature of the model, simulation is used to explore gender differences. All simulations are conducted holding constant the values of the explanatory variables at the population means, so that the gender comparisons reflect only differences in the coefficients of the two models. The simulation results are then used to derive the arc elasticities reported in Table 14.3. As expected, the price elasticity of demand for female care is more elastic than male demand at lower income levels. Furthermore, the difference disappears as income rises. In the lowest income group, the absolute value of the price elasticity for doctors is 58 percent larger for females than for males.

TABLE 14.3 Arc price elasticities by income and gender

Income	Price Range	*Siani*	Government Clinic	Pharmacist	Doctor
Female children					
500	0–15	−0.28	−0.29	−0.30	−0.10
	15–30	−0.60	−0.60	−0.61	−0.25
	30–45	−0.91	−0.91	−0.93	−0.46
1,500	0–15	−0.24	−0.24	−0.25	−0.09
	15–30	−0.49	−0.49	−0.50	−0.20
	30–45	−0.75	−0.75	−0.76	−0.35
2,500	0–15	−0.19	−0.19	−0.19	−0.07
	15–30	−0.38	−0.38	−0.39	−0.15
	30–45	−0.58	−0.58	−0.59	−0.25
3,500	0–15	−0.13	−0.13	−0.14	−0.05
	15–30	−0.26	−0.27	−0.27	−0.10
	30–45	−0.40	−0.40	−0.41	−0.16
Male children					
500	0–15	−0.21	−0.21	−0.21	−0.07
	15–30	−0.43	−0.43	−0.44	−0.17
	30–45	−0.66	−0.66	−0.67	−0.29
1,500	0–15	−0.18	−0.18	−0.19	−0.06
	15–30	−0.37	−0.37	−0.38	−0.14
	30–45	−0.56	−0.57	−0.58	−0.24
2,500	0–15	−0.15	−0.15	−0.16	−0.05
	15–30	−0.31	−0.31	−0.32	−0.11
	30–45	−0.47	−0.47	−0.48	−0.19
3,500	0–15	−0.12	−0.12	−0.12	−0.04
	15–30	−0.24	−0.24	−0.25	−0.09
	30–45	−0.37	−0.37	−0.38	−0.14

NOTE: *Siani* refers to a traditional healer.

TABLE 14.4 Arc income elasticities of demand by demand and gender

	Provider				
Income Range	*Siani*	Government Clinic	Pharmacist	Doctor	Self
Female children					
200–2,000	–0.17	–0.08	–0.16	0.15	–0.19
2,000–3,500	–0.27	–0.15	–0.26	0.20	–0.30
Male children					
500–2,000	–0.09	–0.05	–0.09	0.08	–0.12
2,000–3,500	–0.14	–0.08	–0.14	0.11	–0.19

NOTE: *Siani* refers to a traditional healer.

The corresponding percentage difference is only 14 percent for the highest income group. These comparisons pertain to the 30- to 45-rupee price range, a level that is consistent with doctors' average fee at the time of the survey.

The relative magnitude of price responsiveness for female and male children is similar for traditional healers and pharmacists as well as for clinics that the government provides. Households are more price responsive for these care providers. It is noteworthy that those health providers with the highest absolute values for price elasticities are sources of health care that are considered inferior, as indicated by the income elasticities reported in Table 14.4; for both females and males, the income elasticities are positive only for private doctor care.

Income elasticities are found to be uniformly larger in absolute value for females than for males. Higher-income households appear to be more responsive with changes of income than lower-income households. The model, however, does not predict how income elasticities change with income. Note that the discrete choice model used here exhausts all possibilities. If one choice has a positive income response, at least one other must have a negative response.

These simulations can be used to indicate the predicted probability of choosing each alternative by income level and gender at current average prices per care provider category (Table 14.5). Reading down a column represents how the probability of choosing a particular provider changes as income rises. Reading across a row gives the probability of choosing each provider for a given income class. Each row, therefore, sums to one. The results for females are presented in the upper panel of Table 14.5 and the results for males in the lower panel. Lower-income households seek care more often for males than for females.

More telling is the tendency to use high-quality providers (private doctors) more often for males than for females. Although the probability of a

TABLE 14.5 Predicted probability of choosing a provider by income and gender

		Provider			
Income	*Siani*	Government Clinic	Pharmacist	Doctor	Self
Female children					
500	0.092	0.072	0.059	0.490	0.287
1,000	0.090	0.071	0.057	0.503	0.279
1,500	0.087	0.070	0.056	0.516	0.271
2,000	0.085	0.069	0.054	0.529	0.263
2,500	0.083	0.068	0.053	0.542	0.254
3,000	0.080	0.067	0.051	0.555	0.246
3,500	0.078	0.066	0.050	0.568	0.239
Male children					
500	0.077	0.063	0.044	0.544	0.272
1,000	0.077	0.063	0.043	0.551	0.267
1,500	0.075	0.062	0.043	0.558	0.262
2,000	0.073	0.062	0.042	0.566	0.257
2,500	0.072	0.061	0.042	0.573	0.252
3,000	0.071	0.061	0.041	0.580	0.247
3,500	0.070	0.060	0.040	0.588	0.242

NOTE: *Siani* refers to a traditional healer.

low-income household taking a son to the doctor is 0.054 higher than the probability of its taking a daughter,[6] the probability that only self-care is chosen for the daughter is only 0.015 higher. The remaining difference in the choice of health care provider is in the probability of choosing a provider considered less desirable. These differences disappear as income rises.

Although the differences in health care choice indicated in this table are not dramatic, they pertain to an environment in which the price of health care is low. Moreover, most of the illness incidents from which this estimation is derived are the general day-to-day ailments to which children are susceptible. Cases that are life-threatening often require more expensive hospitalization. The comparatively high price for these treatments may lead to a greater magnitude of gender discrimination and possibly fatal delays in seeking care.

Summary

In this chapter we have examined how gender differences in human capital investments vary across families with different levels of resources. It

6. The probability for the male is 111 percent of that for the female.

has been demonstrated theoretically that the demand for a daughter's human capital will be more income and price elastic under the same conditions that would lead to higher investments in the human capital of males. Moreover, we have found that differences in price elasticities disappear as family resources rise. These results are robust in that they appear in various models that explain differential rates of human capital investment—that is, when the reason for discrimination involves market incentives, parental preferences, or cultural differences in intergenerational transfers. Empirical support for these hypotheses was found in the demand for children's medical care in rural Pakistan. Finally, as indicated previously, the conditional estimates here are lower-bound estimates of long-run responses. Whereas the illustration is based on a specific form of human capital investment, the model is general; the differences in investments observed should apply to other investments, such as education, as well as forms of investments that are difficult to measure, such as child care.

The results imply that general economic growth will assist in reducing differences in investment in human capital for males and females. Existing cross-sectional studies have not found a strong negative correlation between levels of economic development and apparent discrimination (Dyson and Moore 1983; Kynch and Sen 1983; Bardhan 1984; Murthi, Guio, and Drèze 1995). However, this may reflect preexisting differences in the parameters that indicate propensity to remit, marginal returns to human capital investments, or preferences, as well as secular trends in the parameters. Regional differences, then, should not be considered a test of the proposition that gender discrimination declines with income.

Only a limited set of policy instruments can be used to influence household resource allocation. These results indicate that price policy has the potential to reduce gender biases in human capital investment. Moreover, price responsiveness is higher among lower-income households, in which the gender-specific price elasticities are also predicted to have relatively larger differences in absolute value. The theoretical and empirical results indicate a potential, relatively noninvasive, role for policy intervention.

15 Gender Asymmetries in Intrahousehold Resource Allocation in Sub-Saharan Africa: Some Policy Implications for Land and Labor Productivity

JENNIE DEY ABBAS

Declining per capita food and agricultural production in most Sub-Saharan African countries is a source of concern among governments and the international community. The annual growth rate of per capita agricultural production for the region fell from 0.5 percent in the 1961–70 period to –1.8 percent and –0.2 percent in the 1970–80 and 1980–94 periods, respectively (FAO 1995). If Africa is to provide adequate food and employment for its growing population, it must expand agricultural production by at least 4 percent a year. To date, with the exception of hybrid maize, most of the growth in production has been due to expansion of cultivated area rather than increases in yield. Opportunities for further expansion in area are negligible in a number of land-scarce countries such as Burundi, Kenya, Malawi, and Rwanda, where rapidly increasing population densities are leading to land-resource mining and environmental degradation. Even in countries with unexploited land resources, such as Zaire, expansion of cultivated area is an insufficient means for arresting falling per capita food production. Production increases will therefore require a dramatic improvement in productivity of the order of 1–2 percent annually for labor and about 3 percent for land (see, for example, World Bank [1989b]).

Strategies for increasing productivity—whether farmer-instigated or stimulated by "outsiders"—have generally included one or more of the following:

1. modification of existing farming practices for traditional crops through the introduction of improved production inputs, such as higher-yielding seed varieties, fertilizers, and pesticides, often in conjunction with soil conservation measures and new cultural practices;
2. radical changes in crop production technologies involving the development of irrigation infrastructure and the introduction of more advanced, integrated-technology packages (especially for rice and vegetables);
3. (partial) substitution of traditional food or cash crops by higher-value (often new) cash crops, such as cocoa, tobacco, coffee, and tea; and

4. development of more integrated crop-livestock-forestry-fishery systems.

Because women produce 50 percent or more of agricultural output in many Sub-Saharan countries, particularly in eastern and southern Africa, where they manage 20–40 percent of the farms, failure to optimize women's uptake of opportunities for agricultural intensification will have enormous repercussions in aggregate terms on national production and income. In this chapter I analyze gender-differentiated responses to agricultural intensification strategies and discuss the implications of gender for public policy, in order to contribute to the efforts to improve the effectiveness of development assistance to women farmers.

Intrahousehold Gender Asymmetries

Gender asymmetries in intrahousehold resource allocation limit women's ability to adopt productivity-enhancing technologies in three ways.[1] First, women generally obtain rights to use land for household and personal crops through men.[2] Women's rights are not as strong as men's, and they often experience tenure insecurity, particularly if widowed or divorced. Second, women commonly have obligations to provide labor for male-controlled household (and sometimes personal) fields; these obligations often take precedence over women's rights to engage in own-account farming or other income-generating activities. Third, although in theory women generally have the right to dispose of the product and income from their own-account economic activities, in practice they may have relatively little freedom to reinvest their income in productivity-enhancing inputs or labor-saving equipment.

Women's rights to specific productive resources can and do change over time. Furthermore, there may be large differences in the quantity and quality of resources controlled by women within a single community, depending on their socioeconomic class. However, whatever women's socioeconomic status, their rights are generally inferior to those of the men in their households. Subtle social mechanisms and ideologies play an important role in justifying unequal gender relations within the household and the community, and these are further reinforced by policy and institutional biases against women's access to new technologies, inputs, and services, particularly credit and extension.

Labor Productivity

Since land has, until recently, been in relatively ample supply, the main concern of most Sub-Saharan farming systems has been to maximize returns

---

1. See, for example, Guyer (1981, 1986), Sen (1985c), Lele (1986), Cloud and Knowles (1988), Roberts (1988, 1991), Dey (1990), and Whitehead (1990a).

2. Instances have been documented of women owning land (Dey 1980; Cloud and Knowles 1988) and cocoa plantations (Afonja 1986), but this observation tends to apply to relatively small areas.

on labor. The most striking areas of gender asymmetry or conflict or both in intrahousehold and community resource allocation, therefore, tend to revolve around control of household labor as well as access to supplementary non-household labor. The four issues discussed in this section indicate the complex ways in which these gender asymmetries have often prevented women (and their families) from realizing the full potential labor productivity gains expected from agricultural intensification programs.

Gender Asymmetries in the Adoption of Productivity-Enhancing Technologies or Higher-Value Crops

Weaker rights to land, labor, and the income from their own production often prevent women from taking advantage of new productivity-enhancing technologies or higher-value crops. The SEMRY rice project in Cameroon, for example, failed to attract married women as own-account rice producers. Because rice was considered a male crop, women could not have controlled the income resulting from rice production, even if they produced the crop. Women therefore preferred to grow sorghum, despite less advanced technologies and lower returns on their labor, because they controlled the product (Jones 1986).

The underlying dynamics are not simply due to intrahousehold gender inequalities, because female-headed households[3] are often at a serious disadvantage compared with male-headed households in adopting technologies that enhance labor productivity. In Kenya, for instance, where women do most of the work in tea production, female-headed households were only half as likely as male-headed households to adopt tea (the most remunerative cash crop). Bevan, Collier, and Gunning (1989) note that, since about one-third of rural households are female-headed, the impact of this lower propensity to adopt tea is substantial in aggregate terms.

These authors, however, do not explore the underlying reasons for their interesting results. It is clear that labor shortages in female-headed households play a major role. Because 25 percent of married women in rural areas are in polygamous unions (World Bank 1989a), it is likely that female-headed households are smaller in size and are unable to allocate scarce labor to cash crops. Bevan, Collier, and Gunning (1989) also suggest that the absence of a wage labor force precludes the recruitment of nonfamily labor by labor-scarce female- (or male-) headed households. Another possible clue to explain these results is given by the authors' finding that land endowment was a significant influence on tea adoption. Women's inferior access to land could be a constraint on opportunities to plant tea. Other explanatory factors might include

---

3. Unfortunately, none of the studies cited in this chapter, except those of Jones (1985, 1986), differentiates between female-headed households in which the adult male members are migrant workers, and therefore temporarily absent, and households that are headed by women who are divorced, separated, or widowed. The former category of household is likely to have better access to production resources (including cash to hire labor) than the latter.

gender inequalities in access to education, extension, and credit or capital for the initial investment, as well as gender segregation of informal information networks that promote the spread, inter alia, of new agricultural technologies.

The complex socioeconomic factors affecting women's response to new opportunities for agricultural intensification were explored in some detail in a survey of 160 households (of which 26 [16 percent] were female-headed) in the area of Malawi covered by the Lilongwe Land Development Program (Chipande 1987). None of the female-headed households adopted one of the program's main innovations, an improved technology package for fire-cured tobacco; only two took up the second innovation, improved (mainly hybrid) maize. Labor-deficient households (which included all those headed by women) were unwilling to take on these technology packages despite the inducement of credit and extension, because of the risk of poor yields and defaulting on credit repayments. Female-headed households preferred to grow groundnuts, although these required more labor per hectare and gave lower returns on labor than tobacco and maize. Further analysis, moreover, revealed that (1) labor demand for tobacco was far beyond the labor supply of female-headed households; (2) hybrid maize required a greater outlay in inputs and was more risky than groundnuts (factors that weighed heavily with female-headed households, which were significantly poorer than male-headed households); and (3) although the labor input for groundnuts was roughly double that for maize, the labor demand was spread more evenly. Constrained by heavy domestic commitments, female-household heads preferred to minimize peak labor demands and grow a crop with greater labor flexibility than hybrid maize, which has time-specific operations.

Agricultural Technology Change and Loss of Female Control of Production

New technologies introduced to improve productivity on female-controlled crops or land have generally been taken over by men if they brought greater returns than the men's own crops. As a result, women tend to be confined to crops with less advanced technologies and lower returns on labor. The most striking example so far reported concerns The Gambia. Women traditionally had almost exclusive responsibility for rainfed and swamp rice production. But they were largely excluded from control of new rice technologies, which were introduced along with small-scale irrigated rice schemes in the 1970s and a large-scale pump irrigation project owned and managed by the state in the Jahali-Pacharr area in the 1980s.[4] Women lost well-established use and ownership rights to rice land when it was developed for irrigation, although the tenancy titles issued by the government were registered in women's

---

4. For the 1970s, see Dey (1980, 1981); for the Jahali-Pacharr project, see, for example, Carney (1988b), von Braun, Puetz, and Webb (1989), von Braun and Webb (1989), and Webb (1989).

names. As a result rice went from being a crop under female management and control to a household crop under the control of the male household head.[5] Men gained greater control over female labor, as women were obligated to work on (nonpersonal) household, male-controlled crops. In the case of the Jahali-Pacharr project, this resulted in an increase in communal agricultural work for *both* men and women. The increase, however, was relatively greater for women than for men (von Braun and Webb 1989).

The incentives for men to take control of the irrigated rice technology were strong, because the returns on labor were considerably higher than for any other crop. As a result of the irrigation scheme, women were not only prevented from producing the crop with the highest returns on labor but also shifted off the best rice land, on which their labor productivity had been highest.

Women did not readily acquiesce to the loss of their rice land. Their struggles were, however, thwarted by the project management's support for the male household heads' efforts to assert control over the land and technology for household production, despite attempts by the main donor to protect women's traditional rights (Carney 1988b). Women were, nonetheless, insistent on exercising their rights to engage in own-account production: since there was little, if any, uncultivated swamp rice land available, they generally borrowed upland fields, mainly for groundnut and, to a lesser extent, cotton production.

That women adopt strategies to protect their rights to engage in own-account farming and other income-generating activities—despite attempts by development projects to increase the production of household units under male control—is further confirmed by the Mwea settlement scheme in Kenya (Hanger and Moris 1973) and the Volta Valley resettlement project in Burkina Faso (McMillan 1987). Both projects provided land and technology packages for communally cultivated household crops. No consideration was given to women's rights to private fields nor their active role in animal husbandry and trade. As a result, men gained more control over women's activities.

In Mwea, some women managed to borrow land off the scheme to grow beans and vegetables and increased their beer-brewing activities and black market transactions in rice (which, under the tenancy regulations, was to be sold to the scheme). In Burkina Faso, most women had succeeded within a few years in establishing private grain fields (largely off the scheme); several of the older women had built up goat herds and two owned cattle. It is significant that the only crop on which the recommended technology package was consistently applied was the male-controlled household cotton crop—largely because of the extension service's more intensive supervision of cotton, which was used to reimburse settlers' loans.

---

5. Women are rarely household heads in rural areas of The Gambia. Unmarried, divorced, or widowed women are absorbed into extended and frequently polygamous male-headed households.

Gender Differences in Labor Productivity for the
Same Crop and Technology

A number of studies suggest that women often have lower average labor productivity levels than men for the same crop and broad level of technology. Unequal endowments in land, which are well documented in the anthropological literature, are clearly a major causal factor. However, there do not appear to be any studies that show a direct, quantitative link between land endowment and labor productivity, except that by Jackson (1985, cited in Palmer 1991), who notes that women in the Kano River irrigation project area in Nigeria obtained lower yields because they were allocated inferior land. This land was also more fragmented or farther away from the village, thus forcing women to forego productive labor time in walking greater distances.

Saito and Weidermann (1990) indicate that institutional biases against women's access to extension, inputs, and credit, and their generally lower educational levels, militate against their adoption of productivity-enhancing technologies. Moock (1976) found that when female farm managers in the Vihiga Division of Western Kenya enjoyed the same access as men to extension, production inputs, and education, their maize yields were nearly 7 percent higher than those of men. He noted that "women are generally more competent than men in Vihiga as farm managers, which is to say that women produce more output, on average, from a given package of maize inputs" (Moock 1973, cited in Palmer 1991).

A number of studies have considered the production implications of gender differences in labor endowments. Ram and Singh (1988) found that female agricultural labor in the Mossi plateau of Burkina Faso was six times more productive in farming than male labor. Although they were unable to control for men's and women's different endowments, they conjectured that women's significantly younger age and competition between co-wives could partly explain the differences in productivity.

Most of the evidence, however, suggests that women suffer greater labor constraints than men. Smock (1981) reviews evidence indicating that women's lower energy levels, sapped by successive pregnancies and the constant demands of domestic chores and child-care responsibilities, contribute to lower productivity levels.

In Nigeria (Palmer 1991) and Ghana (FAO 1991), women's obligation to attend first to the household or their husbands' fields meant that they were unable to carry out crucial operations on their own fields at the optimum time and were sometimes forced to leave tasks unfinished. In Burkina Faso, women were customarily allowed one day out of every five to tend to their personal fields. However, if men required extra labor for household or their own fields, they could "even take this day from the women" (van Koppen 1990:3).

Von Braun and Webb (1989) found women's average labor productivity in the Jahali-Pacharr area of The Gambia to be lower than men's for the same crops and level of technology. They suggested that this difference could be partly explained by women's reduced access to labor-saving implements and the fact that women generally cultivated smaller plots of land, causing diseconomies of scale. They attributed these circumstances to women's time constraints.

Their data indicate that it is not that female labor per se is less productive, but that the total labor input, consisting of both male and female labor, on female-controlled fields is less productive than that on male-controlled fields (see also Dey 1980).

Probably the most important factor is women's inferior access to labor. Household heads, especially males, have considerably greater financial resources and social influence to recruit, for both household and personal crops, the extra nonhousehold labor needed to increase the area under cultivation and to perform operations at the optimum time in order to maximize yields. They are better placed to hire labor in the casual wage labor market and to take advantage of traditional labor arrangements. For instance, they are able to hire the labor of *kafo* (that is, age-grade groups), which can number as many as 40–60 persons. Similarly, since they control land allocation and household food stores, they effectively control recruitment of "strange farmers" (seasonal labor migrants), who work on their host's fields for three to four days a week in exchange for food and lodging and a plot of land on which to cultivate a personal cash crop.[6] Since women are rarely able to hire labor,[7] they tend to rely more on reciprocal labor exchange[8]—mainly based on kinship and friendship bonds with other women—not to extend the area under cultivation, but to deal with labor peaks.

Von Braun and Webb's findings could also be affected by gender differentials in skill endowments and access to extension. Their data are not disaggregated

---

6. Poor households without adequate land and food to support one or more extra persons during the cultivation season are unable to afford such labor, thus perpetuating socioeconomic stratification between households.

7. Several *kafos* harvesting women's rice crops in 1977–78 were observed. In all cases, the women were ill or pregnant, and, since the crops were for household consumption, the expenses were met by their husbands (Dey 1980).

8. Where labor for personal fields is not reciprocated through labor exchange, it is generally compensated for after harvest through the gift of cloth, part of the crop, or cash payments. Such compensation generally flows from men to women, since men have greater claims on female labor. Similar transactions have been noted in other West African countries, for example, Burkina Faso (McMillan 1987), Cameroon (Jones 1986), Guinea Bissau (Funk 1988), Nigeria (Burfisher and Horenstein 1985; Babalola and Dennis 1988), and Sierra Leone (Leach 1991). It is generally observed that women regard their work for their husbands as an "obligation," whereas any assistance provided by husbands for their wives' personal fields is regarded as "help," that is, voluntary assistance.

for different ethnic groups, but it is possible that the gender productivity differentials for upland crops were biased by the performance of Mandinka women, who were not accustomed to growing upland crops before they lost their rice land. In view of individual responsibility for personal fields and the lack of extension support for women farmers in this area, it is not surprising that these women have not acquired the same skill levels as men.

Women's inconsistent productivity in traditional swamp rice is, however, difficult to explain, since this is traditionally a female crop. The considerable variations in average land and labor productivity (Dey 1980) may be due to the fact that men's fields were in the more productive swamps and they enjoyed greater and more timely access to labor or ploughing services or both.

In her study of a mixed livestock-crop farming system among the Tswana in an area of unpredictable rainfall in Botswana, P. E. Peters (1986) attributed gender differences in labor productivity for the staple crops of sorghum and maize to timely ploughing and planting. The timeliness of these operations depended crucially on access to *both* draught animals and male labor. Households composed only of women and children were smaller and poorer than others and generally owned few, if any, animals. Cattleless male- and female-headed households had access to ploughing-planting services through a variety of nonmarket relations (based on kinship, affinity, coresidence, friendship, or patron-client relations), generally in exchange for providing labor on the lenders' fields. Borrowers achieved lower output and productivity levels, because their fields were ploughed after those of the cattle owners. Citing Fortmann (1983), Peters also noted that female-headed, cattle-owning households ploughed even later than the cattleless households. Substantial male outmigration, attracted by high wage rates prevailing elsewhere, meant there was no male wage labor market in this area. As a result, these cattle-owning female household heads were unable to hire male labor for ploughing and planting and depended on assistance from male relatives, whose first priority was their own fields.

Feldstein and Poats (1990) also pointed to the lack of draught power and labor as major constraints on productivity in female- as compared with male-headed households in Zambia. Households without the resources to hire draught animals had to resort to more time-consuming land preparation by hand, whereas those hiring oxen had to wait until the owners had ploughed their own fields. In both cases, households encountered serious labor bottlenecks at planting time, which led to other productivity-reducing practices, such as broadcasting of sorghum seed instead of planting seeds spaced in furrows.

Furthermore, female-headed households cultivated smaller areas and were less able to benefit from economies of scale. They were also much less likely, as a result of poverty, to purchase maize seed and use fertilizer on maize: 33 percent purchased seed and 56.8 percent used fertilizer, compared with 81 percent and 88 percent, respectively, for men.

Intrahousehold Cooperation and Conflict:
Implications for Labor Allocative Efficiency

Evidence suggests that gender asymmetries in access to household re-sources and the control of crop and livestock products may lead to conflicts of interest between men and women regarding adoption of productivity-enhancing technologies or higher-value crops. Such conflicts may result in inefficiencies in the household allocation of labor, with a corresponding failure to maximize agricultural intensification.

A particularly striking illustration of intrahousehold conflicts over labor allocation is in the SEMRY project in Cameroon (Jones 1985, 1986). Prior to the project, men and women allocated most of their agricultural labor to sorghum production, with each individual responsible for his or her own fields, with little exchange of labor. In contrast to many other farming systems in Sub-Saharan Africa, women had a minimal obligation to work for their husbands: 95 percent of the time women spent cultivating sorghum was on their own fields. Thus, in order to secure female labor needed for the more complex irrigated rice production system, men were forced to compensate their wives with paddy or cash after the sale of the crop. The average rate of compensation proved to be considerably lower than the average returns on labor from rice cultivation and less than the average rates paid to wage laborers transplanting, weeding, or harvesting rice.

Jones (1986) estimated that of an average female labor contribution of about CFA 31,200, husbands paid about CFA 16,900 in compensation. None-theless it seems that "the quantity of sorghum which households forwent on account of rice is more than compensated for, in grain equivalents, by the quantity of paddy retained" and that "the cash women receive from their husbands represents a real increase in their income" (Jones 1986:113). Yet, despite this, she found that many married women allocated less time to rice production than "independent" women (without husbands) and that the time devoted to rice increased with the level of compensation received. Women who received less than the average rate of compensation generally spent more time working as hired labor the following year and less time on their husbands' fields. She also noted (Jones 1985) that the more allocatively efficient house-holds appeared to be those in which wives could exert more pressure in a bargaining situation: senior wives in polygamous households and women whose husbands still owed bride wealth payments to the wives' families (the wives' labor was needed to help accumulate the income to complete these payments).

Similar conflicts and trade-offs have been noted in other instances (Burfisher and Horenstein 1985; McMillan 1987; Carney 1988b; Leach 1991; Cleaver and Schreiber 1994). In the Jahali-Pacharr project in The Gambia, women were compensated for their labor in cash or kind, but at a rate considerably below the actual returns on their labor. Average daily payments for their work on the irrigated rice were roughly equivalent to their labor productivity on their least remunerative cash crop, cotton (US$0.33 per day), despite returns of US$2.32 per day for the rice (von Braun and Webb 1989). Carney (1988b) also observed differences in levels of remuneration between the various ethnic groups participating in the scheme: rates were lower in the Mandinka villages, where women had few alternative sources of income.

Gender conflicts of interest also emerged in research trials in Zambia (Feldstein and Poats 1990). These were conducted to test the intercropping of beans (a female crop) with maize (predominantly a male crop) in fields prepared by tractor or oxen, with a view to saving female labor expended on land preparation, increasing the area under beans, and raising bean yields with fertilizer applied to maize. Although intercropping of beans in the same row or hill with maize led to an increase in bean yields (with no negative effect on maize yields), female farmers were reluctant to adopt the practice since, by intercropping with maize, beans would become a male crop, primarily for cash rather than for use as a relish.

Conflicts also surfaced in village discussions of trial results on farmers' fields of a high-yielding maize variety. Male farmers were very excited by a variety that out-yielded the most commonly cultivated variety and had a number of "agronomic advantages, such as a short maturity period, a short stem enabling easy harvesting by hand, resistance to common maize diseases such as cob rot, and hard kernels, which made it resistant to weevils during storage" (Feldstein and Poats 1990:246). However, women were not happy, since the hard kernels would require longer time for pounding or greater cash expenditure for machine grinding (Feldstein and Poats 1990). Unfortunately, no indication is given of whether or not farmers have subsequently adopted this variety.

Land Productivity

In this section I discuss ways in which the success of public policies and programs, designed to increase land productivity and reduce environmental degradation as population pressure on land grows, is affected by intra- and interhousehold resource allocation.

Land Productivity under Environmentally Sustainable Conditions

Few quantitative studies have investigated the relationship between land productivity and intra- and interhousehold resource allocation. Evidence from Ghana (Bukh 1977) indicates that lack of male labor for clearing dense vegetation led to longer cropping rotations on land that needed fallowing after one to three years. Women were also overcropping land covered with light secondary bush, which they could clear themselves. In areas of high population density, the Guinea Savanna Zone of northern Ghana (FAO 1991), women were usually allocated only land that had already been cultivated for two or three years and that should then have been fallowed. Women practiced a reduced tillage system on this land by planting on the old ridges and minimally disturbing the soil. The inability to make new ridges was attributed to labor shortages. In both cases, reduced fallows led to declining fertility and yields.

Women tend to be pushed onto more marginal land for their own crops when men expand their operations in response to market incentives or government programs that introduce land conservation and water control measures and improved production technologies (Cleaver and Schreiber 1994). Even in cases in which both men and women cultivate marginal land and improved, environmentally sustainable technologies are available for such conditions, women might not have access to these technologies for a number of reasons. They may not have the cash or labor—particularly if they cultivate household food crops or small plots of low-return cash crops—to purchase inputs, such as fertilizers, that enhance land productivity, or to adopt environmentally sound practices, such as alley cropping or terracing. Lack of tenure security is a further disincentive to adopting practices on which the investment may not be recouped for some years. In some areas, women do not have the right to plant trees and are therefore unable to take advantage of either the soil conservation benefits of tree cropping or the possibility of increasing productivity through the use of high-value (often multipurpose) trees (Bruce 1989b). In some cases in which women have reasonable security of tenure, they nevertheless cannot undertake land improvements without first consulting the male head of the clan (FAO 1991). Finally, women's access to improved technologies for enhancing land conservation and land productivity may be seriously constrained by institutional biases in the provision of extension and credit.

Evidence suggests that when development programs ensure tenure security and equitable access to improved technologies, there are likely to be limited, if any, differences in land productivity between men and women. In the SEMRY rice project in Cameroon, for instance, land productivity for independent women's households was 4,270 kilograms per hectare compared with 4,330 kilograms per hectare for male-headed households (Jones 1986).

Attempts to encourage the adoption of long-term land improvement and conservation practices could also be thwarted by possible conflicts of interest within the household. For instance, fallows can be enhanced by sowing a legume after harvest. Subsequently, the new crop would be planted into a mulch of the leaves and small branches of the legume. This practice would, however, require considerably more labor than the traditional slash-and-burn system. The willingness of households to adopt this practice would depend not only on the supply of household and nonhousehold labor but also on whether women felt obliged or encouraged to allocate more labor to male-controlled land and crops (FAO 1991).

Land Titling and Land Productivity

Secure rights to land are essential if the cultivation of perennial crops, adoption of sustainable management practices, and financing of land improvements are to be carried out. However, it is frequently assumed that customary land tenure fails to provide adequate security and, by prohibiting land transfers through sale, discourages efficient land management. The perceived solution is land registration and titling. In addition to enhancing security, this practice is assumed to increase productivity by promoting the development of legal land markets. Land access would be determined by supply and demand factors and entrepreneurial ability, and by the development of rural credit markets, since land could be used as collateral.

The promotion of such land titling throughout Africa should be viewed with considerable concern, not only because of the enormous costs involved in administration but also because there is evidence of the regressive effect of titling on women's productivity and access to land. The spread of land sales, encouraged by titling, has reduced women's land security in Kenya; cases have been recorded of men selling land registered in their names, leaving their mothers destitute (Green 1987; Davison 1988). Women in settlement schemes in Zimbabwe were vulnerable to eviction upon divorce or the death of their husbands (Pankhurst and Jacobs 1988). Titling has also reduced women's ability to exchange plots in order to gain access to several plots in different agroecological environments as a strategy for distributing labor and enhancing its productivity (Green 1987).

Furthermore, titling is often not essential for either tenure security or productivity increases. Sub-Saharan customary land rights systems provide security to the cultivators and their descendants. These systems have successfully adapted to population increases and commercialization through privatization of communal rights, including land sales. Land purchases are becoming more common in a number of countries, such as Ghana, Niger, Rwanda, and Kenya. Using cross-sectional data for some rainfed cropping areas in Ghana, Kenya, and Rwanda in 1987–88, Migot-Adhola et al. (1991) found that, controlling for differences in land quality and household characteristics, there was no relationship between cross-sectional variations in land rights and productivity. The study also indicated that land titling was not sufficient for increasing access to formal credit. In Kenya—despite its 30-year-long experience with land registration—land served little value as collateral, since customary control over land transfer persisted despite the government land registration and titling program, and land transfers to outsiders through sale (or foreclosure) were not always recognized as legitimate. Limited use of formal credit in all three countries was due to weak rural credit markets rather than lack of collateral.

These findings confirmed the results of a survey carried out in the early 1980s in the Kenyan Highlands (Odingo 1989). The possession of title deeds appeared to have no effect on farmers' willingness to make long-term investments in the land or to increase labor productivity through the purchase of farm machinery or improved inputs. Since farming is risky, farmers were averse to using their titles as collateral for bank loans for fear of losing their land. Only a small minority of farmers who had obtained credit had used commercial banks. Furthermore, commercial banks were beginning to demand additional collateral before making loans to farmers.

Nevertheless, titling programs could play a useful role in safeguarding land access by vulnerable groups, especially women. Such programs could protect women's access to land through joint husband-wife titles or by ensuring widows' inheritance of their husbands' titles. In addition, more innovative programs to enhance women's access to credit by developing nonland forms of collateral (such as group guarantees and future crops) are needed.

Concluding Observations: Some Policy Implications

The studies discussed thus far raise both equity and efficiency issues. With regard to equity, agricultural institutions and laws governing land ownership and inheritance rights still tend to discriminate against women. In a number of cases, development interventions designed to promote agricultural intensification have led to an erosion or loss of women's traditional land rights and personal income while increasing male control of female labor. This outcome points to the need for gender-sensitive policy and project design to prevent the introduction of new forms of exploitation of women, ensure their access to modern productive resources and technologies, and protect their traditional rights in agriculture.

Efficiency issues play a central role in determining policy priorities for allocating resources that promote agricultural intensification and ensure sustainable, environmentally sound development. Given the substantial contribution of women to agricultural production in most Sub-Saharan countries, it is vital to ensure that they have the opportunities and incentives to respond to agricultural productivity-enhancing policies and strategies. In some countries, gender roles in agriculture and their associated rights and responsibilities are often sufficiently flexible to adapt to new opportunities and incentives. In other countries, gender asymmetries in intrahousehold resource allocation constrain women (and sometimes their husbands) from taking full advantage of productivity-enhancing technologies. A particular problem is women's more limited control over the amount and timing of labor on their fields. Women's overriding obligations to work on male-controlled crops often mean that they cannot attend to their own crops at the optimum time. Since they rarely own or operate animal-drawn or mechanical equipment, they usually receive these services from men after the latter have tended their own fields, with a correspondingly negative effect on yields. Because of their regular domestic commitments, women are much less able than men to handle agricultural labor peaks that might require very long hours for relatively short periods of time. And they are often unable to hire help to overcome labor bottlenecks because of their lower income levels and inferior access to nonmarket, nonhousehold labor. Where women have been able to defend their rights to cultivate personal crops (for example, in the SEMRY project in Cameroon), inefficiencies in the allocation of male and female household agricultural labor have arisen.

Despite the difficulty of intervening directly in intrahousehold resource allocation, policymakers can nonetheless make an important contribution to raising women's productivity in the following ways:

1. Ensuring that supporting institutions provide unbiased access for men and women to improved inputs (including credit), extension, and general education, and that a legal framework is in place to protect women's rights to and inheritance of land and other productive assets.
2. Promoting research on crops grown by women and, within the context of general farming systems research, taking better account of gender differences in the timing and amount of labor supply and access to labor-saving equipment.
3. Training women in the use of animal-drawn and mechanical equipment and new production technologies, and providing credit to enable them to purchase such equipment as well as productivity-increasing inputs.
4. Ensuring women's equal rights in land titling programs in areas of customary tenure and settlement or irrigation schemes, perhaps through the issuance of joint husband-wife titles.
5. Stimulating the development of formal and informal credit markets that use collateral other than land.
6. Promoting effective private-sector involvement in the distribution of production inputs, a strategy that is likely to be advantageous to small farmers and particularly women, since market-oriented organizations rarely exhibit the gender biases of statal or parastatal institutions.

Finally, there is a need for researchers and policymakers to explore the role of socioeconomic class and marital status in determining women's access to land, labor, draught animals and farm equipment, and educational attainment, and the implications of such access for women's land and labor productivity. Women in richer families have access to larger land areas (often with ownership rights) and are better placed to take advantage of agricultural intensification programs. Agricultural policies and intensification programs will almost certainly need more fine tuning to target poor women farmers, particularly those heading households with no male support.

16 Gender Coalitions: Extrafamily Influences on Intrafamily Inequality

NANCY FOLBRE

Over the past ten years, the microeconomics of the household has experienced a paradigmatic transformation. It is no longer acceptable to ignore inequalities of power and welfare among household members, or to assume that the household itself can be treated as an undifferentiated optimizing unit. Though no paradigmatic shift can be settled once and for all by a barrage of evidence, the burden of proof has been shifted to those who stand by the conventional assumption of familial altruism (Kuhn 1974; Alderman et al. 1995; Hart 1995). Today the microeconomics of household bargaining seems better developed than the macroeconomics of gender- and age-based inequalities. Many economists are modeling the consequences of differences in bargaining power, but few are exploring the causes.

This imbalance is evident in policy discussions. Evidence of gender bias in development planning has been accumulating for decades (Moser 1993; Kabeer 1994). The specific ways in which intrahousehold inequalities can limit and distort public policies have been carefully explained (Haddad and Kanbur 1992; Alderman, Haddad, and Hoddinott, Chapter 17, this volume). But there has been remarkably little discussion of *why* certain policies have been biased not only against women but also against equality in the household. Policymakers themselves are often described as if they were benevolent heads of that larger household known as the state.

In this chapter I argue that it is important to analyze the ways in which gender coalitions seek to influence institutions that affect intrafamily allocation. Individuals do not restrict their pursuit of self-interest to bargaining on the microeconomic level. They also seek to influence public policies and social norms, engaging in forms of collective action designed to protect and advance their position in the family as well as the labor market.

Family Bargaining

The basic hypothesis underlying a bargaining power approach to the family is that there is likely to be a positive relationship among an individual's power, his or her influence on family decisionmaking, and his or her share of family resources (including leisure time). This hypothesis does not imply a complete absence of altruism or positively interdependent preferences in the household. It does, however, imply that self-interest also plays a significant role there (Folbre 1986). Family members may be committed to meeting one another's basic needs but still bargain over allocation within a certain range (Stark 1995). Two questions are of obvious importance: what exactly defines the "power" of family members, and just how self-interested are they?

Economists, not surprisingly, tend to answer these questions in economistic ways. They generally define power in terms of fallback positions, the alternatives available to individuals should they withdraw their family commitments. Yet they devote little attention to how these fallback positions are determined. Similarly, economists generally assume that preferences determining levels of altruism in the family are exogenously given, without asking why they may vary among individuals or change over time. A more interdisciplinary approach to bargaining is less precise but also more ambitious, because it considers the possibility that individuals engage in forms of collective action designed to protect their individual bargaining power.

Before reviewing recent research that illustrates this point, I should explain why I emphasize family rather than household allocation. Both legal rules and implicit contracts pertain primarily to familial relationships rather than to coresidents in a particular physical location. A focus on households is convenient for some purposes, but it threatens to distract from the significant impact of changing family and household boundaries, such as increases in the percentage of families maintained by mothers alone. These families typically suffer from low intrafamily, rather than unequal intrahousehold, income flows. A focus on families also helps accommodate life-cycle rhythms. Since mothers generally invest more time (and often more money) in children than fathers do, the size and reliability of future "paybacks" from nonresident children are especially relevant to their welfare (Bruce, Lloyd, and Leonard 1995).

Social Institutions and Fallback Positions

Economists, almost by definition, focus on wealth and income rather than on social identity. The Nash bargaining approach to modeling relations between husbands and wives, first developed in the early 1980s, defined fallback positions in terms of the utility that individuals would enjoy upon exiting the marriage, largely a function of their relative incomes as single persons (Manser and Brown 1980; McElroy and Horney 1981). Discussion of Becker's "rotten kid" brought to light the importance of the family altruist's control over family assets (Hirshleifer 1977). In both cases, measurable bargaining power is largely a function of stocks of human and nonhuman capital and potential rates of return on them, and it is not significantly affected by the social identity of the bargainer. That Becker assumes that the family altruist is the father and the selfish family member is the "rotten kid" is incidental to his exposition.

Similarly, most empirical challenges to the unitary household hypothesis focus on wealth and income effects. They show, for instance, that some types of income have different effects on consumption or fertility decisions if contributed by a wife than if contributed by a husband (Schultz 1990; Thomas 1990; Browning et al. 1994). The results are quantitatively precise, though they suffer from econometric shortcomings and are inevitably limited by their static, cross-sectional nature (Pitt, Rosenzweig, and Hassan 1990; Behrman 1996). In general, such estimates offer a critique of, rather than an alternative to, the unitary model (Bourguignon and Chiappori 1992). A major problem is that measurable wealth and income are probably poor approximations of actual fallback positions.

The disposable income that an individual will enjoy upon exiting a marriage depends, among other things, on the distribution of the responsibilities and costs of caring for children, the extent of public transfers, and the probability of enjoying a share of another person's income stream through remarriage. These are significantly affected by institutional factors such as family law and public policies regarding child care and income transfers. McElroy (1990) includes these among what she calls "extrahousehold environmental parameters." But the most interesting feature of these parameters is not that they are external to the household, but that they are strongly affected by gender identity. Because mothers are far more likely than fathers to assume custody of children, poor enforcement of the child support responsibilities of an absent parent reduces women's bargaining power. The same may be said of high child-care costs, which reduce the disposable income of a single parent. These are "gender-specific environmental parameters" (GEPs) that work against the interests of women as a group.

Consider the following two examples of GEP effects from Bangladesh. Kabeer's (1995) research on urban Bangladeshi households suggests that women are disadvantaged by a rule that stipulates that they must relinquish custody of children after divorce, a rule that is especially likely to be enforced if they remarry. Pitt and Khandker's (1995) recent empirical analysis of small-scale Grameen Bank–type programs in Bangladesh targeted specifically to women showed that credit supplied to women had a discernibly different impact on family spending and labor supply than credit supplied to men. Some GEPs may not affect the consequences of divorce but are relevant to other fallback definitions. Lundberg, Pollak, and Wales (1995) show that a British decision to send child allowance checks directly to mothers rather than to fathers in the late 1970s was associated with a shift toward relatively greater expenditures on women's and children's goods.

Precisely because GEPs are gender specific, they provide a motive for individuals to engage in gender-specific forms of collective action. Both men and women may foresee family-level benefits from the potential successes of a coalition with others of their gender, designed to modify child custody laws, to increase credit, or simply to improve gender-specific employment opportunities. The number and potential impact of GEPs is even greater if the bargaining game itself is conceptualized as a social, rather than a purely individual, process.

Social Norms and Fallback Positions

Like traditional neoclassical theory, the Nash bargaining approach probably exaggerates the rational choices of optimizing individuals. It is known from experience that the transaction costs of bargaining within the family are high, and the forms of interaction so diverse that mutual responsibilities are difficult to specify in advance (England and Farkas 1986). The fact that relatively few couples draw up a contract governing their relationship confirms that explicit bargaining is limited. When bargaining does take place, it is unlikely to entail constant threats of divorce, which, after some point, either lose credibility or undermine affection.

Thus it seems quite reasonable to suggest that social norms play an important role in family allocation, specifying a set of mutual responsibilities among kin. A number of economists argue that norms are "gendered" in the sense that they rely on a social construction of masculinity and femininity (Folbre 1994; Kabeer 1994, 1995; Hart 1995). Sen (1990) suggests that social perceptions of contributions to the household may be more important than actual contributions in determining bargaining power. This does not imply that household allocation is an entirely norm-driven process, but that the relationship between individual choices and social norms requires serious scrutiny.

Two promising innovations in bargaining theory move in this direction. The separate-spheres model proposed by Lundberg and Pollak (1993; Chapter 5, this volume) defines fallback positions as a noncooperative equilibrium determined by social norms that dictate a certain division of labor based on separate spheres for men and women. Sociological dynamics set the stage for a cooperative bargaining process governed by more individualistic economic logic. If enough couples engage in bargaining, it is easy to see how the fallback norms themselves might be modified. Likewise, the norms themselves affect individual bargaining power. The conjugal contract model proposed by Carter and Katz (Chapter 6, this volume) describes a noncooperative game in which individuals control separate sources of income and maximize consumption of a combination of goods for own and collective consumption. Their responsibilities for collective consumption are specified by a socially determined conjugal contract influenced by "a complex of attitudes, mores, and opportunities exogenous to the household that can be labeled the 'degree of patriarchy'" (103).

Many social norms governing family allocations are gender specific. Consider, for instance, the following normative statement: women should take primary responsibility for children and men should take primary responsibility for earning a market income. One can imagine a household in which the wife wants to work outside the home and the husband wants to spend more time in child care. Both agree that they will be better off if they violate the social norm. One can also imagine a household in which the wife wants to work outside the home but the husband does not want to spend more time in child care. In order to convince him to depart from the norm-based allocation, she may agree to make a "side-payment," such as agreeing to work longer hours overall or devote more of her income to collective consumption. A Bangladeshi woman describes her reasons for handing her earnings over to her husband as follows: "As it is, he is letting me work, how would he feel if I also kept the money?" (Kabeer 1995:17). In this case, the social norm functions as a GEP that reduces her bargaining power.

Institutionalist economists have long described the evolution of norms as mechanisms for solving coordination problems (Schotter 1981). Becker (1981) interprets the emergence of the sexual division of labor in exactly these terms, as an efficient response to differences in male and female endowments. But norms are almost always more efficient for some groups than for others (Ullmann 1977). Even those that initially emerged untainted by any distributional motives are likely to acquire distributional consequences in the course of economic development and changes in relative prices. Individuals and groups often recognize that certain norms work to their own advantage and will defend them as long as the distributional gains outweigh the efficiency losses. Thus it seems likely that men and women will engage in collective efforts to influence social norms as well as more explicit social policies. Their relative success in this process will, in turn, influence intrafamily allocation.

Bargaining and Endogenous Preferences

A more radical change in the analysis of bargaining entails a reconsideration of the role of preferences as well as a broader definition of fallback positions. Microeconomists typically assume that husbands and wives are equally self-interested (or altruistic), in the sense that they place equal weights on the welfare of the other. Becker's (1981) "rotten-kid theorem" is an exception because it assumes that the wealth holder in the family is more altruistic than others. But Sen (1990) points out that the person with the least, rather than the most, bargaining power in a family tends to behave most altruistically. Women may be, on average, more altruistic than men because they have a less "separative" self (England and Kilbourne 1990), or mothers may simply have more love and affection for children than do fathers (Fuchs 1988).

If one accepts the conventional neoclassical assumption that preferences are exogenously given, one must conclude that mothers enjoy a compensating differential: the pleasure of taking responsibility for children counterbalances the increased costs that they incur. But if women have metapreferences that allow them to analyze critically the consequences of their own preferences, they may try to change them, or they may encourage their daughters to be less altruistic than they were. Another interesting possibility is that the process of caring for children creates altruistic preferences, a type of addiction with positive consequences for children (and probably for society) but negative economic consequences for mothers. If addiction reflects a rational, utility-maximizing choice based on full information, the addict feels no regret (Becker, Grossman, and Murphy 1991). But a combination of imperfect information and probabilistic outcomes can explain why individuals often wish they could change (Orphanides and Zervos 1995). Sometimes people wish they could stop caring about others but find they cannot.

How might men and women acquire different preferences? Here again collective action may play a role. Becker and others suggest that parents may inculcate caring preferences in their children, in order to ensure that they themselves are cared for in old age (Becker 1993; Stark 1995). It is economically advantageous for men to augment caring preferences in women by enforcing social norms of female altruism, responsibility, and enjoyment of caring, and punishing deviation from these norms. Likewise, it is economically advantageous for women to augment caring preferences in men. But if men exercise more power than women over the design of the social institutions that inculcate preferences, they will win the caring game (Folbre and Weisskopf 1996).

Gender Coalitions

Economists have been slow to develop theories of collective action, largely because the assumption that most individuals are purely self-interested implies that most collective undertakings will suffer from serious free rider problems. But there is now a growing interest in "rent-seeking" behavior (efforts to claim revenues that are not earned), including investments designed to influence electoral and political outcomes (Krueger 1974; Olson 1975, 1982; Grossman and Helpman 1994). As Becker (1993:372) puts it, "Individuals belong to particular groups—defined by occupation, industry, income, geography, age, and other characteristics—that are assumed to use political influence to enhance the well-being of their members." Neither Becker nor any of the others cited ever mentions groups based on gender. Could men and women simply be added to the list of "interest groups" competing for political power?

Yes and no. They can be added, but not simply. Several aspects of the conventional approach to rent-seeking and lobbying militate against inclusion. Nevertheless a critical analysis of neoclassical reasoning points the way toward a better political economy of family policy.

Rent-Seeking versus Power-Seeking

In her pioneering article on rent-seeking, Krueger (1974) described the efforts of lobbying groups to establish protective tariffs that would allow them to charge a higher price for their goods. Following her example, most neoclassical theorists treat distributional struggle as a form of interference with market-driven outcomes. Rent-seeking groups impose real or meta-phorical taxes that cause a divergence from market equilibrium and create a deadweight loss. Thus it is hardly surprising that an accumulation of such groups would lead to the kind of economic atherosclerosis that Olson (1982) describes.

Some gender-based conflicts can easily be described as rent-seeking. For instance, if male workers create an organization designed to limit women's ability to compete with them in the labor market, they are essentially imposing a tariff on women that lowers overall efficiency, as well as women's earnings and their bargaining power in the household. Similarly, one could argue that affirmative action is a retaliatory form of rent-seeking by women, designed to increase the demand for their labor in the market in order to compensate for previous or current discrimination against them, and to improve their bargaining power in the household.

Many other forms of collective action, however, do not directly pertain to the operation of markets, but to the organization of nonmarket institutions, such as property rights. In this situation, the rent-seeking tariff metaphor is misleading, because there is no deadweight efficiency loss. Take the example of slavery in the southern United States before the Civil War. In 1860, one group (the South) favored it; another group (the North) did not. Slavery allowed one kind of market (the buying and selling of other people) but forbade another (the slave's buying and selling of his or her own labor power). One set of property rights may have been more efficient than the other, but it is not obvious, a priori, which. Influential economic historians argue that slavery in the South was quite efficient, and that it was eliminated for political, rather than economic, reasons (Fogel and Engerman 1974; Fogel 1989).

The family is a nonmarket institution, and once the assumption of perfect familial altruism is relinquished it seems rather clear that the welfare of dependents requires some collective monitoring and enforcement of family responsibilities. Historically state governance of family life has provided a powerful excuse for imposing limits on women's participation in markets. However, women have engaged in collective efforts to redefine family rights and responsibilities. Many feminist struggles in the developing world today focus on property rights, such as married women's rights to control a share of family land or wealth, their own earnings, custody of children in the event of divorce, and claims on the income of fathers for the support of children in the event of nonmarriage or divorce (Folbre 1994). Efforts to improve these property rights do not represent a claim on market-generated allocations but a contest over alternative institutional arrangements.

Such feminist campaigns are not unproductive efforts that reduce overall output. They probably increase the efficiency of production of human capital, not to mention child welfare. They obviously have distributional implications, because they affect the gender-specific environmental parameters described earlier and reduce men's bargaining power in the home. But most economists, lacking any theory other than that which celebrates the efficiency of markets, have little to say about them. The design of family and social policy, like the design of all nonmarket institutions, poses the types of ethical and political questions from which most economists fled when they chose their discipline.

Chosen Groups versus Given Groups

Another obstacle to the economic analysis of gender coalitions lies in the common assumption that individuals join groups for entirely instrumental reasons, after calculating that the probable benefits exceed the probable costs. This assumption may be appropriate to "interest groups," which individuals choose to join for a very explicit purpose and from which they may exit at will. Yet it is far less appropriate to what might be called "given groups"—such as those based on gender, race, class, or nation—to which individuals are exogenously assigned. Exit from such groups is possible, but it is typically difficult and expensive. If I am a woman and I do not like the way women are treated, I cannot just resign from the gender, as if from a club.

Furthermore, the construction of gender identity often entails the development of solidarity, or altruism, among group members, eloquently conveyed by the language of kinship—brotherhood and sisterhood. One can name many "interest groups" based on gender, such as the National Organization of Women in the United States. But card-carrying, dues-paying feminists are the tip of a larger iceberg (or volcano) of less explicit and less instrumental forms of collective action that are coordinated by shared values rather than by explicit political association. The behavior need not be explicitly or consciously feminist. For instance, a woman who encourages another woman to vote for a candidate who supports reproductive rights because it will be good for women as a group is engaging in gender-based collective action.

Efforts to elect or influence public officials may be less important, in the long run, than efforts to contest and modify conventional social norms. It is hard to imagine a set of norms that proved more susceptible to change in the course of economic development than those defining masculinity and femininity. Different points of view are heavily encoded in phrases such as "family values," and claims about efficiency are framed in terms such as the "breakdown" of the family. Gender is by no means the only aspect of social identity that influences this particular debate, but it is a salient one.

Unlike lobbying groups, which generally benefit from a clear presentation of their objectives, many groups that participate in what might be termed political and cultural bargaining over gender roles deny that this is their actual goal. Fundamentalist religious organizations are now playing an increasingly important role in both developed and developing countries. Whether Christian, Islamic, or Jewish, they are remarkably similar in their adherence to traditional gender roles, based on the claim that they are ordained by God. These religious organizations do not fit Becker's definition of a pressure group. Nonetheless they indisputably create pressures that have important consequences for intra-household allocation.

Methodology and Ideology

The most ironic shortcoming of the economic approach to interest groups is that it ignores the ways in which group interests influence economics itself. The progress of scientific research is not determined by elections or lobbying, but it is certainly affected by circles, cliques, and coalitions that struggle to increase their share of power and resources. Funds for research are allocated by individuals whose social identities shape their perception of intellectual priorities. Priorities for the collection of data by governments and multilateral institutions are set by policymakers whose agenda is, inevitably, gendered.

A disproportionate share of economic research on intrahousehold inequality has been conducted by scholars from the developed countries on survey data collected in developing countries. When it comes to something as touchy as gender, it seems more acceptable to study others than ourselves. Much of the intellectual enthusiasm and financial support for research on the status of women derives from what might be called "efficiency" considerations—the hope that improving it will speed both fertility decline and economic development. Conveniently, the distributional costs will be imposed on men in other countries, not our own.

Awareness of the interplay of interests based on nation and class, as well as gender, does not discredit the results of such research. It merely signals the need for a greater awareness of the way in which bargaining power may affect academic as well as household outcomes. Social norms shape professional as well as personal life. Many well-established economists currently enforce strong taboos against interdisciplinary research, nonquantitative methods, and divergence from traditional neoclassical assumptions, making it difficult to develop alternative approaches to intrafamily inequalities. The best strategy for individual researchers willing to challenge these taboos is to demonstrate that the potential efficiency gains from developing a better theory of gender coalitions exceed the distributional losses that might be imposed on those who deny their existence.

Institutionalized Forms of Gender Bias

A growing literature describes public policies that reduce women's bargaining power. Many of these policies were initially developed by states and religious organizations that explicitly restricted women's decisionmaking role. Starting about 150 years ago, feminist groups began systematically contesting institutionalized gender bias. The results have been significant but uneven. In general property rights have received more attention than social norms, but a closer look at existing research could help formulate a more systematic framework for comparative analysis. The following sections discuss particularly salient examples of GEPs.

Property Rights

The advantage of focusing on property rights, which represent a subset of all public policies, is that they are easier to catalogue and have more direct implications for economic outcomes.

RIGHTS TO LAND. Potential for inheritance and co-ownership of marital assets affects women's ability to survive economically outside marriage. Particularly in areas where wage labor is not widespread, lack of independent access to land makes women dependent on male kin. In many areas of Sub-Saharan Africa, widows lack even basic rights to inherit marital property (Potash 1986). Agarwal's (1994a,b) detailed study of land rights in South Asia shows that legal reforms have not always changed actual practices, but it also suggests strategies for improving women's access.

RIGHTS TO MARKET EMPLOYMENT AND EARNINGS. In most countries, married women now have a legal right to control their own earnings. But other restrictions sometimes make it difficult for them to work outside the home. In Saudi Arabia, for instance, women are not allowed to drive.

RIGHTS TO CONTROL OVER REPRODUCTIVE CAPACITIES. Rape within marriage is not a punishable offense in most countries, and women often rely on methods of contraception that require male cooperation. As a result, many women who have already achieved their desired family size may see the possibility of another pregnancy as a threat. Yet modern contraceptives, as well as abortions, are proscribed in many countries. In others, women are vulnerable to forced sterilization and abortion (Hartmann 1987).

RIGHTS TO PROTECTION AGAINST DOMESTIC VIOLENCE. Lack of protection against spousal abuse is a significant political, economic, and public health problem in many countries (Heise, Pitanguy, and Germain 1994). It has obvious implications for bargaining power.

RIGHTS TO CHILD CUSTODY. Historical and comparative data suggest that, in economies in which children make significant contributions to family income, fathers are typically offered custody of them in the event of divorce.

As children become increasingly expensive, legal custody is shifted toward mothers (Folbre 1994).

RIGHTS TO FINANCIAL SUPPORT FROM THE FATHERS OF CHILDREN. Most legal systems outside Sub-Saharan Africa stipulate that a father must provide a minimal amount of financial support for his wife and children. However, this stipulation is seldom enforced, especially in the event of desertion. North-western European countries are unique in enforcing spousal support in the event of divorce or nonmarriage. This is a pressing issue, because the percentage of families maintained by women alone seems to be increasing in north-western Europe, the United States, Latin America, and Sub-Saharan Africa (Folbre 1990, 1994).

RIGHTS TO EDUCATION. Female enrollment rates in primary education have increased rapidly, approaching parity in many areas of the developing world. Nevertheless female children in most countries have a much lower probability than males of completing secondary and postsecondary education (King and Hill 1993).

Other Public Policies

Separate from but related to property rights are public policies that reinforce traditional gender roles by making it more costly for employers to hire women than men and imposing higher taxes on or providing lower benefits for women wage earners. These policies effectively lower women's wages relative to men's.

LAWS AGAINST GENDER DISCRIMINATION. Most countries of the world are signatories of the International Labour Office convention against discrimination in employment. The U.S. experience suggests that antidiscrimination rules can have a significant impact (Beller 1982). However, the U.S. legal system may be better suited than those of other countries to enforcement of such rules through class action suits (Winter 1994). Yet there have been remarkably few studies of the effectiveness or impact of antidiscrimination rules in developing countries.

MATERNITY LEAVES. The International Labour Office's Maternity Protection Convention stipulates that individual employers should not be liable for the cost of maternity benefits. In practice, however, they often pay the bill. Some even require women employees to provide medical certification that they are not pregnant (Anker and Hein 1985; Winter 1994). Even unpaid maternity leaves create disincentives to hire women. Neither paid nor unpaid family leaves from work should be gender specific.

RETIREMENT AND FAMILY ALLOWANCE BENEFITS. The social security systems imported by many countries of Latin America and Sub-Saharan Africa from Europe in the early twentieth century provided direct benefits for a select group of primarily male wage earners in covered employment, and only indirect benefits for women and children, determined by their family relationship to a male wage earner. Furthermore the structure of both taxes and benefits discouraged married women from seeking employment. Only since the 1970s have some European countries taken steps to eliminate discrimination and protect the retirement benefits of women who gain access to benefits through marriage to a covered wage earner (Brocas, Cailloux, and Oget 1990). Family allowances in most countries are paid to male wage earners, and they often provide greater family subsidies for men than for women workers (Folbre 1993).

CHILD-CARE POLICIES. Women typically devote more time and energy to parenting than men. Therefore the degree of public assistance for child care has a significant impact on women's position in both the family and the labor market. In countries like France and Sweden, where substantial public services are provided, women experience much smaller reductions of lifetime earnings as a result of child rearing than in countries like Germany, Great Britain, and the United States (Davies and Joshi 1990).

A Research Agenda

More detailed historical and comparative analysis of gender-biased public policies could shed further light on their evolution. Greater attention should also be devoted to the analysis of social norms, which are closely intertwined with public policies. Community values played an important role in fertility decline in Western Europe (Watkins 1991), and it is worth exploring the ways in which they may affect both community- and household-level bargaining between men and women. Even more pressing is the need to move beyond purely descriptive analysis toward more explicit modeling and hypothesis testing.

Both cross-sectional and longitudinal data that capture variations in public policy could be used to test the impact of GEPs on family allocation. Variations in public policy also require explanation. What kinds of collective action seem to be most successful at resisting or encouraging change? Are policies that are imposed on countries from outside as successful as those that emerge as the result of local grassroots activity? Are increases in women's education and employment levels associated with increases in their participation in women's groups? What are the ramifications of increased age at marriage, increased nonmarriage, and fertility decline for men's and women's perceptions of their own gender interests?

These questions will require time, patience, and imagination to answer. In the meantime, economists should recognize that they cannot simply be delegated to other disciplines. The burden of proof must be shifted to those who are reluctant to challenge the status quo. Why should public policies not promote equal access to education and wage employment? Why should the cost of children not be equally divided between men and women? Why should the state not guarantee all children a basic right to health, education, and economic opportunity?

17 Policy Issues and Intrahousehold Resource Allocation: Conclusions

HAROLD ALDERMAN, LAWRENCE HADDAD, AND
JOHN HODDINOTT

As seen from the preceding chapters, the costs of neglecting the process of intrahousehold resource allocation are often high. This is a categorical statement, not a statement about adopting or rejecting any particular model or class of models. It suggests that the process of policy analysis should begin with the following questions: How do individuals form family units? What norms govern the functioning of family units? How are these rules revised as circumstances change? In this spirit, we now recapitulate ways in which policy formulation and implementation can be improved by considering intrahousehold allocation.

Resource allocation processes are complex, and no single approach can be expected to be valid in all cultures or for all policy questions. Indeed a few caveats to policymakers are included here: just as ignoring intrahousehold allocation can result in errors, miscalculations will occasionally arise from basing actions on an incomplete understanding. However, whether or not they are understood, intrahousehold allocation processes occur in many spheres of action. There should be no reason why errors from ignoring intrahousehold processes are *inherently* less dangerous than errors from acting on the basis of the limited information given. In this concluding chapter we reiterate this point in the context of one—but hardly the only—key debate in this field, that of the advantages of targeting programs to women. Yet the risks involved in misunderstanding intrahousehold allocation are a powerful incentive to further research. Suggestions are given regarding ways in which the range of uncertainty in understanding household allocation processes can be reduced.

Policy and Modeling of Intrahousehold Resource Allocation

Whereas many of the chapters in this book explore alternatives to unitary models of the household, others indicate that this challenge has encouraged researchers to broaden the applications of this model. Consider, for example, the choice of instruments to use for poverty alleviation. Under a welfarist

275

approach to poverty alleviation, lump-sum transfers are generally more efficient than price subsidies, if decisionmaking is unitary. Under a nonwelfarist
scenario, with unitary decisionmaking, the efficiency of transfers holds when
planners' objectives (weights on individual welfare) match those of the household (Tobin 1970), although Ross (1988) illustrates how such differences of
objectives can make in-kind transfers efficient interventions. If the two sets of
preferences do not match—possibly because of some externalities in investments or because policymakers (or a subset) have a different preference for
female survival than do some households in the society at large—then there is
still a range of interventions in wage and price policy that may be used in the
context of unitary decisionmaking to shift household allocation closer to social
objectives.

Much of the literature on gender discrimination in health and schooling
can be viewed in this context. For example, the findings of Rosenzweig and
Schultz (1982) imply an impact on female child survival if credible policies
can be found to narrow male-female wage gaps. Similarly, Duraisamy and
Malathy (1991), Gertler and Glewwe (1992), Alderman et al. (1996), and
Alderman and Gertler (Chapter 14, this volume) imply roles for price policy in
health and schooling allocation across boys and girls without a need to shift
relative control of income. These are cases in which, as Pitt discusses in
Chapter 2, individual prices can be identified or plausibly proposed.

If, however, household allocation is collective, it makes little sense to
discuss a match between the preferences of the planners and those of the
household; under this model, households may have behaviors, but they do not
have a common preference. In a technical sense, interventions that aim to shift
budget allocations merely weigh individuals' utility differently than does the
household head. However, from a practical standpoint, it may not be useful to
focus on the preference of one individual for, say, investment in children; only
under rather special circumstances do the preferences of a single individual
determine resource allocation. Welfarist objectives are more difficult to determine in the absence of a "standard" household utility function. Thus the current
inability to distinguish between alternative collective models limits exact measurement of the welfare effects of policy.

However, this situation does not prohibit identification of four areas of
policy in which neglect of the decisionmaking process could have serious
consequences in terms of policy failure:

1. Different models predict different effects of public transfers made to the
   household. The unitary model predicts that the impact of such transfers is
   unaffected by the identity of the recipient, whereas collective models
   suggest that the identity of the recipient will change purchasing patterns.
2. Not only is the identity of the recipient important when the government is
   considering transfers, the response of nonrecipients must also be consid-

ered. The nature of interactions between household members will determine whether public transfers are mitigated or enhanced by changes in private income-sharing behavior, as shown in the second set of examples given later in this section. Unitary as well as collective models treat this topic; the range of issues and predictions, however, differs across models.

3. In addition to predicting that the impact of transfers is neutral with respect to which household member is the recipient, household models that presume information sharing and joint production imply that the response to many other policy initiatives will be recipient independent. This presumption gives rise to two potential policy failures: (1) the nonadoption of particular policies that appear beneficial in the aggregate and (2) unintended costs arising from policies that are adopted.

4. The unitary model depicts as impotent a number of policy initiatives that neither directly affect the technology of production nor affect household preferences, but which may have a major impact on allocation decisions. For example, laws on property rights within marriage and upon inheritance as well as the efficacy of enforcement may have long policy handles, as predicted under some models of intrahousehold allocation.

These four categories of policy failure are illustrated in the following sections.

Targeting of Transfers and Income-Source Dependence

The claim that household decisions are independent of the identity of the individual receiving income (income-source independence) has been refuted in a number of settings.[1] The implications of this refutation for public transfers are illustrated by the following quotations:

> Many participants in the public debate concerning actual government transfers take it for granted that intrafamily distribution will vary systematically with the control of resources. When the British child allowance system was changed in the mid-1970s to make child benefits payable in cash to the mother, it was widely regarded as a redistribution of family income from men to women and was expected to be popular with women. (Lundberg and Pollak, Chapter 5, this volume, 76)

> Indeed, so convinced did some Ministers become that a transfer of income "from the wallet to the purse" at a time of wage restraint would be resented by male workers, that they decided at one point in 1977 to defer the whole child benefit scheme. (Brown 1984:64).

Compared with the creation of a new instrument that so overtly transfers income "from the wallet to the purse," other programs may achieve the same objective under a nonwelfarist banner. Food stamps, which often are found to

---

1. This evidence is reviewed by Thomas (Chapter 9) and by Hoddinott, Alderman, and Haddad (Chapter 8).

influence spending in a manner different from cash, despite models that show their theoretical equivalence (Senauer and Young 1986), may be an illustration. Food stamps are not directed at women per se, but because women are the main food purchasers, the delivery mechanism creates an entitlement to the transfers.

Similar considerations are at play, for instance, in deciding whether labor should be remunerated with food or cash in a public works scheme. One of the many factors entering into the decision is the likely profile of program participants. When the nature of the work and the level of the wage offered are such that the participants are predominantly male, some have argued that remuneration should be in the form of food, owing to differences in male and female expenditure patterns.

The importance of the class of potential policy failures centered on control of income is likely to grow as social safety nets are designed to ameliorate the short-run negative impacts of economic adjustment. Newman, Jorgensen, and Pradhan (1991) found that in Bolivia, the Social Emergency Fund activities, mainly targeted at the construction industries, did bolster the incomes of the poorest in a cost-effective manner. But the Fund had only a 2 percent female participation rate. The untested assumption seems to have been that fund income would trickle down to wives, mothers, and children or that they would be better served through credit and other programs in which female participation was substantial.

A recent perspective on nonpooled incomes is presented by Browning (1994). He models savings within a two-person household in which wives are younger than their husbands and have longer life expectancies. Thus individuals have different preferences for savings. This approach results in household savings rates that are functions of individual income and age disparities. The models also predict that the household's response to pensions and insurance is not neutral to internal income distribution.

Moreover, if preferences are not unitary, some collective models imply price elasticities that differ from conventional demand theory.[2] Most price policy, however, is designed on the basis of models that use a representative consumer or a few sets of consumers based on region and income to portray an entire economy. In the presence of unitary preferences, it is not apparent that refined estimates of demand elasticities from further disaggregation of households will lead to new price instruments. However, if preferences are not unitary, gender- or age-specific price indexes exist, and price movements can reallocate resources within households. Therefore, when targeted income-transfer programs are costly to administer, price policy may be more efficient than lump-sum transfers.

---

2. For example, Nash bargaining models imply a different set of restrictions on the Slutsky matrix than standard models.

Intrahousehold Distribution and the Offsetting of Policy Goals

In the initial discussion of policy issues, it was noted that changes in private behavior may offset public transfers (see Cox and Jakubson [1995] for a recent review). In models such as that of Barro (1974), altruism on the part of private agents undoes the effect of government policies that increase the incomes of the current generation at the expense of future generations. If intergenerational altruism, one form of the unitary model, is replaced with exchange motives, this result no longer holds.

Cox and Jimenez (1990) illustrate this feature. Consider a hypothetical family with young members residing in towns and old members living in rural areas. Transfers are made by the altruist "young" to the old, and individual consumption is a function of aggregate income. Suppose a social security program that taxes the young and subsidizes the old is introduced, leaving aggregate income unchanged. This might well lead to a reduction in urban-rural remittances, with consumption by individual members unchanged. However, suppose that these young-to-old transfers are undertaken in exchange for some in-kind service (such as home production). When an urban wage tax (the social security program) is introduced, with the proceeds used to subsidize rural wages, the opportunity cost for a rural resident providing a service will increase. As a result, the urban household members must transfer higher amounts to their elders. This is the opposite result of that predicted by the altruistic unitary model.

The empirical work of Quisumbing (1994b) and Altonji, Hayashi, and Kotlikoff (1992) as well as Cox and Jimenez (1992) has been motivated, in part, by a desire to test the policy implications of such a model of inter-generational altruism. An analogous possibility exists for intrahousehold transfers from husbands to wives. Although the polar position of perfect altruism may be hard to defend, the degree of partial crowding out is not measured in most models. This situation again makes assessment of the impact of targeted transfers imprecise.[3]

It is noted that a number of recent innovations in this field are modeled in terms of monitoring or the sequence of individual (or generational) decisions made, conditional on decisions made by other household members. For example, Rosenzweig and Wolpin (1993, 1994) study transfers across generations in which the moves of the parental generation are conditional on observing the younger generation (and, in their 1994 paper, the government). Such studies can be applied to residential choices and to predict the impact of private transfers in response to changes in government transfers.

---

3. Similarly, although there is evidence that women's limited access to credit affects the allocation of inputs to agriculture, given that in some communities men purchase a portion of the inputs used by women, the net impact of targeted credit for crops controlled by women is likely to be less than expected, owing to reallocation by males.

Attempts to reallocate food in the light of targeted nutrition programs also fall under this broad category of policies, for which an understanding of intrahousehold allocation may be crucial to program success. A recent empirical example of this issue within the framework of the unitary model is provided by Pitt, Rosenzweig, and Hassan (1990). This study illustrates the adaptability of unitary models to a range of issues of intrahousehold allocation. They suggest that if returns to activities are responsive to health and effort, it makes sense for the household to allocate marginal calories to healthy men. They also find that in some seasons, individuals with the best health endowments are taxed in the sense that their larger allocation of calories does not fully compensate them for their effort. Thus, within the context of shared preferences, they show that households may reallocate so that consumption is more equitable than work effort. Thus they measure the role that equity as well as efficiency plays in household allocation (see also Pitt and Rosenzweig 1990).

Intrahousehold Ramifications of Policy Initiatives: Agricultural Productivity

A number of examples of the nonadoption of policies designed to improve crop technology reflect failure to appreciate intrahousehold allocation of responsibilities (Quisumbing 1994a). Jones (1986), summarized by Dey Abbas (Chapter 15, this volume), reported the results of a project in Cameroon to encourage women to produce rice. In the study area, rice was considered a "male" crop. Any income generated from it would have been controlled by men, even if the crop had been produced by women. Consequently few women entered into rice cultivation. Instead they continued to grow sorghum, despite its lower returns, because women controlled the harvested product. In Zambia households were encouraged to intercrop maize, a "male" crop, with beans, a "female" crop (Poats 1991). Researchers hoped that households would take advantage of the well-known complementary nutritional benefits of the two crops. In addition they hoped that the overall amount of weeding time would be diminished, through the simultaneous weeding of both crops. However, women opposed this innovation because if beans were planted on land normally allocated to maize, they would lose ownership of the beans and the men would benefit from the cash generated by their sale.

Udry et al. (1995) and Udry (1996) generalize on the misallocation of resources within farm households. They note that intrahousehold inefficiency in Burkina Faso can account for a loss of 10–20 percent owing to misallocation of currently used inputs. This conclusion was framed in terms of a static technology; over time, greater misallocation might come from inefficiencies in adapting new techniques.

That extension workers routinely ignore women farmers when new technology is introduced is well documented. For example, in Malawi Gladwin and McMillan (1989) found that a groundnut seed multiplication project was introduced to male household heads, despite the fact that groundnuts were recognized as a women's crop, whereas tobacco, cotton, and hybrid maize were considered men's crops. Extension agents argued that the program was "too complicated" for women to understand. The exclusion of women from the project resulted in a loss of cash crop income for the wives of program participants.

Similar examples of the overly narrow focus on one household member can be found that pertain to resource management (Alderman et al. 1994). Garrett and Espinosa (1988) document an illustration from Ecuadorean Indian communities. In these communities, both men and women traditionally own and control land and animals, with control being governed by a complex set of property rights within the family. When an erosion control system was being designed, the technicians consulted only the male household members. During the implementation phase, women demonstrated against the project and refused to permit their fields to be divided by the trench.

A similar failure of policy occurred in the context of a reforestation initiative in the Dominican Republic. The initiative was predicated on the assumption that men and women used wood for the same purposes. Fortmann and Rocheleau (1989) note that this reforestation project did not consider the possibility that men's needs from the forest might differ from women's needs; consequently only men were consulted. As a result, the intercropping of cash and subsistence crops and the planting of indigenous and exotic pines for watershed management and timber were emphasized. Women were consulted only during a midproject evaluation, and it turned out that their needs were not met by the project. Women needed trees for fuel and for palm frond fiber for basket weaving. The scarcity of fuel forced some women to give up their cassava bread processing operations owing to time constraints. These needs were not addressed.

In contrast, a project in Togo to encourage soybean production succeeded precisely because it took into account the collective nature of household behavior (Dankelman and Davidson 1986). At the outset, the project was targeted to women. Exchange visits were arranged between soybean- and non–soybean-growing villages. Workshops were organized in women's homes (it was argued that homes are more effective training places than is an unfamiliar urban center). Women returned to their villages after these workshops to train other women. In addition, soybeans were not introduced as a cash crop. They were promoted as legumes that could be used to make sauces. Thus men did not become interested in cultivating soybeans and even allowed women to utilize small plots of land for soybean cultivation.

The nonadoption of new technology in the area of family planning is another example of the failure of a deliberately targeted initiative to achieve its stated goals. Most fertility research assumes that the household can be treated as a unitary decisionmaking unit (so-called "one-sex" models), even though married men and married women may have very different ideas about how many children they want. Rao and Greene (1993) model the fertility decision as a "two-sex" decision. They use a bargaining approach to examine how "credible threats" (that is, the ability to support oneself outside marriage) affect fertility decisions and find that increased female earnings decrease fertility, whereas increased male earnings raise fertility. They conclude that men's characteristics must not be ignored in the study of fertility determinants.[4] Similarly, evaluators found the most successful family planning centers in Thailand to be those that made a point of seeking male participation in classes (ICRW 1990).

Ignoring the "Long Reach" of Policy

Perhaps the most underrated drawback of relying on the unitary model for policy guidance is that a number of potentially powerful policy handles are disabled. Under the unitary model, policymakers affect intrahousehold resource allocation primarily through changes in prices and income. As argued earlier, even the role of income policies is more limited if the unitary model is valid than otherwise. Moreover, some, but not all, collective approaches suggest that additional policy handles, often with a very long reach, are available to the policymaker. The "long-reach" policy handles depend on the existence of rights that are credible in the sense that should they be violated, they obligate action. However, the policy handles do not depend on this action for their effectiveness.

To see this, consider the following model in the context of more equitable access to common property resources (CPRs). Within a household, there are two individuals, each with access to a production function that produces output as the result of two task inputs. There is comparative advantage in the tasks, so it pays to cooperate and specialize in tasks. But how are the gains from cooperation to be divided? Let the fallback option for each individual be identified with the outcome of working alone. Now suppose that the government introduces a scheme that guarantees better access for all to CPRs. How will this affect intrahousehold inequality and, in particular, the well-being of a woman with poorer preintervention access? If the income that could be generated from improved access is higher than what a woman could previously have earned on her own, but is still less than the income from cooperation, the access will result in improved equity in the household. This is the case even if the common property is not actually used. What is remarkable is that the scheme has a long reach—it equalizes intrahousehold allocation by altering outside options, despite the failure to exercise those options (Haddad and Kanbur 1992).

---

4. The identification they use to distinguish bargaining from education effects—differences in opportunities to marry due to age-specific sex ratios—is subject to challenge. Nevertheless their approach to the question adds a new dimension to the literature.

Of course the credibility of the guaranteed access is at the heart of the matter. If rationing limits the ability of women to raise their fallback utility, then there will not be an impact on intrahousehold allocation. Other intrahousehold allocation issues also come into play—if improved access is guaranteed only for married women, the threat points outside the marriage are unaffected by the policy choice. Improved access to CPRs for women outside as well as inside marriage will result in CPR reforms that are better able to alter intrahousehold resource allocation.

Similarly, programs that raise the equality of access to credit, even if the credit is not utilized, may affect intrahousehold resource allocation. A number of successful programs allow women to enter into agreements as individuals rather than as wives (often on the basis of shared liability with other women, as in the Grameen Bank program in Bangladesh).[5] This class of programs can be viewed as a subset of the category of programs creating property rights.

More generally, many collective models imply that changes in the legal environment have an indirect impact on family allocation through changes in relative bargaining position as well as the direct impact when the laws are applied. Thus Folbre (Chapter 16, this volume) calls for a review of gender bias in law as a foundation for social policy. She points out pervasive biases in divorce and child support laws that cause intrafamily and intragenerational inequality. Moreover, in many societies, there is a particular need for property rights that allow women to hold assets as individuals rather than as wives and trustees for minor children. Agarwal (1994a,b) provides an extensive discussion of this issue in the context of South Asia.

While concluding, along with others, that legislative reforms can have far-reaching effects on the welfare of children and adult women, Folbre also acknowledges that such biases in civil law often reflect preexisting biases in common law and religious strictures. Sen (1990) takes this observation one step further. Often the legal and social inequalities reflect perceived legitimacy as seen by women as well as men. This situation, in turn, parallels perceptions of relative contributions to the household in which cash earnings are valued more than unpaid labor. Women often do not see themselves as being "entitled" to a larger share of household resources. This view, in turn, leads to inequalities in investments in physical and human capital and a feedback cycle that reinforces inequalities that is difficult to break.

---

5. Goetz and Sen Gupta (1994) present evidence that men gain some control over these loans. However, even if this is the case, the implications for a woman's position in the household depend on the process by which these funds are transferred as well as her potential to retain the funds if the marriage breaks up. The transfer of control over a loan as part of an exchange can have a far different impact on a woman's well-being than if this control is taken by coercion. Although Pitt and Khandker (1994) do not address the issue of extrahousehold environmental parameters, they show that credit affects human capital investments differently, depending on gender.

This situation implies, first, that legislative solutions to intrahousehold inequalities must overcome the biases of male policymakers (Folbre, Chapter 16, this volume). Moreover, it indicates that, were a coalition of advocates of increased rights for women and children able to achieve a success in civil law, enforcement of those laws would most likely be problematic. Thus although "getting the legal environment right" may be a cornerstone in a program to achieve greater intrahousehold equality, other measures that change incentives and that change perceptions of entitlement might be necessary to achieve the full potential of such legal reforms.

So far this discussion of "long-reach" policies has implicitly relied upon McElroy's extra household environmental parameters (EEPs), a feature of Nash-bargained collective models. However, alternative collective models indicate different roles for EEPs. For example, the most general form of the sharing rule in Browning et al. (1994) does not have the "long-reach" implication, although sharing rules that are Nash bargained can be considered. It should also be remembered that Nash cooperative-bargaining models may indicate no effect if a policy changes the distribution of transfers within a union but has no effect on the threat point. Lundberg and Pollak (Chapter 5, this volume) indicate that this could happen if there were a shift in the distribution of child support supplements from fathers to mothers that left the distribution of support payments to mothers in the event of a divorce intact. In this example, the entitlement influences the woman's position within a marriage in a manner similar to a CPR. Since the shift does not affect the situation in the event of household breakup (by assumption), it has no influence in the Nash cooperative model.

Caveats

Although a number of policy measures fail to reach their potential because of neglect of intrahousehold decisionmaking processes, there are risks associated with policies that attempt to take these into account. In particular, individuals and households will respond to new positions taken by governments and nongovernmental organizations. Given the difficulty of anticipating all such moves, there is a risk of adverse impacts, even when efforts have been made to address intrahousehold allocation.

An example of this in The Gambia is provided by von Braun and Webb (1989). In the early 1980s, rice irrigation was introduced to an area of swamp rice production in order to raise yields, commercialize the product, and raise women's share of household income. However, an initiative intended to raise female income ended up reducing it. Previously women had been the rice growers. Yield increases transformed the status of rice from a private crop under the control of women into a communal crop under the control of men. The choice of technology and the attempts by donors to protect female rights were based on observed outcomes of household decisions, which left the production of rice under the control of women. However, the process of decisionmaking was not fully understood and rights were not sufficiently protected by the project's management. Thus males in the community were able to shift the equilibrium of resource allocation to reflect preproject preferences and to take control over the new resources offered by the project. It is not, of course, clear that a fuller model of household resource allocation would have led to measures to ensure that the donor's intentions were realized. Nevertheless, a perspective that viewed individuals as interdependent (rather than as independent agents) might have led to an expectation of responses by males to changes in women's assets and productivity.[6] Lundberg and Pollak (Chapter 5, this volume) discuss this issue in more detail.

Although more experience and research on intrafamily allocation will lessen the probability of similar unwanted results in the future, considerable uncertainty is likely to remain for some time. Does this mean that it is too risky to use the analyses currently available? Kuhn (1970) points out that whereas the Copernican model of the universe initially resolved a number of the anomalies that had accrued within the Ptolemaic system, it did not immediately offer improved predictive power over the often convoluted ad hoc extensions of the older model. Although it is not claimed that a shift to collective models rivals the Copernican revolution as a change in world view, an analogy to the Ptolemaic view in the unitary model can be seen; despite the accumulated evidence against income pooling, the unitary model, bolstered by ad hoc assumptions, retains an impressive ability to explain the new body of evidence on inequality within the household. Moreover, in many cases, both policy and research will be unaffected by the choice of models; Occam's razor argues that in these cases the simplest approach be taken.

Nevertheless, although the risk of incorrectly analyzing a complex policy measure must always be carefully assessed, it is contended that this judgment must include a scrutiny of the consequences of *not* taking into consideration intrahousehold decisionmaking as well as potential errors that such consideration might introduce. This point is elaborated from the perspective of the implication of collective models for targeting of transfers.

It has been argued that the greater error is the failure to consider intra-household allocation in any form, with any tool. However, it is also argued that the unitary approach imposes limitations and that a researcher should be cognizant of those liabilities. Under many circumstances, acceptance of a unitary model of the household, when it is inappropriate, has more serious

---

6. It is also not clear that any current model of bargaining or sharing would have predicted the virtual seizure of control that occurred. Nevertheless, the example suggests that in economics, as in chemistry, a disturbance of an equilibrium leads to processes that tend to restore the equilibrium.

consequences for policy than the false rejection of such a model (this point is argued in Alderman et al. [1995]).

In the area of targeted interventions, consider the targeting of resources to women. False rejection of the collective model implies (erroneously) that targeting resources to women is pointless; thus an efficient means of directing resources to women and children is foregone. False rejection of the unitary model implies that the costs of targeting could have been avoided. Even if there is a wide confidence interval on the differences entailed by collective models, most imply either more or, at least, no less investment in children from increasing resources controlled by women than the unitary model.[7] Thus, unless there are significantly higher costs to targeting programs to women in poor households, rather than to poor households as a unit, the available evidence may be considered adequate to indicate that false rejection of the collective model is the more serious error. An exception, however, might occur if, in addition to different rates of investment in children, males and females have different gender biases toward these investments (Thomas 1994). Under such a circumstance, a targeting of transfers may leave some children worse off.

To be sure, few programs that target women are costless. For example, they may impose extra time burdens on women, reducing the welfare of the woman herself and possibly that of her children. Although most studies indicate that increased earnings for women offset any negative effects of reduced time for child care—an important factor in the production of nutrition and health (Leslie 1988)—such studies do not analyze the impact of an increased time burden that shifts rather than increases total household resources. Thus greater precision in measuring the benefits of intrahousehold targeting may be necessary to determine optimal program design.

Regarding nonadoption of development initiatives, the consequences of the false rejection of the collective model in terms of nonadoption or adoption with unintended effects have been noted. False rejection of the unitary model again implies that the costs of understanding the needs and constraints of all household members could have been avoided.

For long-reach policy handles, false rejection of the collective model eliminates many policy instruments that could have far-reaching and profound effects on the lives of the most vulnerable of household members. False rejection of the unitary model means that these long handles are not connected to the policy machine, and energy will be wasted in pulling on them. Regarding intergenerational transfers, false rejection of the collective model implies that

---

7. Conversely, it may be possible to conceive of cases in which an increase in resources controlled by males has a negative impact on investments in children owing to changes in bargaining or sharing rules that offset the male's (presumed) nonnegative marginal propensity to invest. This has been alleged concerning increases in incomes from cash cropping. However, these scenarios also generally presume a decrease of other incomes.

the effect of the tax policy is the opposite of its intent: instead of reducing urban-to-rural remittance flows, the urban wage tax–rural wage subsidy has increased urban-to-rural remittance flows. A false rejection of the unitary model will again lead to impact's being the opposite of intent, although the relative magnitude of each false rejection is hard to predict.

Research Directions

There is a growing body of empirical work on intrahousehold allocation, but it is still limited in scope. There is not a body of research from which to derive generalizations. More important, since the diversity of social structures almost assuredly rules against such generalizations, few studies have been replicated over a range of conditions and cultures. In addition to examining whether intrahousehold allocation processes are invariant to the policy regime the household faces, there is a need for policy research to focus on other institutions, such as the extended family, community, and other social groupings.

Most econometric studies of intrahousehold allocation are based on cross-sectional data. Generally these studies do not address how households or other social groupings are formed or dissolved. Yet one of the valuable features of the contributions by McElroy and Lundberg and Pollak (Chapters 4 and 5, this volume) is the linkage they establish between allocation within the household and the processes of household formation and dissolution. Though demographers have long been concerned with such issues, within economics there exist fewer empirical studies, based on the framework developed by Becker (1973, 1974a) and Becker, Landes, and Michael (1977), and, with the exception of Handa (1995), these generally pertain to developed countries.[8]

Further work, particularly from developing countries, can be regarded as promising from both a research and a policy standpoint. For example, in very different contexts and using different methodologies, both Ainsworth (1992) and Rosenzweig and Wolpin (1993) indicate that families consider coresidency and transfers across households as part of a continuum of options used to invest in the education of family members. More generally, allocations within households (such as labor usage or the composition of expenditures) may reflect implicit agreements made at the time a union was formed or coresidency established, subject to new information (including unanticipated income and fertility shocks). The process of living in a union reduces asymmetries of information and also creates human and physical capital specific to the partnership.

Furthermore, the time path of transfers and services often creates incentives to renege on agreements—a classic example being a spouse abandoned

---

8. Cameron (1995) provides a recent review of the economics literature in this area, particularly for developed countries.

after having invested in the human capital of the other. Although there have been a number of theoretical and empirical advances regarding the importance of extrahousehold links and the dynamic processes of conjugal agreements and incentives to renegotiate, both topics remain a priority for the analysis of both intra- and intergenerational distribution.

This theme relates to the issue of household headship. Female-headed households are often perceived as a vulnerable group and one to which policy measures should be directed. This view is too simplistic. There may be a strong correlation between female headship and poverty as in Buvinic et al. (1992), some correlation as in Quisumbing, Haddad, and Peña (1995), little correlation as in Louat, Grosh, and van der Gaag (1993), or some interaction between headship and welfare at low income levels (Kennedy and Peters 1992). However, the processes by which households become male or female headed are rarely random; instead, they are often the result of conscious decisions made by men and women. Such processes will affect observed outcomes. As Bruce and Lloyd (Chapter 13, this volume) note, existing work rarely takes these processes into account.

An additional specific area for further research is indicated in the review of tests of income pooling and collective models in Chapter 8 (Hoddinott, Alderman, and Haddad). One interesting possibility would be an experiment in which, conditional on having a household qualified for a transfer—say, on conventional means testing criteria—the transfer would be assigned randomly to men and women within the household. The experiment would monitor how the assignment affects spending as well as whether the restriction to a specified family member affects participation or other time allocation. Such an experiment could assist in settling the debate over income pooling, since it would avoid identification on potentially endogenous labor or investment choices.

Another area in which work would be valuable would be empirical studies of labor allocation within a collective framework. There have been a few studies in developed countries, notably Kooreman and Kapteyn (1990) and Kooreman (1994), but these have not been replicated in a developing-country context. As discussed by Carter and Katz and by Dey Abbas (Chapters 6 and 15, this volume), the absence of labor pooling can explain why policies that increase household income, but require reallocation of labor between "male" and "female" activities or crops, often fail. The few econometric studies from this perspective (Jones 1983; von Braun and Webb 1989; Jacoby 1995; Udry 1996) indicate considerable scope for work in developing this issue. A particular advantage of the approach Udry employs is that it deals, in part, with marginal returns on purchased inputs; there is a long empirical tradition of investigating allocative efficiency when prices are exogenous.

A related approach would be to apply the model of labor allocation in cooperatives as set out by Sen (1966), Putterman (1980, 1981, 1986), and Putterman and DiGiorgio (1985) to households. Alternatively, labor allocation could be thought of in terms of a principal-agent model (Haddad, Hoddinott, and Alderman 1994:22–27).

Finally, there is a need for greater collaboration between economists and social scientists in other disciplines. Much of the literature on households employs concepts based on social interactions that differ from those standard in economic analysis. For example, Sen (1985a) notes that bargaining among members is also a function of their perceived contribution to the household. The individual perceived as making the larger contribution can expect to obtain an outcome more favorable to him or her. This situation may place women at a particular disadvantage, as much of their contribution may take the form of nonmarket labor, which is less visible than wage employment. The distinction between actual and perceived behavior is rarely made in economic models of household behavior, though Woolley (1992) is a recent exception.

A number of studies on intrahousehold allocation recognize the importance of dynamic cultural processes. For example, Hart (1995) argues that distinctions such as sharing versus not sharing or household versus not household are sharper than they need to be. She recognizes a dynamic process in which social aggregations form and reform as well as redefine the norms of interaction.

In another context, Folbre (Chapter 16, this volume) suggests that public policy is not separate from inequalities in the household; policy can easily be shown to cause that inequality, but it is also a reflection of the attitudes that determine household allocation. Similarly, Sen (1990) sees a second feedback loop in which perceptions of self and personal welfare are both causes and results of inequalities. Understanding the first loop may allow one to determine at which points the system is most subject to intervention and at which points economic and legal reforms can work in synergism. From a research standpoint, these interactions imply a broader set of tools than is often used by a single discipline. Promising areas for such work include (1) the use of information collected in a qualitative manner and yet accessible to "quantifiers," such as the creation of variables for "respect," "status," or "apparent prosperity," and (2) an investigation of the cultural norms that often override the intent of social legislation. These norms link to the second feedback loop depicted by Sen.[9]

---

9. Sen's (1990) discussion of perceived interests and perceived legitimacy raises a number of ethical issues that can only be alluded to here. It can be presumed that most readers of this volume are comfortable with the advocacy of individual rights (usually of children or exploited women) implied in most policy prescriptions. However, in some cases, social policy attempts to promote rights that individuals do not currently see as legitimately theirs, although they—or their daughters—may do so once the feedback cycle is reversed. With sense of self, and intrahousehold allocation endogenous over the long run, there is a clear conceptual distinction between dynamic welfare consideration and paternalism. However, the measurement of the effect of interventions in such a context may require new research tools.

Interdisciplinary work may help define the data requirements for research.[10] Hart (1995) argues that the conceptual framework of a researcher limits data collection in a manner that often precludes institutional analysis. This theme is also taken up by Guyer (Chapter 7, this volume). Here again, interdisciplinary work on methods, as well as analysis, might reap rich rewards.

Conclusion

The focus of this concluding chapter has been on the policy implications of intrahousehold resource allocation. Elsewhere in the book, it has been stressed that regardless of the model used, it is incorrect to assume that policies designed to ameliorate household poverty are sufficient for the alleviation of individual poverty, and that individual poverty can be alleviated without due regard to household processes. In this chapter, this claim is extended to contend that errors in understanding intrafamily allocation processes may result in the nonadoption of beneficial policies, in policies having unintended consequences, and in the loss of policy handles.

Although it is acknowledged that the diversity and complexity of human society make it hard to derive universal guidelines on how to incorporate intrahousehold allocation process into policy, it is also ventured that the policy failures associated with accepting unitary models when they are inappropriate are often more serious than those associated with erroneously accepting collective models. In making this claim, the approach has been illustrative rather than exhaustive.

Just over a decade ago, a conference on intrahousehold resource allocation (published in Rogers and Schlossman [1990]) examined whether going inside the "black box" of the household would yield any useful insights. One objective of this book has been to argue that from a policy perspective, the answer is an emphatic "yes." A second has been to suggest that, in many cases, a broadening of conceptual models (for example, collective rather than unitary models) and research methods (for example, the integration of qualitative and quantitative methods) may reap rich rewards. However, considerable work remains. Although it has been argued that the collective framework may often be the most appropriate means of analyzing intrahousehold issues, the choice of model under different circumstances is still not clear. Such difficulties are compounded by the fact that by their nature, the results of gender and intrahousehold analyses are specific to cultural, social, and institutional settings and are thus difficult to generalize. Perhaps one way forward would be to apply a common conceptual approach to the analysis of a set of policy-oriented case

10. For more on the data collection implications of intrahousehold research, see Levin, Ralston, and Haddad (1993).

studies from a regionally diverse set of countries. Hypotheses could be developed on the basis of different conceptual models and tested with and without the benefit of additional intrahousehold data. This approach would permit an assessment of the trade-offs between additional policy insights (and the mistakes avoided) and the costs of such an extended analysis. It is hoped that the chapters in this volume will stimulate such work.

References

Abdullah, M. 1983. Dimensions of intrahousehold food and nutrient allocation: A study of a Bangladeshi village. Ph.D. diss., Faculty of Medicine, London University, London.

Acharya, M., and L. Bennett. 1983. *Women and the subsistence sector: Economic participation in household decisionmaking in Nepal.* World Bank Working Paper 526. Washington, D.C.: World Bank.

Afonja, S. 1986. Land control: A critical factor in Yoruba gender stratification. In *Women and class in Africa,* ed. C. Robertson and I. Berger. New York and London: Holmes & Meier.

Agarwal, B. 1994a. Gender and command over property: A critical gap in economic analysis and policy in South Asia. *World Development* 22 (10): 1455–1478.

———. 1994b. *A field of one's own: Gender and land rights in South Asia.* Cambridge: Cambridge University Press.

Ainsworth, M. 1992. *Economic aspects of child fostering in Côte d'Ivoire.* Living Standards Measurement Study 92. Washington, D.C.: World Bank.

Alderman, H., and M. Garcia. 1993. *Poverty, household food security, and nutrition in rural Pakistan.* Research Report 96. Washington, D.C.: International Food Policy Research Institute.

Alderman, H., and C. H. Paxson. 1992. *Do the poor insure? A synthesis of the literatures on risk and consumption in developing countries.* Policy Research Working Paper 1008. Washington, D.C.: World Bank.

Alderman, H., and D. Sahn. 1993. Substitution between goods and leisure in a developing country. *American Journal of Agricultural Economics* 75 (4): 875–883.

Alderman, H., J. Behrman, D. Ross, and R. Sabot. 1996. Decomposing the gender gap in cognitive skills in a poor rural economy. *Journal of Human Resources* 31 (1): 229–254.

Alderman, H., L. Haddad, J. Hoddinott, and S. Vosti. 1994. Strengthening agricultural and natural resource policy through intrahousehold analysis: An introduction. *American Journal of Agricultural Economics* 76 (5): 1208–1212.

Alderman, H., P.-A. Chiappori, L. Haddad, J. Hoddinott, and R. Kanbur. 1995. Unitary versus collective models of the household: Is it time to shift the burden of proof? *World Bank Research Observer* 10 (1): 1–19.

Altman, J. 1973. Observational study of behavior: Sampling methods. *Behavior* 44: 227–265.

Altonji, J., F. Hayashi, and L. Kotlikoff. 1992. Is the extended family altruistically linked? Direct tests using micro data. *American Economic Review* 82 (5): 1177–1198.

Anker, R., and C. Hein. 1985. Why Third World urban employers usually prefer men. *International Labour Review* 124 (1): 73–90.

Anker, R., and C. Hein, eds. 1986. *Sex inequalities in urban employment in the Third World.* New York: St. Martin's.

Appadurai, A., ed. 1986. *The social life of things: Commodities in cultural perspective.* Cambridge: Cambridge University Press.

Apps, P. 1981. *A theory of inequality and taxation.* Cambridge: Cambridge University Press.

––––––. 1982. Institutional inequality and tax incidence. *Journal of Public Economics* 18 (2): 217–242.

Apps, P. F., and G. S. Jones. 1986. Selective taxation of couples. *Zeitschrift für National-ökonomie* 5 (Supplement): 63–74.

Apps, P., and R. Rees. 1988. Taxation and the household. *Journal of Public Economics* 35 (3): 355–369.

Apps, P., and E. Savage. 1989. Labour supply, welfare rankings, and the measurement of inequality. *Journal of Public Economics* 39 (3): 335–364.

Arrow, K. 1963. *Social choice and individual values,* 2d ed. New Haven, Conn., U.S.A.: Yale University Press.

Ashenfelter, O., and J. Heckman. 1974. The estimation of income and substitution effects in a model of family labor supply. *Econometrica* 42: 73–85.

Ashworth, J., and D. Ulph. 1981. Household models. In *Taxation and labour supply,* ed. C. V. Brown. London: Allen and Unwin.

Axelrod, R. 1984. *The evolution of cooperation.* New York: Basic Books.

Babalola, S. O., and C. Dennis. 1988. Returns to women's labor in cash crop production: Tobacco in Igboho, Oyo State, Nigeria. In *Agriculture, women, and land: The African experience,* ed. J. Davison. Boulder, Colo., U.S.A., and London: Westview.

Bardhan, P. K. 1984. *Land labor and rural poverty.* Oxford: Oxford University Press.

Barro, R. 1974. Are government bonds net wealth? *Journal of Political Economy* 82 (6): 1095–1117.

Bates, R. H. 1990. Capital, kinship, and conflict: The structuring influence of capital in kinship societies. *Canadian Journal of African Studies* 24 (2): 151–164.

Beaton, G., and H. Ghassemi. 1982. Supplementary feeding programs for young children in developing countries. *American Journal for Clinical Nutrition* 34 (4) (Supplement): 863–916.

Becker, G. 1965. A theory of the allocation of time. *Economic Journal* 75: 493–517.

––––––. 1973. A theory of marriage: Part I. *Journal of Political Economy* 81 (4): 813–846.

––––––. 1974a. A theory of marriage: Part II. *Journal of Political Economy* 82 (2): S11–S26.

––––––. 1974b. A theory of social interactions. *Journal of Political Economy* 82 (6): 1063–1093.

————. 1981. *A treatise on the family.* Cambridge, Mass., U.S.A.: Harvard University Press.

————. 1993. Preference formation within families. Paper presented at the meetings of the American Economic Association, January 6.

Becker, G., and N. Tomes. 1976. Child endowments and the quantity and quality of children. *Journal of Political Economy* 84 (4, Part 2): S143-S162.

Becker, G., M. Grossman, and K. Murphy. 1991. Rational addiction and the effect of price on consumption. *American Economic Review* 81 (2): 237–241.

Becker, G., E. Landes, and R. T. Michael. 1977. An economic analysis of marital instability. *Journal of Political Economy* 85 (6): 1141–1187.

Begg, C., and J. Berlin. 1988. Publication bias: A problem in interpreting medical data. *Journal of Royal Statistical Society* 151 (3): 419–463.

Behrman, J. 1988a. Nutrition, health, birth order, and seasonality: Intrahousehold allocation in rural India. *Journal of Development Economics* 28 (7): 42–63.

————. 1988b. Intrahousehold allocation of nutrients in rural India: Are boys favored? Do parents exhibit inequality aversion? *Oxford Economic Papers* 40 (1): 32–54.

————. 1990. *The action of human resources and poverty on one another.* Living Standards Measurement Study 74. Washington, D.C.: World Bank.

————. 1996. Intrahousehold distribution and the family. In *Handbook of population and family economics,* ed. M. Rosenzweig and O. Stark. Amsterdam: North-Holland.

Behrman, J. R., and A. Deolalikar. 1988. Health and nutrition. In *Handbook of development economics,* ed. H. Chenery and T. N. Srinivasan. Amsterdam: North-Holland.

————. 1989. Seasonal demands for nutrient intakes and health status in rural south India. In *Seasonal variability in Third World agriculture,* ed. D. E. Sahn. Baltimore: Johns Hopkins University Press for the International Food Policy Research Institute.

————. 1990. The intrahousehold demand for nutrients in rural South India: Individual estimates, fixed effects, and permanent income. *The Journal of Human Resources* 25 (4): 665–696.

————. 1995. Are there differential returns to schooling by gender? The case of Indonesian labour markets. *Oxford Bulletin of Economics and Statistics* 57 (1): 97–117.

Behrman, J., R. Pollak, and P. Taubman. 1982. Parental preferences and provision for progeny. *Journal of Political Economy* 90 (1): 52–75.

Behrman, J. R., M. R. Rosenzweig, and P. Taubman. 1994. Endowments and the allocation of schooling in the family and in the marriage market: The twins experiment. *Journal of Political Economy* 102 (6): 1131–1174.

Beller, A. H. 1982. The impact of equal opportunity policy on sex differentials in earnings and occupations. *American Economic Review* 72 (2): 171–175.

Bender, D. R. 1967. A refinement of the concept of household: Families, coresidence, and domestic functions. *American Anthropologist* 69 (5): 493–504.

Benjamin, D. 1992. Household composition, labor markets, and labor demand: Testing for separation in agricultural household models. *Econometrica* 60 (2): 287–322.

Bennholdt-Thomsen, V. 1988. Investment in the poor: An analysis of World Bank policy. In *Women: The last colony,* ed. M. Mies, V. Bennholdt-Thomsen, and C. von Werlhof. London: Zed.

Ben-Porath, Y. 1979. The F-connection: Families, friends, and firms and the organization of exchange. *Population and Development Review* 6: 1–30.

Bentley, M. E., M. T. Boot, J. Gittelsohn, and R. Y. Stallings. 1994. *The use of structured observations in the study of health behavior.* Occasional Paper 27. The Hague, the Netherlands: International Reference Centre, International Water and Sanitation Centre.

Bentley, M. E., K. L. Dicken, S. Mebrahtu, B. Kayode, G. A. Oni, C. C. Verzosa, K. H. Brown, and J. R. Idowu. 1991a. Development of a nutritionally adequate and culturally appropriate weaning food in Kwara State, Nigeria: An interdisciplinary approach. *Social Science and Medicine* 33 (10): 1103–1112.

Bentley, M. E., R. Y. Stallings, M. Fukumoto, and J. A. Elder. 1991b. Maternal feeding behavior and child acceptance of food during diarrhea, convalescence, and health in the Central Sierra of Peru. *American Journal of Public Health* 81 (1): 43–47.

Bergstrom, T. 1989. A fresh look at the rotten kid theorem—and other household mysteries. *Journal of Political Economy* 97 (5): 1138–1159.

Bergstrom, T., L. Blume, and H. Varian. 1986. On the private provision of public goods. *Journal of Political Economy* 29 (February): 25–49.

Bernard, H. R. 1988. *Research methods in cultural anthropology.* Newbury Park, Calif., U.S.A.: Sage.

Bernard, H. R., P. J. Pelto, O. Werner, J. Boster, A. K. Romney, A. Johnson, C. R. Ember, and AA. Kasakoff. 1986. The construction of primary data in cultural anthropology. *Current Anthropology* 27 (4): 382–396.

Bernheim, B. D., and O. Stark. 1988. Altruism within the family reconsidered: Do nice guys finish last? *American Economic Review* 78 (5): 1034–1045.

Bernheim, B. D., A. Shleifer, and L. Summers. 1985. The strategic bequest motive. *Journal of Political Economy* 93 (6): 1045–1076.

Berry, S. S. 1989. Social institutions and access to resources. *Africa* 59 (1): 41–55.

Besley, T. 1993. *Savings, credit, and insurance.* Discussion Paper 167. Princeton, N.J., U.S.A.: Woodrow Wilson School of Public and International Affairs, Princeton University.

Bevan, D. L., P. Collier, and J. W. Gunning. 1989. *Peasants and governments: An economic analysis.* Oxford: Oxford University Press.

Binmore, K., A. Rubinstein, and A. Wolinsky. 1986. The Nash bargaining solution in economic modelling. *Rand Journal of Economics* 17 (2): 176–188.

Bjorn, P., and Q. Vuong. 1984. *Simultaneous models for dummy endogenous variables: A game theoretic formulation with an application to household labor force participation.* Working paper. Pasadena, Calif., U.S.A.: California Institute of Technology.

———. 1985. *Econometric modeling of a Stackelberg game with an application to household labor force participation.* Working paper. Pasadena, Calif., U.S.A.: California Institute of Technology.

Blood, R., and D. Wolfe. 1960. *Husbands and wives: The dynamics of married living.* New York: Free Press.

Blumberg, R. L. 1987. Income under female versus male control: Differential spending patterns and the consequences when women lose control of returns to labor. World Bank, Washington, D.C. Mimeo.

————. 1988. Income under female versus male control: Hypotheses from a theory of gender stratification and data from the Third World. *Journal of Family Issues* 9 (1): 51–84.

————. 1991. Income under female versus male control: Hypotheses from a theory of gender stratification and data from the Third World. In *Gender, family, and economy,* ed. R. L. Blumberg. Newbury Park, Calif., U.S.A.: Sage.

Blundell, R., and A. Lewbel. 1991. The information content of equivalence scales. *Journal of Econometrics* 50 (1–2): 49–68.

Bohannan, P. 1963. *Social Anthropology.* New York: Holt, Rinehart, and Winston.

Bolles, L. 1986. Economic crisis and female-headed households in urban Jamaica. In *Women and change in Latin America,* ed. J. Nash and H. Safa. South Hadley, Mass., U.S.A.: Bergin and Garvey.

Boserup, E. 1970. *Women's role in economic development.* New York: St. Martin's.

Boskin, M., and L. Kotlikoff. 1985. Public debt and U.S. saving: A new test of the neutrality hypothesis. *Carnegie-Rochester Conference Series on Public Policy* 23: 55–86.

Bouis, H. E. 1994. The effect of income on demand for food in poor countries: Are our food consumption data bases giving us reliable estimates? *Journal of Development Economics* 44 (1): 199–226.

————. 1996. A food demand system based on demand for characteristics: If there is curvature in the Slutsky matrix, what do the curves look like and why? *Journal of Development Economics* 51: 239–266.

Bouis, H. E., and L. J. Haddad. 1990. *Agricultural commercialization, nutrition, and the rural poor: A study of Philippine farm households.* Boulder, Colo., U.S.A.: Lynne Rienner.

————. 1992. Are estimates of calorie-income elasticities too high? A recalibration of the plausible range. *Journal of Development Economics* 39 (2): 333–364.

Bouis, H. E., L. Haddad, and E. Kennedy. 1992. Does it matter how we survey demand for food? Evidence from Kenya and the Philippines. *Food Policy* 17 (5): 349–360.

Boulier, B. L. 1977. Children and household economic activity in Laguna, Philippines. *Journal of Philippine Development* 4 (2): 195–222.

Bourguignon, F. 1984. Rationalité individuelle ou rationalité stratégique: Le cas de l'offre familiale de travail. *Revue Economique* 35: 147–162.

Bourguignon, F., and P.-A. Chiappori. 1992. Collective models of household behavior: An introduction. *European Economic Review* 36: 355–364.

Bourguignon, F., M. Browning, and P.-A. Chiappori. 1994. Identifying intrahousehold decision processes. McMaster University, Hamilton, Ontario, Canada. Mimeo.

Bourguignon, F., M. Browning, P.-A. Chiappori, and V. Lechène. 1993. Intrahousehold allocation of consumption: A model and some evidence from French data. *Annales d'Economie et de Statistiques* 29: 137–156.

Bradley, C. 1988. The problem of domestic violence in Papua New Guinea. In *Guidelines for police training on violence against women and child sexual abuse.* London: Commonwealth Secretariat, Women and Development Programme.

Braun, J. von. 1988. Effects of technological change in agriculture on food consumption and nutrition: Rice in a West African setting. *World Development* 16 (9): 1083–1098.

Braun, J. von, and P. Webb. 1989. The impact of new crop technology on the agricultural division of labor in a West African setting. *Economic Development and Cultural Change* 37 (3): 513–534.

Braun, J. von, D. Puetz, and P. Webb. 1989. *Irrigation technology and commercialization of rice in The Gambia: Effects on income and nutrition.* Research Report 75. Washington, D.C.: International Food Policy Research Institute.

Brenner, R. 1985. *The Brenner debate. Agrarian class structures and economic development in pre-industrial Europe.* Cambridge: Cambridge University Press.

Breusch, T. S., and A. R. Pagan. 1980. The Lagrange multiplier test and its applications to model specification in econometrics. *Review of Economic Studies* 47: 225–238.

Brocas, A.-M., A.-M. Cailloux, and V. Oget. 1990. *Women and social security. Progress towards equality of treatment.* Geneva: International Labour Office.

Brown, J. C. 1984. *Family income support Part 2: Children in social security.* Studies of the Social Security System 3. London: Policy Studies Institute.

Browning, M. 1983. Necessary and sufficient conditions for conditional cost functions. *Econometrica* 51 (3): 851–856.

———. 1994. The savings behavior of a two-person household. Department of Economics, McMaster University, Hamilton, Ontario, Canada. Mimeo.

Browning, M., and P.-A. Chiappori. 1995. *Efficient intrahousehold allocation: A general characterization and empirical tests.* Working paper. Paris: Département et Laboratoire d'Économie Théorique et Appliquée (DELTA).

Browning, M., and C. Meghir. 1991. The effects of male and female labor supply on commodity demands. *Econometrica* 59 (4): 925–951.

Browning, M., F. Bourguignon, P.-A. Chiappori, and V. Lechène. 1994. Income and outcomes: A structural model of intrahousehold allocation. *Journal of Political Economy* 102 (6): 1067–1096.

Bruce, J. 1989a. Homes divided. *World Development* 17 (7): 979–992.

———. 1989b. *Community forestry: Rapid appraisal of tree and land tenure.* Rome: Food and Agriculture Organization of the United Nations.

Bruce, J., C. Lloyd, and A. Leonard. 1995. *Families in focus: New perspectives on mothers, fathers, and children.* New York: Population Council.

Bruce, N., and M. Waldman. 1990. The rotten-kid theorem meets the Samaritan's dilemma. *Quarterly Journal of Economics* 105 (1): 155–166.

Bukh, J. 1977. *Women in food production, food handling, and nutrition.* Copenhagen: Centre for Development Research.

Burfisher, M. E., and N. Horenstein. 1985. *Sex roles in the Nigerian Tiv farm household.* West Hartford, Conn., U.S.A.: Kumarian.

Buvinic, M., J. P. Valenzuela, T. Molina, and E. Gonzales. 1992. The fortunes of adolescent mothers and their children: The transmission of poverty in Santiago, Chile. *Population and Development Review* 18 (2): 269–297.

Cain, M. 1986. The consequences of reproductive failure: Dependence, mobility, and mortality among the elderly of rural South Asia. *Population Studies* 40 (3): 375–388.

Cameron, S. 1995. A review of economic research into determinants of divorce. *British Review of Economic Issues* 17 (41): 1–22.

Carney, J. 1988a. Struggles over crop rights and labor within contract farming households in a Gambian irrigated rice project. *Journal of Peasant Studies* 15: 334–349.

————. 1988b. Struggles over land and crops in an irrigated rice scheme: The Gambia. In *Agriculture, women, and land: The African experience,* ed. J. Davison. Boulder, Colo., U.S.A., and London: Westview.

Carter, M. R., and J. Kalfayan. 1989. *A general equilibrium exploration of agrarian class structure and production relations.* Agricultural Economics Staff Paper 279. Madison, Wis., U.S.A.: University of Wisconsin–Madison.

Chamberlain, G. 1977a. Education, income and ability revisited. In *Latent variables in socio-economic models,* ed. D. J. Aigner and A. S. Goldberger. Amsterdam: North-Holland.

————. 1977b. An instrumental variable interpretation of identification in variance-components and MIMIC models. In *Kinometrics: Determinants of socio-economic success within and between families,* ed. P. Taubman. Amsterdam: North-Holland.

————. 1980. Analysis of covariance with qualitative data. *Review of Economic Studies* 47 (1): 225–238.

Chamberlain, G., and Z. Griliches. 1975. Unobservables with a variance components structure: Ability, schooling and the economic success of brothers. *International Economic Review* 16: 422–450.

Chambers, R., R. Longhurst, and A. Pacey. 1981. *Seasonal dimensions to rural poverty.* London: Frances Pinter.

Chayanov, A. 1966. *The theory of the peasant economy,* ed. D. Thorner, B. Kerblay, and R. Smith. Homewood, Ill., U.S.A.: Richard Irwin.

————. 1986. *A. V. Chayanov and the theory of peasant economy.* Madison, Wis., U.S.A.: University of Wisconsin Press.

Chen, L., E. Huq, and S. D'Souza. 1981. Sex bias in the family allocation of food and health care in rural Bangladesh. *Population and Development Review* 7 (1): 55–70.

Chiappori, P.-A. 1988a. Nash-bargained household decisions: A comment. *International Economic Review* 29 (4): 791–796.

————. 1988b. Rational household labor supply. *Econometrica* 56 (1): 63–89.

————. 1990a. Nash-bargained household decisions: A rejoinder. *International Economic Review* 32: 761–762.

————. 1990b. La fonction de demande de biens collectifs: Théorie et application. *Annales d'Economie et de Statistiques* 26: 28–42.

————. 1992. Collective labor supply and welfare. *Journal of Political Economy* 100 (3): 437–467.

————. 1993. Traditional versus collective models of household behavior: What can data tell us? Paris: Département et Laboratoire d'Économie Théorique et Appliquée. Mimeo.

Chipande, G. H. R. 1987. Innovation adoption among female-headed households. *Development and Change* 18 (2): 315–327.

Claudio, V. S., P. E. DeGuzman, M. S. Oliveros, and G. P. Dimaano. 1982. *Basic nutrition for Filipinos.* Manila: Merriam Corporation.

Clay, E. J., and B. B. Schaffer, eds. 1984. *Room for manoeuvre: An exploration of public policy in agriculture and rural development.* London: Heinemann.

Cleaver, K., and G. Schreiber. 1994. The population, agriculture, and environment nexus in Sub-Saharan Africa. Washington, D.C.: World Bank.

Clemhout, S., and H. Y. Wan, Jr. 1977. *Symmetric marriage, household decisionmaking, and impact on fertility.* Working Paper 152. Ithaca, N.Y., U.S.A.: Cornell University.

Cloud, K., and J. B. Knowles. 1988. Where can we go from here? Recommendations for action. In *Agriculture, women, and land: The African experience,* ed. J. Davison. Boulder, Colo., U.S.A., and London: Westview.

Cohen, A. 1969. *Custom and politics in urban Africa. A study of Hausa migrants in Yoruba towns.* Berkeley, Calif., U.S.A.: University of California Press.

Conti, A. 1979. Capitalist organization of production through non-capitalist relations: Women's role in a pilot settlement scheme in Upper Volta. *Review of African Political Economy* 15/16: 75–92.

Coreil, J., A. Augustin, E. Holt, and N. A. Halsey. 1989. Use of ethnographic research for instrument development in a case-control study of immunization use in Haiti. *International Journal of Epidemiology* 18 (4) (Supplement 2): s33–s37.

Cox, D. 1987. Motives for private income transfers. *Journal of Political Economy* 95: 508–546.

Cox, D., and G. Jakubson. 1995. The connection between public transfers and private interfamily transfers. *Journal of Public Economics* 75 (1): 129–167.

Cox, D., and E. Jimenez. 1990. Achieving social objectives through private transfers: A review. *World Bank Research Observer* 5 (2): 205–218.

———. 1992. Social security and private transfers in developing countries: The case for Peru. *World Bank Economic Review* 6 (1): 155–171.

Cox, D., and M. Rank. 1992. Inter-vivos transfers and intergenerational exchange. *Review of Economics and Statistics* 74 (2): 305–314.

Crabtree, B. F., and W. L. Miller, eds. 1992. *Doing qualitative research.* Newbury Park, Calif., U.S.A.: Sage.

Crawford, D. L., and R. A. Pollak. 1989. Child care policy. University of Pennsylvania, Philadelphia, Pa., U.S.A. Mimeo.

Crawford, V. P., and E. M. Knoer. 1981. Job matching with heterogeneous firms and workers. *Econometrica* 49 (2): 437–450.

Cronk, L. 1989. Low socioeconomic status and female-biased parental investment: The Mukogodo example. *American Anthropologist* 91: 414–429.

Cumper, G., and S. Daly. 1979. *Family law in the Commonwealth Caribbean.* Mona, Kingston, Jamaica: University of the West Indies.

Dankelman, I., and J. Davidson. 1986. *Women and the environment in the Third World: Alliance for the future.* London: Earthscan.

Das Gupta, M. 1987. Selective discrimination against female children in rural Punjab, India. *Population and Development Review* 13 (1): 77–101.

Daunton, M. J. 1990. Housing. In *The Cambridge social history of Britain, 1750–1950,* vol. 2, ed. F. M. I. Thompson. Cambridge: Cambridge University Press.

Davies, H., and H. Joshi. 1990. *The foregone earnings of Europe's mothers.* Discussion Paper 24. London: Birkbeck College, University of London.

Davison, J. 1988. Who owns what? Land registration and tensions in gender relations of production in Kenya. In *Agriculture, women, and land: The African experience,* ed. J. Davison. Boulder, Colo., U.S.A., and London: Westview.

Deaton, A. 1986. Demand analysis. In *Handbook of econometrics,* ed. Z. Griliches and M. D. Intriligator. Amsterdam: North-Holland.

————. 1988. Quantity, quality, and spatial variation of price. *American Economic Review* 78 (3): 418–430.

————. 1989. Looking for boy-girl discrimination in household expenditure data. *World Bank Economic Review* 3 (1): 1–15.

————. 1995. Inequality within and between households in growing and aging economies. In *Critical issues in Asian development,* ed. M. G. Quibria. Oxford: Oxford University Press for the Asian Development Bank.

Deaton, A. S., and J. Muellbauer. 1980. *Economics and consumer behavior.* Cambridge: Cambridge University Press.

Defense for Children International–USA. 1991. *The effects of maternal mortality on children in Africa: An exploratory report on Kenya, Namibia, Tanzania, Zambia, and Zimbabwe.* New York.

Demange, G., and D. Gale. 1985. The strategy structure of two-sided matching markets. *Econometrica* 53 (4): 873–888.

Deolalikar, A., and W. Vijerberg. 1987. A test of heterogeneity of family and hired labor in Asian agriculture. *Oxford Bulletin of Economics and Statistics* 49: 291–305.

Desai, S., and D. Jain. 1992. *Maternal employment and changes in family dynamics: The social context of women's work in rural South India.* Research Division Working Paper 39. New York: Population Council.

————. 1994. Maternal employment and changes in family dynamics: The social context of women's work in rural South India. *Population and Development Review* 20 (1): 115–137.

DeTray, D. 1988. Government policy, household behavior, and the distribution of schooling: A case study of Malaysia. *Research in Population Economics* 6: 303–336.

Dey, J. 1980. Women and rice in The Gambia: The impact of irrigated rice development projects on the farming system. Ph.D. diss., University of Reading.

————. 1981. Gambian women: Unequal partners in rice development projects? *Journal of Development Studies* 17 (3): 109–122.

————. 1990. Gender issues in irrigation project design in Sub-Saharan Africa. Paper presented at the International Workshop on Design for Sustainable Farmer-Managed Irrigation Schemes in Sub-Saharan Africa, Wageningen Agricultural University, the Netherlands, 5–8 February.

Doan, R. M., and L. Bisharat. 1990. Female autonomy and child nutritional status: The extended family unit in Amman, Jordan. *Social Science and Medicine* 31 (7): 783–789.

Dor, A., P. Gertler, and J. van der Gaag. 1987. Nonprice rationing and choice of health care provider in rural Côte d'Ivoire. *Journal of Health Economics* 6 (2): 291–304.

Dow, W. 1995. Unconditional demand for curative health inputs: Does selection on health status matter in the long run? Rand Corporation, Santa Monica, Calif., U.S.A. Mimeo.

Drèze, J., and A. K. Sen. 1989. *Hunger and public action.* London: Oxford University Press.

Duncan, G. 1987. A simplified approach to m-estimation with application to two-stage estimators. *Journal of Econometrics* 34: 373–389.

Duraisamy, P., and R. Malathy. 1991. Impact of public programs on fertility and gender-specific investments in human capital of children in rural India: Cross-sectional and time series analyses. In *Research in population economics,* vol. 7, ed. T. P. Schultz. Greenwich, Conn., U.S.A., and London: JAI.

Dwyer, D., and J. Bruce, eds. 1988. *A home divided: Women and income in the Third World.* Stanford, Calif., U.S.A.: Stanford University Press.

Dyson, T., and M. Moore. 1983. On kinship structure, female autonomy, and demographic behavior in India. *Population and Development Review* 9 (1): 35–60.

Eggebeen, D., and D. T. Lichter. 1991. Race, family structure, and changing poverty among American children. *American Sociological Review* 56 (6): 801–817.

Ellis, F. 1988. *Peasant economics.* Cambridge: Cambridge University Press.

Elster, J. 1989. Social norms and economic theory. *The Journal of Economic Perspectives* 3 (4): 99–117.

Encarnacion, J. 1990. Consumer choice of qualities. *Economica* 57 (1): 63–72.

England, P., and G. Farkas. 1986. *Households, employment, and gender: A social, economic, and demographic view.* New York: Aldine.

England, P., and B. Kilbourne. 1990. Feminist critiques of the separative model of the self: Implications for rational choice theory. *Rationality and Society* 2 (2).

Engle, P. L. 1990. Intrahousehold allocation of resources: Perspectives from psychology. In *Intrahousehold resource allocation: Issues and methods for development policy and planning,* ed. B. L. Rogers and N. P. Schlossman. Tokyo: United Nations University Press.

———. 1991. Mother's work and child care in peri-urban Guatemala: Nutritional effects. *Child Development* 62.

———. 1993. Influences of mother's and father's income on children's nutritional status in Guatemala. *Social Science and Medicine* 37 (11): 1303–1312.

Erchak, G. 1984. Cultural anthropology and spouse abuse. *Current Anthropology* 25: 331–332.

Evans, A. 1991. Gender issues in household rural economics. *IDS Bulletin* 22: 51–59.

Evenson, R., B. Popkin, and E. King-Quizon. 1979. *Nutrition, work, and demographic behavior in rural Philippine households.* Economic Growth Center Discussion Paper 308. New Haven, Conn., U.S.A.: Yale University.

FAO (Food and Agriculture Organization of the United Nations). 1991. *Ghana: Land and water resource management study. Annex 2: The socioeconomic framework.* Rome.

———. 1995. FAOSTAT. <http://www.fao.org>.

FAO/WHO/UNU (Food and Agriculture Organization of the United Nations/World Health Organization/United Nations University). 1985. *Energy and protein requirements.* Report of the Joint Consultative Meeting of Experts from FAO/WHO/UNU. Geneva: World Health Organization.

Fapohunda, E., and M. Todaro. 1988. Family structure, implicit contracts, and the demand for children in southern Nigeria. *Population and Development Review* 14: 571–594.

Farmer, A., and J. Tiefenthaler. 1995. Fairness concepts and the intrahousehold allocation of resources. *Journal of Development Economics* 47 (2): 179–189.

Feldstein, H. S., and S. V. Poats. 1990. *Working together. Gender analysis in agriculture.* West Hartford, Conn., U.S.A.: Kumarian.

Ferguson, J. 1988. Cultural exchange: New developments in the anthropology of commodities. *Cultural Anthropology* 3 (4): 488–513.

———. 1992. The cultural topography of wealth: Commodity paths and the structure of property in rural Lesotho. *American Anthropologist* 94: 55–73.

Filmer, D. 1995. The intrahousehold allocation of health and cognitive skills in developing countries. Ph.D. diss., Department of Economics, Brown University, Providence, R.I., U.S.A.

Fogel, R. 1989. *Without consent or contract: The rise and fall of American slavery.* New York: W. W. Norton.

Fogel, R., and S. Engerman. 1974. *Time on the cross: The economics of American Negro slavery.* Boston: Little, Brown.

Folbre, N. 1984. Market opportunities, genetic endowments, and intrafamily resource distribution: Comment. *American Economic Review* 74 (3): 518–520.

———. 1986. Hearts and spades: Paradigms of household economics. *World Development* 14 (2): 245–255.

———. 1990. Women on their own: Global patterns of female headship. In *Women and international development annual,* vol. 2, ed. R. S. Gallin and A. Ferguson. Boulder, Colo., U.S.A.: Westview.

———. 1993. Women and social security in Latin America, the Caribbean, and Sub-Saharan Africa. Report to the International Labour Office. Department of Economics, University of Massachusetts, Amherst, Mass., U.S.A. Mimeo.

———. 1994. *Who pays for the kids? Gender and the structures of constraint.* New York and London: Routledge.

Folbre, N., and T. Weisskopf. 1996. Did father know best? Markets, families, and the supply of caring labor. Department of Economics, University of Massachusetts, Amherst, Mass., U.S.A. Mimeo.

Fortin, B., and G. Lacroix. 1993. *Test of noncooperative and cooperative models of labor supply.* Working Paper. Quebec, Canada: Université Laval.

Fortmann, L. 1983. Who plows? The effect of economic status on women's participation in agriculture in Botswana. Mimeo.

Fortmann, L., and D. Rocheleau. 1989. Why agroforestry needs women: Four myths and a case study. In *Women's role in forest resource management: A reader.* Bangkok, Thailand: Food and Agriculture Organization of the United Nations, Regional Wood Energy Development Program in Asia.

Fried, E. S., and S. Settergren. 1986. The effects of children on wives' and husbands' allocation of time. Paper presented at the Annual Meeting of the Population Association of America, San Francisco.

Friedman, J. W. 1986. *Game theory with applications to economics.* New York: Oxford University Press.

Friedmann, H. 1980. Household production and the national economy: Concepts for the analysis of agrarian formations. *Journal of Peasant Studies* 7 (2): 158–184.

Fuchs, V. 1988. *Women's quest for economic equality.* Cambridge, Mass., U.S.A.: Harvard University Press.

Funk, U. 1988. Land tenure, agriculture, and gender in Guinea-Bissau. In *Agriculture, women, and land: The African experience,* ed. J. Davison. Boulder, Colo., U.S.A., and London: Westview.

Furstenberg, F. F., and A. J. Cherlin. 1991. *Divided families: What happens to children when parents part.* Cambridge, Mass., U.S.A.: Harvard University Press.

Garcia, M. 1990. Resource allocation and household welfare: A study of personal sources of income on food consumption, nutrition and health in the Philippines. Ph.D. diss., Institute of Social Studies, The Hague, the Netherlands.

Garcia, M., and P. Pinstrup-Andersen. 1987. *The pilot food subsidy scheme in the Philippines: Its impact on income, food consumption, and nutritional status.* Research Report 61. Washington, D.C.: International Food Policy Research Institute.

Garfinkel, I., and S. S. McLanahan. 1986. *Single mothers and their children: A new American dilemma.* Washington, D.C.: Urban Institute Press.

Garg, A., and J. Morduch. 1997. Sibling rivalry, resource constraints, and the health of children. *Journal of Population Economics.* Forthcoming.

Garrett, P., and P. Espinosa. 1988. Phases of farming systems research: The relevance of gender in Ecuadorian sites. In *Gender issues in farming systems research and extension,* ed. S. Poats, M. Schmink, and A. Spring. Boulder, Colo., U.S.A.: Westview.

Gertler, P., and P. Glewwe. 1992. The willingness to pay for education for daughters in contrast to sons: Evidence from rural Peru. *World Bank Economic Review* 6 (1): 171–188.

Gertler, P., L. Locay, and W. Sanderson. 1987. Are user fees regressive? The welfare implications of health care financing proposals in Peru. *Journal of Econometrics* 36: 67–80.

Ghai, Y., R. Luckham, and F. Snyder. 1987. *The political economy of law: A Third World reader.* Delhi: Oxford University Press.

Gilgun, J. F., K. Daly, and G. Handell, eds. 1992. *Qualitative methods in family research.* Newbury Park, Calif., U.S.A.: Sage.

Gillespie, S., and G. McNeill. 1992. *Food, health, and survival in India and developing countries.* Delhi: Oxford University Press.

Gittelsohn, J. 1989. Intrahousehold food allocation in rural Nepal. Ph.D. diss., University of Connecticut. Ann Arbor, Mich., U.S.A.: University Microfilms, Inc.

―――. 1991. Opening the box: Intrahousehold food allocation in rural Nepal. *Social Science and Medicine* 33 (10): 1141–1154.

―――. 1996. Qualitative research in field trials. In *Field trials of health interventions in developing countries: A toolbox,* 2d ed., ed. P. G. Smith and R. H. Morrow. London: Macmillan.

Gladwin, C. 1989. *Ethnographic decision tree modelling.* Qualitative Research Methods Series No. 19. Newbury Park, Calif., U.S.A.: Sage.

Gladwin, C., and D. McMillan. 1989. Is a turnaround in Africa possible without helping African women to farm? *Economic Development and Cultural Change* 37 (2): 345–369.

Glendon, M. A. 1989. *The transformation of family law: State, law, and family in the United States and Western Europe.* Chicago: University of Chicago Press.

Goetz, A. M., and R. Sen Gupta. 1994. Who takes the credit? Gender, power, and control over loan use in rural credit programs in Bangladesh. Institute of Development Studies, University of Sussex, Falmer, U.K. Mimeo.

Goldberger, A. S. 1969. Directly additive utility and constant marginal budget shares. *Review of Economic Studies* 36 (April): 251–254.

Goldin, C. 1990. *Understanding the gender gap: An economic history of American women.* Oxford: Oxford University Press.

Goodenough, W. 1956. Componential analysis and the study of meaning. *Language* 32: 195–216.

Goody, J. 1982. *Cooking, cuisine, and class: A study of comparative sociology.* Cambridge: Cambridge University Press.

Graham, M. A., and A. Larme. 1992. Food allocation and child health in rural Peru. Paper presented at American Anthropological Association meeting, San Francisco, 2–6 December.

Green, J. K. 1987. *Evaluating the impact of consolidation of holdings, individualization of tenure, and registration of title: Lessons from Kenya.* LTC Paper 129. Madison, Wis., U.S.A.: University of Wisconsin.

Gross, D. A., and B. A. Underwood. 1971. Technological changes and caloric costs: Sisal agriculture in northeastern Brazil. *American Anthropologist* 73 (3): 725–740.

Grossman, G. M., and E. Helpman. 1994. Protection for sale. *American Economic Review* 84 (4): 833–850.

Guyer, J. 1980. *Household budgets and women's incomes.* African Studies Center Working Paper 28. Boston: Boston University.

———. 1981. Household and community in African studies. *African Studies Review* 24 (2/3): 87–137.

———. 1986. Intrahousehold processes and farming systems research: Perspectives from anthropology. In *Understanding Africa's rural households and farming systems,* ed. J. L. Moock. Boulder, Colo., U.S.A., and London: Westview.

———. 1993. Wealth in people and self-realization in equatorial Africa. Boston University, Department of Anthropology, Boston. Mimeo.

Guyer, J. I., and P. Peters. 1987. Introduction. Special issue on Conceptualizing the household: Issues of theory and policy in Africa. *Development and Change* 18 (2): 197–213.

Haaga, J. G., and J. B. Mason. 1987. Food distribution within the family: Evidence and implications for research and programs. *Food Policy* 12 (2): 146–161.

Haddad, L. 1990. Gender and poverty in Ghana. Development Economic Research Centre, University of Warwick. Mimeo.

Haddad, L., and J. Hoddinott. 1994a. Household resource allocation in the Côte d'Ivoire: Inferences from expenditure data. In *Poverty and rural development,* ed. T. A. Lloyd and W. O. Morrissey. London: Macmillan.

———. 1994b. Women's income and boy-girl anthropometric status in the Côte d'Ivoire. *World Development* 22 (4): 543–553.

Haddad, L., and R. Kanbur. 1990. How serious is the neglect of intrahousehold inequality? *Economic Journal* 100 (402): 866–881.

———. 1992. Intrahousehold inequality and the theory of targeting. *European Economic Review* 36 (2): 372–378.

———. 1993. The value of intrahousehold survey data for age-based nutritional targeting. *Annales d'Economie et de Statistique* 29: 65–81.

Haddad, L., and T. Reardon. 1993. Gender bias in the allocation of resources within households in Burkina Faso. A disaggregated outlay equivalent analysis. *Journal of Development Studies* 29: 260–276.

Haddad, L., J. Hoddinott, and H. Alderman. 1994. *Intrahousehold resource allocation: An overview.* World Bank Policy Research Working Paper 1255. Washington, D.C.: World Bank.

Haddad, L. J., R. Kanbur, and H. E. Bouis. 1992a. Do better-off households exhibit lower intrahousehold inequality? Energy intake and energy expenditure data from the Philippines. Paper presented at the Institut National de la Recherche Agronomique Conference on Household Economy and Modelling the Family Farm in Agriculture, Montpellier, France, 4–6 December, 1991.

———. 1992b. Intrahousehold inequality and average household well-being: Evidence on calorie intakes and energy expenditures from the Philippines. International Food Policy Research Institute, Washington, D.C. Mimeo.

Haddad, L. J., C. Peña, A. Quisumbing, and A. Slack. 1995. Poverty and nutrition within households: Review and new evidence. Report to the World Health Organization. International Food Policy Research Institute, Washington, D.C.

Hampel, F. 1974. The influence curve and its role in robust estimation. *Journal of the American Statistical Association* 69: 383–393.

Handa, S. 1995. The determinants of female headship in Jamaica: Results from a structural model. Department of Economics, University of the West Indies-Mona, Kingston, Jamaica. Mimeo.

Hanger, J., and J. Moris. 1973. Women and the household economy. In *Mwea: An irrigated rice settlement in Kenya,* ed. R. Chambers and J. Moris. Munich: Weltforum Verlag.

Harriss, B. 1989a. *Differential female mortality and health behavior in India.* Luca d'Agliano–Queen Elizabeth House Development Studies Working Paper 13. Oxford: Oxford University Press.

———. 1989b. Differential female mortality and health care in South Asia. *Journal of Social Studies* 44: 1–123.

———. 1990. The intrafamily distribution of hunger in South Asia. In *The political economy of hunger,* vol. 1, *Entitlement and well-being,* ed. J. Drèze and A. Sen. Oxford: Clarendon.

———. 1991. *Poverty and child nutrition in South India.* New Delhi: Concept.

Harsanyi, J., and R. Selten. 1988. *A general theory of equilibrium selection in games.* Cambridge, Mass., U.S.A.: MIT Press.

Hart, G. 1995. Gender and household dynamics: Recent theories and their implications. In *Critical issues in Asian development: Theories, experiences, and policies,* ed. M. G. Quibria. Oxford: Oxford University Press.

Hart, K. 1982. On commoditization. In *From craft to industry: The ethnography of proto-industrial cloth production,* ed. E. Goody. Cambridge: Cambridge University Press.

Hart, O., and B. Holmström. 1987. The theory of contracts. In *Advances in economic theory,* ed. T. Bewley. Cambridge: Cambridge University Press.

Hartmann, B. 1987. *Reproductive rights and wrongs: The global politics of population control and reproductive choice.* New York: Harper and Row.

Hartmann, H. I. 1981. The family as the locus of gender, class, and political struggle: The example of housework. *Signs* 6 (3): 366–394.

Haugerud, A. 1982. The limits of household analysis in the study of agricultural production: A central Kenyan case. Paper presented at the 81st annual meeting of the American Anthropological Association, Washington, D.C.

Heise, L. 1992. Violence against women: The missing agenda. In *Women's health: A global perspective,* ed. M. Koblinsky, J. Timyan, and J. Gray. Boulder, Colo., U.S.A.: Westview.

Heise, L. L., with J. Pitanguy and A. Germain. 1994. *Violence against women: The hidden health burden.* World Bank Discussion Paper 255. Washington, D.C.: World Bank.

Henn, J. K. 1988. The material basis of sexism: A mode of production analysis. In *Patriarchy and class: African women in the home and the workplace,* ed. S. Stichter and J. Parpart. South Hadley, Mass., U.S.A.: Bergin and Garvey.

Hill, P. 1972. *Rural Hausa. A village and a setting.* Cambridge: Cambridge University Press.

Hirshleifer, J. 1977. Shakespeare vs. Becker on altruism: The importance of having the last word. *Journal of Economic Literature* 15 (2): 500–502.

Hochschild, A. 1990. *The second shift.* New York: Avon.

Hoddinott, J. 1992a. Rotten kids or manipulative parents: Are children old age security in western Kenya? *Economic Development and Cultural Change* 40 (3): 545–565.

———. 1992b. Modelling remittance flows in Kenya. *Journal of African Economies* 1 (2): 206–232.

———. 1993. A model of migration and remittances applied to western Kenya. Trinity College, Oxford University, Oxford. Mimeo.

———. 1996. Testing cooperative bargaining models of household behavior: Divorce law reform and female suicide in Canada. Oxford University, Oxford. Mimeo.

Hoddinott, J., and L. Haddad. 1991. Household expenditures, child anthropometric status, and the intrahousehold division of income: Evidence from the Côte d'Ivoire. Research Program in Development Studies Discussion Paper 155. Princeton, N.J., U.S.A.: Woodrow Wilson School of Public and International Affairs, Princeton University.

———. 1995. Does female income share influence household expenditures? Evidence from the Côte d'Ivoire. *Oxford Bulletin of Economics and Statistics* 57 (1): 77–96.

Horney, M. J., and M. McElroy. 1988. The household allocation problem: Empirical results from a bargaining model. In *Research in population economics,* vol. 6, ed. T. P. Schultz. Greenwich, Conn., U.S.A., and London: JAI.

Horton, S. 1986. Child nutrition and family size in the Philippines. *Journal of Development Economics* 23 (1): 161–176.

Horton, S., and B. Miller. 1987. The effect of gender of household head on food expenditure: Evidence from low-income households in Jamaica. University of Toronto, Toronto, Ontario, Canada. Mimeo.

———. 1989. The effect of gender of household head on food expenditures: Evidence from low-income households in Jamaica. Paper presented at the Conference on Family, Gender Differences, and Development, Yale University, New Haven, Conn.

Hubback, E. 1949. The family allowances movement, 1924–1927. In *Family allowances,* a new edition of *The disinherited family,* ed. E. Rathbone, 278–288. London: Allen and Unwin.

Humphrey, C., and S. Hugh-Jones. 1992. *Barter, exchange, and value: An anthropological approach.* Cambridge: Cambridge University Press.

ICRW (International Center for Research on Women) Task Force. 1989. *Strengthening women: Health research priorities for women in developing countries.* Washington, D.C.

ICRW (International Center for Research on Women). 1990. *Effects of improved height monitoring feedback during pregnancy in a Khmer refugee camp in Thailand.* Maternal Nutrition Health Care Program Report 16. Washington, D.C.

Jackson, C. 1985. *The Kano River irrigation project: Women's roles and gender differences in development.* West Hartford, Conn., U.S.A.: Kumarian.

Jackson, J. 1982. Stresses affecting women and their families. In *Women and the family,* ed. J. Massiah. Cave Hill, Barbados: Institute for Social and Economic Research, University of the West Indies.

Jacoby, H. 1995. The economics of polygyny in Sub-Saharan Africa: Female productivity and the demand for wives in Côte d'Ivoire. *Journal of Political Economy* 103 (5): 938–971.

Jaeckel, L. A. 1972. Estimating regression coefficients by minimizing the dispersion of residuals. *Annals of Mathematical Statistics* 42: 1020–1034.

Jick, T. D. 1979. Mixing qualitative and quantitative methods: Triangulation in action. *Administrative Science Quarterly* 24: 602–611.

Johnson, A. 1990. Time allocation research: The costs and benefits of alternative methods. In *Intrahousehold resource allocation,* ed. B. Rogers and N. Schlossman. Tokyo: United Nations University Press.

Jones, C. 1983. The mobilization of women's labor for cash crop production: A game theoretic approach. *American Journal of Agricultural Economics* 65 (5): 1049–1054.

————. 1985. The mobilization of women's labor for cash crop production: A game theoretic approach. In *Women in rice farming.* Aldershot, U.K., and Brookfield, Vt., U.S.A.: Gower Publishing Company for the International Rice Research Institute.

————. 1986. Intrahousehold bargaining in response to the introduction of new crops: A case study from North Cameroon. In *Understanding Africa's rural households and farming systems,* ed. J. L. Moock. Boulder, Colo., U.S.A., and London: Westview.

Junankar, P. 1989. The response of peasant farmers to price incentives: The use and misuse of profit functions. *Journal of Development Studies* 25: 169–182.

Kabeer, N. 1991. *Alternative approaches to the household economy?* Institute of Development Studies Discussion Paper 288. Brighton, U.K.: University of Sussex.

————. 1992. Beyond the threshold: The policy relevance of intrahousehold research. Paper presented at the IFPRI/World Bank Conference on Intrahousehold Resource Allocation: Policy Issues and Research Methods, 12–14 February, Washington, D.C.

————. 1994. *Reversed realities. Gender hierarchies in development thought.* London: Verso.

————. 1995. *Necessary, sufficient, or irrelevant: Women, wages, and intrahousehold power relations in urban Bangladesh.* Working Paper 25. Brighton, U.K.: Institute of Development Studies, University of Sussex.

Kaiser, L. L., and K. G. Dewey. 1991. Migration, cash cropping, and subsistence agriculture: Relationships to household food expenditures in rural Mexico. *Social Science and Medicine* 33 (10): 1113–1126.

Kamerman, S. B., and A. J. Kahn. 1989. Single-parent, female-headed families in western Europe: Social change and response. *International Social Security Review* 1/89: 3–35.

Kanbur, R. 1991. *Linear expenditure systems, children as public goods, and intrahousehold inequality.* Discussion Paper 104. Coventry, U.K.: Development Economics Research Centre, University of Warwick.

Kanbur, R., and L. Haddad. 1994. Are better off households more unequal or less unequal? *Oxford Economic Papers* 46 (3): 445–458.

Kapteyn, A., and P. Kooreman. 1992. Household labor supply: What kind of data can tell us how many decisionmakers there are? *European Economic Review* 36: 379–390.

Katona-Apte, J. 1983. The significance of intrahousehold food distribution patterns in food programs. *Food and Nutrition Bulletin* 5 (4): 35–42.

Katz, E. G. 1992. Intrahousehold resource allocation in the Guatemalan Central Highlands: The impact of nontraditional agricultural exports. Ph.D. diss., University of Wisconsin–Madison, Madison, Wis., U.S.A.

———. 1994. The impact of nontraditional agriculture on income and food availability in Guatemala: An intrahousehold perspective. *Food and Nutrition Bulletin* 15 (4): 295–302.

———. 1995. Gender and trade within the household: Observations from rural Guatemala. *World Development* 23 (2): 327–342.

Kennedy, E., and H. Alderman. 1987. Comparative analyses of nutritional effectiveness of food subsidies and other food-related interventions. International Food Policy Research Institute and WHO-UNICEF, Washington, D.C.

Kennedy, E., and B. Cogill. 1987. *Income and nutritional effects of the commercialization of agriculture in southwestern Kenya.* Research Report 63. Washington, D.C.: International Food Policy Research Institute.

Kennedy, E., and P. Peters. 1992. Household food security and child nutrition: The interaction of income and gender of household head. *World Development* 20 (8): 1077–1085.

Kenya, Government of. 1982. *Statistical Abstract of Kenya.* Nairobi: Central Statistical Office.

Killingsworth, M. 1983. *Labour supply.* Cambridge: Cambridge University Press.

King, E. M., and M. A. Hill, eds. 1993. *Women's education in developing countries: Barriers, benefits, and policies.* Baltimore and London: Johns Hopkins University Press for the World Bank.

Kniesner, T. J. 1976. An indirect test of complementarity in a family labor supply model. *Econometrica* 44: 651–659.

Koenig, D. 1982. Women's work and social stratification in the rural Malian household. Paper presented at the 81st annual meeting of the American Anthropological Association, Washington, D.C.

Kooreman, P. 1994. Estimation of econometric models of some discrete games. *Journal of Applied Econometrics* 9 (3): 255–268.

Kooreman, P., and A. Kapteyn. 1990. On the empirical implementation of some game theoretic models of household labor supply. *Journal of Human Resources* 25 (4): 584–598.

Kotlikoff, L., and J. Morris. 1991. Why don't the elderly live with their children? A new look. In *Issues in the economics of aging,* ed. D. Wise. Chicago: University of Chicago Press.

Koussoudji, S., and E. Mueller. 1983. The economic and demographic status of female-headed households in rural Botswana. *Economic Development and Cultural Change* 31 (July): 831–859.

Krotki, K. 1986. Reported masculinity ratio in Pakistan: A triumph of anthropology and economics over biology. *Pakistan Development Review* 24 (4): 267–297.

Krueger, A. O. 1974. The political economy of the rent-seeking society. *American Economic Review* 64 (3): 291–303.

Kuhn, T. 1970. *The structure of scientific revolutions.* Chicago: University of Chicago Press.

———. 1974. The structure of scientific revolutions. In *International Encyclopedia of Unified Science.* Chicago: University of Chicago Press.

Kumar, S. 1979. *Impact of subsidized rice on food consumption and nutrition in Kerala.* Research Report 5. Washington, D.C.: International Food Policy Research Institute.

———. 1983. A framework for tracing policy effects on intrahousehold food distribution. *Food and Nutrition Bulletin* 5 (4): 13–15.

Kynch, J., and A. Sen. 1983. Indian women: Well-being and survival. *Cambridge Journal of Economics* 7 (3/4): 363–380.

Lam, D. 1988. Marriage markets and assortative mating with household public goods: Theoretical results and empirical implications. *Journal of Human Resources* 23 (Fall): 462–487.

Leach, M. 1991. Locating gendered experience: An anthropologist's view from a Sierra-Leonean village. *IDS Bulletin* 22 (1): 44–50.

Lee, L.-F., and M. Pitt. 1986. Microeconometric demand systems with binding non-negativity constraints: The dual approach. *Econometrica* 54 (5): 1237–1242.

Lele, U. 1986. Women and structural transformation. *Economic Development and Cultural Change* 34 (2): 195–221.

Leonard, W. 1991. Household-level strategies for protecting children from seasonal food scarcity. *Social Science and Medicine* 33 (10): 1127–1134.

Leslie, J. 1988. Women's work and child nutrition in the Third World. *World Development* 16 (11): 1341–1362.

Leuthold, J. 1968. An empirical study of formula resource transfers and the work decision of the poor. *Journal of Human Resources* 3: 312–323.

Levin, C., K. Ralston, and L. Haddad. 1993. Intrahousehold-related policy research: Implications for data collection. In *Data needs for food policy in developing countries,* ed. J. von Braun and D. Puetz. Washington, D.C.: International Food Policy Research Institute.

Levinson, D. 1989. *Family violence in cross-cultural perspective.* London: Sage.

Levi-Strauss, C. 1949. *Les Structures Élémentaires de la Parente.* Paris: Mouton.

———. 1969. *The raw and the cooked.* New York: Harper and Row.

Lewis, O. 1959. *Five families: Mexican case studies in the culture of poverty.* New York: Basic Books.

Lim, L. L. 1990. The status of women and international migration. United Nations Expert Group Meeting on International Migration Policies and the Status of Female Migrants, 27–30 March 1990, San Miniato, Italy.

Lipton, M. 1983. *Poverty, undernutrition, and hunger.* World Bank Staff Working Paper 597. Washington, D.C.: World Bank.

Lloyd, C. B. 1993. *Family and gender issues for population policy.* Research Division Working Paper Series 48. New York: Population Council.

———. 1995. *Household structure and poverty: What Are the Connections?* Research Division Working Paper Series 74. New York: Population Council.

Lloyd, C. B., and A. K. Blanc. 1996. Children's schooling in Sub-Saharan Africa: The role of fathers, mothers, and others. *Population Development Review* 22 (2): 265–298.

Lloyd, C. B., and S. Desai. 1992. Children's living arrangements in developing countries. *Population Research and Policy Review* 11 (3): 193–216.

Lloyd, C. B., and A. J. Gage. 1995. High fertility and the intergenerational transmission of gender inequality: Children's transition to adulthood in Ghana. In Women and Demographic Change in Sub-Saharan Africa, ed. A.-M. Jensen and P. Makinwa-Adebusoye. Liège, Belgium: Ordina.

Lloyd, C. B., and A. J. Gage-Brandon. 1993a. Does sibsize matter? Implications of family size for children's educational opportunities and work responsibilities in Ghana. In *Fertility, family size, and structure: Consequences for families and children,* ed. C. B. Lloyd. New York: Population Council.

———. 1993b. Women's role in maintaining households: Family welfare and sexual inequality in Ghana. *Population Studies* 47 (1): 115–131.

Lopez, R. 1986. Structural models of the farm household that allow for interdependent utility and profit maximizing decisions. In *Agricultural household models: Extensions, applications, and policy,* ed. I. Singh, L. Squire, and J. Strauss. Baltimore: Johns Hopkins University Press.

Louat, F., M. Grosh, and J. van der Gaag. 1992. Is participation in rural public works gender-differentiated? The case of India's Employment Guarantee Scheme. Paper presented at the IFPRI/World Bank Conference on Intrahousehold Resource Allocation: Policy Issues and Research Methods, 12–14 February, Washington, D.C.

———. 1993. *Welfare implications of female headship in Jamaican households.* Living Standards Measurement Study 96. Washington, D.C.: World Bank.

Lucas, R., and O. Stark. 1985. Motivations to remit: Evidence from Botswana. *Journal of Political Economy* 93 (5): 901–918.

Luce, R., and H. Raiffa. 1957. *Games and decisions: Introduction and critical survey.* New York: John Wiley and Sons.

Lundberg, S. 1988. Labor supply of husbands and wives: A simultaneous equations approach. *Review of Economics and Statistics* 70 (2): 224–235.

Lundberg, S., and R. A. Pollak. 1993. Separate spheres bargaining and the marriage market. *Journal of Political Economy* 101 (6): 988–1010.

Lundberg, S. J., R. A. Pollak, and T. J. Wales. 1995. Do husbands and wives pool their resources? Evidence from the U.K. child benefit. Department of Economics, University of Washington, Seattle, Wash. Mimeo.

Macpherson, S., and J. Midgley. 1987. *Comparative social policy and the Third World.* New York: St. Martin's.

Mahajan, A. 1990. Instigators of wife battering. In *Violence against women,* ed. S. Sood. Jaipur, India: Arihant.

Mahieu, R. 1989. Principes Economiques et Société Africaine. *Revue Tiers Mondes* 30: 725–753.

Malinowski, B. 1922. *Argonauts of the Western Pacific.* London: Routledge.

Manser, M., and M. Brown. 1980. Marriage and household decisionmaking: A bargaining analysis. *International Economic Review* 21 (1): 31–44.

Martin, P., and P. Bateson. 1986. *Measuring behavior: An introductory guide.* Cambridge: Cambridge University Press.

Mason, B. J. 1985. Jamaican working-class women: Producers and reproducers. *Review of Black Political Economy* 14 (2/3): 259–275.

Mauss, M. 1925. *The gift: Forms and functions of exchange in archaic societies.* New York: Norton (1969 Translation).

McElroy, M. B. 1981. Appendix: Empirical results from estimates of joint labor supply functions of husbands and wives. In *Research in labor economics,* vol. 14, ed. R. G. Ehrenberg. Greenwich, Conn., U.S.A.: JAI.

———. 1985. The joint determination of household membership and market work: The case of young men. *Journal of Labour Economics* 3: 293–316.

———. 1990. The empirical content of Nash-bargained household behavior. *Journal of Human Resources* 25 (4): 559–583.

McElroy, M. B., and M. J. Horney. 1981. Nash-bargained household decisions: Toward a generalization of the theory of demand. *International Economic Review* 22 (2): 333–349.

———. 1990. Nash-bargained household decisions: Reply. *International Economic Review* 31 (1): 237–242.

McFadden, D. 1981. Econometric models of probabilistic choice. In *Structure analysis of discrete data with econometric applications,* ed. C. F. Manski and D. McFadden. Cambridge, Mass., U.S.A.: MIT Press.

McGreevey, W. 1990. *Social security in Latin America: Issues and options for the World Bank.* World Bank Discussion Paper 110. Washington, D.C.: World Bank.

McMillan, D. E. 1987. Monitoring the evolution of household economic systems over time in farming systems research. *Development and Change* 18 (2): 295–314.

Messer, E. 1983. The household focus in nutritional anthropology: An overview. *Ecology of Food and Nutrition* 5 (4): 2–12.

———. 1990. Intrahousehold allocation of resources: Perspectives from anthropology. In *Intrahousehold resource allocation: Issues and methods for development policy and planning,* ed. B. L. Rogers and N. P. Schlossman. Tokyo: United Nations University Press.

Midgley, J. 1984. *Social security, inequality, and the Third World.* New York: John Wiley and Sons.

Migot-Adholla, S., P. Hazell, B. Blarel, and F. Place. 1991. Indigenous land rights systems in Sub-Saharan Africa: A constraint on productivity? *World Bank Economic Review* 5 (1): 155–175.

Moltedo, C. 1989. *Estudio sobre violencia domestica en mujeres pobladoras chilenas.* Santiago, Chile: CUSO.

Molyneux, M. 1986. Mobilization without emancipation? Women's interests, state, and revolution. In *Transition and development: Problems of Third World socialism,* ed. R. R. Fagen, C. D. Deere, and J. L. Coraggio. New York: Monthly Review Press.

Moock, P. 1973. Managerial ability in small-farm production: An analysis of maize yields in the Vihiga Division of Kenya. Ph.D. diss., Columbia University, New York.

————. 1976. The efficiency of women as farm managers: Kenya. *American Journal of Agricultural Economics* 58 (5): 831–835.

Morgan, R. 1984. *Sisterhood is global.* New York: Anchor.

Morse, J., ed. 1992. *Qualitative health research.* Newbury Park, Calif., U.S.A.: Sage.

Mortensen, D. T. 1982a. The matching process as a noncooperative bargaining game. In *The economics of information and uncertainty,* ed. J. J. Mccall. Chicago: University of Chicago Press for National Bureau of Economic Research.

————. 1982b. Property rights and efficiency in mating, racing, and related games. *American Economic Review* 72 (December): 968–979.

————. 1988. Matching: Finding a partner for life or otherwise. *American Journal of Sociology* 94 (Supplement): S215-S240.

Moser, C. 1993. *Gender planning and development: Theory, practice, and training.* New York: Routledge.

Mulder, M. B., and T. M. Caro. 1985. The use of quantitative observational techniques in anthropology. *Current Anthropology* 26 (3): 323–335.

Murthi, M., A.-C. Guio, and J. Drèze. 1995. *Morality, fertility, and gender bias in India.* Development Economics Programme Discussion Paper 61. London: London School of Economics.

Nash, J. 1950. The bargaining problem. *Econometrica* 18 (April): 155–162.

————. 1953. Two-person bargaining games. *Econometrica* 21: 128–140.

National Center for Health Statistics. 1976. *Growth charts.* Washington, D.C.: U.S. Department of Health and Human Services, Public Health Service, Health Resources Administration.

Netting, R. 1984. Introduction. In *Households: Comparative and historical studies of the domestic group,* ed. R. M. Netting, R. R. Wilk, and E. J. Arnould. Berkeley, Calif., U.S.A.: University of California Press.

Neuhouser, K. 1989. Sources of women's power and status among the urban poor in contemporary Brazil. *Signs* 14 (3): 685–702.

Newman, J., S. Jorgensen, and M. Pradhan. 1991. How did workers benefit from Bolivia's Emergency Social Fund? *World Bank Economic Review* 5 (2): 367–393.

Odingo, R. S. 1989. The dynamics of land tenure and agrarian systems in Kenya. A study of the Nakuru, Kericho, and Machakos areas of the Kenyan Highlands. In *The dynamics of land tenure and agrarian systems in Africa.* Rome: Food and Agriculture Organization of the United Nations.

Ojofeitimi, E. O., and M. O. Adelekan. 1984. Partnership with fathers in combatting malnutrition: Their views as to causes and treatment of protein-energy malnutrition. *Child Care, Health Development* 10: 61–66.

Olsen, W. 1990. Long-term fieldwork in South India: Five mistakes I'm glad I made. Paper presented at the workshop on Locality-Based Fieldwork in Developing Countries, Queen Elizabeth House, Oxford.

Olson, M. 1975. *The logic of collective action: Public goods and the theory of groups.* Cambridge, Mass.: Harvard University Press.

————. 1982. *The rise and decline of nations. Economic growth, stagflation, and social rigidities.* New Haven, Conn.: Yale University Press.

Ongaro, W. 1988. Adoption of new farming technology: A case study of maize production in western Kenya. Unpublished Ph.D. diss., University of Gothenburg, Sweden.

Oppen, M. von, P. P. Rao, and K. V. S. Rao. 1985. The impact of market access on agricultural productivity in India. In *Agricultural markets in the semi-arid tropics.* Hyderabad: International Crops Research Institute for the Semi-Arid Tropics.

Orphanides, A., and D. Zervos. 1995. Rational addiction with learning and regret. *Journal of Political Economy* 103 (4): 739–758.

Osmani, S. R. 1990. Nutrition and the economics of food: Implications of some recent controversies. In *The Political Economy of Hunger,* vol. 1, ed. J. Drèze and A. Sen. New York: Oxford University Press.

Pacey, A., and P. Payne. 1984. *Nutrition and agricultural development.* London: Hutchinson.

Pagan, A. 1984. Econometric issues in the analysis of regression with generated regressors. *International Economic Review* 25 (February): 241–247.

Pahl, J. 1983. The allocation of money and the structuring of inequality within marriage. *Sociological Review* 31 (May): 237–262.

Pakistan, Ministry of Planning and Development, Technical Assistance Project Cell. 1987. Health sector in Pakistan: A financing and expenditure study. Report of a study by Institute of Health Economics and Technology Assessment and United Computers, Islamabad.

Palmer, I. 1991. *Gender and population in the adjustment of African economies: Planning for change.* Women, Work, and Development Working Paper 19. Geneva: International Labour Organization.

Pankhurst, D., and S. Jacobs. 1988. Land tenure, gender relations, and agricultural production: The case of Zimbabwe's peasantry. In *Agriculture, women, and land: The African experience,* ed. J. Davison. Boulder, Colo., U.S.A., and London: Westview.

Paolisso, M., and S. Regmi. 1992. Economic anthropology and the study of intra-household resource allocation: Some methodological examples from Nepal. Paper presented at the IFPRI/World Bank Conference on Intrahousehold Resource Allocation: Policy Issues and Research Methods, 12–14 February, Washington, D.C.

Papademetriou, D., and P. L. Martin, eds. 1991. *The unsettled relationship: Labor migration and economic development.* New York: Greenwood.

Parsons, D. 1983. On the economics of intergenerational control. *Population and Development Review* 10: 41–53.

Paterson, R. 1985. Modelling the division of labor and assets within peasant households. M.Sc. extended essay, Oxford University.

Payne, P. R. 1994. Not enough food: Malnutrition and famine. In *Food,* ed. B. Harriss and R. Hoffenberg. Oxford: Blackwell.

Payne, P., and M. Lipton. 1994. *How Third World rural households adapt to dietary energy stress: The evidence and the issues.* Food Policy Review 2. Washington, D.C.: International Food Policy Research Institute.

Pelletier, D., L. Msukwa, and U. Ramakrishnan. 1991. Nutrition in project planning: Intrahousehold risks and determinants. *Food Policy* 16 (2): 127–139.

Pelto, P. J., and G. H. Pelto. 1978. *Anthropological research: The structure of inquiry,* 2d ed. New York: Cambridge University Press.

Peña, C. 1996. Intrahousehold food distribution in Bukidnon, a southern Philippine province. Ph.D. diss., Boston University, Boston.

Peshkin, A. 1988. Understanding complexity: A gift of qualitative inquiry. *Anthropology and Education Quarterly* 19: 415–424.

Peters, H. E. 1986. Marriage and divorce: Informational constraints and private contracting. *American Economic Review* 76 (3): 437–454.

Peters, P. E. 1986. Household management in Botswana: Cattle, crops, and wage labor. In *Understanding Africa's rural households and farming systems,* ed. J. L. Moock. Boulder, Colo., U.S.A., and London: Westview.

Pike, K. 1956. Towards a theory of the structure of human behavior. In *Estudios Antrologicos en Homenaje al Doctor Manuel Gamio.* Mexico City: Direccion General de Publicaciones, Universidad Nacional Autonoma de Mexico.

Pinstrup-Andersen, P., ed. 1988. *Food subsidies in developing countries: Costs, benefits, and policy options.* Baltimore: Johns Hopkins University Press.

Pitt, M. M. 1996. The impact of group-based credit for the poor on the intrahousehold distribution of nutritional outcomes in Bangladesh. Department of Economics, Brown University, Providence, R.I., U.S.A. Typescript.

Pitt, M., and S. Khandker. 1994. Household and intrahousehold impacts of the Grameen Bank and similar targeted credit programs in Bangladesh. World Bank, Washington, D.C. Mimeo.

———. 1995. The impact of group-based credit programs on poor households in Bangladesh: Does the gender of participants matter? Department of Economics, Brown University, Providence, R.I., U.S.A. Mimeo.

Pitt, M., and V. Lavy. 1992. The intrahousehold allocation of medical care in Ghana. Paper presented at the IFPRI/World Bank Conference on Intrahousehold Resource Allocation: Policy Issues and Research Methods, 12–14 February, Washington, D.C.

———. 1995. The intrahousehold allocation of medical care in low-income countries. Brown University, Providence, R.I., U.S.A. Mimeo.

Pitt, M., and M. Rosenzweig. 1985. Health and nutrient consumption across and within farm households. *Review of Economics and Statistics* 67 (May): 212–222.

———. 1986. Agricultural prices, food consumption, and the health and productivity of Indonesian farmers. In *Agricultural household models,* ed. I. Singh, L. Squire, and J. Strauss. Baltimore: Johns Hopkins University Press.

———. 1990. Estimating the intrahousehold incidence of illness: Child health and gender inequality in the allocation of time. *International Economic Review* 31 (4): 969–989.

Pitt, M., M. Rosenzweig, and M. D. Hassan. 1990. Productivity, health, and inequality in the intrahousehold distribution of food in low-income countries. *American Economic Review* 80 (5): 1139–1156.

Piwoz, E. G., and F. E. Viteri. 1985. Studying health and nutrition behavior by examining household decisionmaking, intrahousehold distribution, and the role of women in these processes. *Food and Nutrition Bulletin* 7 (4): 1–31.

Poats, S. V. 1991. *The role of gender in agricultural development.* Issues in Agriculture 3. Washington, D.C.: Consultative Group on International Agricultural Research.

Pollak, R. 1969. Conditional demand function and consumption theory. *Quarterly Journal of Economics* 83 (1): 70–78.

———. 1985. A transaction cost approach to families and households. *Journal of Economic Literature* 23 (June): 581–608.

Pollak, R., and M. Wachter. 1975. The relevance of the household production function and its implications for the allocation of time. *Journal of Political Economy* 83 (2): 255–277.

Potash, B., ed. 1986. *Widows in African societies: Choices and constraints.* Stanford, Calif., U.S.A.: Stanford University Press.

Puetz, D. 1991. Agricultural supply response in The Gambia: A sectoral, household, and intrahousehold analysis. Ph.D. diss., Department of Agricultural Economics, Bonn University.

Putterman, L. 1980. Voluntary collectivization: A model of producers' institutional choice. *Journal of Comparative Economics* 4 (2): 125–157.

———. 1981. On optimality in collective institutional choice. *Journal of Comparative Economics* 5 (4): 392–403.

———. 1986. *Peasants, collectives, and choice: Economic theory and Tanzania's villages.* Greenwich, Conn., U.S.A.: JAI.

Putterman, L., and M. DiGiorgio. 1985. Choice and efficiency in a model of democratic semi-collective agriculture. *Oxford Economic Papers* 37 (1): 1–21.

Quisumbing, A. 1994a. Gender differences in agricultural productivity: A survey of empirical evidence. World Bank, Washington, D.C. Mimeo.

———. 1994b. Intergenerational transfers in Philippine rice villages: Gender differences in traditional inheritance customs. *Journal of Development Economics* 43 (2): 167–195.

Quisumbing, A., L. Haddad, and C. Peña. 1995. Gender and poverty: New evidence from 10 developing countries. Food Consumption and Nutrition Division Discussion Paper 9. International Food Policy Research Institute, Washington, D.C. Mimeo.

Raikes, A. 1990. *Pregnancy, birthing, and family planning in Kenya: Changing patterns of behavior.* Copenhagen: Centre for Development Research.

Ram, R., and R. Singh. 1988. Farm households in rural Burkina Faso: Some evidence on allocative and direct return to schooling, and male–female labor productivity differentials. *World Development* 16 (3): 419–424.

Ramirez, C. O. 1987. *La mujer. Su situacion juridica in veintiseis paises Americanos.* Cordoba, Argentina: Marcos Lerner.

Randolph, S., R. D. Ely, L. H. Allen, A. Chavez, and G. H. Pelto. 1991. The assessment of caloric adequacy. *Food Nutrition Bulletin* 13 (1): 3–7.

Rao, V. J. 1994. Wife beating, its causes and its implications for nutrition allocation in children: An economic and anthropological case study of a rural South Indian community. Department of Economics, Williams College, Williamstown, Mass., U.S.A. Mimeo.

Rao, V. J., and M. Greene. 1993. Marital instability, intrahousehold bargaining, and their implication for fertility in Brazil. Population Research Center, University of Chicago, Chicago. Mimeo.

Rasmusen, E. 1989. *Games and information.* Oxford: Blackwell.

Razavi, S. 1990. Fieldwork in your home country. Paper presented at the workshop on Locality-Based Fieldwork in Developing Countries, Queen Elizabeth House, Oxford.

Reinhardt, N. 1988. *Our daily bread.* Berkeley, Calif., U.S.A.: University of California Press.

Reyna, S. 1979. The rationality of divorce: Marital instability among the Barma of Chad. In *Cross-cultural perspectives of mate-selection and marriage,* ed. S. Reyna. Westport, Conn., U.S.A.: Greenwood.

Richards, A. I. 1956. *Chisungu. A girls' initiation ceremony among the Bemba of Northern Rhodesia.* London: Faber and Faber.

Roberts, P. 1979. The integration of women into the development process: Some conceptual problems. *IDS Bulletin* 10 (3): 60–67.

———. 1988. Rural women's access to labor in West Africa. In *Patriarchy and class: African women in the home and the work force,* ed. S. B. Stichter and J. L. Parpart. Boulder, Colo., U.S.A., and London: Westview.

———. 1991. Anthropological perspective on the household. *IDS Bulletin* 22 (1): 60–66.

Rogers, B. L. 1990. The internal dynamics of households: A critical factor in development policy. In *Intrahousehold resource allocation: Issues and methods for development policy and planning,* ed. B. L. Rogers and N. P. Schlossman. Tokyo: United Nations University Press.

———. 1991. Female headship in the Dominican Republic: Alternative definitions and implications for food consumption and nutrition. Manuscript, Tufts University School of Nutrition, Medford, Mass., U.S.A.

———. 1993. The internal dynamics of households: A critical factor in development policy. Report submitted to U.S. Agency for International Development. Tufts University School of Nutrition, Medford, Mass., U.S.A. Mimeo.

Rogers, B., and N. Schlossman, eds. 1990. *Intrahousehold resource allocation.* Tokyo: United Nations University Press.

Rosenhouse, S. 1989. *Identifying the poor: Is "headship" a useful concept?* Living Standards and Measurement Survey, Working Paper 58. Washington, D.C.: World Bank.

Rosenzweig, M. 1986a. Program interventions, intrahousehold distribution, and the welfare of individuals: Modeling household behavior. *World Development* 14 (2): 233–243.

———. 1986b. Birth spacing and sibling inequality: Asymmetric information within the family. *International Economic Review* 27 (1): 55–76.

———. 1988. Risk, implicit contracts, and the family in rural areas of low-income countries. *Economic Journal* 98: 1148–1170.

———. 1991. *Risk and the family.* Kuznets lectures. New Haven, Conn., U.S.A.: Economic Growth Center, Yale University.

Rosenzweig, M., and T. P. Schultz. 1982. Market opportunities, genetic endowments, and intrafamily resource distribution: Child survival in rural India. *American Economic Review* 72 (4): 803–815.

———. 1983. Estimating a household production function: Heterogeneity, the demand for health inputs, and their effects on birth weight. *Journal of Political Economics* 91 (5): 723–746.

―――. 1984. Market opportunities, genetic endowments, and intrafamily resource distribution of resources: Reply. *American Economic Review* 74: 521–522.

Rosenzweig, M., and K. Wolpin. 1991. The scope for policy intervention. *Journal of Econometrics* 50 (1/2): 205–228.

―――. 1993. Intergenerational support and the lifecycle incomes of young men and their parents: Human capital investments, coresidence, and intergenerational financial transfers. *Journal of Labor Economics* 11 (1): 84–112.

―――. 1994. Parental and public transfers to young women and their children. *American Economic Review* 84 (5): 1195–1212.

Ross, J. 1992. The intrahousehold distribution of malnutrition: An alternative indicator of intrahousehold resource distribution. Ph.D. diss., Cornell University, Ithaca, N.Y., U.S.A.

Ross, T. 1988. *On the relative efficiency of cash transfers and subsidies.* Hoover Institution Working Paper E-8-20. Stanford, Calif., U.S.A.: Stanford University.

Roth, A. E., and M. A. O. Sotomayor. 1990. *Two-sided matching: A study of game-theoretic modeling and analysis.* Cambridge: Cambridge University Press.

Rubinstein, A. 1982. Perfect equilibrium in a bargaining model. *Econometrica* 50 (January): 97–109.

Rutz, H. J., and B. S. Orlove. 1989. *The social economy of consumption.* Monographs in economic anthropology, No. 6. New York: University Press of America.

Ryan, J. G., P. D. Bidinger, R. N. Prahlad, and P. Pushpamma. 1984. *The determinants of individual diets and nutritional status in six villages of South India.* ICRISAT Research Bulletin 7. Hyderabad: International Crops Research Institute for the Semi-Arid Tropics.

Sahn, D. 1990. *Malnutrition in Côte d'Ivoire.* Social Dimensions of Adjustment in Sub-Saharan Africa Working Paper No. 4. Washington, D.C.: World Bank.

Saito, K. 1991. Extending help to women farmers in LDCs. *Finance and Development* 28 (3): 29–31.

Saito, K., and J. Weidermann. 1990. *Agricultural extension for women farmers in Africa.* Working Paper 398. Washington, D.C.: World Bank.

Samba, K., and J. Gittelsohn. 1991. Improving child feeding practices in The Gambia: A report of research conducted by The Gambian Food and Nutrition Association. Report prepared for The Gambia Food and Nutrition Association.

Samuelson, P. 1956. Social indifference curves. *Quarterly Journal of Economics* 70 (February): 1–22.

―――. 1965. *Foundations of economic analysis.* New York: Atheneum.

Sanjek, R. 1982. The organization of households in Adabraka: Toward a wider comparative perspective. *Comparative Studies in Society and History: An International Quarterly* 24 (1): 57–103.

Sathar, Z. 1987. Seeking explanations for high levels of infant mortality in Pakistan. *Pakistan Development Review* 26 (1): 55–70.

Schotter, A. 1981. *The economic theory of social institutions.* London: Cambridge University Press.

Schultz, T. P. 1985. School expenditures and enrollments, 1960–1980: The effects of income, prices, and population. In *Population growth and economic development,* ed. D. Johnson and R. Lee. Madison, Wis., U.S.A.: University of Wisconsin Press.

————. 1989. Women and development: Objectives, framework, and policy interventions. Department of Economics, Yale University, New Haven, Conn., U.S.A. Typescript.

————. 1990. Testing the neoclassical model of family labor supply and fertility. *Journal of Human Resources* 25 (4): 599–634.

————. 1991. Economic aspects of marriage and fertility in the United States. Yale University, New Haven, Conn., U.S.A. Mimeo.

Schultz, T. W. 1964. *Transforming traditional agriculture.* New Haven, Conn., U.S.A.: Yale University Press.

Schwarz, G. 1978. Estimating the dimension of a model. *Annals of Statistics* 6: 461–464.

Scrimshaw, S., and E. Hurtado. 1987. *Rapid assessment procedures: Anthropological approaches to increasing program effectiveness.* Los Angeles: University of California at Los Angeles Latin American Center Publications.

Sen, A. 1966. Labour allocation in a cooperative enterprise. *Review of Economic Studies* 33: 361–371.

————. 1970. *Collective choice and social welfare.* San Francisco: Holden-Day.

————. 1983. Economics and the family. *Asian Development Review* 1 (2): 14–26.

————. 1985a. Women, technology, and sexual divisions. *Trade and Development* 6: 195–213.

————. 1985b. *Commodities and capabilities.* Amsterdam: Elsevier.

————. 1985c. *Women, technology, and sexual division.* Study prepared at the request of the UNCTAD Secretariat and INSTRAW, UNCTAD/TT/79.

————. 1990. Gender and cooperative conflicts. In *Persistent inequalities: Women and world development,* ed. I. Tinker. New York: Oxford University Press.

Sen, A., and S. Sengupta. 1983. Malnutrition of rural children and the sex bias. *Economic and Political Weekly* 18 (19): 855–864.

Senauer, B., and M. Garcia. 1992. An intrahousehold analysis of a Philippine food subsidy program. Paper presented at the International Food Policy Research Institute/World Bank Conference on Intrahousehold Resource Allocation, 12–14 February, Washington, D.C. Mimeo.

Senauer, B., and N. Young. 1986. Impact of food stamps in food expenditures. *American Journal of Agricultural Economics* 68 (1): 37–43.

Senauer, B., M. Garcia, and E. Jacinto. 1988. Determinants of the intrahousehold allocation of food in the rural Philippines. *American Journal of Agricultural Economics* 70: 170–180.

Shubik, M. 1989. Cooperative games. In *The new Palgrave: Game theory,* ed. J. Eatwell, M. Milgate, and P. Newman. New York: Norton.

Singh, I., L. Squire, and J. Strauss, eds. 1986. *Agricultural household models: Extensions, applications, and policy.* Baltimore: Johns Hopkins University Press.

Smock, A. C. 1981. Women's economic roles. In *Papers on the Kenyan economy: Performance, problems, and policies,* ed. T. Killick. Nairobi and London: Heinemann.

Solomons, N. W., and J. Barrows. 1991. Intrahousehold distribution of food in the Guatemalan vitamin A intervention: Anthropological component, Interim Report, Phase I. International Eye Foundation, Bethesda, Md.

Spiro, H. 1985. *The Ilora farm settlement in Nigeria.* West Hartford, Conn., U.S.A.: Kumarian.

Spradley, J. P. 1979. *The Ethnographic Interview.* Chicago: Holt, Rinehart, and Winston.

SSA (Social Security Administration), United States Department of Health and Human Services. 1990. *Social security programs throughout the World—1989.* Research Report 62. Washington, D.C.: U.S. Government Printing Office.

Stanton, B., and J. Clemens. 1987. Twenty-four-hour recall, knowledge-attitude-practice questionnaires, and direct observations of sanitary practices: A comparative study. *Bulletin of the World Health Organization* 63 (2): 217–222.

Stapleton, D. C. 1990. Implicit marriage markets with collective goods. University of Maryland, College Park, Md., U.S.A. Mimeo.

Stark, O. 1991. *Migration of labor.* Oxford and Cambridge: Blackwell.

———. 1995. *Altruism and beyond: An economic analysis of transfers and exchanges within families and groups.* Cambridge: Cambridge University Press.

Stark, O., and R. Lucas. 1988. Migration, remittances, and the family. *Economic Development and Cultural Change* 36: 465–481.

Stone, E. 1981. *Women and the Cuban revolution.* New York: Pathfinder.

Stone, L. 1977. *The family, sex, and marriage in England 1500–1800.* New York: Harper and Row.

Strathern, M. 1988. *The gender of the gift: Problems with women and problems with society in Melanesia.* Berkeley, Calif., U.S.A.: University of California Press.

Strauss, J., and K. Beegle. 1995. Intrahousehold allocation: A review of theories, empirical evidence, and policy issues. Department of Economics, Michigan State University, Ann Arbor, Mich., U.S.A. Mimeo.

Strauss, J., and D. Thomas. 1995. Human resources: Empirical modeling of household and family decisions. In *Handbook of development economics,* ed. J. Behrman and T. N. Srinivasan. Amsterdam: North Holland.

Subramanian, S., and A. Deaton. 1990. *Gender effects in Indian consumption patterns.* Discussion Paper 147. Princeton, N.J.: Woodrow Wilson School of Public and International Affairs, Princeton University.

Sugden, R. 1989. Spontaneous order. *Journal of Economic Perspectives* 3 (Fall): 85–97.

Svedberg, P. 1990. Undernutrition in Sub-Saharan Africa: Is there a gender bias? *Journal of Development Studies* 26 (3): 469–486.

Tambiah, S. J. 1984. *The Buddhist saints of the forest and the cult of amulets.* Cambridge: Cambridge University Press.

Tauchen, H., A. Witte, and S. Long. 1991. Domestic violence: A nonrandom affair. *International Economic Review* 32 (May): 491–511.

Thadani, V. N. 1978. The logic of sentiment: The family and social change. *Population and Development Review* 4 (3): 457–499.

Thirsk, J. 1978. *Economic policy and projects: The development of consumer society in early modern England.* Oxford: Clarendon.

Thomas, D. 1990. Intrahousehold resource allocation: An inferential approach. *Journal of Human Resources* 25 (4): 635–664.

———. 1991. *Gender differences in household resource allocation.* Living Standards Measurement Survey Working Paper 79. Washington, D.C.: World Bank.

————. 1992. The distribution of income and expenditures within the household. *Annales d'Economie et de Statistiques* 29: 109–136.

————. 1994. Like father, like son: Like mother, like daughter: Parental resources and child height. *Journal of Human Resources* 29 (4): 950–988.

Thomas, D., and C. Chen. 1994. *Income shares and shares of income*. Labor and Population Working Paper 94-08. Santa Monica, Calif., U.S.A.: Rand Corporation.

Thomas, D., R. Schoeni, and J. Strauss. 1995. *Parental investments in schooling: The roles of gender and resources in urban Brazil*. Santa Monica, Calif., U.S.A.: Rand Corporation. Mimeo.

Thomas, D., J. Strauss, and M. Barbosa. 1991. Income and price elasticities of the demand for food. *Pesquisa e Planejamento Economico* (Brazil) 21 (2): 305–354.

Thomas, D., J. Strauss, and M. H. Henriques. 1990. Survival rates, height-for-age, and household characteristics in Brazil. *Journal of Development Economics* 33 (2): 197–234.

Thomas, N. 1991. *Entangled objects. Exchange, material culture, and colonialism in the Pacific*. Cambridge, Mass., U.S.A.: Harvard University Press.

Tobin, J. 1970. On limiting the domain of inequality. *Journal of Law and Economics* 13 (2): 263–277.

Tripp, R. 1981. Farmers and traders—some economic determinants of nutritional status in northern Ghana. *Journal of Tropical Pediatrics* 27: 15–22.

Tzannatos, Z. 1991. Potential gains from the elimination of gender differentials in the labor market. In *Women's employment and pay in Latin America: Part I. Overview and methodology*, ed. Z. Tzannatos and G. Psacharopoulos. Regional Studies Program, Report 10. Washington, D.C.: World Bank, Latin America and the Caribbean Technical Department.

Udry, C. 1996. Gender, agricultural production, and the theory of the household. *Journal of Political Economy* 104 (5): 1010–1046.

Udry, C., J. Hoddinott, H. Alderman, and L. Haddad. 1995. Gender differentials in farm productivity: Implications for household efficiency and agricultural policy. *Food Policy* 20 (5): 407–423.

Ullmann, M. 1977. *The emergence of norms*. Oxford: Clarendon.

Ulph, D. 1988. *A general noncooperative Nash model of household consumption behavior.* Working paper. Bristol, U.K.: University of Bristol, Department of Economics.

USDA (United States Department of Agriculture). 1986. *Nationwide food consumption survey: Continuing survey of food intakes by individuals*. Human Nutrition Information Service, NCFS, CSFII, No. 86-3. Washington, D.C.

van Koppen, B. 1990. Women and the design of irrigation schemes: Experiences from two cases in Burkina Faso. Paper presented at the International Workshop on Design for Sustainable Farmer-Managed Irrigation Schemes in Sub-Saharan Africa, Wageningen Agricultural University, The Netherlands, 5–8 February.

Vasconcellos, M. 1983. *Objetivos, descricao e metodologia usada no ENDEF*. Rio de Janeiro: Instituto Brasilieri de Geografia e Estatistica.

Wales, T., and A. Woodland. 1983. Estimation of consumer demand systems with binding non-negativity constraints. *Journal of Econometrics* 21: 263–285.

Walker, T. S., and J. G. Ryan. 1990. *Village and household economies in India's semi-arid tropics*. Baltimore and London: Johns Hopkins University Press.

Warner, R., G. Lee, and J. Lee. 1986. Social organization, spousal resources, and marital power: A cross-cultural study. *Journal of Marriage and the Family* 48: 121–128.

Warr, P. G. 1983. The private provision of a public good is independent of the distribution of income. *Economic Letters* 13 (2/3): 207–211.

Waterlow, J., R. Buzina, W. Keller, J. Lane, M. Nichman, and J. Tanner. 1977. The presentation and use of height and weight data for comparing the nutritional status of groups of children under the age of ten years. *Bulletin of the World Health Organization* 55: 489–498.

Watkins, S. 1991. *From provinces into nations: Demographic integration in western Europe, 1870–1960.* Princeton, N.J.: Princeton University Press.

Webb, P. 1989. *Intrahousehold decisionmaking and resource control: The effects of rice commercialization in West Africa.* Working Papers on Commercialization of Agriculture and Nutrition 3. Washington, D.C.: International Food Policy Research Institute.

Weiner, A. B. 1992. *Inalienable possessions: The paradox of keeping-while-giving.* Berkeley, Calif., U.S.A.: University of California Press.

Weller, S. C., and A. K. Romney. 1988. *Systematic data collection.* Qualitative Research Methods Series No. 10. Newbury Park, Calif., U.S.A.: Sage.

Werner, O., and G. M. Schoepfle. 1987. *Systematic field work,* vols. 1 and 2. Newbury Park, Calif., U.S.A.: Sage.

Wheeler, E. 1991. Intrahousehold food and nutrition allocation. *Nutrition Research Reviews* 4: 69–81.

White, H. 1980. A heteroskedasticity-consistent covariance matrix and a direct test for heteroskedasticity. *Econometrica* 48 (4): 817–838.

Whitehead, A. 1981. "I'm hungry, mum": The politics of domestic budgeting. In *Of marriage and the market: Women's subordination internationally and its lessons,* ed. K. Young, C. Wolkowitz, and R. McCullagh. London: Routledge and Kegan Paul.

———. 1984. Beyond the household? Gender and kinship-based resource allocation in a Ghanaian domestic economy. Paper presented at the workshop on Conceptualizing the Household: Theoretical, Conceptual, and Methodological Issues, Harvard University, Cambridge, Mass., U.S.A.

———. 1990a. Rural women and food production in Sub-Saharan Africa. In *The political economy of hunger,* vol. 1, ed. J. Drèze and A. Sen. Oxford: Clarendon.

———. 1990b. Food crisis and gender conflict in the African countryside. In *The food question: Profits versus people?* ed. H. Bernstein, B. Crow, M. Mackintosh, and C. Martin. London: Earthscan.

Whyte, W. F., ed. 1991. *Participatory action research.* Newbury Park, Calif., U.S.A.: Sage.

Winter, C. 1994. *Gender discrimination in the labor market and the role of the law: Experiences in six Latin American countries.* Report No. 13201-LAC, Latin American and the Caribbean Technical Department. Washington, D.C.: World Bank.

Wolf, D. L. 1990. Daughters, decisions, and domination: An empirical and conceptual critique of household strategies. *Development and Change* 21 (1): 43–74.

Wolf, E. 1969. *Peasant wars of the twentieth century.* New York: Harper and Row.

Woolley, F. 1988. *A noncooperative model of family decisionmaking.* Discussion Paper No. TIDI/125. London: London School of Economics.

———. 1992. New approaches to testing economic models of the household. Carleton University, Ottawa, Ontario, Canada. Mimeo.

World Bank. 1989a. *Kenya: The role of women in economic development.* Washington, D.C.

———. 1989b. *Sub-Saharan Africa. From crisis to sustainable growth.* Washington, D.C.

———. 1990. *World development report 1990.* Oxford: Oxford University Press.

———. 1994. *Averting the old age crisis: Policies to protect the old and promote growth.* New York: Oxford University Press.

Contributors

Harold Alderman is a senior economist in the Policy Research Department of the Poverty and Human Resources Division of the World Bank. He was formerly a research fellow at the International Food Policy Research Institute.

Howarth E. Bouis is a research fellow in the Food Consumption and Nutrition Division of the International Food Policy Research Institute. His research has focused on factors influencing food demand in developing countries and the interface of household resource allocation decisions and nutrition outcomes.

Judith Bruce received training as an anthropologist from Harvard University and is currently the director of the Program on Gender, Family, and Development in the Programs Division of the Population Council. She has devoted most of her 25-year career to the promotion of programs and policies that will increase girls' and women's access to valued resources, improve their reproductive health, and enhance the quality of their lives. Subjects of her writings and research include the quality of family planning and reproductive health care, the broadening of population policy beyond family planning, women's roles in the context of family dynamics, and, most recently, a broadened approach to adolescent programming.

Michael R. Carter is a professor in the Department of Agricultural and Applied Economics at the University of Wisconsin–Madison, where he has also directed the Global Studies Research Program. He has held visiting positions with the Corporation for Latin American Economic Research in Santiago, Chile, and the University of the Pacific in Lima, Peru. His research focuses primarily on the distributional impacts of agrarian economic growth and transformation.

Pierre-André Chiappori, an economist, is a senior researcher at the Centre National de la Recherche Scientifique at the Département et Laboratoire d'Économie Théorique et Appliquée. He has been a visiting professor at the

325

University of Chicago. His research has mainly been in the areas of household behavior, contract and insurance theory, and redistribution policies.

Jennie Dey Abbas is chief of the Rural Institutions and Participation Service of the Food and Agriculture Organization of the United Nations (FAO). As a socioeconomist, she undertook numerous consultancies in Africa and assisted the International Rice Research Institute in setting up a regional network to study women in rice farming systems before joining FAO in 1985. Her main area of research has been intrahousehold resource allocation, particularly its implications for the introduction of improved water management systems and other agricultural technologies.

Nancy Folbre, professor of economics at the University of Massachusetts at Amherst, has served as a consultant on gender and development for the Population Council, the United Nations Human Development Report Office, and the World Bank. Her research explores the interface between feminist theory and political economy in a variety of different ways. In addition to numerous articles published in academic journals, she is the author of *Who Pays for the Kids? Gender and the Structures of Constraint* (Routledge, 1994) and an associate editor of the *Journal of Feminist Economics.*

Paul Gertler is a professor of economics, finance, and public policy at the Haas School of Business and the School of Public Health at the University of Calfornia at Berkeley. Before joining Berkeley, he was a senior economist at RAND. He also serves as the health economics editor for the *Journal of Human Resources.* In 1995 Dr. Gertler received the Kenneth Arrow Award for the best article published in health economics. His research interests include health, education, and population issues.

Joel Gittelsohn, assistant professor of international health at the Johns Hopkins University, is a medical anthropologist who specializes in the use of qualitative and quantitative information to design, implement, and evaluate health and nutrition intervention programs. He integrates qualitative and quantitative approaches to better understand culture-based beliefs and behaviors and how these factors influence the success or failure of dietary and life-style modification strategies. He applies these methods and interventions to assist nongovernmental organizations in developing interventions to improve women's health, to prevent obesity and diabetes among American Indians, to prevent nutrient deficiencies in Nepalese children and women, and to improve infant feeding in diverse settings.

Jane I. Guyer is director of the Program of African Studies and professor of anthropology at Northwestern University. Her research focuses on the division of labor in the political economy of expanding food-supply hinterlands around major cities, particularly in southern Cameroon and western Nigeria. Her fieldwork in producer communities has been combined with social historical research on the history of money, taxation, and economic regulation.

Lawrence Haddad is the director of the Food Consumption and Nutrition Division of the International Food Policy Research Institute (IFPRI). He was previously a research fellow at IFPRI and, before joining the institute, a lecturer in quantitative development economics in the economics department at the University of Warwick, England. His research focuses on the micro-econometrics of the household in agriculture and human resource development as related to food policy issues in developing countries.

Barbara Harriss-White is the reader in development studies and director of graduate studies at Queen Elizabeth House, Oxford University, having former-ly held a research fellowship in the Department of Human Nutrition at the London School of Hygiene and Tropical Medicine, London University. She has long-standing field research interests in rural development, agrarian markets, and social welfare in South Asia.

John Hoddinott is a research fellow in the Food Consumption and Nutrition Division of the International Food Policy Research Institute (IFPRI). He was formerly a university lecturer in economics and a fellow and tutor at Lady Margaret Hall, Oxford University. From 1990 to 1997 he was also a research officer at Oxford's Centre for the Study of African Economies.

Elizabeth G. Katz is an assistant professor of economics at Barnard College, Columbia University. Her research is focused on the theoretical development of intrahousehold models, as well as applications of intrahousehold analysis of key rural development issues, including agricultural commercialization, land tenure, and rural-urban migration.

Cynthia B. Lloyd, an economist, is currently a senior associate and director of social science research in the Research Division of the Population Council. She was formerly chief of the Fertility and Family Planning Studies Section of the Population Division at the United Nations and prior to that assistant professor of economics at Barnard College. Her major research interests are family and gender issues.

Shelly Lundberg is a professor of economics at the University of Washington. Her principal research areas are labor economics and the economics of household behavior, and her work includes studies of discrimination and inequality, family decisionmaking and intrahousehold distribution, and the relationship between labor market outcomes and fertility.

Marjorie B. McElroy received her Ph.D. from Northwestern University and has spent most of her academic career at Duke University, where she is currently a professor in and chair of the Department of Economics. She has worked on a variety of applied microeconomic applications, including production and consumption and financial economics. Her current research focuses on labor economics and the economics of the family with special attention to the interplay of family decisions, the sources of bargaining power, and marriage markets.

Sangeeta Mookherji is currently a doctoral candidate at the Johns Hopkins University School of Hygiene and Public Health in the Department of International Health, with a concentration in health systems management. She was previously a Health and Child Survival Fellow, working in Dhaka, Bangladesh, with the Urban Maternal and Child Health–Family Planning Extension Project as operations research manager. Her research has focused on using qualitative methods to study economic issues, such as cost recovery and health service quality.

Christine L. Peña is an economist (long-term consultant) in the Africa Technical Human Development 1 Division of the World Bank. She was formerly a visiting researcher in the Food Consumption and Nutrition Division of the International Food Policy Research Institute. Her work has focused mainly on household economics, particularly intrahousehold resource allocation modeling, empirical analysis, and policy (health, nutrition, and education) issues; she has also investigated the incorporation of gender analysis into development policy.

Mark M. Pitt is a professor of economics and an associate of the Population Studies and Training Center at Brown University. He has worked primarily on issues of household behavior in the developing countries using household survey data. His recent research has focused on health and demographic behavior, program evaluation, and the household and intrahousehold impacts of microcredit programs for the poor.

Robert A. Pollak is the Hernreich Distinguished Professor of Economics at Washington University in St. Louis. He was formerly on the faculty of the University of Pennsylvania and the University of Washington in Seattle. His research interests include environmental policy, allocation within the family, demography, consumer demand analysis, and the theory of the cost-of-living index.

Duncan Thomas has a joint appointment at RAND and the University of California–Los Angeles, where he is a senior economist and professor of economics, respectively. He was formerly an associate professor at Yale University. His primary area of research is the economics of household decisionmaking with particular emphasis on the health and well-being of children. Most of his empirical research uses household survey data from developing countries.

Index

Abdullah, M., 195
Abortion, 272
Accra, Ghana, 214n
Acharya, M., 175
Activity level, 32, 33t, 35
Adelekan, M. O., 225
Adolescents, nutrition and, 187, 191–92, 204, 210
Affirmative action, 73, 269
Afonja, S., 250n
Africa: assets in, 123; capitalism and, 124; maternal mortality in, 225; North, 218, 220t, 221; Sub-Saharan, *see* Sub-Saharan Africa
Agarwal, B., 272, 283
Age: medical care demand and, 239, 242; nutrition and, 195–96, 197, 200, 202, 204, 205, 208, 210
Agricultural productivity, 249–62, 280–82, 284–85. *See also* Labor productivity; Land productivity
Aid to Families with Dependent Children, 77
Ainsworth, M., 287
Alcohol, 216, 217
Alderman, H., 1, 3, 5, 14–15, 45, 55n, 118, 134, 139, 240, 242, 263, 276, 277n, 281, 286, 288, 289
Allowance system, 80n
Altman, J., 174
Altonji, J., 135, 279
Altruism models, 4, 40, 53, 263, 264–65; assumptions of, 78; bargaining model overlap with, 61–62; child-care allowances/ subsidies and, 76, 92; child care and, 268; evidence on, 135–36; family utility models and, 55–57; generous altruists in, 56;

health outcomes and, 144, 163; intergenerational, 15, 279; rotten-kid theorem and, 6–7, 55n,78, 135, 264–65, 267; stingy altruists in, 56
Altruistic preferences, 42, 43n
Anker, R., 273
Anthropology, 11–12, 124–25, 165–78; determinants of change in resource allocation and, 175–76; direct observation in, 166, 167, 173–74, 177; local concepts and terms in, 168–71; local perspectives on resource allocation and, 171–72; local systems for differential valuation of individuals and, 173; modeling resource decisionmaking in, 175; qualitative methods in, 165–67, 177; quantitative methods in, 165, 167; of wealth, 113, 114–16
Anthropometric status, 196, 198, 200, 204–5, 208; fair share and, 181; income and, 146, 158–59, 160t, 163; measuring individual, 195–96
Appadurai, A., 116, 124
Apps, P., 7, 14, 39n
Arrow, K., 82n
Ashenfelter, O., 134
Ashworth, J., 10, 39n
Asia, 218, 220t, 221; South, 231, 272, 283
Asset creation, 10, 113–14
Asset income, 146, 148t, 149, 156
Asset management, 10, 113–14
Assets, 112–25; incompatibility with receipt of benefits, 117; local and historical specificity of, 123–24; multifaceted nature of small-scale, 117–18, 121–22
Assignable goods, 50–51
Assortative mating, 5, 53, 88
Autonomy, in conjugal contract model, 97

329

86; methodological issues in determining, 181; regression analysis of, 189–92. *See also* Food allocation; Nutrition

Fallback positions: social institutions and, 264–66; social norms and, 266–67

Family allowance benefits, 273–74

Family decisions, 54–61; cooperative bargaining models of, 57–59; family utility models of, 54–57, 61; Pareto-only approach to, 60; relationship among models of, 60–61; transactions cost approach to, 60

Family size, 197, 211

Family utility models, 54–57, 61

Farkas, G., 266

Farmer, A., 181n

Farm size, 197–98, 199, 201, 209

Fast days, 195

Feast days, 195

Feldstein, H. S., 256, 25856

Ferguson, J., 115

Fertility, 132, 136–37, 223, 281–82

Filmer, D., 37n

Fixed-effects procedure, 26

Flexibility, 167

Focus groups, 166, 167

Fogel, R., 269

Folbre, N., 11, 15, 213n, 223, 264, 266, 268, 269, 273, 274, 283, 284, 289

Food allocation, 170, 171, 177–78; determinants of change in, 175–76; endowments and, 32–37; household head influence on, 216–17. *See also* Fair share; Nutrition

Food consumption patterns, 182

Food expenditures, 182–86

Food prices, 199, 202, 205

Food share to energy share ratio (FS/ES), 186–87, 191

Food stamps, 277–78

F-optimal points, 65–66, 67, 68–69, 70–71

Fortin, B., 134

Fortmann, L., 256, 281

France, 133, 140, 274

Free lists, 166, 171–72

Fried, E. S., 225

Friedman, H., 108

Friedman, J. W., 98

Full income concept, 226

Fundamentalist religious organizations, 271

Funk, U., 135n, 255n

Furstenberg, F. F., 225

Gage-Brandon, A. J., 213n, 215, 219, 220, 222

Gale, D., 62, 65n, 72

Gambia, 15, 130, 171; agricultural productivity in, 252–53, 255, 284–85

Game theory, 7, 8, 40, 53, 61, 65

Garcia, M., 14, 130, 240, 242

Garg, A., 231

Garrett, P., 281

Gender: agricultural productivity and, 249–62, 280–82, 284–85; assets and, 113–14; bargaining and, 264–68; conditional demand and, 25–28; in conjugal contract model, 105, 108–10; fair share measures and, 187, 190–91f; health outcomes and, *see* Health outcomes; of household heads, *see* Household heads; human capital investments and, *see* Human capital investments; income impact of, 137–40; institutionalized forms of bias, 272–74; medical care demand and, *see* Medical care demand; nutrition and, *see* Nutrition

Gender coalitions, 268–71

Gender discrimination laws, 273

Gender-specific environmental parameters (GEPs), 265–66, 267, 272, 274

Generous altruists, 56

GEPs. *See* Gender-specific environmental parameters

Germain, A., 272

Germany, 274

Gertler, P., 1, 5, 14, 237, 243, 276

Ghai, Y., 211

Ghana: agricultural productivity in, 254, 258, 259, 260; children living away from mothers in, 218t; health care in, 37; household heads in, 215–16, 219, 220; nutrition in, 231

Ghana Living Standards Measurement Survey, 219n

Ghar, 169

Ghassemi, H., 14

Gift, The, 115

Gilgun, J. F., 167

Gittelsohn, J., 2, 11–12, 141, 167, 170, 171, 173, 174, 176

Given groups, 270–71

Gladwin, C., 135, 175

Glewwe, P., 276

Goetz, A. M., 283n

Goodenough, W., 168

Goody, J., 115

Government clinics, 242, 244t

Graham, M. A., 170

Grameen Bank, 265, 283

Great Britain, 274

LIBRARY OF CONGRESS CATALOGING-IN-PUBLICATION DATA

Intrahousehold resource allocation in developing countries: models, methods,
    and policy / edited by Lawrence Haddad, John Hoddinott, and Harold Alderman.
       p.   cm.
    Includes bibliographical references and index.
    ISBN 0-8018-5572-1 (hardcover: alk. paper)
     1. Households—Developing countries—Econometric models. 2. Households—
Economic aspects—Developing countries. 3. Consumption (Economics)—
Developing countries—Mathematical models. I. Haddad, Lawrence James.
II. Hoddinott, John. III. Alderman, Harold, 1948– .
HC59.7.I5947 1997
339.2′2—DC21   96-6720
                                                            CIP

DATE DUE

Intrahousehold Resource Allocation in Developing Countries